THE
ABC-CLIO
COMPANION TO

The American Peace Movement in the Twentieth Century

Demonstrators protest at Selective Service headquarters, 15 October 1969.

THE
ABC-CLIO
COMPANION TO

The American Peace Movement in the Twentieth Century

*Christine A.
Lunardini*

ABC-CLIO

Library of Congress Cataloging-in-Publication Data

Lunardini, Christine A., 1941–
    The ABC-CLIO companion to the American peace movement in the
twentieth century/Christine A. Lunardini.
       p.   cm. — (ABC-CLIO companions to key issues in American
history and life)
    Includes bibliographical references and index.
    1. Peace movements—United States—History—20th century.
I. Title. II. Series.
JX1961.U6L83   1994 327.1'72'09730904—dc20   94-10405

    ISBN 0-87436-714-X

99 98 97 96 95 94   10 9 8 7 6 5 4 3 2 1

ABC-CLIO, Inc.
130 Cremona Drive, P.O. Box 1911
Santa Barbara, California 93116-1911

To Maureen and Steve,
true supporters of the Arts and Letters,
with appreciation and gratitude

ABC-CLIO Companions to Key Issues in American History and Life

The ABC-CLIO Companion to the American Labor Movement
Paul F. Taylor

The ABC-CLIO Companion to the Civil Rights Movement
Mark Grossman

The ABC-CLIO Companion to Women in the Workplace
Dorothy Schneider and Carl J. Schneider

The ABC-CLIO Companion to Women's Progress in America
Elizabeth Frost-Knappman

*The ABC-CLIO Companion to the American Peace Movement
in the Twentieth Century*
Christine A. Lunardini

Forthcoming

The ABC-CLIO Companion to the Environmental Movement
Mark Grossman

The ABC-CLIO Companion to the Media in America
Daniel Webster Hollis, III

Contents

Preface

Americans have always been active in the peace movement, both at home and internationally. Since the turn of the century, the peace movement has responded to world crises with nothing less than zealous dedication and a variety of proposals for maintaining world peace. Indeed, referring to a U.S. peace "movement" can be somewhat misleading because it implies that those who worked on behalf of the peaceful resolution of conflict have always been like-minded about solutions. Nothing could be further from the truth. Peace advocates have embraced a range of ideologies—from pure pacifism regardless of the circumstance, to belief in "just" wars, to the advancement of containment theory—and have included such seemingly diametric opposites as internationalists and isolationists. Peace advocates have both proposed reliance on international peacekeeping organizations and have insisted on maintaining self-determination in order to avoid conflict. They have both rejected and embraced weapons development, world organizations, and people-to-people programs.

This volume will acquaint readers with the people and organizations that have fueled the U.S. peace movement in the late-nineteenth through the twentieth century. The biographical profiles of individuals ranging from Jane Addams to Linus Pauling illuminate not only their dedication to peace, but also the breadth and depth of their commitment to a variety of social, political, philosophical, ethical, and moral issues. As we learn about the individuals, it is clear that many of the movers and shakers in the peace community could no more isolate their impulse to be involved in something bigger than themselves than they could isolate the elements of the air they breathed. For these people, the relationship between a variety of issues seemed perfectly clear and required that they make contributions on as many fronts as possible. The organizations that were created by such activists reflect their diverse backgrounds and interests. Many of the organizations are still thriving; others evolved or disbanded as times changed. Whether or not one agrees or disagrees with their strategies and philosophies, it is difficult to come away with less than admiration for those who dedicated much of their lives to the quest for world peace.

Deciding which entries to include in the dictionary proved to be very easy in many instances and much more difficult in others. My goal in selecting entries was to include organizations and individuals who were truly advocates of peace and not merely objectors to a particular conflict. Although some people and organizations fell into both categories, there were many instances where the distinction was quite clear. The Vietnam

War created a particularly difficult case, because—in that conflict more than in any other—there were probably more individuals than usual who were involved in war protests but who did not necessarily have a general commitment to peace. Similarly, in looking over the list of U.S. recipients of the Nobel Peace Prize, I omitted individuals more identifiable as the architects of conflict rather than as pursuers of peace. It seemed to me that Henry Kissinger did not really belong in the same category as Jane Addams, for example, although both received Nobel Peace Prizes. Organizations were selected according to influence, effectiveness, and—sometimes, but not always—their status as a national rather than a local group. Undoubtedly, there are entries that I have overlooked or erroneously passed over. I can only hope that there will be another opportunity to include relevent entries.

Both the Pace University Library and the New York Public Library have been generous in providing materials necessary to complete this volume. I would also like to thank several people who have provided assistance and encouragement, including Maureen Callahan, Catherine Clinton, Elizabeth Frost Knappman, Steve Victore, Noah Callahan-Bever, Chloe Callahan-Flintoft, Pat and Kevin Donahue, Helen Close, Donna Lunardini, Maureen Keating Tsuchiya, Elyn and Barry Rosenthal, and Jonathan and Abigail Lunardini. A special thanks also to my editors at ABC-CLIO, Jeffrey Serena and Sallie Greenwood, and to the outstanding job done by Impressions, a division of Edwards Brothers.

Introduction

From the earliest days of U.S. nationhood, there has been a minority of the population that could be characterized as advocates of peace. Then, as now, those who counted themselves part of that minority rarely agreed on reasons or means, and only sometimes would they even acknowledge that all factions sought the same goal. Usually, peace advocates would agree on the principle but not necessarily on the specifics. The movement lacked cohesion and sometimes had different goals, different degrees of dedication and political sophistication, and different ideas regarding effective strategies. Indeed, it is more accurate to characterize the peace movement at certain times during the twentieth century as a protest movement. Pacifism, particularly as preached and practiced by members of the so-called peace churches—the Quakers, Brethren, and Mennonites—embraces an across-the-board resistance to any type of violence in order to settle disputes, whether civil or international. Not all peace advocates, however, are pacifists. In fact, pacifists are in the minority. In the twentieth century, members of the peace movement have included pacifists, those who advocate world government, internationalists, those who object to a specific hostile action on either political or moral grounds, and those who campaign for weapons reductions or the elimination of specific types of weapons. Depending on the time and the circumstance, the peace movement in the United States has fluctuated markedly; at times it has had very few active participants, and at other times a significant minority of the population has been involved. In truth, there has never been a monolithic peace movement in the United States with a single goal and with all participants agreeing on the means of reaching that goal. Even though the peace movement has always included disparate factions, it is nevertheless useful to refer to it as though it were a single, identifiable movement.

In the early twentieth century, until World War I, members of the peace movement included pacifists and those who tended to advocate a particular means of avoiding international conflict. There was a great deal of grass-roots support for peace plans. The Mohonk Conferences at Lake Mohonk in New York state annually drew the movers and shakers in the peace movement for roundtable discussions on world government, forced arbitration to settle international conflict, possible peacekeeping organizations, and education campaigns. Philanthropists like Andrew Carnegie were more than willing to establish large endowments to ensure that peace research would be vigorously supported. Moreover, a surprising number of prominent individuals, men and women alike, were willing to invest their time, energy, and money, when possible, year after year in an effort to find meaningful solutions. Highly visible people like Carnegie, Jane Addams, and Emily Greene Balch (the latter two ultimately won Nobel Peace Prizes) did their level best to make the cause of peace both urgent and fruitful. Organizations like the foremost pre–World War I group, the American Peace Society, which was founded in the nineteenth century, sponsored campaigns, conferences, and literature—all aimed at promoting peace.

Ironically, most wars in the twentieth century in which the United States became involved proved to be troublesome for the peace movement. The most consistent opponents of war were the church-grounded pacifists, but even some pacifists found it difficult to remain dispassionately opposed to war when confronted with what they perceived as forces bent on destroying the civilized world. Faced with German aggression in World War I, pacifists and peace advocates alike felt compelled to suspend principle in order to deal with the situation at hand. Not all pacifists renounced their conviction. Some organizations came into being precisely to provide advice and protection for those who did express their opposition to the war. The Fellowship of Reconciliation, founded in Europe, established a U.S. branch and eventually became an important element in counseling war opponents; later, during World War II, it worked with the government to establish alternative service camps for conscientious objectors. The American Civil Liberties Union (ACLU) was also born out of concern that conscientious objectors and opponents of World War I would be treated harshly unless there were a watchdog agency to protect their rights and interests. The great majority of

previously avowed peace advocates, however, saw no other recourse but to support their country in time of war.

The next resurgence of the peace movement coincided with the disillusionment caused by the outcome of "the-war-to-end-all-wars." Far from stabilizing Europe, the Treaty of Versailles helped to create a new set of tensions and perpetuated old resentments. The only thing that seemed certain was that the peace in Europe was temporary. The political turmoil in Europe, coupled with the publication of several exposés that purported to prove that events had been manipulated by arms manufacturers interested only in their profits, left many Americans believing that they had been duped by both politicians and profiteers. Peace advocates who had supported the war were especially intent on renouncing war under any circumstance. Both individuals and organizations renewed efforts to find peaceful methods of conflict resolution.

Although many pacifist groups did maintain their opposition to war, the challenge of fascism and nazism, which flourished in Germany and Italy and threatened to engulf the entire world if left unchecked, once again forced members of the U.S. peace community to deal with the horror of another world war. Despite previous vows to refuse participation in future wars, most peace advocates concluded that Adolf Hitler and his Nazi party had to be stopped militarily before true peace could be achieved. Peace advocates did not forget lessons learned from World War I. They lobbied both for a just peace and for the creation of a peacekeeping organization like the League of Nations, which U.S. politicians refused to endorse or join after World War I.

Once again, the aftermath of war helped to set the stage for new conflicts. After World War II, the emergence of two superpowers—the United States and the Soviet Union—ensured that proponents of peace would have to redouble their efforts. The atomic bombs that brought an abrupt end to the war in the Pacific also heralded a new and more terrifying threat to world peace, indeed to world existence: the threat of a nuclear holocaust. For the next 50 years the peace movement focused primarily on two issues. The first dealt with nuclear weapons and how to control and eliminate them. Out of this need, the Nuclear Freeze Movement was born. It soon became one of the more successful grass-roots efforts in U.S. peace movement history. The second issue had less to do with advocating peace than it did with opposing a particular military engagement: the Vietnam War. Although both efforts ultimately sought the same peaceful goal, the Vietnam War proved to be one of the most divisive episodes in U.S. history, while the Nuclear Freeze Movement united a variety of otherwise disparate individuals and organizations in a common opposition to nuclear annihilation.

At times, the peace movement that emerged in response to the Vietnam War seemed to spend as much time settling internal strife as it did protesting the war. There was a clear lack of cohesion because of the array of goals that worked to divide rather than unify the movment. For all of the activity and publicity that attended antiwar actions, support for the movement was soft and transitory. Nor was the idealism that characterized much of the Nuclear Freeze Movement tied to any specific political remedy. Protesters had a ready list of grievances, but few suggestions for how to effect change. When Jonathan Schell, author of the influential book *The Fate of the Earth*, was asked how to organize and implement the "new politics," which he identified as crucial to saving the planet, he responded that he could not "presume" to tell anyone how to accomplish that end. If idealism characterized the Nuclear Freeze Movement, a certain amount of naïveté was another characteristic. Many nuclear freezers tended to place the blame for the arms race and nuclear stockpiling solely on the shoulders of the United States, without regard for the part played by the Soviet Union. In all instances, the consequence of the conflicts and naïveté was that most Americans never embraced either movement. Moreover, public opinion remained fairly constant regarding this issue.

International events over the past five years have produced a rapidly changing political landscape that is truly astonishing in its structure and detail. Not the least astonishing is the radically different popular perception of peace and war and the apparent diminishing role of nuclear stockpiles in a "brave new world." The breakup of the Soviet Union and the breaking of its long-held control over Eastern Europe has had consequences that make it clear that efforts to find peaceful resolutions to international conflict are as necessary now as they have always been. Although the threat of a nuclear war pitting one superpower against another superpower has virtually disappeared, the reality of a world littered with the nuclear remains of a decades-long arms race is, at the very least, sobering.

Abbot, Willis John (1863–1934)

John Abbot, a lawyer by training but a journalist by profession, was born in New Haven, Connecticut. After earning a law degree from the University of Michigan in 1884, Abbot moved to New Orleans, where he reported news for the New Orleans *Times-Democrat*. For the next 15 years, Abbot worked for a succession of newspapers, including the *New York Tribune*, the *Kansas City Evening News*, the *Chicago Evening Mail*, and the *Chicago Times*. He was also involved in politics, notably as campaign manager for Henry George, when George ran for mayor of New York in 1897.

Abbot became the editorial page editor of William Randolph Hearst's *New York Journal* during the Spanish-American War, in the heyday of yellow journalism. His career kept him moving about as he became editor (and part owner) of the Battle Creek, Michigan, *Pilgrim;* chief editorial writer of Hearst's *New York American*, political writer for the *Chicago Tribune*, and employee of the New York *Sun* and the *Chicago American*.

A staunch supporter of the Allies in World War I, Abbot left the *Chicago American* when the newspaper took the stand that the Germans' sinking of the *Luisitania* was a legitimate action. In 1921, Abbot was asked to take over the reins of the *Christian Science Monitor*, which was then suffering from the effects of prolonged litigation between the trustees and the board of directors. Abbot helped to rebuild the failing newspaper. Under his editorship, the *Monitor* spearheaded a campaign objecting to repeal of the Eighteenth Amendment. From 1922 to 1925, Abbot worked closely with peace advocates to promote the *Christian Science Monitor* peace plan. The plan advocated subjecting property to conscription for war, a radical idea that both houses of Congress considered.

Perhaps as a consequence of his association with yellow journalism, Abbot also worked to promote ethics in journalism. He retired as editor of the *Monitor* in 1927 but remained associated with the paper as a member of the editorial board and as a special contributing editor. Abbot died in Brookline, Massachusetts, on 19 May 1934.

Reference Starr, Harris E., *Dictionary of American Biography*, supp. 1 (1944).

Abbott, Lyman (1835–1922)

As editor of the *Outlook*, Lyman Abbott became one of the leading proponents of the social gospel developed and promulgated during the late-nineteenth century. Abbott, like other advocates of the social gospel, believed that Christians had a duty and responsibility to apply the teachings of Christ not only in the context of religion, but to society, economic life, social institutions, and individuals. Armed with this new moral ethic, the reformers sought to solve the problems generated by a rapidly industrializing society whose ills included poverty, crime, over-crowding, and homelessness.

Abbott was born in Roxbury, Massachusetts, and graduated from New York University in 1853. As a young man, he was drawn to the ministry, but he spent several years immediately after college working in his brother's law offices while he prepared to become a Congregationalist minister. During this period he began writing for various periodicals. Through his writing, Abbott helped to shape the social gospel as much as it shaped him, and he was able to convey to his readers a sense of logical progression in a world that sometimes seemed to be

1

changing drastically without purpose or direction. Long a protégé of Henry Ward Beecher, Abbott succeeded Beecher as editor of the *Christian Union* (later renamed the *Outlook)*. Abbott also succeeded Beecher as pastor of the Plymouth Church in Brooklyn when Beecher died.

Having lived through the Civil War, Abbott was profoundly interested in the twin issues of war and peace. In *Christianity and Social Problems*, a collection of Abbott's essays published in 1896, he addressed the question of war in a Christian society. Abbott believed that war was not consistent with social progress and that individuals could not make the decision to engage in violence against evil. Governments, as protectors of the people, could determine when a war was necessary. Thus, Abbott—although he was a peace advocate—was not a pacifist. He embraced the concept of international law and compulsory arbitration of conflict as a primary means of keeping nations from engaging in war. Abbott became an active participant in the annual International Arbitration Conferences at Lake Mohonk, New York. He was also an early and avid supporter of The Hague Tribunal, the first world court established in 1899. At the same time as he promoted peace, Abbott supported the United States during World War I, believing that Germany had demonstrated extremly uncivilized behavior, particularly in its decision to engage in submarine warfare. Given those circumstances, Abbott believed that the United States had little choice but to respond with force. He continued to work for and advocate international law and arbitration until his death on 22 October 1922.

References Brown, Ira B., *Lyman Abbott, Christian Evolutionist* (1953); Josephson, Harold, ed., *Biographical Dictionary of Modern Peace Leaders* (1985).

Abzug, Bella Savitsky (1920–)
Bella Savitsky Abzug, a lawyer and politician, was born in New York City to Russian-Jewish émigré parents in 1920. She was educated in public schools and graduated from Hunter College in 1942. As a college student, she supported the Republicans in the Spanish Civil War and protested against fascism. After college, Abzug entered Columbia University School of Law and earned an LL.D. in 1947. After passing the New York State Bar exam, she went into private practice, but her cases were anything but private. She defended civil rights cases in the South as well as writers accused of un-American activities during the McCarthy era.

In the 1960s, Abzug became active in the peace movement, the antinuclear movement, and the women's movement. She founded the Women Strike for Peace (WSP) (1961) and served as its national legislative director from 1961 to 1970. She also founded the National Women's Political Caucus and served as its chairperson.

After more than two decades as an activist, Abzug decided to run for Congress in 1971. She served there for three terms, gaining the nickname "Bellicose Bella" because of her vocal advocacy of welfare rights, consumer and environmental protection, full employment, jobs programs, and aid to Israel. Her flamboyance made her a national figure, and she was as well known for her work on behalf of women as she was for her work in Congress.

Running for the Senate in 1976 against Daniel Patrick Moynihan brought an end to her congressional career. She lost the Senate race by a narrow margin and, in 1977, she ran for mayor of New York City, losing that race as well.

Abzug continues to lobby for the causes she believes in. She has been a long-standing member of the National Organization of Women, Americans for a Democratic Society, and the American Civil Liberties Union (ACLU). She continues to write on politics and women's issues, and has written several books, including *Gender Gap: Bella Abzug's Guide to Political Power for Women* (1984).

See also Women Strike for Peace.

Congressional campaign poster for Bella Abzug

References Abzug, Bella, *Ms. Abzug Goes to Washington* (1972); Uglow, Jennifer S., ed., *The Continuum Dictionary of Women's Biography* (1989).

Addams, Jane (1860–1935)

Although Jane Addams lived slightly more than half her life in the nineteenth century, it is much more accurate to describe her as a luminary of the twentieth century, and although she is better known as the founder of Hull House and the social welfare movement in the United States, she worked equally hard to promote peaceful solutions to world conflict.

Addams, born in Cedarville, Illinois, belonged to the first generation of college-educated women. Ancestors on both sides of her family had arrived in this country before the Revolutionary War. Addams grew up with a sense of responsibility that was heightened after her graduation from Rockford Seminary in 1877. She briefly attended the Women's Medical College in Philadelphia but soon discovered that medicine was not her calling. Feeling adrift, she traveled to Europe twice, both times bringing back a stronger sense of where she could be most useful. After the second trip, Addams returned to Chicago and, with her longtime friend Ellen Gates Starr, opened Hull House. It was the first settlement house in the United States, modeled on London's Toynbee Hall, and was intended as a place where immigrants and the poor—both buffeted by the changing demands of rapid industrialization—could come for education, help, and training. Hull House became a model for similar settlement houses in other U.S. cities.

One of Addams's skills was her ability to bring together some of the best minds in the country, many of whom were women, and all of whom went away from Hull House with energy, ideas, and a determination to help make changes where they would be most useful to society. It was the birth of American progressivism and the ideal of improving conditions in order to create an equitable society where opportunity was open to everyone, not just the privileged few.

Addams believed that the "moral energy of women" could be brought to bear on a number of critical issues. Thus, she worked tirelessly for women's suffrage in order to give women the means to effect change via the ballot box. And, as early as 1907, in a book entitled *Newer Ideals of Peace*, Addams likened the multicultural district in Chicago where Hull House was located with the world at large. Learning from the immigrants who were forced by geography to find ways to coexist and to capitalize on cultural diversity, Addams advocated applying those lessons to world internationalism as a force for peace. When World War I began in Europe, she turned her full attention to peaceful solutions. She was elected first chairwoman of the newly formed Women's Peace Party (WPP) in 1915. That same year, she was elected president of the International Congress of Women at The Hague, which sought to persuade world statesmen to enlist neutral nations in ongoing mediation between belligerents.

When the United States entered the war, Addams did not stop working for peace. Perceived as un-American, she was vilified by many and was expelled by the Daughters of the American Revolution. Despite criticisms leveled at her,

Jane Addams

Addams refused to abandon her principles. She did, however, lecture nationally for Herbert Hoover's Food Administration. Hoover's efforts to provide relief for people in war-torn countries, including the Belgian relief program he initiated in 1915, earned him Addams's lifelong admiration.

Her peace efforts continued long after the war ended in 1919. The Women's International League for Peace and Freedom elected Addams president in 1919, a post that she held until her death. She also supported Carrie Chapman Catt's National Committee on the Cause and Cure of War, organized in 1925. Because of her dedication to seeking what the philosopher William James characterized as the moral equivalent of war, the Nobel Peace Prize Committee awarded Addams the Nobel Peace Prize in 1931, an honor that she shared with Nicholas Murray Butler of Columbia University. She immediately donated her share of the monetary award, $16,000, to the Women's International League for Peace and Freedom.

Jane Addams died on 21 May 1935. At the time of her death she was recognized worldwide as a humanitarian and as a woman whose life work derived from both a conviction of pragmatic necessity and a sense of moral responsibility.

See also Women's Peace Party.

References Addams, Jane, *Twenty Years at Hull-House* (1910); James, Edward T., et al., eds., *Notable American Women, 1607–1950: A Biographical Dictionary* (1971); Lasch, Christopher, *The New Radicalism in America, 1889–1963: The Intellectual as a Social Type* (1965).

Allen, Devere (1891–1955)

Devere Allen was born in Providence, Rhode Island, and became a journalist immediately after graduating from Oberlin College in 1917. A pacifist and opponent of World War I, he edited a publication called *The Rational Patriot* from 1917 to 1918. For the next three years he edited *Young Democracy*. In 1921, Allen was asked to edit *The World To-*morrow, first as managing editor and then, beginning in 1925, as editor, a position he held with short interruptions.

In 1930 he spent several months in Europe as a special correspondent for U.S. newspapers and magazines, and in 1931 and 1932 he was assistant editor of *The Nation*, before returning to *The World Tomorrow*, in 1933. Throughout this period, Allen became more and more involved in Socialist politics. In 1932, and again in 1934, he ran unsuccessful campaigns for the U.S. Senate from the state of Connecticut as a Socialist party candidate. He also ran for governor in 1938, this time on the Labor party ticket, but again he did not succeed.

In 1930, Allen wrote a book entitled *The Fight For Peace,* in which he advocated pacifist solutions for world conflict, and in 1932 he wrote *Will Socialism End the Evil of War?* Allen's pacifism was rooted in his membership in the Society of Friends, one of the historic peace churches, and he was a member of the Friends's service organization, the Fellowship of Reconciliation (FOR). Allen was also a member of the planning committee of the American League against War and Fascism, which was founded in 1933. Efforts by the founders to bring together the politically divergent elements in the peace movement did not succeed for very long. A league meeting that featured a Socialist demonstration was disrupted by Communists, and shortly thereafter Allen and other pacifists and Socialists withdrew from the organization.

Allen continued to work through a variety of peace and Socialist organizations, including the American Civil Liberties Union (ACLU) and the Americans for Democratic Action (ADA), in an effort to promote peace through pacifism. Even during World War II, he continued to investigate cooperative methods for resolving conflict and in 1943 published *The Caribbean Laboratory of World Cooperation*. Despite disappointment at the development of the Cold War and the nuclear arms race, Allen remained hopeful that war would ultimately be perceived as an unacceptable solution to conflict. He died on 27 August 1955 in Connecticut.

References *Who Was Who in America?* (1972); Wittner, Lawrence S., *Rebels against War: The American Peace Movement 1941–1960* (1969).

America First Committee

Even before war in Europe was declared in September 1939, Franklin Delano Roosevelt had discussed the probability of war and had began to make appropriate plans. His commitment to shoring up the Allies's resources resulted in the Lend Lease Program. A number of measures affecting the United States more directly were taken throughout 1940, including national defense tax measures aimed at producing nearly a billion dollars a year. The public was not eager, however, to play a direct role in the conflict. Even the effort to provide aid to the beleaguered democracies required an enormous public relations effort. The Committee to Defend America by Aiding the Allies, under the able chairmanship of Kansas editor William Allen White, was instrumental in promoting favorable sentiment.

Those who were even opposed to providing financial aid to the Allies—in order to counter what they believed was unwise intervention in a European problem—organized the America First Committee in July 1940. The chairman was a mid-westerner, General Robert E. Wood, the former president of Sears Roebuck. Members included prominent Americans such as Charles Lindbergh, Senator Gerald Nye, and Senator Burton Wheeler. The America First Committee lobbied to keep the United States out of the war and to maintain neutrality. It drew its support from a disparate coalition of reactionaries (including a small fringe of Nazi sympathizers and anti-Semites) and moderate conservatives. In addition, left-leaning pacifists, who did not necessarily agree with the political philosophy of the America Firsters but who believed that preventing the spread of war was fundamental, also joined the coalition. America First advocates never preached disarmament; instead, they consistently endorsed an "impregnable" defense, which, in their view, meant increasing armaments. Debate between the America First Committee and the Committee to Defend America by Aiding the Allies, which was often bitter in nature, continued up to 7 December 1941.

References Cole, Wayne S., *Roosevelt and the Isolationists, 1932–1945* (1983); Wittner, Lawrence S., *Rebels against War: The American Peace Movement 1941–1960* (1969).

American Civil Liberties Union (ACLU)

Founded originally in 1915 as the Civil Liberties Bureau (CLB) of the American Union against Militarism (AUAM) by Crystal Eastman, her assistant, Roger Baldwin, and Norman Thomas. When the AUAM disbanded in 1921, the CLB became the American Civil Liberties Union (ACLU). The founders were concerned that the civil liberties of antiwar spokespersons and conscientious objectors (COs) were being denied.

Initially, the ACLU advised COs of their legal rights and assisted and defended them in camps, but as Norman Thomas pointed out, the ACLU always had a broader agenda in mind as well. In *The World Tomorrow*, which Thomas edited, he wrote, "There is a region in human life where the commandment of the state does not run." To Thomas and Baldwin, the ACLU was created to defend "the privilege of men everywhere to choose their way of life and obedience." This mandate has by necessity meant that the ACLU often takes unpopular stands on issues when it perceives that a minority is being deprived of its constitutional rights by the majority. The ACLU has consistently defended the rights of COs, the rights of individuals or groups to protest against the government in war and peace, and the rights of individuals and groups to publicly advocate unpopular causes. For example, the ACLU came to the assistance of anti–Vietnam War protesters when they were being denied a permit to demonstrate; appealed to the U.S. Supreme Court on behalf of Congresswoman Elizabeth Holtzman when she tried to obtain an injunction that would have halted bombing in Cambodia; defended on several occasions the rights of Ku Klux Klan members to publicly demonstrate; and defended the rights of so-called skinheads to parade through Jewish neighborhoods in Skokie, Illinois. Regardless of public opinion, the ACLU has played a positive role throughout its history in its determination to protect the civil liberties of all citizens, not just the majority.

See also Baldwin, Roger Nash; Eastman, Crystal; Thomas, Norman.

References DeBenedetti, Charles, ed., *Peace Heroes in Twentieth Century America* (1988); Zaroulis, Nancy, and Gerald Sullivan, *Who Spoke Up? American Protest against the War in Vietnam 1963–1975* (1984).

American Friends Service Committee (AFSC)

Founded in 1917 by U.S. Quakers to relieve the suffering of European victims of World War I as well as to provide an alternative service for Quakers and other conscientious objectors (COs), the American Friends Service Committee (AFSC) was the action organization of the Society of Friends. The Society of Friends—a centuries-old religious organization dedicated to peaceful coexistence—still sponsors and supports the AFSC.

The AFSC descended from the Friends War Victims Relief Committee, organized after the Franco-Prussian War in 1870–1871, to assist war victims in France. Many American COs worked as ambulance and relief workers in Europe during World War I and, at the request of Quaker Herbert Hoover, the head of the

U.S. Food Administration, helped to distribute food and services to a million impoverished children in Germany and Austria. Following the war, the AFSC continued to work throughout Europe by helping to rebuild the devastated continent.

With the onset of worldwide depression in the 1930s, the AFSC transferred its major activity back to the United States, where it perceived an equally pressing need. During Hitler's rise to power, the AFSC, under the direction of its longtime chairman, Henry Cadbury, worked to help relocate refugees from fascism in Europe. It also sent workers to Spain during the Spanish Civil War to distribute food to both sides. A linchpin of AFSC philosophy was to make every effort to support and preserve the self-respect of all recipients of its aid and to help people to help themselves. Thus, the AFSC sought to help the victims of war on all sides of a conflict.

During World War II, American COs were recognized legally but were restricted to alternative service within the United States. The AFSC helped to administer nearly 50 camps in which 2,400 men participated in civilian public service (CPS) programs. Participants, only one-quarter of whom were Quakers, served in forestry camps, as social workers, and in hospital wards; they even participated in medical experimentation, working without pay except for room and board and a $25-per-month allowance. Once the war ended, many AFSC workers joined other Quakers doing relief work in Europe, India, China, and Japan.

During both the Korean and the Vietnam wars, the AFSC continued to serve as an important forum for COs, offering both advice and counsel to those who sought alternative service. Because of its long history of dedication to peace, the Nobel Peace Prize Committee awarded the Nobel Peace Prize to the AFSC and its British counterpart, the Friends Service Committee, in 1947. Although news of the award prompted Clarence Pickett, the organization's executive secretary, to caution his staff to "beware when men think well of you," he observed that, "in an age when increasingly the state [is] held to be supreme, the prize has gone . . . to that way of life which holds each individual to be a child of God and therefore of supreme value."

See also Cadbury, Henry Joel; Pickett, Clarence Evan.

References Abrams, Irwin, *The Nobel Peace Prize and the Laureates: An Illustrated Biographical History 1901–1987* (1988); Bacon, Margaret, *Let This Life Speak: The Legacy of Henry Cadbury* (1987); Meyer, Robert S., *Peace Organizations Past and Present* (1988).

American League against War and Fascism

Organized in 1933, the American League against War and Fascism was a coalition of liberal and left-wing organizations united to oppose war and the Fascist governments in Europe that threatened the peace. It had a paper membership of several million members, but—because it included such disparate groups as the American Communist Party and old-line pacifists—securing cooperation within the organization was difficult. Within a year of its founding, members of the American Communist Party broke up a Socialist demonstration at a league meeting in New York City. After that, several important groups left the league, including the Socialist groups, most pacifists, and the National Association for the Advancement of Colored People. Nevertheless, the league remained fairly vigorous throughout the decade, periodically sponsoring huge demonstrations and sending out newsletters nationwide to both farm and labor groups.

Reference Wittner, Lawrence S., *Rebels against War: The American Peace Movement 1941–1960* (1969).

American League for the Limitation of Armaments

See American Union against Militarism.

American Movement for World Government (AMWG)

In 1945, a book written by Emery Reves, entitled *The Anatomy of Peace*, analyzed the causes of war and made a strong case for building peace on a global level. Reves argued that modern technology had rendered the concept of a sovereign nation-state obsolete. The book was published just before atomic bombs were dropped on Hiroshima and Nagasaki, bringing Japan to the surrender table and ending World War II. In light of the destructive nature of nuclear weapons, Reves's argument seemed to many people to be prescient at the very least. It was out of this concern that the American Movement for World Government (AMWG) grew.

Although the AMWG was not incorporated as an organization until 1970, it had flourished as a movement throughout the 1950s and 1960s. Its objective was to educate the American public on the need for a democratic, federal world government created either through a world constitutional convention or by transforming the United Nations (U.N.) into an effective government. To this end, the AMWG established a speaker's bureau and an educational forum for peace groups, churches, and schools. World Government Seminars are held in New York City each May, sponsored by the AMWG publication *World Peace*. The World Government Center headquarters also oversees publication of a quarterly newsletter, *Peace Bulletin*. In August 1987, the AMWG cosponsored the International Bicentennial Symposium on Strengthening the United Nations. The delegates who met in Philadelphia to attend the conference received a *Declaration of Interdependence*, written by members of the AMWG and based loosely on the U.S. Declaration of Independence. Initiating changes in the structure of the U.N. continues to be a primary goal of the AMWG.

Reference Meyer, Robert S., *Peace Organizations Past and Present* (1988).

American Peace Award

In 1923, *Ladies Home Journal* Editor Edward William Bok sponsored a contest to find the best practical solution for maintaining peace and cooperation among nations. The contest was open to all and the prize was to be an award of $100,000. The winner was to receive half immediately, with the remaining $50,000 to be paid when and if Congress approved the plan. The contest attracted worldwide attention and several hundred thousand peace plans were submitted to the jury. Of those, 22,165 proposals met all of the contest requirements. The winning proposal was submitted by Charles Herbert Levermore, a longtime peace advocate, who had dedicated much of his life to international peace. The prize jury submitted Levermore's plan to the public, for its approval or disapproval, through 800 newspapers and 300 magazines. Under the contest rules, Levermore's name was withheld until the public vote was counted. The referendum resulted in a vote of 608,090 votes for the Levermore plan.

Levermore's plan contained three provisions: (1) the United States should join the Permanent Court of International Justice; (2) without officially joining the League of Nations, the United States should use the machinery of the league as "an instrument of mutual counsel," assuming no obligation to interfere with political questions of policy or international administration of foreign states; and (3) international law should be revised in order to renew the existing rules of the law of nations, thereby providing, in time, a broad and recognized code for maintaining international justice and for defining the social rights and duties of nations. Levermore never received the second half of the prize award, because the Congress never approved the plan.

See also Bok, Edward William; Levermore, Charles Herbert.

References National Cyclopaedia of American Biography, vol. 6 (1967); Starr, Harris E., ed., *Dictionary of American Biography*, supp. 1 (1944); Wynner, Edith, and Georgia Lloyd, *Searchlight on Peace Plans: Choose Your Road to World Government* (1944).

American Peace Society (APS)

The American Peace Society (APS), founded in Boston in 1828, was one of the oldest and most respected of the peace organizations active in the first half of the twentieth century. The APS always had a strong Christian emphasis, as illustrated in its original statement of purpose: "The society, being founded on the premise that all war is contrary to the spirit of the gospel, shall have for its object to illustrate the inconsistency of war with Christianity." Almost from its conception, the APS advocated an international court of arbitration to which all nations could turn in order to resolve disputes without resorting to war. It was, nevertheless, an essentially conservative organization within the spectrum of peace organizations. During the period of U.S. neutrality during World War I, for example, the APS refrained from taking a stand on the difficult political and diplomatic questions confronting proponents of peace.

The APS experienced a period of rapid growth when Benjamin Franklin Trueblood took over the duties of general secretary in 1892. At that point, membership in the APS stood at about 400, and its publication, *Advocate of Peace*, had a circulation of just over 1,000 copies. When Trueblood stepped down in 1915, membership had risen to 8,000, and the publication enjoyed a circulation of 11,500. Moreover, under Trueblood's direction, *Advocate of Peace* had become an influential forum in the peace community. Particularly in the era preceding World War I, the APS's reputation as the premier peace organization attracted almost every prominent peace advocate in the United States, including David Starr Jordan, Hamilton Holt, Edwin Ginn, Edwin Doak Mead, and Lucia

Ames Mead. The society was represented at every major national and international peace conference of the era, and its members frequently took the lead in promoting internationalism and arbitration.

See also Trueblood, Benjamin Franklin.

Reference Patterson, David S., *Toward a Warless World: The Travail of the American Peace Movement 1887–1914* (1976).

American School Peace League

Founded in 1908 by Fannie Fern Phillips Andrews, the league was intended to promote peace by introducing principles of international justice and fraternity into the curricula of U.S. schools. By 1915 it had branches in 40 states, primarily because of the energy of Andrews and her fellow peace workers, including Lucia Ames Mead.

The National Education Association urged all teachers to cooperate with the league, and in 1912, the U.S. commissioner of education, Philander P. Claxton, invited Andrews to serve as special advisor in his bureau. The movement spread to Europe, with French teachers organizing a similar league. On a trip to England in 1914, Andrews helped organize the School Peace League of Great Britain and Ireland.

The league distributed circulars, leaflets, and booklets for classroom use. The material included poetry, endorsements for peace from statesmen and military leaders, accounts of peace activity, information regarding other peoples and cultures, and a series of programs, including pageants and essay contests that were designed to further the message of international peace. Following the outbreak of World War I, the league—fearful of a potential backlash—officially changed its name to the American School Citizenship League. Although it was most active as an organization in its early years, the league continued to function until 1950.

See also Andrews, Fannie Fern Phillips.

References Andrews, Fannie Fern Phillips, *Memory Pages of My Life* (1948); James, Edward T., et al., eds., *Notable American Women, 1607–1950: A Biographical Dictionary* (1971).

American Union against Militarism (AUAM)

(Originally organized in early 1915 as the American League for the Limitation of Armaments.) With the outbreak of World War I in Europe, American progressive reformers grew increasingly alarmed at the call for U.S. military preparedness and the possibility of involvement in the war. This was particularly true of women reformers, who viewed any war as antithetical to the reform impulse. Convinced that all wars were forms of injustice, Lillian Wald, Oswald Garrison Villard, and Norman Mattoon Thomas, among others, organized the league to help concentrate opposition to Woodrow Wilson's preparedness program. In April 1916 the league changed its name to the American Union against Militarism (AUAM).

The AUAM had the support of an impressive array of progressive reformers and Socialists, including Jane Addams, Paul Kellogg, Amos Pinchot, Crystal Eastman, Max Eastman, Stephen Wise, Frederick Howe, Louis Lochner, Florence Kelley, Helen Keller, Hamilton Holt, Fanny Villard, and James Mauer. It advocated complete neutrality on the part of the United States, published antimilitarist essays, lobbied in Washington against preparedness, opposed conscription, and campaigned against U.S. imperialism in Latin America. Branches sprang up in every major city in the country within one year. Members were primarily engaged in lobbying members of Congress and the White House. They also distributed over half a million pieces of antipreparedness literature. On all their speaking tours around the country, AUAM members sported the official mascot, a papier-mâché dinosaur called Jingo, who wore a collar around his neck with the legend: "All Armor Plate—No Brains." Jingo became something of a national celebrity, and the AUAM theme song, "I Didn't Raise My Boy to Be a Soldier," became a national hit.

Once the United States entered the war, a major concern of AUAM members was the disregard for the civil liberties of those who continued to express opposition. Crystal Eastman, the organization's executive director, along with her assistant, Roger Baldwin, and Norman Thomas, established the Civil Liberties Bureau (CLB) of the AUAM in order to protect the civil liberties of those who were being harassed by the government for their opposition to the war. The CLB ultimately became the American Civil Liberties Union (ACLU).

See also Thomas, Norman Mattoon; Villard, Oswald Garrison; Wald, Lillian.

References DeBenedetti, Charles, ed., *Peace Heroes of Twentieth Century America* (1986); Knock, Thomas J., *To End All Wars: Woodrow Wilson and the Quest for World Order* (1992); Whitman, Alden, ed., *American Reformers* (1985).

Americans for Democratic Action (ADA)

Originally called the Union for Democratic Action, the Americans for Democratic Action (ADA) was organized following the 1940 Socialist party convention. In that year, the Socialist party platform called for absolute neutrality and opposition to military appropriations. Although the Socialists condemned Adolf Hitler, the party contended that just because the British and French were engaged in the war against Hitler, that did not render it a holy war. Opposition to this stand within the Socialist party caused what became known as the "silent split," with some New York Socialists joining the Committee to Defend America by Aiding the Allies and another faction organizing the Union for Democratic Action. The union supported Allied participation in World War II because its members were too horrified at the atrocities being committed by the Nazis and because they believed that the alternative—an Axis victory—would always pose a threat to peace and freedom.

The renamed ADA did not hold its first official conference until March 1947. By then, ADA membership was composed of moderate liberals like James Wechsler, who supported the Truman Doctrine and who opposed the Henry Wallace liberals who had been alienated by President Harry S Truman's efforts to rally western support against the Soviet Union. The ADA liberals were not enamored of Truman and, indeed, many of them banded with Democratic party leaders in an effort to persuade Truman to step down as a candidate. Efforts were made to enlist the candidacy of, among others, Dwight D. Eisenhower, but in the end, the ADA and the Democratic party supported Truman, who went on the win the 1948 election.

During the Vietnam War, ADA members supported efforts in 1967 to stop the bombing of North Vietnam and to advocate peace negotiations. A group calling itself Negotiations Now!, which was backed by the ADA, sought a candidate for the presidency, either Democratic or Republican, who would be more flexible in negotiating with the North Vietnamese than was President Lyndon Johnson. Former New York antiwar congressman Allard Lowenstein took over as ADA president following Johnson's 1969 retirement. Under Lowenstein, the ADA sponsored an unusual protest in 1972, which enjoyed the participation of some of Lowenstein's former colleagues from the U.S. House and Senate. Speakers at the 1972 rally included senators Edward Kennedy, John Tunney, and Alan Cranston and representatives Bella Abzug, Robert Drinan, and Edward Koch. The ADA membership is still composed primarily of a broad spectrum of liberals.

See also Lowenstein, Allard.

References DeBenedetti, Charles, ed., *Peace Heroes in Twentieth Century America* (1988); Wittner, Lawrence S., *Rebels against War: The American Peace Movement 1941–1960* (1969); Zaroulis, Nancy, and Gerald Sullivan, *Who Spoke Up? American Protest against the War in Vietnam, 1963–1975* (1984).

Andrews, Fannie Fern Phillips (1867–1950)

Fannie Fern Phillips Andrews, a scholar and educator, focused both her professional activity and private life on efforts to secure lasting peace. Born in Nova Scotia,

Canada, and raised in Lynn, Massachusetts, Andrews was one of seven children of William Wallace Phillips and Anna Maria (Brown) Phillips. Her mother, an active Baptist and a member of the Women's Christian Temperance Union (WCTU), imbued in Andrews a zeal for activism. After graduating from Salem Normal School in 1884, Andrews began her teaching career. She also continued her own education. She enrolled at Radcliffe College, where she earned a B.A. in 1902 and a Ph.D. in 1923. In 1890 she married Edwin Gasper Andrews. The couple was childless, thus providing Andrews greater opportunity to pursue reform activities.

In 1908, Andrews founded the American School Peace League in the Boston public schools. Her goal was to promote peace through education. The league eventually had branches in 40 states, but efforts to expand internationally were cut short by the United States's entry into World War I. Throughout that conflict, Andrews worked with the League to Enforce Peace as well as with an international group called the Central Organization for a Durable Peace. *Freedom of the Seas*, which Andrews wrote, was published in 1917 under the auspices of that organization. By that time, she had come to the attention of President Woodrow Wilson, and in 1918 Wilson tapped Andrews to attend the Paris Peace Conference. Her hope was that the covenant of the League of Nations would provide for an international bureau of education. It did not. Disappointed, Andrews persisted, and in the 1920s, such a bureau was established. Fittingly, President Franklin Delano Roosevelt appointed Andrews as the official U.S. delegate to the bureau meetings in 1934 and 1936.

In the 1930s, Andrews began gathering information for a study on international diplomacy. The study was never completed, however. Fannie Andrews died in Somerville, Massachusetts, on 23 January 1950.

See also American School Peace League.

References Andrews, Fannie Fern Phillips, *Memory Pages of My Life* (1948); James, Edward T., et al., eds., *Notable American Women, 1607–1950: A Biographical Dictionary* (1971).

Antiballistic Missile Treaty

In 1972, as part of the general Strategic Arms Limitation Talks (SALT), an antiballistic missile (ABM) treaty agreement was achieved and entered into. President Richard M. Nixon traveled to Moscow in May 1972 to meet with Soviet Premier Leonid Brezhnev. The SALT agreement signed by the two world leaders had been worked out in advance by subordinates from both sides. It called for severe limitations on ABM systems, which, in any event, had a questionable defensive effectiveness. The agreement also froze intercontinental ballistic missile (ICBM) deployment on both sides at the levels that existed when the treaty was signed. In return for its cooperation, the Soviet Union was granted the right to purchase large quantities of U.S. wheat, a condition that caused domestic grain prices to increase sharply. The pact was to last for only five years.

References Link, Arthur S., et al., eds., *The American People: A History* (1981); Meyer, Robert S., *Peace Organizations, Past and Present* (1988).

Artists for Survival (AFS)

Artists for Survival (AFS), founded in Waltham, Massachusetts, in January 1972, remained a relatively small organization that nevertheless managed to make itself known through a series of art and poster campaigns designed to encourage a halt to the nuclear arms race. In an effort to make an "emotional and intellectual" appeal to the public, AFS held numerous exhibits, including exhibitions at the Senate and House of Representatives and Harvard Medical School. Its Posters for Peace rallies helped to initiate several poster exchanges between school children in the United States and Soviet Union. AFS was also active as a participant in the Nuclear Freeze Movement.

See also Nuclear Freeze Movement.

References Kaltefleiter, Werner, and Robert L. Pfaltzgraff, eds., *The Peace Movement in Europe and the United States* (1985); Schell, Jonathan, *The Fate of the Earth* (1982); Whitman, Alden, ed., *American Reformers* (1985); DeBeneditti, Charles, ed., *Peace Heroes in Twentieth Century America* (1988).

Athletes United for Peace (AUFP)

In 1983, Athletes United for Peace (AUFP) was founded to promote peace through sports contacts between the United States and the Soviet Union. The organization hosted a visit by Soviet athletes who participated in the Kansas relays, held at the University of Kansas in Lawrence in 1983. Out of that event, a "Declaration of American and Soviet Athletes United for Peace" was issued. The "Lawrence Declaration" was signed by athletes from more than 40 countries and helped to initiate a series of AUFP conferences held around the world, including in West Germany and Japan. The organization eventually built up a membership of more than 500 athletes.

Reference Wank, Solomon, ed., *Doves and Diplomats: Foreign Offices and Peace Movements in Europe and America in the Twentieth Century* (1978).

Baez, Joan (1941–)

Folk singer Joan Baez, born in Staten Island, New York, in 1941, grew up in California. Both of her grandfathers were ministers, and both parents were academics. After graduating from high school in Los Angeles, Baez returned to the East to attend Boston University. She abandoned her academic career when she began singing in coffee houses in Cambridge. Her career as a folk singer took off after her first appearance at the Newport Folk Festival in 1959.

Her long association with protest singer Bob Dylan began shortly thereafter. It was Baez who introduced Dylan to the world when she invited him to appear at her concerts. Their relationship was both professional and personal, and Baez made famous many of Dylan's compositions.

In the early 1960s, Baez began to emerge as a vocalist for social causes. A fixture at the civil rights rallies and marches of that era, she became associated with the song "We Shall Overcome," which became the movement's anthem. Baez was also an active pacifist. She founded the Institute for the Study of Non-Violence in Carmel, California, in 1965. As an activist in the antiwar movement, Baez refused to pay income taxes and made countless appearances at rallies. She was married briefly to student antiwar leader David Harris in 1968.

Baez has remained a committed pacifist and peace advocate. Since 1974 she has been a member of the advisory council of Amnesty International. She also helped to found Humanitas, the international human rights commission, in 1979.

References Baez, Joan, *Daybreak* (1968); Baez, Joan, *And a Voice to Sing With* (1987); Uglow, Jennifer S., ed., *The Continuum Dictionary of Women's Biography* (1989).

Bailey, Hannah Clark Johnson (1839–1923)

In her seventies and eighties, Hannah Bailey's lifelong dedication to peace and pacifism led her to direct the most comprehensive woman's peace movement of the late nineteenth century and early twentieth century. Born Hannah Johnson at Cornwall-on-Hudson, New York, she was the oldest of 11 children. Her father was a minister in the Society of Friends. Hannah and her siblings were raised on the pacifist principles of Quakerism.

Although her own education was somewhat limited, Hannah taught school throughout the 1860s before marrying Melvin Bailey, a Maine factory owner. She remained active in the Quaker church throughout her marriage, was a member of the Women's Christian Temperance Union (WCTU), and was involved in a variety of WCTU reform issues, most related to women. From 1891 to 1897, Bailey served as president of the Maine Woman Suffrage Association, and from 1894 to 1899 she was also the treasurer of the National Council of Women. All of this was carried on as Bailey was directing a peace campaign through the WCTU, which had been initiated in 1887, when the organization created a Department of Peace and Arbitration. Bailey served as superintendent of the new department and, with the able assistance and support of WCTU President Frances Willard, she began to advocate pacifism.

Highly organized and focused, Bailey kept up a voluminous correspondence with WCTU branches in the United States and abroad. She published two monthly newsletters: one for adults, called *Pacific Banner*, and another, *Acorns*, for children. In addition, Bailey saw to it that literature was distributed through Sunday

School classes in churches throughout the country. She also maintained a speakers bureau that sent out lecturers to spread the pacifist message and went on speaking tours herself. Bailey organized petitions to Congress, urging arbitration in international crises, and strongly advocated that parents refrain from giving their children toys that might glorify war, such as toy guns. Bailey continued her campaign for pacifism right up to the eve of World War I.

Forced to retire in 1916 because of her advancing age, Bailey was greatly distressed when the WCTU endorsed the United States's entry into the war. Thereafter, ill health kept her out of the public domain. Hannah Bailey died in Portland, Maine, in 1923.

References James, Edward T., et al., eds., *Notable American Women, 1607–1950: A Biographical Dictionary* (1971); *The National Cyclopaedia of American Biography*, vol. 10 (1967).

Balch, Emily Greene (1867–1961)

In recognition of a lifetime of activism on behalf of peace, Emily Greene Balch was awarded the Nobel Peace Prize in 1946. Even at her advanced age, Balch was not yet ready to retire and remained active well into her eighties. Her sense of service in the public good extended back to her earliest years.

Balch was born near Boston, Massachusetts, and was the second of six children of Francis Vergnies Balch and Ellen Maria (Noyes) Balch. Both her parents were progressive reformers who made selflessness the highest ideal in the family. Encouraged by her parents, Balch graduated in the first class at Bryn Mawr College in 1889. Determined to put her education to good use, she carved out a career in economics, studying first in Paris as the first Bryn Mawr European Fellow. Balch followed up with a year at Harvard Annex (1893), a year at the University of Chicago (1895), and a year at the University of Berlin (1896). Her teaching career was spent at Wellesley College, where she started as a grader in Katherine Coman's economics course and rose to a full professorship and department chairperson in economics and sociology by 1913. Throughout that period, Balch was an active participant in causes ranging from immigration to labor to socialism.

Both her academic career and the focus of her activism were profoundly altered with the outbreak of World War I. She accepted Jane Addams's invitation to attend a meeting of American and European women leaders at The Hague in order to discuss peaceful solutions to the conflict. The American Women's Peace Party (WPP) was one of the outgrowths of that meeting; thereafter, Blach devoted all her time to pacifist activism. Because of her refusal to stand down after the United States entered the war, Balch's name became associated with a variety of peace groups ranging from conservative to radical. In 1917 she helped to found the Emergency Peace Federation, leaving herself open to charges of being un-American. But it was her vocal support of the People's Council of America that forced her to choose principle over career security. Because of the council's association with bolshevism and socialism, Wellesley's board of trustees voted to postpone consideration of Balch's reappointment. The anti-Red hysteria that erupted at the end of the war had claimed Balch. She refused to protest the decision, as some of her colleagues urged. "I am obliged to give up the happiness of full and unquestioned cooperation where the responsibility of choice is mine," she said. Balch joined the Fellowship of Reconciliation (FOR) during the war and became increasingly drawn to Quakerism, a philosophy that went beyond pacifism to a spiritual communion between individuals. In this, she found a common ground for working out the solutions that divided people.

In May 1919, Balch attended the International Congress in Zurich and helped to found the Women's International League for Peace and Freedom (WILPF). The remainder of her life was devoted to work with the WILPF. Balch succeeded Jane Addams as president of the league's U.S. branch in 1931 and became the honorary international president in 1937. An avowed feminist, she believed in the effectiveness of women working together to secure social change. During her years with the WILPF she addressed leaders of government and groups concerned with international issues.

Her support of U.S. involvement in World War II was reluctant and was based on her concern for the plight of European Jews. During the war, she lobbied on behalf of German Jews and interned Japanese Americans. All of Balch's concerns helped to secure for her the Nobel Peace Prize, an honor that she never sought and hugely deserved. Balch died the day after her ninety-fourth birthday, on 9 January 1961.

See also Emergency Peace Federation; Women's International League for Peace and Freedom.

References Randall, M. M., *Improper Bostonian: Emily Greene Balch* (1964); Sicherman, Barbara, et al., eds., *Notable American Women, The Modern Period: A Biographical Dictionary* (1980).

Baldwin, Roger Nash (1884–1981)

For more than half a century, Roger Nash Baldwin led the American Civil Liberties Union (ACLU) and remained its spiritual leader until his death at the age of 97.

Baldwin was born in Wellesley, Massachusetts. He was a brilliant student and graduated from Harvard University in 1904. A year later he earned his law degree at the University of Washington Law School. Baldwin found St. Louis agreeable and remained there for several years, first taking a job on the faculty of Washington University and then working on behalf of children in the St. Louis Juvenile Court system. He was chief probation officer for the Juvenile Court from 1907 to 1910 and served on a variety of commissions, including the St. Louis Children's Commission.

Baldwin was an early opponent of World War I, and his predilection for social activism brought him into contact with people like Crystal Eastman and Norman Thomas, founders of the American Union Against Militarism (AUAM). Fearful that those who opposed the war were in danger of the government curtailing their civil liberties, Baldwin, Eastman, and Thomas organized a Civil Liberties Bureau (CLB) of the AUAM in 1915. Throughout the war, the CLB took up the cause of conscientious objectors (COs) and antiwar activists. The issue was particularly vital to Baldwin, because he had been imprisoned for a year for failure to submit to the draft. In 1921 the CLB became the ACLU, an independent and nonpartisan organization dedicated to defending the principles contained in the Bill of Rights. Its agenda, therefore, extended way beyond upholding the rights of COs and war resisters. Baldwin, who had taken over as executive director of the CLB in 1917, became executive director of the ACLU in 1921 and remained in that position until 1950. From 1950 to 1955 he served as national chairman; thereafter, he was the unofficial advisor for the ACLU.

Under Baldwin's tutelage, the ACLU became synonymous with civil liberties. The scope of Baldwin's interest quickly became clear in the 1920s, when the ACLU came to the legal defense of Nicola Sacco and Bartolomeo Vanzetti, the two immigrant shoemakers who were accused of robbery and murder in a case that achieved nationwide notoriety. The ACLU also came to the defense of Tennessee biology teacher John Scopes in the famous Monkey Trial that pitted William Jennings Bryan, arguing for the teaching of creationism, against Clarence Darrow, who defended Scopes's right to teach evolution. In Baldwin's view, cases like these, which tested the limits of civil liberties, were exactly why an ACLU was necessary. Baldwin also defended the publishers of James Joyce's *Ulysses,* when that book was banned from the United States as obscene.

During World War II, in addition to providing advice and assistance to COs and war resisters, Baldwin and the ACLU came to the defense of the Japanese Americans interred in concentration camps. After the war, Baldwin served as an advisor on civil liberties for the occupation forces in Japan, Germany, Austria, and Korea. He never pulled back from representing even the most unpopular causes when he was persuaded that an important constitutional right was involved. Thus, the ACLU has taken up the cause of neo-Nazis, the Ku Klux Klan, and individuals accused of terrorism.

During his lifetime, Baldwin received numerous awards from organizations as well as governments. He also spent several years teaching part time at the New School for Social Research in New York and wrote numerous articles, pamphlets, and books. Baldwin died on 26 August 1981.

See also American Civil Liberties Union.

References Current Biography (1981); DeBenedetti, Charles, ed., *Peace Heroes in Twentieth Century America* (1988); *New York Times* (27 August 1981); Wittner, Lawrence S., *Rebels against War: The American Peace Movement 1941–1960* (1969); Zaroulis, Nancy, and Gerald Sullivan, *Who Spoke Up? American Protest against the War in Vietnam 1963–1975* (1984).

Baltimore Four

On 27 October 1967, Father Philip Berrigan and three companions walked into the Maryland selective service headquarters in Baltimore and, before clerks could react, proceeded to pour a mixture of human and animal blood over the files of potential draftees. It was the first such raid on a selective service office and, consequently, received prominent media attention. The Baltimore Four were tried in federal court and convicted. For his part in the raid, Philip Berrigan was sentenced to six years in prison.

See also Berrigan Brothers; Catonsville Nine.

Reference Lieberman, Mark, *The Pacifists: Soldiers without Guns* (1972).

Baptist Peace Fellowship of North America (BPFNA)

The founding of the Baptist Peace Fellowship of North America (BPFNA) dates back to World War II, when American Baptists formed a support group in order to provide advice and encouragement to their coreligionists who believed that the tenets of their religion forbade participation in the war. A relatively small organization with less than 1,000 members throughout the war years, the fellowship continued its program after the Allied victory, shifting its focus from support of conscientious objectors (COs) to support of the antinuclear movement.

At the same time, members began advocating rapprochement with Russia and a lessening of Cold War tensions. In 1983 a delegation of American and Southern Baptists visited the Soviet Union, meeting with Baptists from that country and reaffirming their belief in working for peace through religious ties. Shortly thereafter, the American and Southern Baptists combined to form a fellowship for all North American Baptists. Expressing the deep conviction that the BPFNA was a response to a "call by God to witness the Gospel of Peace," the fellowship reconfirmed the goal of uniting Baptist Christians in order to help "bring peace to a warring world." The program set out by the leadership included the establishment of peace groups at regional and state levels as well as the local church level to bring together peace groups for common purposes, to encourage active peacemaking among members, to work with other peace groups, and to share activities and concerns with the international community.

Reference Meyer, Robert S., *Peace Organizations Past and Present* (1988).

Barney, Nora Stanton Blatch (1883–1971)

As a young engineering student at Cornell University (1901–1905), Barney organized a women's suffrage club on campus. Her perserverance in pursuing a male-dominated career and her energy in campaigning for women's suffffrage at the same time as she maintained honor student status at Cornell were, in part, a legacy from her famous grandmother and equally well-known mother. Barney was the granddaughter of Elizabeth Cady Stanton, the extraordinary nineteenth century women's rights advocate and mentor of Susan B. Anthony, and the daughter of Harriot Stanton Blatch, an influential campaigner for suffrage in the three decades leading up to ratification of the Nineteenth Amendment.

When Barney graduated from Cornell in 1905, she was the first woman to receive a Cornell degree in civil engineering. Through two marriages and while raising three children, Barney pursued a varied career as an engineer, an architect, a real estate developer, and a volunteer for those causes in which she held a deep and abiding belief. As an engineer, Barney worked for both private and public concerns, including the New York Public Service Commission and, later, the Public Works Administration in Connecticut and Rhode Island during the New Deal years. As an architect and real estate developer, she designed and built many residences in the wealthy suburban community of Greenwich, Connecticut, where she lived with her second husband and children for many years. As a suffrage advocate, she was prominent at rallies and marches, gathered signatures for petitions, made street-corner speeches, and rode in parades. After the Nineteenth Amendment became law, Barney took up the campaign for an Equal Rights Amendment as proposed by Alice Paul and the National Woman's Party in 1923.

Barney's concern for world peace ignited during World War II. Her ideas on creating a democratic house of world government that she hoped would cut through nationalism and ideology were published in 1944 in a pamphlet entitled *World Peace through a People's Parliament.*

Central to her world government ideal was an equal role for women. During the Korean War, Barney again urged a peaceful solution to the conflict and an immediate cease-fire. Nora Barney died on 18 January 1971, still committed to equality for women and world peace.

References *New York Times* (20 January 1971); Sicherman, Barbara, et al., eds., *Notable American Women, The Modern Period: A Biographical Dictionary* (1980).

Bartholdt, Richard (1855–1932)

Richard Bartholdt, a native of Germany, emigrated to Brooklyn, New York, in 1872. He worked as a pressman and proofreader for several foreign-language periodicals before returning briefly to Germany to study law. Upon his return to the United States, Bartholdt continued his career in journalism, and in 1884 he was made editor of the St. Louis (Missouri) *Tribune*, a German-language newspaper.

Bartholdt entered politics in 1888, losing the Republican party nomination to Congress. From 1890 to 1892 he served as a member of the school board and as president of the board in St. Louis. He succeeded in enacting a number of reforms in the school system during his tenure. In 1893 he ran once again for Congress, this time winning Missouri's 10th congressional district seat. In Congress, Bartholdt's interests focused on labor, foreign affairs, infrastructure building, and the tariff, but as World War I loomed, he felt more and more conflicted. In the early days of the war, he presented Germany's side in Congress on several occasions.

He declined to run for an eleventh term in 1914 and turned his efforts to peace instead. He had worked tirelessly for arbitration of international disputes almost from his first term in Congress. He made dozens of trips abroad, attending numerous conferences of the Interparliamentary Union for the Promotion of International Arbitration.

While in Congress, he formed an American Group of the Interparliamentary Union in 1903, serving as its president for eleven years. In 1904 he was elected as its president. Bartholdt also attended the annual arbitration conferences at Lake Mohonk, New York, and lectured widely on the topic. He was a member of Henry Ford's "Peace Ship," an effort to persuade European countries to enact a cease-fire by Christmas of 1915.

Bartholdt continued, after the war, to work for international arbitration. Unbound by party considerations, he chose to support progressive candidate Robert La Follette in 1924 and Democrat Al Smith in 1928. But his dedication and integrity won him the friendship and confidence of six U.S. presidents in both political parties. He carried on voluminous correspondence with advocates of peace and arbitration throughout the world until his death in St. Louis on 19 March 1932.

References *The National Cyclopaedia of American Biography* vol. 25 (1967); Patterson, David S., "An Interpretation of the American Peace Movement, 1898–1914." In *Peace Movements in America*, ed. Charles Chatfield (1973).

Beals, Charles E. (1869–1931)

A clergyman born in Stoughton, Massachusetts, Charles Beals spent his life ministering to his congregations and working for peaceful solutions to world problems. As a student of mechanical engineering at the Massachusetts Institute of Technology, Beals's interests shifted to religion, and he eventually graduated from Drew Theological Seminary in 1892. Beals and his wife, Nellie Vernon Drake, and their four children served in a number of churches throughout Massachusetts.

In 1908 Beals resigned from the Prospect Street Church in Cambridge to become field secretary for the American Peace Society (APS). He was made director of the Central-West Department of the society in 1912. He was also secretary of the Chicago Peace Society from 1910 to 1914. Although Beals did not suspend his peace work, he returned once again to the ministry, accepting a post as pastor of Church of Unity in Worcester, Massachusetts, in 1915. He organized the second National Peace Congress in Chicago in 1909 and entirely reorganized the Chicago Peace Society in 1910. He was also a fixture at the annual Lake Mohonk arbitration conferences from 1908 to 1913.

As for many other peace advocates, World War I was an enormous disappointment to Beals. He continued to advocate peace, particularly as a contributing editor to *The Nation* in 1919. But in the 1920s, Beals concentrated more on church organization and conferences. Beals died in East Taunton, Massachusetts, on 4 October 1931, but his dedication to international peace ensured him a lasting reputation as one of the influential figures in the U.S. peace movement.

References Patterson, David S., "An Interpretation of the American Peace Movement, 1898–1914." In *Peace Movements in America*, ed. Charles Chatfield (1973); *Who Was Who in America*, vol. 1 (1943).

Bender, Harold Stauffer (1897–1962)

Harold Bender, born in Elkhart, Indiana, became the foremost Mennonite scholar of his day. After graduating from Goshen College in 1918, he went on to the Garrett Biblical Institute, Princeton Theological Seminary, and Princeton University. He also did postgraduate work in Germany before returning to Goshen College as a professor of Bible and church history.

The Mennonite Church, one of the historic peace churches, preached a literal discipleship in its role as the faithful church. As such, Mennonites believed in the "gospel of peace" and advocated living according to that gospel. Bender, who had established himself as the chief theologian of the Mennonite vision, followed the teachings of a literal discipleship by becoming an activist in the peace movement. Bender's role as a leader in the peace churches movement helped him to shape the movement in at least one significant way. He served on the executive committee of the Mennonite Central Committee (MCC), the main agency for peace service in the church. He was also chairman of the Peace Problems Committee in his church. At the Historic Peace Churches Conference in 1935, Bender began working with other church peace activists in creating a U.S. program of alternative service for conscientious objectors (COs). As chairman of the Mennonite Central Peace Committee, Bender continued to work closely with other peace church activists on the National Service Board for Religious Objectors (NSBRO).

Although Bender's alternative service concept served all COs during and after World War II, young male Mennonites were especially well represented, even among peace church members. Three out of every five young male Mennonites declared themselves COs during World War II and accepted alternative service. Bender, a committed pacifist himself, was disappointed that fully two-fifths of young Mennonites chose to participate in the military. Nevertheless, his ideas regarding alternative service proved to be a significant contribution to the cause of peace, and Bender continued his peace work after the war. He was an active participant in the International Fellowship of Reconciliation (FOR). From 1944 until his death on 21 September 1962, he also served as dean of the Goshen College Biblical Seminary.

References Josephson, Harold, ed., *Biographical Dictionary of Modern Peace Leaders* (1985); Wittner, Lawrence S., *Rebels against War: The American Peace Movement 1941–1960* (1969).

Berger, Victor L. (1860–1929)

At the age of 18, in 1878, Victor Berger immigrated from his native Austria-Hungary to the United States. A committed Socialist who believed that the fundamental cause of war was the capitalist economic system, Berger settled in Milwaukee and began teaching in a local high school. Berger was never dogmatic in his political beliefs—a characteristic that sometimes proved as troublesome for his Socialist colleagues as his socialism was for mainstream Americans.

Berger left teaching to work as a journalist, eventually becoming editor of the *Wisconsin Vorwarts*, the *Social Democratic Herald*, and finally the *Milwaukee Leader*. He dabbled in third-party politics for a time before founding the Socialist Party of America, the party that nominated Eugene Debs for president several times—including in 1912, when the Socialists garnered fully 10 percent of the popular vote. Berger himself served in the U.S. House of Representatives as a member of the Socialist party from 1911 to 1913 and again from 1923 to 1929.

In his role as editor, Berger consistently editorialized in favor of peace. Likewise, in Congress he leaned heavily toward issues that involved questions of peace. He introduced a resolution to

Victor L. Berger

withdraw U.S. troops from Mexico. During World War I, which he condemned, Berger helped draft his party's position paper in 1915. With a list of particulars not dissimilar to those of every other peace group, the Socialists called for an immediate end to the war, universal disarmament, and an international peace-keeping organization.

Because of his ties to socialism, his advocacy for peace caused Berger to be convicted for conspiracy to violate the Espionage Act, and he was prohibited from taking the seat in Congress that he had won in the 1918 election. A special election to fill the seat was held, and Berger won that race as well, but to no avail, as the Congress was determined not to seat him. Eventually, the Supreme Court overturned his conspiracy conviction.

Berger opposed militarism, standing armies, the national guard, the arms race, and the lack of any real structure for international arbitration, but he was not a pacifist. Berger accepted the idea of wars of liberation and believed in social revolution. Unlike many of his Socialist colleagues, Berger also accepted the idea of wars of national self-defense. He was pragmatic enough to realize that working people identified with their nations rather than with an amorphous international working class, as most Socialists believed. And although he held out the hope that a future internationalism would produce a united worldwide working class, in the situation as it existed, Berger advocated citizen armies for self-defense against both external agressors and internal oppressors. Views such as these almost cost Berger his position on the Socialist party executive committee. After his reelection to the House of Representatives, Berger served there as a member of the Socialist party until his death on 7 August 1929.

Reference Miller, Sally M., *Victor Berger and the Promise of Constructive Socialism* (1973).

Berrigan Brothers

Daniel and Philip Berrigan, priests and brothers, were among the most visible of the antiwar protesters during the Vietnam era. Born in Syracuse, New York, in 1921 and 1923 respectively, the Berrigans came from a close-knit family of Irish Catholics and grew up in a home where poetry and radical labor politics were constant passions. Dan Berrigan was thin and shy; Phil Berrigan was tall and athletic. In 1939, Dan announced his decision to become a priest and enter the Society of Jesus. The Jesuits appealed to his desire to live a life of service in the community. He spent the next 13 years at a seminary in Poughkeepsie, New York, and was ordained in 1952.

During those years, Philip Berrigan had two experiences that that helped to shape his own future. He had been drafted in 1943 and had spent some time at a southern base. He saw firsthand and for the first time how appalling the conditions of segregation and poverty were in which African Americans lived and became determined to help change those conditions. Two years in combat also convinced him that war was an unacceptable solution to conflict. On his return to the United States, Philip Berrigan attended Holy Cross College and then entered the Society of Saint Joseph, following Daniel into the priesthood. He chose the Josephites because they worked with African Americans, and his first assignment after ordination was to teach school in New Orleans. He quickly acquired a reputation as a "troublemaker" within the religious community when he began taking part in civil rights demonstrations. In 1964 he was reassigned to Newburgh, New York.

Like his brother, Daniel Berrigan had also involved himself in civil rights activity, but—what was more problematic for the Jesuits—Daniel Berrigan began calling for reform within the Catholic Church. By 1965 both brothers began to speak out against U.S. involvement in Vietnam. They were the first Catholic priests to sign a "declaration of conscience" opposing around-the-clock bombing and the war in general. Philip Berrigan was ordered by the Josephites to stop making public statements regarding the war. His refusal resulted in another transfer, this time to a Baltimore ghetto parish.

On 27 May 1967, after a series of escalating demonstrations, Philip Berrigan and three companions entered the selective service headquarters in Baltimore and poured blood over the files of potential draftees. They were quickly arrested and became known as the Baltimore Four. Eventually, Philip Berrigan was sentenced to six years in prison for his part in the raid.

Daniel Berrigan, in the meantime, had also been arrested in Ithaca, New York, for participating in a demonstration at Cornell University. On 17 May 1968, the two brothers and seven others, later referred to as the Catonsville Nine, staged a raid on the Catonsville, Maryland, selective service office, this time removing files from the office, dousing them with napalm, and igniting them. Found guilty of destroying government property, Philip Berrigan was sentenced to three and a half years and Daniel to three years in prison.

The actions that the Berrigans took initiated a wave of direct-action confrontations by members of the peace movement who were commonly called the Catholic left. Most notable were raids on selective service offices in Milwaukee and Chicago, which resulted in the destruction of a combined total of 50,000 draft records, and on the Dow Chemical Company, the manufacturer of napalm used in Vietnam. In addition, J. Edgar Hoover, director of the F.B.I., claimed in November 1970 that the Berrigans were masterminds of a plot to kidnap Henry Kissinger, reportedly to force the government to stop the around-the-clock bombing of Hanoi. Hoover's charges were never substantiated. The Berrigans' appeal was turned down by the U.S. Supreme Court, but before the brothers could be incarcerated, they disappeared. Philip and another member of the Baltimore Four were arrested on 21 April, twelve days after going underground. Daniel managed to elude the FBI until August, when agents arrested him on

Block Island, Rhode Island, where he had gone to visit friends. Both brothers were sent to federal prison to serve out their sentences.

See also Baltimore Four; Catonsville Nine.
Reference Lieberman, Mark, *The Pacifists: Soldiers without Guns* (1972).

Bethe, Hans Albrecht (1906–)

A brilliant theoretical physicist whose accomplishments included the discovery of what makes the sun shine, Hans Albrecht Bethe was born in Strasbourg, Alsace-Lorraine. His was a family of scientists and doctors, and he earned his Ph.D. from the University of Munich by age 22. Bethe's brilliance was easily detected early on, and it was no surprise that he used the newly developed system of quantum mechanics to solve previously enigmatic problems while still a graduate student.

Bethe's career in the German university system might have proceeded uninterrupted had it not been for Adolf Hitler and the rise of nazism. Bethe, whose mother was a Jew, was one of many scientists who left Germany in the 1930s. The young physicist went first to England, where he secured a teaching position at the University of Manchester before taking a position of the University of Bristol. In 1935, Bethe accepted a position as assistant professor at Cornell University in the United States. It was while he was at Cornell that Bethe worked out the theory of what made the sun shine, a theory that held up to a variety of proofs. Bethe continued to excite the scientific community with his discoveries. In 1940, *Time* magazine described Bethe as "one of Nazi Germany's greatest gifts to the United States."

Bethe was one of the scientists chosen to develop an atomic bomb at the highly secret Los Alamos Laboratory during World War II. He was placed in charge of the theoretical physics department. The work that he and his colleagues did was so important that the predictions supplied by Bethe's team became the ground upon which all other divisions in the project conducted their work.

The atomic bombs had barely fallen on Hiroshima and Nagasaki before a group of scientists—including Albert Einstein and Hans Bethe—who had helped develop the bomb formed the Emergency Committee of Atomic Scientists (ECAS) in 1946. Deeply concerned that the United States not engage in an arms race or continue to develop more powerful weapons of destruction without first directing its vast resources toward international cooperation, the scientists eventually came to oppose the development of the hydrogen bomb. Bethe hoped at first that international control of atomic energy might provide a reasonable answer to limiting the production of atomic weapons; however, as the Cold War intensified in the years immediately following World War II, it became more and more clear that another war—a far more lethal one—was very possible. Consequently, Bethe began to side with those who supported statesman George Kennan's Containment Theory as being the most logical and possible method of controlling nuclear proliferation. Containment of Russia became U.S. policy, but Hans Bethe never relinquished his deeply held belief that the indiscriminate development of nuclear weapons was folly for mankind.

Unlike Edward Teller, whose views eventually prevailed, Bethe did not believe that scientists had no moral obligation to decide whether or not hydrogen bombs should be developed. Bethe, along with other scientists like Albert Einstein and Linus Pauling, continued to protest the development of nuclear weapons. In the Cold War atmosphere that, by the 1950s had become impervious to rational thought on all sides, Bethe and many of his colleagues had to endure unfair and unfounded attacks on their patriotism.

See also Emergency Committee of Atomic Scientists.

References *Current Biography* (1950); *Time* (29 January 1940); Wittner, Lawrence S., *Rebels against War: The American Peace Movement 1941–1960* (1969).

Beyond War

In 1962, a group of people in San Fransisco who were concerned about the world their children would inherit, organized an informal discussion group called Creative Initiative. Creative Initiative sponsored at-home discussion groups focusing on issues that included population control and the environment and which became the impetus for local projects related to those issues. Creative Initiative functioned in this manner for approximately 20 years, until 1982. At that time, members began to pay particular attention to nuclear war and the dire consequences of such an eventuality. With a new focus, the group also changed its name to Beyond War.

Characterizing itself as an "idea rather than an organization," Beyond War has thousands of members working throughout the country to spread the idea that war is obsolete, that all life on earth is interrelated and therefore must be mutually protected and nourished, and that it is imperative to begin building a world beyond war. Members of the organization take seriously the observation made by Albert Einstein in 1946 that "the unleashed power of the atom has changed everything save our modes of thinking, and we thus drift toward unparalleled catastrophes."

In an effort to change people's thinking, Beyond War sent its members out as missionaries. Families relocated for year-long sabbaticals, during which time they delivered their message in both formal and informal settings. As part of their mission, these families trained local families to take over and continue the program in their own communities. Originally, there was no effort in Beyond War to affect or develop legislation; the organization did not engage in lobbying efforts, nor did it subscribe to partisanship. An annual award, the Beyond War Award, is given yearly to individuals or organizations who make outstanding contributions to helping realize the goal of a world beyond war. During the first several years of the award, recipients included the National Council of Catholic Bishops, Physicians for the Prevention of Nuclear War, the Five Continent Peace Initiative, and the Contadora Group.

In October 1985, Beyond War used satellite communications to bring together more than 15,000 members who had already trained as discussion group leaders to plan future programs. In 1987, departing from previous policy, Beyond War sent a task force to Washington to lobby congressmen, senators, think tanks, policy makers, labor unions, foundations, and public organizations. With a well-developed program intended to educate others on the question of the obsolescence of war and the irreparable damage nuclear war would cause, and using the example of Central America as an example of how even conventional war is not a viable solution to conflict, members of Beyond War spoke with hundreds of elected officials, public officials, heads of foundations, and prominent individuals. The organization continues to spread the ideas developed since 1962. A monthly newsletter entitled *On Beyond War* keeps members informed of ongoing programs.

Reference Meyer, Robert S., *Peace Organizations Past and Present* (1988).

Bishops' Pastoral Letter

On 3 May 1983, the American Conference of Bishops of the Catholic Church issued a major statement on nuclear war to all of its congregations across the country. The Bishops' Pastoral Letter on War and Peace, called "The Challenge of Peace: God's Promise and Our Response," was a remarkable departure from traditional, official Catholic support for government policy. Although the pastoral letter was not an authoritative church teaching, the bishops did draw on church documents to support their position on nuclear war, including Pope John XXIII's encyclical, *Pacem in Terris*, and Vatican Council II.

The Catholic Church, which, in its very early existence had been a pacifist church, had long relied on the just war theory, formulated by St. Augustine (A.D. 354–430). The just war theory was an attempt on the part of Christian theologians to limit the brutality of war, without going so far as to embrace pacifism, and to set standards for determining what constituted an acceptable war and what constituted an unacceptable war. The U.S. bishops applied the just war theory to nuclear weapons and came to three central conclusions. They argued first that the use of nuclear weapons violated just war criteria. Second, in their view, a just war precluded any intention to use nuclear weapons. And third, the bishops acknowledged a "strictly conditional moral acceptance of nuclear deterrence"; possession of nuclear weapons was acceptable only if that possession was accompanied by serious efforts to secure disarmament.

The pastoral letter also discussed the implications of the conclusions drawn regarding nuclear weapons for individual conscience. It called upon Catholics, especially those in the military, to determine if they could, in good conscience, take part in preparing for a possible nuclear war. It offered clear praise for conscientious objectors (COs).

Reaction to the letter in the United States was mixed. Many Catholics applauded the bishops for taking the initiative, and very few people could object to the stated desire for ultimate disarmament. Some critics, however, considered the letter a clear threat to implementation of the government's nuclear policy. Moreover, not all Catholic prelates agreed with the letter. Some bishops felt that it was too strong an indictment of government policy. Nevertheless, the letter was a product of the growing Catholic peace and justice movement that had been gaining strength since the late 1970s and which included nonviolent resistance to U.S. policy in Central America, the establishment of peace and justice offices in many U.S. dioceses, and symbolic acts of protest—like those of the Plowshares Movement, which entered factories manufacturing weapons parts, thereby forcing authorities to arrest them.

References Kaltefleiter, Werner, and Robert L. Pfaltzgraff, eds., *The Peace Movement in Europe and the United States* (1985); Seeley, Robert, *The Handbook of Nonviolence* (1986).

Bok, Edward William (1863–1930)

When Edward Bok took over as editor of *The Ladies Home Journal* at the age of 26, the Dutch-born immigrant had already established his reputation in the publishing field. Born in den Helder, Holland, Bok and his family immigrated to New York in 1870. Bok, an avid reader, derived his first ideas about the potential for personal success in the United States from reading biographies of successful Americans. His most salient impression was that most of them had come from extremely modest circumstances and, by

Edward Bok

hard work and ingenuity, had realized remarkable success. Bok vowed to do the same. He worked from the age of 10 to help support his family, and at 13 he quit school entirely. He began his career in publishing by delivering newspapers, reporting on children's birthday parties, and eventually writing short biographies of great Americans for a souvenir card company.

In 1884 he began working for Charles Scribner's Sons. Eventually, Bok and a partner started their own newspaper syndicate, beginning with a weekly article by Henry Ward Beecher. Bok also began to focus on women readers and their interests. It was Bok who developed the concept of a "woman's page" that was quickly picked up by newspapers across the country. When Scribner's began publishing *Scribner's Magazine*, Bok was placed in charge of advertising. He was not averse to taking on any task that would promote the magazine, including the writing of advertisements for a then–little-known book that quickly became famous—*Looking Backward* by Edward Bellamy. It was this kind of attention to detail that helped to establish a reputation for Bok. But when, in 1889, publishing magnate Cyrus Curtis asked Bok to take over as editor of the relatively new *Ladies Home Journal*, Bok was advised by almost everyone to turn it down. Bok chose to take on the task of building the magazine and essentially created the format for women's magazines.

Recognizing early on that women's interests included home and family but also extended beyond to the worlds of literature, art, health, politics, and a host of other interests, Bok accommodated these interests in the pages of the *Ladies Home Journal*. He also elevated the magazine by announcing in 1892 that the *Journal* would no longer accept advertisements from patent medicine manufacturers. It was a risky step, because patent medicine was the mainstay of advertising revenue at the time. A resulting flurry of lawsuits eventually helped to bring about passage of the Food and Drug Act in 1906, about which Bok always expressed pride. He remained with the *Journal* until his retirement in 1920. When he retired, the *Journal* had a circulation of 2 million and advertising revenues of about $1 million per issue. His autobiography, released in 1920, *The Americanization of Edward Bok*, became a nationwide best-seller and won for Bok the Pulitzer Prize in 1921.

Bok, who was one of the nation's most active civilian workers during World War I, involved himself in a variety of civic and social causes, one of which was sponsoring a contest, called the American Peace Award, in 1923. The contest asked contestants to submit a workable plan for preventing future wars between the United States and other countries. Bok put up prize money of $100,000, half to be awarded on selection of the winning proposal and the other half to be awarded when Congress approved the proposal. The contest attracted worldwide attention and several hundred thousand entries were submitted. The winner was Charles Levermore, himself a noted peace advocate. Levermore's plan was never approved by Congress, but the ideas he suggested would all eventually be incorporated through the United States's participation in the United Nations (U.N.). Bok remained an activist until his death on 9 January 1930.

See also American Peace Award.

References The National Cyclopaedia of American Biography, vol. 6 (1967); Starr, Harris E., ed., *Dictionary of American Biography*, supp. 1 (1944); Wittner, Lawrence S., *Rebels against War: The American Peace Movement 1941–1960* (1969).

Bok Award
See American Peace Award.

Bok Prize
See American Peace Award.

Borlaug, Norman (1914–)
A nutritionist and the first head of the United Nations (U.N.) Food and Agriculture Organization, Norman Borlaug received the Nobel Peace Prize in 1970 for his successful efforts to increase agricultural production through the application of scientifically researched methods. In awarding the prize to Borlaug, the committee noted that "more than any other single person in this age, he has helped to provide bread for a hungry world. We have made this choice in the hope that providing bread will also give the world peace."

Armed with a Ph.D. in plant pathology, Borlaug accepted an invitation from the Rockefeller Foundation in 1944 to join a team of research scientists bound for Mexico at the request of the Mexican Ministry of Agriculture. Borlaug helped to develop a short-stemmed dwarf wheat particularly suited to Mexican environmental conditions that produced an unusually rich yield. His success with wheat and other staple crops in Mexico attracted a steady stream of young scientists anxious to study with him and to export his methods to numerous other underdeveloped countries, including Afghanistan, India, Turkey, Pakistan, and Morocco. By 1970, when Borlaug received his Peace Prize, approximately 25 million acres in countries around the world were planted according to his methods. The harvest from that combined acreage helped to feed 500 million people.

Borlaug was credited with creating a "green revolution," something that he underplayed, because, in his opinion, such a revolution would merely be ephemeral if the problem of human reproduction could not be brought under control. Nevertheless, Borlaug noted that he was "optimistic for the future of mankind . . . since man is potentially a rational being."

References Abrams, Irwin, *The Nobel Peace Prize and the Laureates: An Illustrated Biographical History, 1901–1987* (1988); Josephson, Harold, ed., *Biographical Dictionary of Modern Peace Leaders* (1985).

Boss, Charles Frederick, Jr. (1888–1965)
One of the more gratifying moments of Charles Boss's career as a peace

advocate came when he was designated an accredited observer at the United Nations (U.N.) Charter Conference in 1945. A longtime proponent of just such a world peacekeeping organization, Boss spoke and wrote enthusiastically on behalf of internationalism and the U.N. throughout his career.

Born in Washington, D.C., Boss was educated at George Washington University, Boston University, Harvard Graduate School, American University, and Northwestern University. He became a Methodist minister and church leader and served as superintendent of the Church School Administration of the General Board of Education from 1926 to 1928, as director of the Bureau of Research of the General Board of Education from 1928 to 1933, and as the executive secretary and then general secretary of the Methodist Board of World Peace from 1936 to 1957.

As a young churchman beginning his career at the height of the Progressive Movement, Boss had no qualms about involving himself politically to achieve the goals he believed in. In the late 1930s, as World War II first threatened and then became reality, Boss worked with a group of clergymen determined to foster an alternative service program for conscientious objectors (COs). He served on the National Service Board for Religious Objectors (NSBRO), and his Methodist Board of World Peace was the only nonhistoric peace church pacifist group in the NSBRO.

After the war, Boss continued to speak out against universal military training and for international abolition of conscription. As a committed internationalist, Boss served as leader of the World Conference of Christian Youth, first in Amsterdam in 1939 and again in Oslo in 1947. Much of his post–World War II career, however, was dedicated to the success of the U.N. Appearing before Congress on several occasions, Boss consistently advocated cessation of unilateral action and support for U.N. action. In 1953 the Carnegie Peace Center cooperated with Boss in establishing a Methodist U.N. Office at the center.

Boss never accepted the inevitability of the Cold War. Although he was sometimes accused of naïveté in his dismissal of realpolitik, he firmly believed that a rapprochement with the Soviet Union was possible. Long before détente was seriously considered as a possibility, Boss argued on its behalf. In his honor, the U.N. Church Center renamed one of its rooms the Boss Room. Charles Boss died in Alexandria, Virginia, on 13 December 1965.

References Harmon, Nolan B., ed., *The Encyclopedia of World Methodism* (1974); Josephson, Harold, ed., *Biographical Dictionary of Modern Peace Leaders* (1985).

Bourne, Randolph Silliman (1886–1918)

An intellectual beacon whose writing and literary criticism helped to define his generation, Randolph Bourne's entire professional career lasted less than a decade. Born in Bloomfield, New Jersey, Bourne had physical deformities that might have crushed a weaker spirit. Suffering from dwarfism compounded by a markedly hunched back, he knew at an early age that he would have to find his own way to overcome a life of almost certain despair. Working in a sweatshop, he saved enough money to finance a college education at Columbia University with the help of a partial scholarship. He was already 23 when he entered Columbia, and almost from the first moment, he found the intellectual milieu that he had longed for.

While he was an undergraduate, several of Bourne's essays were published in the *Atlantic Monthly*. By the time he graduated in 1912, he had already established himself as a literary intellectual. Columbia awarded him a fellowship that allowed him to travel in Europe for a year. There he met many of the leading socialists, including H. G. Wells and George Bernard Shaw.

The foreign experience had an enormous influence on Bourne. When he returned to the United States after Germany declared war, he took a position as educational editor of the *New Republic*, thanks to the efforts of Charles Beard. Bourne was deeply distressed over the war in Europe and the prospect of the United States entering the war. When that possibility became fact in April 1917, Bourne wrote a series of articles published in the *Seven Arts* that were critical of the United States' entry into the war and of the entire Allied war policy. The articles staked out for Bourne a role as the country's foremost intellectual critic of foreign policy. He was particularly distressed when his colleagues at the *New Republic* and elsewhere rapidly jettisoned their previously held beliefs about war and peace and endorsed the war. Bourne accused them of betraying their intellectual heritage.

Bourne was in the process of writing an essay entitled "The State" when he contracted influenza during the epidemic of 1918. He died at the age of 32 on 22 December 1918, leaving in his final essay the warning that "war is the health of the state."

Reference Josephson, Harold, ed., *Biographical Dictionary of Modern Peace Leaders* (1985).

Bowman, Rufus David (1899–1952)

Rufus Bowman, born into the Church of the Brethren on 23 January 1899, learned early the tenets of this historic peace church grounded in pacifism. A native of Dayton, Virginia, Bowman subscribed wholeheartedly to his church's teachings. After graduating from Bridgewater College in 1923, he went on to Yale Divinity School, graduating in 1926. He returned to school later on, first to do graduate work at Catholic University in 1937 and then to earn a Ph.D. from Northwestern University in 1944.

His first ministerial position took him back home to Virginia, where he performed the duties of pastor at a church in Roanoke after his graduation from Yale. It wasn't long before the promising young pastor came to the attention of the national office, and in 1929 he was called to Elgin, Illinois, to direct the Christian education program for the national Church of the Brethren. It was an opportunity that Bowman did not squander.

During World War I, much to Bowman's disappointment, the Church of the Brethren had been ambivalent at best in its resolve to maintain a traditional pacifistic stance. Bowman determined to strengthen that resolve. Using his position as national education director, the young clergyman encouraged church members to embrace the traditional peace position. He took every opportunity to participate in the interdenominational peace movement and served on the executive committee of the Emergency Campaign for Peace. He was also a member of the National Council for the Prevention of War. His work with activists in the historic peace church meetings, which included Mennonites and Friends, gained him a reputation within the movement. He wrote numerous articles on peace, and his attendance at international peace conferences in Cambridge, England and Geneva provided him with ideas for helping to establish a program of alternative service for conscientious objectors (COs).

Bowman's familiarity with political issues convinced him by the mid-1930s that war was an almost certain prospect. He worked with other members of the historic peace churches to convince President Franklin Delano Roosevelt of the necessity to establish a Civilian Public Service (CPS) program. Bowman's doctoral dissertation, written during the war, became the authoritative study on Brethren response to war when it was published in 1944 as *The Church of the Brethren and War, 1708–1941*. After the war he continued writing and collecting material for a book on the CPS program. Bowman died in 1952 before he could complete work on that book.

References Josephson, Harold, ed., *Biographical Dictionary of Modern Peace Leaders* (1985); Wittner, Lawrence S., *Rebels against War: The American Peace Movement 1941–1960* (1969).

Bridgeman, Raymond Landon (1848–1925)

Raymond Bridgeman was born in Amherst, Massachusetts. He graduated from Amherst College in 1871 and attended Yale University Graduate School for two years. While at Yale, Bridgeman was a newspaper correspondent and eventually went on the lecture circuit, speaking on a variety of subjects, including world politics. The Massachusetts Agricultural College (later the University of Massachusetts) selected Bridgeman as the first series lecturer on world politics.

Bridgeman was a prolific author, and several of his books were widely read by those involved in the peace movement, including *The Master Idea* (1899), *Loyal Traitors* (1903), *World Organization* (1905), and *The First Book of World Law* (1911). He died in Auburndale, Massachusetts, on 20 February 1925.

References Patterson, David S., "An Interpretation of the American Peace Movement, 1898–1914." In *Peace Movements in America*, ed. Charles Chatfield (1973); *Who Was Who in America*, vol. 1 (1943).

Bryan, William Jennings (1860–1925)

Born on the eve of the Civil War, on 19 March 1860, in Salem, Illinois, William Jennings Bryan chose early in life to follow his father into public service. Silas Bryan—a state senator, judge, and a member of the state constitutional convention in 1870—provided the example of dedicated public service that his son would emulate and surpass.

A lawyer, congressman, senator, two-time presidential nominee, and secretary of state during Woodrow Wilson's first administration, Bryan was a dynamic orator of both power and eloquence. Bryan's impassioned free silver speech at the 1896 Democratic convention, in which he vowed that he would not allow his opponents to "crucify mankind upon a cross of gold," so galvanized the convention that he was nominated for president

the following day. Although he lost that campaign and the campaign of 1900, he remained a powerful figure in the Democratic party. In 1912 it was Bryan who was able to persuade the Nebraska delegation to vote for Wilson on the fourteenth ballot of a deadlocked convention. In return, Wilson named Bryan secretary of state. As war clouds were forming in Europe in 1914, Bryan found himself in a position to directly influence the course of world events.

As secretary of state, Bryan proposed a program for the prevention of war through "treaties of investigation." Nations would agree, Bryan explained, not to declare war until an international commission of inquiry could investigate and report on the dispute. Three-quarters of the world's nations agreed in principle with Bryan's proposal and entered into agreement with the United States, binding themselves to avoid war by first submitting to arbitration. A notable exception to the agreement was Germany. Bryan also worked to resolve the long-standing dispute with Columbia over the Panama Canal.

When World War I broke out, despite Bryan's efforts to the contrary, his pacifist principles would not allow him to compromise his efforts to keep the United States out of the war. As Wilson prepared to notify Germany that the United States would defend its rights if Germany violated U.S. neutrality through an aggressive act, Bryan could not in good conscience support the stand. His profound belief in the prevention of war compelled him to resign as secretary of state in June 1915. Because of his actions, Bryan was condemned from all quarters for walking away from the government at such a crucial time and for possibly harming the prestige of President Wilson.

Bryan ended his long career in 1925 when he agreed to work with the prosecution in the famous Scopes "monkey trial" in Tennessee. A staunch anti-evolutionist, Bryan was pitted against Clarence Darrow in what was arguably the era's

William Jennings Bryan

most sensational trial. The emotional defense of creationism took a toll on the 65-year-old Bryan from which he was unable to recover. He died suddenly at the close of the trial in Dayton, Tennessee, on 26 July 1925.

References Coletta, Paola, *William Jennings Bryan*, 3 vols. (1964–1969); *The National Cyclopaedia of American Biography*, vol. 19 (1967).

Buddhist Peace Fellowship (BPF)

Founded in 1978, the Buddhist Peace Fellowship (BPF) was created specifically to bring a Buddhist perspective to the peace movement and to bring the peace movement to the Buddhist community. The BPF's goals enumerated by its founders include: raising peace and ecology concerns among U.S. Buddhists, creating projects through which members can respond to the issues, offering avenues to promote friendship between U.S. and world Buddhists, serving as a liaison to existing Buddhist peace and ecology programs, and bringing the Buddhist perspective to contemporary peace and ecology movements.

The first non–Judeo-Christian group to affiliate with the Fellowship of Reconciliation (FOR), the BPF is one of 16 religious peace fellowships. Its activities have included campaigns opposing the political repression of Buddhists as well as participation in disarmament efforts, ecology, and human rights actions. The BPF publishes a quarterly newsletter and offers assistance to local groups in developing appropriate projects. Although the local chapters operate within broad guidelines established by the BPF, they nevertheless retain much of their autonomy.

Reference Meyer, Robert S, *Peace Organizations Past and Present* (1988).

Bunche, Ralph J. (1904–1971)

In 1949, as chief mediator for the United Nations (U.N.), Ralph Bunche accomplished what many world leaders believed was impossible. He successfully negotiated an armistice ending Arab-Jewish hostilities over Palestine. To be sure, the armistice eventually broke down, but Bunche had, nevertheless, accomplished something that was nothing short of miraculous. For his efforts, Bunche was awarded the Nobel Peace Prize in 1950.

An African American native of Detroit, Bunche grew up at a time when it was still acceptable for people to exhibit prejudice against nonwhites. Were it not for his grandmother, Bunche might never have lived up to his potential in so remarkable a fashion. Urged by her to stand up for his rights and to reject indignities—and to do so without bitterness—Bunche won an athletic scholarship to UCLA. When he graduated summa cum laude in 1927, he was a member of Phi Beta Kappa. He went on to Harvard to complete graduate work.

Rather than accept an invitation from any one of a number of white institutions that sought him out, Bunche chose to teach at Howard University. After establishing a department of political science there, Bunche accepted a Rosenwald

Fellowship to do research for his own Ph.D. In 1934 he became the first African American to earn a Ph.D. in political science. Over the next several years, Bunche cemented his reputation as an expert on race relations. His book, *A World View of Race*, prompted the noted social scientist Gunnar Myrdal to invite Bunche's collaboration on a two-year study of blacks in the United States. The project led to publication of Myrdal's landmark treatise, *An American Dilemma*.

By then, World War II was underway, and Bunche joined the Office of Strategic Services. Secretary of State Cordell Hull was instrumental in Bunche's ultimate move to the State Department, where he served as the department's colonial problems troubleshooter. Before long, he was appointed acting chief in the Office of Political Affairs, the highest post held by an African American in the State Department.

In 1946, U.N. Secretary-General Trygve Lie asked Bunche to organize and direct the Trusteeship Division of the U.N. Secretariat. With the Arab-Jewish conflict over Palestine exploding as it did following the end of World War II, Bunche was the logical person to take on the task of mediation. He had been on the receiving end of prejudicial behavior in his own life and possessed the attributes necessary for such a job. In fact, he himself had defined the qualities required of effective mediators: "They should be biased against war and for peace. They should have a bias which would lead them to believe in the essential goodness of their fellowman and that no problem of human relations is insoluble. They should be biased against suspicion, intolerance, hate, religious and racial bigotry." After nearly a year of grueling negotiations, Bunche returned home to a hero's welcome, complete with a ticker tape parade through the streets of New York and an official Ralph Bunche Day in Los Angeles.

Bunche remained with the U.N., turning down President Harry S Truman's offer to appoint him assistant secretary of state. Accepting his Nobel Prize, Bunche described the U.N. as the "greatest peace effort in human history." He implored the West to help translate peace into "bread, rice, shelter, health and education, as well as freedom and human dignity," predicting that Asia and Africa, with their vast numbers, would become a "dominant factor in the future world pattern of life." Bunche resigned from the U.N. as under secretary-general in October 1971 and died two months later on 9 December 1971.

Reference Abrams, Irwin, *The Nobel Peace Prize and the Lauraeates: An Illustrated Biographical History, 1901–1987* (1988).

Burton, Theodore Elijah (1851–1929)

As a fixture in Republican party circles in Ohio and Washington for over four decades, Theodore Burton gained a well-earned reputation for integrity, common sense, and loyalty. He was born in Jefferson, Ohio, and graduated from Oberlin College before heading off to Chicago to read law. He returned to Ohio in 1875 and for the next 40 years maintained an intermittent practice in Cleveland, which he left frequently to serve as U.S. representative (1889–1890, 1895–1908, 1921–1928) and U.S. senator (1909–1915, 1928–1929).

Burton quickly gained a reputation as a politician who rejected machine politics and special interests. At the same time, he became known as a stalwart advocate for peace and internationalism. During his first term in Congress in 1889, the Interparliamentary Union was founded, and Burton became an avid supporter. The union, dedicated to peaceful resolutions of international disputes, eventually enlisted Burton as a member of its Executive Committee from 1904 to 1914, and again from 1921 to 1929. Burton and his colleague, Richard Bartholdt, another peace movement supporter, founded the U.S. branch of the Interparliamentary Union. Burton was also a longtime supporter of the Permanent Court of International Justice and fought arduously for United States inclusion in the court.

Although Burton often fought long and hard to set limits on military spending and arms buildups, he was not a pacifist. He opposed most preparedness bills and fought against the naval cruiser buildup program in 1926, but he nevertheless believed in maintaining an adequate defense and in the necessity of possessing arms to ensure that defense. Although he hated the idea of war, he nevertheless supported U.S. involvement in World War I.

His high-profile support of peace measures (including the Kellogg-Briand Pact), his tenure as president of the American Peace Society (APS) from 1911 to 1916, and his advocacy of internationalism combined with his rational approach to these issues made Burton, in the eyes of President Calvin Coolidge, the ideal nominee for delegate to the League of Nations Conference on the Traffic in Arms that was held in Geneva in 1925. During the course of conference sessions, Burton became the most prominent spokesman for outlawing the use of poison gas.

One of Burton's last major projects was organizing a World Conference on International Justice in Cleveland in 1928. The conference celebrated the centennial of the APS, of which Burton was then president. Burton was reelected to the U.S. Senate in 1928, but his term was cut short when he died in Washington on 28 October 1929.

Reference Josephson, Harold, ed., *Biographical Dictionary of Modern Peace Leaders* (1985).

Butler, Nicholas Murray (1862–1947)

In 1931, in the midst of his tenure as president of Columbia University, Nicholas Murray Butler, already hailed as the architect of Columbia's vault into the pantheon of U.S. universities, was honored for his equally monumental work on behalf of world peace when he, along with Jane Addams, was awarded the Nobel Peace Prize. Butler, who was born in Elizabeth, New Jersey, graduated from Columbia in 1882 and went on to earn an M.A. (1893) and a Ph.D. (1884) from the institution with which he was destined to forge a lifelong association.

After a brief period in Berlin and Paris, Butler returned to Columbia as an assistant tutor (1886–1889). He went on to become an adjunct professor of philosophy and a professor of philosophy and education. In 1889, he founded the *Educational Review* and served as its first editor for 29 years. The *Review* became a showcase for the scholarly opinions of the leading educators not only in the United States but around the world. In the meantime, Butler founded what ultimately became Columbia Teacher's College and served as its first president from 1886 to 1891. A brief bout of ill health forced his resignation as president. In the ensuing years, Butler continued editing the

Nicholas Murray Butler

Educational Review. He also launched the *Great Educators Series,* a series of biographies of world-renowned educators. In 1894 he started the Teacher's Professional Library.

In 1901, Butler was asked to take over the presidency of Columbia University. For the next four and a half decades, he worked tirelessly to make Columbia a respected center for intellectual growth, academic inquiry and discovery, and the pursuit of excellence. He attracted a faculty second to that of no other similar institution, he made Columbia's graduate schools into centers of scholarship, and he expanded the physical plant of the university after overseeing its move to its present site on Morningside Heights in New York City.

If Butler had accomplished nothing else, his stewardship of Columbia would have been sufficient to bring him acclaim, but—like many successful people of his generation—he put as much energy into a wide variety of civic and philanthropic endeavors. As an advocate of international arbitration and world peace, Butler exerted a profound influence in the nation and the world. He served as president of the Lake Mohonk Conference on International Arbitration in 1907 and from 1909 to 1912.

It was also Butler who, in 1910, persuaded Andrew Carnegie to establish the Carnegie Endowment for International Peace. Butler served as a trustee of the foundation from 1911 until his death and was a director from 1911 to 1945. During his period of leadership, international relations clubs were founded in cities throughout the country and abroad. He helped to establish international alcoves in libraries throughout the world and helped to set up an exchange program for both students and professors, between the United States and other countries.

Although Butler was a strong advocate of world peace, he was not a pacifist. He strongly supported the United States's entry into both world wars to fight against what he characterized as savage dictatorships. Butler strongly supported the League of Nations, even though he was consulted on and helped to frame the Senate's reservations to the Treaty of Versailles, which Woodrow Wilson refused to accept and which ultimately led to the failure to ratify the treaty.

Butler was also a prolific writer. He wrote extensively on the peace movement and the quest for permanent peace. His works include: *The International Mind* (1913), *The Basis of a Durable Peace* (1917), *A World in Ferment* (1918), *The Path to Peace* (1930), *The Family of Nations* (1938), and *Why War?* (1940). In addition to the Nobel Peace Prize, Butler was given honorary degrees from universities around the world and bestowed with medals of merit from governments around the world. He died in New York City on 7 December 1947.

Reference *National Cyclopaedia of American Biography,* vol. 34 (1967).

Cadbury, Henry Joel (1883–1974)

Henry Cadbury's life as a peace activist bracketed his academic career as professor of divinity at Harvard University. However, his peace activities were hardly peripheral to either the peace movement or to his own life. Born in Philadelphia, Cadbury graduated from Haverford College before going on to earn an M.A. and a Ph.D. at Harvard. As a Quaker, Cadbury was a member of one of the historic peace churches and took his religious beliefs seriously, incorporating them into both his personal and professional lives.

In 1917, Cadbury was one of the founders of the American Friends Service Committee (AFSC), which was organized to provide alternative service for conscientious objectors (COs) and to relieve the suffering of European victims of World War I. By that time, Cadbury had returned to Haverford, his alma mater, to take up a teaching position. The following year, after writing a letter that was published in the Philadelphia *Public Ledger*, Cadbury found himself a victim of the "100 percent Americanism" campaign initiated when the United States entered the war in the hope of vitiating potential opposition to the war. Cadbury's letter took to task those who engaged in anti-German hatred. The college, succumbing to pressure from those who considered Cadbury a traitor, suspended the young Quaker. Instead of backing off, Cadbury threw himself into work for the AFSC. Some years later, from 1928 to 1934, and again from 1944 to 1960, Cadbury served as chairman of the organization. He was chairman when the AFSC received a Nobel Peace Prize in 1947. Eventually, Haverford reinstated Cadbury, but in the early 1930s he accepted a position at Harvard, having by then become a noted biblical scholar.

He never stopped writing about peace and throughout his lifetime published numerous articles in peace journals, including *Christian Century* and *Fellowship*. After his retirement from Harvard in 1954, he devoted most of his time to peace work. Much of his work during the latter years revolved around efforts to bring about an end to the Cold War. Cadbury died in Haverford, Pennsylvania, on 7 October 1974.

See also American Friends Service Committee.

References Abrams, Irwin, *The Nobel Peace Prize and the Laureates: An Illustrated Biographical History, 1901–1987* (1988); Bacon, Margaret, *Let This Life Speak: The Legacy of Henry Cadbury* (1987); Josephson, Harold, ed., *Biographical Dictionary of Modern Peace Leaders* (1985).

Caldicott, Helen (1938–)

When she was a 14-year-old in her native Australia, Helen Broinowski read Nevil Shute's nuclear doomsday thriller, *On the Beach*. The possibility of just such an occurrence had a profound effect on the future physician, radicalizing her forever as an anti–nuclear weapons advocate.

Caldicott was born in Melbourne. At the age of 17, she entered the University of Adelaide Medical School. Six years later, she had earned the equivalent of an American M.D. degree. After marrying her husband, William Caldicott, in 1962, she went into private practice until 1966, when Harvard Medical School offered her a three-year fellowship in nutrition. Shortly after her return to Australia, a near fatal bout of hepatitis caused Caldicott to reevaluate her life goals. Convinced that she owed more to the world than a provincial medical practice, Caldicott became a pediatrician after doing the requisite internships and specialized in the treatment of cystic fibrosis.

Her growing commitment to human survival was inspired not only because of her love for her own children and the children born with cystic fibrosis that she treated but also because of the example of Bertrand Russell, a man who, in her words, "faced up to the dangers of the atomic age and, despite all odds, dedicated himself to ridding the earth of nuclear weapons."

In 1971, Caldicott learned that France was conducting atmospheric atomic bomb testing in the South Pacific, in contravention of the 1962 International Atmospheric Test Ban Treaty. Her outrage prompted her to write letters to newspapers, protesting the situation. Her letters drew so much support that when France scheduled its next test, television news programs asked her to comment on the health hazards involved in such testing. Over the next year, with each of four subsequent tests by France, Caldicott became more and more vocal, exposing an Australian report that showed high levels of radiation in South Australian drinking water, commenting on the dangers of radiation—especially to young children—and noting the higher levels of radiation found in rainwater. Because of her persistence, other scientists condemned the testing, consumers boycotted French products, and France was ultimately taken before the International Court of Justice at The Hague. Eventually, France stopped atmospheric testing.

Caldicott was also responsible for the Australian Council of Trade Unions' passage of a resolution banning the mining, transporting, or selling of uranium. The ban lasted from 1975 to 1982, when, according to Caldicott, multinational corporations persuaded the council that it was selfish not to sell uranium to an energy-hungry world.

The Caldicotts, meanwhile, immigrated permanently to the United States in 1977. Caldicott became a fellow in the cystic fibrosis clinic at Boston's Children's Hospital Medical Center. In addition, she was an instructor in pediatrics at Harvard Medical School. In 1978, Caldicott, by then a member of Physicians for Social Responsibility (PSR), a nearly defunct organization that had been founded in 1962, organized a meeting in her home, intent on reviving the PSR. It remained relatively low-key until the near-meltdown of Three Mile Island nuclear power plant near Philadelphia in March 1978. Coincidentally, the PSR ran an advertisement in the *New England Journal of Medicine* at the same time. The two events resulted in an immediate membership increase of more than 500 physicians. Over the next several years, membership grew steadily at the rate of 250 a week. The main spokesperson for PSR remained Helen Caldicott, who also became its president.

In 1982, the National Film Board of Canada produced a documentary entitled *If You Love This Planet*, which featured Caldicott speaking to a group in Plattsburgh, New York, urging them to shut down a nearby Strategic Air Command base. The film won an Oscar. Caldicott also was featured on a one-hour "Nova" segment produced by WGBH/Boston, a Public Broadcast System television station.

Caldicott believes very much in teaching people through love. In so doing, she is applying what she calls the "positive feminine principle" of "nurturing, caring, protective instinct." This principle has proved to be both influential and distracting to friend and foe alike. Ironically, although she was one of Ronald Reagan's most vocal critics on the issue of nuclear weapons, she was the only antinuclear advocate to have a one-on-one meeting with the former president for more than an hour. Reagan's daughter, Patti Davis, a Caldicott admirer, persuaded Reagan to grant Caldicott an interview in 1983. Although she was not successful in changing Reagan's mind, she did come away with a new awareness of what she called his "dark side," which emerged whenever he spoke about communism.

Caldicott's style led her to resign from PSR in 1983. The organization had grown exponentially after she revived it and served as its president, but its growth and increased membership also made it a more conservative organization, whose members did not always embrace Caldicott's emotional style. Amid sufficient internal criticism, Caldicott resigned the presidency, stating, "I can't in good conscience change what I think and believe—and I can't change the way I express myself." Caldicott remained a member of PSR and continues to travel widely, speaking out against both nuclear weapons and nuclear energy. She has also written widely on the subject. Her best-selling *Nuclear Madness, What You Can Do* was published by Autumn Press in 1978 and Bantam Books in 1980. In addition to her speaking tours in the United States, Caldicott has traveled throughout the world, founding the Medical Campaign Against Nuclear War and the Women's Party for Survival in England. She helped to establish similar organizations in West Germany, the Netherlands, Belgium, and Scandinavia. She has also toured in New Zealand, Japan, and Russia. From the young girl reading about nuclear catastrophe in *On the Beach* to the relentless advocate for nuclear disarmament, Helen Caldicott's has been an important voice in the peace movement.

References *Christian Science Monitor* (28 December 1982); *Current Biography* (1983); DeBenedetti, Charles, ed., *Peace Heroes in Twentieth Century America* (1988); *Washington Post* (26 February 1983).

Call, Arthur Deerin (1869–1941)

Arthur Call was born in Fabius, New York, and graduated from Cortland State College and Brown University in preparation for a career in teaching and public school administration. From 1896 to 1912, Call served as principal of several public schools in New York and New England and as a superintendent of schools in systems in Holliston, Medway, and Sherborn, Massachusetts, and Ansonia and Hartford, Connecticut. From 1906 to 1912, Call was also the president of the Connecticut Peace Society and a member of the executive board of the American Peace Society (APS).

After 1912 he devoted his life to the cause of international peace. When he was asked to accept the post of executive director of the APS, Call resigned his position as superintendent of schools and moved to Washington, D.C., in 1912. In 1915 he took over as editor of the society's publication, *Advocate of Peace through Justice*. Representing the APS, Call attended national conferences in Baltimore, St. Louis, and San Francisco and international peace congresses in The Hague, Luxembourg, London, and Berlin—both prior to and following World War I.

In addition to his other commitments, Call was a director of the International Peace Bureau in Berne from 1915 to 1930. Beginning in 1920, Call also served for 21 years as executive secretary of the U.S. branch of the Interparliamentary Union. As executive secretary, he directed the twenty-third conference of the union held in Washington, D.C., in 1925. In appreciation of his work on behalf of peace in Latin America, Call received a gold medal from the government of Peru, and in 1926 the government of France honored him by making him a chevalier of the Legion of Honor.

Call lectured widely, advocating international peace and arbitration, and wrote *Our Country and World Peace* in 1926. In addition, he wrote several school texts and numerous pamphlets. His accumulated years of dedication to peace carved for him a permenent place in the peace movement. Call died in Silver Spring, Maryland, on 23 October 1941, on the eve of United States's entry into World War II.

References National Cyclopaedia of American Biography, vol. 31; Patterson, David S., "An Interpretation of the American Peace Movement, 1898–1914." In *Peace Movements in America*, ed. Charles Chatfield (1973).

Call to Resist Illegitimate Authority

Seeking to bring attention to mounting opposition to the Vietnam War, 158 professors, authors, clergy, and other professionals signed a statement entitled "A Call to Resist Illegitimate Authority." The statement, coauthored by Marcus Raskin, of the Institute for Policy Studies in Washington, D.C., was made public in October 1967. It was not markedly different in tone or content from hundreds of similar statements that had circulated over the previous several months. Basically, it discussed the legal and moral arguments against the Vietnam War, and it encouraged resistance by those sympathetic to its message. In particular, it encouraged draft resistance. In part, it stated: "We will continue to lend our support to those who undertake resistance to this war. We will raise funds to organize draft resistance unions, to supply legal defense and bail, to support families and otherwise aid resistance to the war in whatever ways may seem appropriate."

Among the call's signers were William Sloan Coffin, Jr., the Yale chaplain; Dr. Benjamin Spock, the preeminent baby doctor; Mitchell Goodman; Michael Ferber; and Raskin. All of the signatories pledged to engage in civil disobedience the week of 16 October, which they designated as Stop the Draft Week. Draft resisters were also promised sanctuary in churches and synagogues if they so desired. Although the document itself was not particularly new, it did become the basis for an indictment against Spock, Coffin, Goodman, Ferber, and Raskin that was handed down by a federal grand jury in Boston on 5 January 1968. The five became known as the Boston Five.

Spock had erroneously predicted that the federal government was not likely to indict the signers, citing the improbability of idictment as an indication of the moral bankruptcy of the government's position. Spock had miscalculated the government's desire to send a message to war resisters. The trial took place in May and June 1968 and resulted in a conviction of four of the five defendants. Raskin was acquitted. Ultimately, the U.S. Court of Appeals overturned the conviction, but the trial itself was disappointing to those who had hoped it would be the vehicle for testing the legality of the Vietnam War. As Spock noted after the trial, "The purpose of the trial was not so much to punish us as to intimidate other people."

References Spock, Benjamin, *Decent and Indecent* (1969); Van Doren, Charles, ed., *Webster's American Biographies* (1974); Zaroulis, Nancy, and Gerald Sullivan, *Who Spoke Up? American Protest against the War in Vietnam 1963–1975* (1984).

Campaign for United Nations Reform

Critical of nations—particularly the powerful United States and the Soviet Union—who refused to abandon selfish vested interests in favor of cooperative world interest, the World Federalist Association (WFA) in 1975 launched the Campaign for United Nations Reform. Noting that the United Nations (U.N.) Charter allows procedures that could assure world peace, campaign director Eric Cox pointed out that without adequate "funding, structure, and authority to guarantee 'an orderly and safe world,'" the U.N. remained ineffective.

Cox identified the United States and the Soviet Union as the two nations most bound by narrow nationalism, although they were not the only ones. The campaign listed a total of 14 steps identified as necessary to prevent the U.N. from fading into obscurity as had the League of Nations. The steps were aimed at providing structures that would allow the U.N. to carry through its decisions, thus strengthening the organization. When Franklin Stark became president of the campaign in 1984, a review of the original suggestions took place. With minor revisions, the same steps were advocated again. The revised 14-point program, published in 1987, includes:

1. Improved General Assembly decision making
2. Modification of the veto in the Security Council
3. An International Disarmament Organization
4. Improved dispute settlement procedures
5. Improved peacekeeping capability
6. Adequate and stable U.N. revenues
7. Greater reliance on the International Court of Justice
8. An International Criminal Court to try hijackers and terrorists
9. Improved human rights machinery
10. Improved environmental and conservation programs
11. International authority for areas not under national control
12. Strengthened world trade and monetary systems
13. Consolidation of the U.N. Development Program
14. Administrative reform of the U.N. system

The campaign has also endorsed the idea of a People's Assembly in the United Nations, composed of elected officials responsible to the people of the world, just as the General Assembly is responsible to the nations of the world.

Reference Meyer, Robert S., *Peace Organizations Past and Present* (1988).

Campaign for World Government (CWG)

The Campaign for World Government (CWG) professes to be the oldest world federalist organization. In 1924, and again in 1937, the CWG called for heads of state to initiate a conference, with invited experts on voting practices, to formulate the best approach for all nations to elect representatives to a World Constitution Convention. In lieu of action by official heads of state, the CWG advo-

cated committees of experts to choose delegates to the convention. The purpose of a World Constitution Convention was to establish a Federation of Nations. Plans for implementation were suspended during World War II, but world federalists resumed efforts when the conference on the establishment of a United Nations (U.N.) was taking place at Dumbarton Oaks in 1945. The federalists argued for a federalist form of world government rather than the association under consideration. In their view, the fundamental problem with a U.N. was that it retained protection of national sovereignty rather than striving to construct a true one-world government that would impose a system of controls over all nations. As late as 1984, a questionnaire sent by the CWG to all members and prospective members of the House and Senate revealed that the responses most favorable to world federalists were in answer to questions involving reform of the U.N. and extending "government by consent of the governed" to world affairs.

Reference Meyer, Robert S., *Peace Organizations Past and Present* (1988).

Capen, Samuel Billings (1842–1914)

Samuel Capen believed that exporting Christian values to foreign countries would produce both a lasting peace and a greatly expanded market for U.S. goods. At the same time, Capen did not characterize himself as an expansionist, because he believed that open markets would be simply a fortuitous circumstance growing out of a stable, peaceful environment. However Capen's motives are interpreted, he did place a premium on finding peaceful solutions to world conflict and participated actively in major peace organizations.

Capen was born in Boston, Massachusetts. His formal education was limited to high school, from which he graduated in 1858. Starting from scratch, Capen managed to build a moderately successful carpet manufacturing business, but his real love was the foreign missionary movement. A devout Congregationalist, Capen began teaching Sunday School and developed his interest in the missions. By 1899 he was elected president of the American Board of Commissioners of Foreign Missions, which at the time was the largest Protestant missionary organization. His mission work fed his desire to promote the cause of peace. He was one of several individuals who, beginning in 1895, became fixtures at the annual Lake Mohonk Conference on International Arbitration.

Over time, Capen served as a vice-president of the American Peace Society (APS), president of the Massachusetts Peace Foundation, and a director of the World Peace Foundation. Along with Lake Mohonk colleagues, including Edward Everett Hale and Benjamin Trueblood, Capen advocated support for a permanent international court of arbitration and deplored massive military spending. On 29 January 1914, while on a tour of China as a representative of both the World Peace Foundation and the American Board of Foreign Missions, Capen died.

Andrew Carnegie

References Josephson, Harold, ed., *Biographical Dictionary of Modern Peace Leaders* (1985); Marchland, C. Roland, *The American Peace Movement and Social Reform, 1898–1918* (1972).

Carnegie, Andrew (1837–1919)

When Andrew Carnegie wrote *The Gospel of Wealth* in 1900, he not only articulated his beliefs about the responsibilities of the wealthy to society, he also defined his own character in a way that a recitation of his commercial successes could not have adequately conveyed. Carnegie firmly believed that those who accumulated great wealth had a responsibility to distribute the surplus wealth in such a way as to benefit the community from which the wealth was derived. In his view, a person who died with accumulated wealth that he or she had not made provisions to distribute, "died in disgrace."

Carnegie, born in Dunfermline, Scotland, immigrated to the United States with his family in 1848. In 1849, Carnegie went to work in a cotton textile factory as a bobbin boy, earning $1.40 per week. When his father died, he became the family provider, a task he accepted with a great sense of responsibility. He gradually worked his way out of the textile factory and into a telegraph office, where he worked as a messenger boy. While there, he also learned telegraphy and eventually beame an operator, earning about $300 per year. The superintendent of the Pennsylvania Railroad, a frequent visitor to the telegraph office, offered Carnegie a 20 percent salary increase to come and work for the railroad. Carnegie did, and his career was thereafter set on a course that would lead to enormous success, first in the railroad industry and then as the founder of United States Steel.

Under Carnegie's leadership, his steel company gradually grew to the point where it overtook production in Great Britain, the world's leading steel producer of that era, and went on to become the foundation of a steel industry that out-produced in quantity and quality all other steel-producing nations combined. In the process, Carnegie amassed enormous wealth.

In 1901 he sold his steel interests and turned his attention to philanthropy. He was the best example of his admonition to spend money for the public good. He endowed countless libraries throughout the world, established philanthropic foundations, and endowed many of them, including the Carnegie Foundation for the Advancement of Teaching, the Carnegie Institution of Washington, the Carnegie Corporation of New York, and the Carnegie United Kingdom Trust. In 1910, Carnegie established a $10 million fund to found and support the Carnegie Foundation for International Peace. Since its inception, the foundation has sponsored numerous international conferences and has promoted the cause of world peace and international arbitration. Andrew Carnegie donated a total of $350 million to civic and social causes in the course of his lifetime. He died on 11 August 1919 in Lenox, Massachusetts.

References Malone, Dumas, ed., *Dictionary of American Biography*, vol. 2 (1936); Morris, Richard B., ed., *Encyclopedia of American History*, vols. 9, 11, 30 (1976).

Catholic Peace Fellowship (CPF)

The Catholic Peace Fellowship (CPF) was founded in 1964 by a group of Catholic activists, including Philip and Daniel Berrigan, Martin Corbin, Thomas Cornell, and James Forest. Affiliated with the much older Fellowship of Reconciliation (FOR), the CPF was founded in the hope that it would strengthen ties between Catholic peace advocates and other Christian groups. Impetus for the CPF came from the Second Vatican Council and the statements made by Pope John XXIII on the necessity of peaceful solutions to world conflict.

The CPF focused on educating Catholics in the principles of nonviolence. It also provided more practical services, including draft counseling. As the war in Vietnam intensified, the CPF also became a forum for speaking out against U.S. policy. The CPF never gained official acceptance by the Catholic Church, and CPF members represented a fairly small percentage of U.S. Catholics. Its founders saw the fellowship as a way to integrate the spiritual lives and the social responsibilities of its members and, ideally, as a new force for social activism within the Catholic Church.

See also Berrigan Brothers.

References DeBenedetti, Charles, ed., *Peace Heroes in Twentieth Century America* (1988); Klejment, Anne, "The Berrigans: Revolutionary Christian Nonviolence." In *Peace Heroes in Twentieth Century America*, ed. Charles DeBenedetti (1988).

Catholic Worker

The Catholic Worker movement was founded by Dorothy Day and Peter Maurins in 1933. The two began publishing a periodical called *The Catholic Worker* as a forum for their views on the neccessity of direct action on behalf of the poor and the homeless. The periodical spawned the movement. The Catholic Worker, a radical pacifist group, established Houses of Hospitality, the first of which was located in New York City's Lower East Side, where people were fed, clothed, and sheltered. By the mid-1930s, *The Catholic Worker* had a circulation of 110,000, Houses of Hospitality in 30 cities nationwide, and a series of farming communes.

In 1935, a branch of the British PAX movement was organized at the Mott Street (New York City) headquarters of the Catholic Worker. The purpose was to study Catholic teaching on the morality of war. This association helped to establish the Catholic Worker as a leading voice for Catholic militant pacifism.

Catholic Workers staged the first anti–Vietnam War rally in New York City in August 1963. The protest, organized by Thomas Cornell, lasted for ten days. For the first nine days, Cornell and fellow Catholic Worker Christopher Kearns walked up and down past the East Sixties residence of Vietnam's permanent United Nations (U.N.) observer, carrying signs protesting the Diem government in South Vietnam. On the tenth day, Cornell and Kearns were joined, at their request, by about 250 protesters—mostly students—representing several peace organizations. The ABC television network filmed the protest and ran it on the nightly news for the first time. The Catholic Worker was one of the sponsoring organizations of the Times Square Vigil, initiated in October 1964 to protest the war. Participants in the vigils vowed to return every Saturday until the war ended.

See also Dorothy Day.

References Wittner, Lawrence S., *Rebels against War: The American Peace Movement 1941–1960* (1969); Zaroulis, Nancy, and Gerald Sullivan, *Who Spoke Up? American Protest against the War in Vietnam 1963–1975* (1984).

Catonsville Nine

On 27 May 1968, nine antiwar protesters, led by Philip and Daniel Berrigan, walked into the Selective Service Local Board No. 33, in Catonsville, Maryland. While astonished clerks looked on, the demonstrators filled baskets with files on 300 potential draftees. The protesters carried the baskets outside, poured napalm over them, and ignited the files. No one resisted when the authorities arrived to arrest the demonstrators. A statement issued by the Catonsville Nine, as they were known, revealed that their protest was leveled not only against the government's war in Vietnam but also against the Catholic Church and other religious groups for refusing to speak out against the war. "Today, we enter Local Board No. 33 at Catonsville, Maryland, to seize Selective Service Records and burn them with napalm manufactured by ourselves. . . . We destroy these records not only because they exploit our young, but because they represent misplaced power concentrated in the ruling class of America. . . . We confront the Catholic Church, other Christian bodies, and the synagogues of America with their silence and cowardice

in the face of our country's crimes," the statement read. "We are convinced that the religious bureaucracy in this country is racist, is an accomplice in war, and is hostile to the poor."

In addition to the Berrigans, the participants included David Darst, a Christian brother and teacher; John Hogan, a Maryknoll brother; Tom Lewis, an artist-activist; Thomas and Marjorie Melville, who had worked in Guatemala as Maryknoll missionaries; George Mische, a former Alliance for Progress worker; and Mary Moylan, a nurse who had worked as a midwife in Uganda. All were well educated and had extensive theological training and experience. None could be described as irresponsible or motivated by personal desires other than that of bringing about an end to the war.

On 7 October 1968, the Catonsville Nine were tried in Maryland. The Berrigans and the other protesters used the forum of the trial to outline their opposition to the Vietnam War. Philip Berrigan expressed the sentiments of all nine defendants when he recorded in his journal: "One does not look for justice in this court, one hopes for a forum. The greatest good that can be extracted from that courtroom is conviction, and the greatest evil, acquittal." After a trial that produced a thousand pages of testimony, the Catonsville Nine were found guilty of trespassing and willfully destroying government property. Philip Berrigan was sentenced to three and a half years, to run concurrently with his six-year conviction for a similar action in Baltimore. Daniel Berrigan was sentenced to three years. The remaining six defendants were each sentenced to lesser terms.

Catonsville led to a series of other actions over the next several months by the so-called Catholic left. Ten thousand draft records were napalmed in Milwaukee in September 1968. In May 1969, 40,000 draft records were burned in Chicago, and in June 1969 a group of nuns and priests walked into the Washington headquarters of the Dow Chemical Company and poured blood over hundreds of files. Dow Chemical manufactured napalm used in Vietnam.

See also Baltimore Four; Berrigan Brothers.

References DeBenedetti, Charles, ed., *Peace Heroes in Twentieth Century America* (1988); Klejment, Anne, "The Berrigans: Revolutionary Christian Nonviolence." In *Peace Heroes in Twentieth Century America*, ed. Charles DeBenedetti (1988); Lieberman, Mark, *The Pacifists: Soldiers without Guns* (1972).

Catt, Carrie Clinton Lane Chapman (1859–1947)

Carrie Chapman Catt was born in Ripon, Wisconsin. Wisconsin, on the eve of the Civil War, was still considered the frontier. As she grew up, Catt learned to be independent and self-reliant in both thought and action. Her disdain for the limitations placed on women was clear from an early age. When her father denied her request to attend college after high school, Catt got a job teaching and saved money to enroll at the University of Iowa. She worked her own way through school at a time when most women did not even think about college and when those who did, did so only with the support of parents and family.

Catt's life work was spent in the women's suffrage movement, in which she became a major force. As Susan B. Anthony's successor, she took over the reins of the National American Woman Suffrage Association (NAWSA) in 1890, at a time when the organization was faltering and dispirited. A superb organizer and a tireless worker, Catt arranged her personal life to suit her career. A second marriage in 1890 to George Catt, whom she had first met when they were classmates in Iowa, was undertaken only after both signed a prenuptial agreeement. (A first marriage to Leo Chapman in 1885 ended less than two years later, when Chapman contracted typhoid while on a trip to California.) The agreement gave Catt freedom for two months in the spring and two months in the fall to suspend marital obligations so that she could

Carrie Chapman Catt

work full time for the suffrage cause. The agreement also demonstrated Catt's willingness to do the unconventional in order to pursue goals that she believed were fundamental. Although the fight for suffrage would not end until ratification of the Nineteenth Amendment in 1920, and although other forces—including the emergence of a militant wing of the movement—helped to shape the final years of struggle, Carrie Chapman Catt remained an active leader. Her contributions to the cause of women's suffrage were immeasurable—indeed, some would say crucial.

Catt's reform interests extended beyond suffrage. She was an avowed pacifist as well. She joined with Jane Addams in 1915 to found the Women's Peace Party (WPP). Her efforts on behalf of peace, however, were less linear and consistent than those on behalf of suffrage. Despite her pacifism, for instance, she chose to support Woodrow Wilson and U.S. involvement in World War I. Her rationale for compromising her principles was her belief that the expediency of backing the war effort would demonstrate to lawmakers and voters that women deserved to have the vote. She was galvanized to further action when the League of Nations proposal was rejected by Congress. At a meeting of the League of Women Voters (LWV) in Cleveland in 1921, Catt appealed to women to use the vote to help put an end to all wars. In 1924 she spearheaded a group, which represented several women's organizations, to promote a program for peace and disarmament. She helped organize a Conference on the Cause and Cure of War, which met in Washington, D.C., in 1925. Among those who supported and attended the conference was Jane Addams. From 1925 to 1939 the conference met annually as the Committee on the Cause and Cure of War, with Catt serving as chairwoman until 1932. By then, Catt was already in her seventies. She spent her last years in New Rochelle, New York, and died there on 9 March 1947.

See also Committee on the Cause and Cure of War; Women's Peace Party.

References James, Edward T., et al., eds., *Notable American Women, 1607–1950: A Biographical Dictionary* (1971); Peck, Mary Grey, *Carrie Chapman Catt* (1975).

Center for Defense Information (CDI)

In the two decades since its founding in 1972, the Center for Defense Information (CDI) has grown into one of the most respected forums for defense analysis. It is considered an impeccable and impartial source for independent analysis of defense policies and their actual and potential impact on world order. A project of the Fund for Peace, the CDI is composed of retired upper- and middle-echelon military personnel and civilians trained in military analysis, all working under the direction of retired Admiral Gene R. La Rocque and united in the fundamental belief that there are no winners in a nuclear war.

The CDI supports effective military defense. At the same time, it clearly identifies excessive military spending and works toward eliminating wasteful spending and reducing military influence on domestic and foreign policy. The CDI is supported entirely by the public and accepts no contributions from government or defense industries. Its reputation is such that it regularly fulfills requests for information from the Pentagon, the State Department, and congressional committees, including the Senate and House Armed Service committees, and the House Foreign Affairs Committee.

The *Defense Monitor*, published ten times a year, is widely quoted by other media and is often read into the *Congressional Record*. The CDI has produced three films dealing with the danger of nuclear war and has published the *Nuclear War Prevention Kit*. It sponsors a speakers bureau, internships, conferences, and seminars. Most recently, the CDI has focused on the shift from an arms race that drove military spending to military spending that has driven the arms race. Admiral La Rocque has urged Congress on several occasions to take the profit motive out of military spending as an important step in decreasing the possibility of nuclear war.

Reference Meyer, Robert S., *Peace Organizations Past and Present* (1988).

Center for Innovative Diplomacy (CID)

In 1983, three Stanford University graduates—Hal Harvey, a civil engineer; Eric Horvitz, a physician; and Michael Shuman, a lawyer—founded the Center for Innovative Diplomacy (CID) in order to reduce the risk of nuclear war. In 1986, two groups—Local Elected Officials of America and Local Elected Officials for Social Responsbility—merged with the CID, setting the stage for a program called the LEO Project and increasing the CID's membership rolls to nearly

5,000, including more than 1,000 mayors, city council persons, and other elected officials.

The core of the LEO Project is to advocate reductions in military spending and the rechanneling of funds for rebuilding cities and the infrastructure while reducing the national debt. Its members are united in the belief that continued massive military spending is potentially catastrophic in terms of possible weapons use and immediately destructive domestically, because funds needed to deal with everything from ecology to education to health care are diverted to military uses instead.

The CID also sponsors other innovative programs, including the Municipal Foreign Policy, which urges state and local government officials to become more involved in foreign affairs on the theory that actions undertaken by the U.S. government directly effect the well-being of citizens on the local level politically, economically, or culturally. It also advocates that cities suspend investment in companies engaged in the production of mass destruction weapons. The Citizen Diplomacy Project is an effort to involve individuals in peacemaking activities by urging them to develop an agenda and to find local networks to work through. PeaceNet is CID's global computer network through which peace groups around the world can be in instant communication. Using computers helps to lessen significantly the cost of disseminating information by reducing the need for costly printing and mailings. The Alternative Security Project seeks to promote the idea that the United States should be working to increase the security of all nations, including traditional adversaries. Overall, the CID's mandate is to reduce the "risks of nuclear and conventional war by encouraging greater citizen participation in foreign affairs."

Reference Meyer, Robert S., *Peace Organizations, Past and Present* (1988).

Center for War/Peace Studies

The Center for War/Peace Studies was founded in 1966. Its motto is: "Applied Research Toward a World of Peace with Justice." With a mandate to seek out new ideas and social inventions in order to achieve greater cooperation among the nations of the world, the center chose study issues on the basis of whether the issue was critical to progress toward a world of peace with justice. The center initially settled on four areas of concern:

1. The Law of the Sea, including the question of global sharing of ocean resources beyond national boundaries
2. Disarmament
3. Peace in the Middle East
4. International decision-making processes

A key element in reforming the United Nations (U.N.), proposed by Richard Hudson, the center's executive director, would be the "binding triad system of global decision-making." The essence of the triad system as proposed by Hudson was that while the General Assembly would still be able to make important decisions by a single vote, that vote would, however, contain three simultaneous majorities. The majority vote would have to include two-thirds of the nations present and voting as well as two-thirds of the nations that make regular contributions to the U.N. budget. A resolution could be adopted, therefore, only with the approval of most of the countries in the world, most of the world's population, and most of the world's political, economic, and military powers. The triad system would also make the decisions of the General Assembly binding rather than recommendations, as they are under the current system.

Although the center seeks reform in order to make the U.N. an organization that can act effectively as a true mediator and arbitrator of world conflicts, free from the intrusion of national interests, the triad system contains elements that can also retard any effective action by the U.N. Unless budgetary contributions can be distributed more equally among nations, the richest contributors will wield greater power. Requiring a two-thirds vote from three different constituencies can also make even the most modest resolutions difficult to secure. Nevertheless, the center continues to press for an organization that will respond in a fair and imaginative way to world conflicts.

Reference Meyer, Robert S., *Peace Organizations Past and Present* (1988).

Center on Law and Pacifism

The Center on Law and Pacifism is a national service organization that provides counseling to individuals and groups in need of legal and theological advice because of activities arising out of their religious convictions that have placed them at odds with the law. The organization was founded in Philadelphia in 1978 in response to religious and conscientious war tax resistance and civil disobedience. The center advocates peaceful approaches to issues such as militarism, war taxes, ecology, poverty, and abortion. It employs three forms of action: (1) it provides legal research, opinion, and counsel and acts as a court representative for those who solicit its services; (2) it sponsors education workshops and classes in law, theology, and criminal justice, and helps clients to prepare legal briefs in order to represent themselves in the legal system; and (3) it supports community activists engaged in religious pacifist activities, peace groups involved in disarmament campaigns, and legislation intended to provide conscientious objector (CO) status to war tax withholders.

Reference Meyer, Robert S., *Peace Organizations Past and Present* (1988).

Central Committee for Conscientious Objectors (CCCO)

Organized in 1948 by peace groups, including the War Resisters League

(WRL), to oppose the Selective Service Act of 1948. The Central Committee for Conscientious Objectors (CCCO) provided counseling as well as legal help for people who were discharged from the military, either because they were conscientous objectors or for other reasons. They also tried to reach potential draftees and enlistees before individuals were committed, with information on conscientious objection and on military life in general. The CCCO made information on discharge requirements available to those who wished for the information. In order to act as an advocate for conscientous objectors, the CCCO helped to train 3,000 military lawyers and counsellors.

References Josephson, Harold, ed., *Biographical Dictionary of Modern Peace Leaders* (1985); Wittner, Lawrence S., *Rebels against War: The American Peace Movement 1941–1960* (1969).

Central Organization for a Durable Peace

The Central Organization for a Durable Peace, an international group with representatives from nations around the world, was founded at The Hague in the spring of 1915. Its statement of purpose emphasized pacifism and liberal principles as requisite for the "new diplomacy" that the organization believed would emerge as a consequence of World War I. Departing from strict pacifism, the organization expressed a willingness to accept military sanctions against countries that started hostilities without first making a good faith effort to resolve a dispute by submitting to international arbitration or making some other appeal to the existing peace machinery. The organization disbanded after the Treaty of Versailles.

Reference Patterson, David S., *Toward a Warless World: The Travail of the American Peace Movement 1887–1914* (1976).

Chicago Seven

During the Democratic National Convention held 26–29 August 1968, thousands of antiwar protesters converged on

Chicago. Chicago mayor Richard Daley double-shifted his entire police force, called out 5,000 National Guard troops, and had another 7,000 army troops on call in the event of trouble. The ensuing events—characterized later by many who investigated the episode as a "police riot"—resulted in disruption of the convention and nationwide television coverage of Chicago police, under orders from Dailey, employing brutal force in subduing the protesters.

President Lyndon Johnson ordered Ramsey Clark to investigate the riot to see if indictments against any of the protesters might be in order. In Clark's opinion, there was no substantial evidence to suggest that blame for inciting a riot could be laid at anyone's doorstep. Other law and order officials came to the same conclusion. After Richard M. Nixon was inaugurated in 1969, however, his attorney general, John Mitchell, decided to press the case. Under Mitchell's direction, the grand jury returned indictments

against eight of the demonstraters who had been arrested in Chicago. The defendants were charged with violation of the Civil Rights Act of 1968 for crossing state lines in order to incite a riot.

The eight arrested were: Tom Hayden, the founder of Students for a Democratic Society (SDS); Abbie Hoffman and Jerry Rubin (Yippies); Rennie Davis, a member of National Mobilization; David Dellinger, Lee Winer, and John Froines, all of whom were longtime peace advocates; and Bobby Seale of the Black Panthers. Known at first as the Chicago Eight, the name was changed to the Chicago Seven when only seven of the eight original defendants actually came to trial.

The trial began in Chicago on 24 September 1969, with Judge Julius Hoffman presiding. Judge Hoffman set the tone for the months-long trial by denying the request of four of the defending attorneys to withdraw from the case shortly before it began. When the lawyers did not show

Demonstrators march at Watergate, protesting the trial of the Chicago Seven.

up in court on 24 September, Hoffman charged them with contempt of court and ordered two of the attorneys jailed. After several hours behind bars, the attorneys were freed by order of the 7th Circuit Court of Appeals. Ultimately, William Kunstler of the American Civil Liberties Union (ACLU) and Leonard Weinglass served as defense attorneys.

The trial itself was a circus such as had never before been seen in a U.S. court of law. The defendants took every opportunity to express their opposition to the proceedings. During the course of the trial, Hoffman found all the defendants and their attorneys guilty of contempt of court. While the jury was deliberating, Judge Hoffman handed down 125 contempt citations to defendants and lawyers alike. Kunstler and Weinglass were sentenced to 6 of the 12 years in prison that were imposed by Hoffman for the 125 contempt citations. During the trial, defendant Bobby Seale, who refused to sit quietly through the proceedings, was ordered gagged and shackled by Hoffman, who ultimately declared a mistrial in Seale's case and order him bound over for retrial at a later date. Hoffman also sentenced Seale to four years for contempt of court. The trial ended on 18 February 1970, with a controversial verdict returned by the jury. All defendants were acquitted of conspiracy charges, two of the defendants were acquitted of all charges, and the remaining five were found guilty only of crossing state lines to incite a riot. Hoffman sentenced all to the maximum—five years in prison and a $5,000 fine. On appeal, all the verdicts were overturned by higher courts.

See also Davis, Rennie; Dellinger, David; Hayden, Tom.

References The American Annual: An Encyclopedia of the Events of 1968, 1969, 1970 (1969, 1970, 1971); *New York Times* (28–30 August 1968).

Children as Teachers of Peace Foundation
See Children as the Peacemakers Foundation (CPF).

Children as the Peacemakers Foundation (CPF)
Founded in San Francisco in 1982 by Patricia Montandon, the organization was known first as the Round Table Foundation, then as the Children as Teachers of Peace Foundation. The purpose of the Children as the Peacemakers Foundation (CPF) is to promote world peace through the interaction of children and adults in peace-related activities.

The CPF sponsors two major programs, one of which is its World Peace Mission. This program enables children to meet with heads of state and with youth organizations in order to convey their hopes for peace. One participant, 11-year-old Samantha Smith of Maine, after corresponding with both President Ronald Reagan and Soviet Premier Mikhail Gorbachev, toured the Soviet Union at the invitation of the Soviets in 1983. In turn, the World Peace Mission sponsored the much-publicized U.S. visit by Soviet schoolgirl Katerina Lycheva in 1986. In addition, the CPF organized missions to 20 countries, which included meetings with the heads of state of the Soviet Union, China, West Germany, and with the Pope.

The CPF also sponsors an Annual International Children's Peace Prize. The prize honors children from ages six to 11 for their efforts on behalf of peace. Since its inception, more than 15,000 children have participated in the annual contest by submitting original works of art, essays, poetry, music, dance, and sculpture dedicated to furthering the cause of world peace. Children from more than 35 countries have been awarded the coveted Children as the Peacemakers glass sculpture.

Reference Meyer, Robert S., *Peace Organizations Past and Present* (1988).

Children's Crusade
While President Lyndon Johnson continued to pursue the Vietnam War as strenuously as ever in 1967, opposition was reaching a critical point. Allard

Lowenstein, an antiwar activist responsible for mobilizing thousands of students against the war, sought a suitable alternative candidate to run against Johnson. Senators George McGovern of South Dakota and Robert Kennedy of New York, both critical of the war, turned down Lowenstein's suggestion that they run for president in 1968. Senator Eugene McCarthy, from Oregon, a member of the Senate Foreign Relations Committee, also spoke with Lowenstein. McCarthy, considered one of the Senate's true intellectuals, a former English teacher and published poet, had already begun to consider entering the race. Johnson's under secretary of state, Nicholas Katzenbach, while testifying before the Foreign Relations Committee in August 1967, had been particularly heated in his responses to Johnson's misuse of the Gulf of Tonkin Resolution. As he left the hearing room, McCarthy spoke briefly with a reporter, commenting on the "wild" nature of Katzenbach's testimony, adding, "There is only one thing to do—take it to the country."

In October, McCarthy told Lowenstein that he would enter the race. By the time he announced his candidacy on 30 November, Lowenstein was already mobilizing an army of students to respond to his call. They went to New Hampshire en masse, ready to knock on every single door in the state. Initially, a somewhat dubious press characterized the campaign as the "children's crusade," certain that college students, no matter how well-intentioned, would be unable to persuade voters to turn away from Lyndon Johnson. Many of the students "came clean for Gene," which was to say that they cut their long hair, trimmed beards and sideburns, and dressed as neatly as possible without being hypocrites. They worked up to 16 hours a day, passing out literature, speaking with people, and going door-to-door. All told, more than 10,000 students from over 100 colleges and universities worked in New Hampshire on behalf of the McCarthy campaign. Most

Senator Eugene McCarthy

of them believed in the system, as did Lowenstein. The McCarthy campaign represented for them one final opportunity to prove that the system could work.

When McCarthy won 40 percent of the vote and 21 of 24 delegates, Lowenstein and his student volunteers felt vindicated, at least briefly. Later, Robert Kennedy wrote to Lowenstein, noting that McCarthy "knew the lesson of [the poet] Emerson and taught it to the rest of us: 'They did not yet see, and thousands of young men as hopeful, now crowding to the barriers of their careers, do not yet see, that if a single man plant himself on his convictions and then abide, the huge world will come round to him.'"

References Current Biography (1971); White, Theodore, *The Making of the President 1968* (1969); Zaroulis, Nancy, and Gerald Sullivan, *Who Spoke Up? American Protest against the War in Vietnam 1963–1975* (1984).

Civilian-Based Defense Association (CBDA)

The Civilian-Based Defense Association (CBDA) adopted that name in 1987. Prior to 1987 the organization was known as the Association for Transarmament Studies and had originally been founded as the Omaha Peace Association. The

CBDA advocates nonviolent, civilian-based defense as an alternative to a military defense—a radical notion in a world bound by the proliferation of nuclear weapons.

The CBDA coined the term *transarmament* and has sought to develop the concept of transarmament, which calls for putting aside military defense in favor of a prepared nonviolent civilian defense that would act to preserve freedom against possible internal or external efforts to cause the downfall of the government. The CBDA has strived to initiate research in order to judge the potential of transarmament as a defense concept. It publishes a quarterly newsletter, *The Civilian-Based Defense News & Opinion*, which acts as a forum for promoting its goals.

Reference Meyer, Robert S., *Peace Organizations Past and Present* (1988).

Clark, Grenville (1882–1967)

Grenville Clark used his wealth and position to advance the cause of world peace. Born in New York City, Clark graduated from Harvard (1903) and Harvard Law School (1906). He worked at the law firm of Carter, Ledyard and Milburn, where Franklin Delano Roosevelt was also a clerk. Clark, although he was not a brilliant or original lawyer, did earn a reputation as hard-working and energetic. He opened his own law firm with partners Elihu Root, Jr., the son of the secretary of state, and Francis Bird.

When the war in Europe began, Clark helped to found the Military Training Camps Association. Although the camps were criticized for being elitist, they ultimately provided about 80 percent of the officers who served in World War I and were the forerunner of the Reserve Officers Training Corp (ROTC). As a lieutenant colonel in the adjutant general's office, Clark helped to train 130,000 technicians. Although he supported preparedness, he also was a firm believer in the necessity of actively pursuing peace. He was a proponent of world government and an opponent of peacetime selective service. Even throughout World War II, Clark worked to interest friends and colleagues in and out of the government in the concept of world federation.

Following World War II, Clark and Harvard law professor Louis B. Sohn privately printed a publication called *Peace through Disarmament and Charter Review*. It advocated revision of the United Nations (U.N.) Charter and compulsory membership in the organization. Ultimately, Clark and Sohn published a book entitled *World Peace through World Law: Two Alternative Plans* (1958). One plan called for revision of the U.N. Charter. The second plan called for a new world security and development organization. Soon after it was published, many involved in the peace movement believed that future peace efforts required consulting the Clark-Sohn book.

Failing health curtailed Clark's activities in his latter years, but his efforts to promote peace gave rise to some lobbying on his behalf for the Nobel Prize. Clark died at his home in Dublin, New Hampshire, on 13 January 1967.

References Cousins, Norman, and J. Garry Clifford, eds., *Memoirs of a Man* (1975); Malone, Dumas, ed., *Dictionary of American Biography*, supp. 6 (1956).

Clergy and Laity Concerned (CALC)

During the Vietnam War, as in other times when the United States was involved in war, criticism of government policy by individuals and organizations was often met with accusations of disloyalty, or worse. Since its founding in 1965, Clergy and Laity Concerned (CALC) has argued strenuously that keeping silent in the face of government wrongdoing would be un-American. It has, therefore, consistently exercised its perceived responsibility to openly oppose government policy, not only in Vietnam but regarding other issues as well.

In the nearly three decades since it was founded, CALC has grown into an organization with 30,000 supporters in chapters throughout the country. It is both interfaith and interracial. Its original concern over Vietnam has broadened to embrace general issues of justice, poverty, and human rights—regardless of their venue—insofar as U.S. domestic or foreign policy is concerned.

During the Vietnam War, CALC was a moving force behind the mobilization against war campaign. It has also maintained an active role in the antinuclear campaign, opposing the nuclear arms race and supporting a nuclear freeze. Concerned particularly with weapons development and an arms buildup initiated primarily to increase military strength or to perpetuate the profits of arms manufacturers, CALC has waged a long battle against the testing and production of nuclear weapons. As a consequence, CALC has been willing to face armed opposition in carrying out its tactic of civil disobedience.

In the view of CALC members, spending trillions of dollars on weapons has diverted both funds and energy sorely needed to help eradicate social injustice and has resulted in increased poverty and hunger. It has long been a sponsor of a broad-based coalition to make the public aware of the problems of poverty. One of CALC's goals is to build grass-roots support for solutions to these problems. A program begun during the Vietnam War, the Peace Sabbath, has been expanded into a Peace with Justice Week, thus providing churches and synagogues with a powerful forum for discussing and advocating peace with justice.

Reference Meyer, Robert S., *Peace Organizations Past and Present* (1988).

Coalition for a New Foreign and Military Policy

Founded in 1976, the Coalition for a New Foreign and Military Policy sought to enlist both grass-roots support and organizational expertise in order to promote a program to reduce military spending, protect human rights, advocate arms control, and demilitarize U.S. foreign policy. Since its inception, the coalition has grown to include 55 member organizations and draws heavily from church movements of all denominations as well as from minority, human rights, and peace groups. The coalition organizes workshops, seminars, and outreach groups that work with member organizations to monitor and pressure members of Congress on key legislative issues related to peace and military spending. It has been particularly active on issues such as U.S. sanctions against South Africa, military intervention in Central America, and Star Wars funding. In addition, the coalition has been particularly critical of U. S. military actions, including the bombing of Libya in 1986.

Reference Day, Alan, ed., *Peace Movements of the World: An International Directory* (1986).

Coffin, William Sloane, Jr. (1924–)

William Sloane Coffin, Jr. was born into an affluent New York family. His father owned a Fifth Avenue furniture store, his uncle was president of Union Theological Seminary and a member of the Yale Corporation. When he was nine, Coffin's father died, and the family moved to Carmel, California. William returned East in 1939 to attend Phillips Academy in Andover, Massachusetts. He attended Yale's Music School for a year before joining the United States Army in 1943.

Due to his skill with languages, Coffin eventually found himself as a junior officer in Germany, working as liaison with the Soviets at the war's end. He also found himself caught up in Operation Keelhaul, whereby 3,000 Soviets who had defected from Stalinist Russia were to be turned back over to the Russians, presumably to face death. The evening before the unwitting Soviets were to be shipped back to Russia, Coffin was assigned the unenviable task of attending a party. As he sat alongside the doomed men, Coffin had an urge to warn them of their fate. But he did not. He kept silent and thereby missed an opportunity to possibly save lives. The consequences of his inaction haunted him. He returned to Yale to finish his degree and intended to join the CIA as an anti-Stalinist operative.

Coffin, who had never been particularly religious, found himself wrestling with the problem of good and evil. He took a short detour on his way to Washington to attend a weekend conference at Union Theological Seminary, where the speakers included Reinhold Niebuhr. In a flash, Coffin wired the CIA, delaying his work there, and enrolled at Union, where he spent the next year. Even then, he remained uncertain about the ministry, and from 1950 to 1953, Coffin did work for the CIA. Finally, he entered Yale Divinity School, where he studied with Richard Niebuhr, Reinhold Niebuhr's son, among others. In 1956 he returned to Phillips Academy for a year, serving as chaplain before moving on to Williams College for another year. In 1958, Coffin returned once again to Yale, where he would remain this time for 18 years.

From the start, Coffin's ministry was characterized by activism. He was among the first freedom riders in the civil rights movement, and he was an advisor to and the first director of the Peace Corps field training center. The Vietnam War presented him with his greatest challenge. Coffin, one of the founders of the Clergy and Laity Concerned (CALC) about Vietnam, opened his Yale chapel as a sanctuary for draft resisters. In October 1967, Coffin and Dr. Benjamin Spock led a peace rally in Boston, during which 944 potential draftees handed over their draft cards to protest what they believed was an unjust war. Coffin turned the cards over to the Department of Justice. The following year, Coffin, Spock, and other leaders were convicted of conspiracy in violation of the Selective Service Act, a conviction that was overturned on appeal two years later.

In 1972, Coffin was a member of a Committee of Liaison that traveled to Hanoi to accompany prisoners of war returning to the United States. After an 18-year chaplaincy at Yale, Coffin resigned in 1976 and a year later was appointed senior minister of the prestigious pro-activist Riverside Church in New York City. He continued to work with the CALC on issues related to arms control and nuclear disarmament. He also remained active in social causes ranging from peace to poverty, a characteristic that the Riverside Church committee had sought when filling the senior minister position.

During the Carter administration, when U.S. hostages were captive in Tehran, the Iranians chose several Americans to visit the hostages and to report on their well-being. Because of his Vietnam activism, Coffin was among the delegates whom the Iranians asked to visit the hostages. On the eve of his departure, Coffin delivered a sermon at Riverside Church in the course of which he lamented Carter's decision to impose economic sanctions on Iran, comparing the decision to former President Lyndon Johnson's bombing of the North Vietnamese. It was by far his most controversial sermon, and Coffin drew the anger of many parishioners and others who read about the incident later. It is characteristic of Coffin's deep commitment to justice and peace, as well as his determination never to repeat the mistake he had made regarding Operation Keelhaul, that the activist clergyman did not let potential criticism censor his beliefs and his responsibility to speak out.

See also Clergy and Laity Concerned; SANE/FREEZE.

References Coffin, William Sloane, *Once to Every Man* (1977); *Current Biography* (1980); Zaroulis, Nancy, and Gerald Sullivan, *Who Spoke Up? American Protest against the War in Vietnam 1963–1975* (1984).

Committee for Enrollment against War

The Committee for Enrollment against War was organized in 1922 by Jessie

Wallace Hughan, a noted pacifist and socialist. The committee was formed under the auspices of the Fellowship of Reconciliation (FOR) in order to enlist popular support against war as a means of settling international disputes. Hughan and fellow FOR members, dismayed over the ongoing dislocation that resulted from World War I and its aftermath, hoped to influence Americans and Europeans alike to seek peaceful solutions.

See also Hughan, Jessie Wallace.

References Chatfield, Charles, *For Peace and Justice: Pacifism in America, 1914–1941* (1971); Sicherman, Barbara, et al., eds, *Notable American Women, The Modern Period: A Biographical Dictionary* (1980).

Committee for Non-Violent Action (CNVA)

The Committee for Non-Violent Action (CNVA) was founded in 1957 by members of the War Resisters League (WRL), with a specific mandate to protest against nuclear weapons. The CNVA was considered the direct action arm of the peace movement, ideally working in conjunction with the public education arm of the movement, SANE.

The CNVA actually grew out of the World War II experiences of radical pacifists who had wanted no part of the war and no part of the Civilian Public Service (CPS) camps created by the historic peace churches and the government to provide alternative forms of service for pacifists. By 1957, when there appeared to be renewed interest in peace because of the alarming developments in nuclear weapons testing, the CNVA was an organization whose time had finally arrived. Using direct-action methods, members of the CNVA engaged in activities such as sailing into the nuclear testing zone in the Pacific Ocean in 1958 and in 1962, trespassing onto a nuclear test base in Nebraska in 1959, and organizing a protest at the New London, Connecticut, home base of the Polaris nuclear submarine in 1960. The CNVA members worked in New London trying to persuade both

workers on the base as well as local residents of the moral and ethical implications of building missiles armed with nuclear warheads. Although residents were at first hostile to the CNVA campaign, converts gradually emerged. The CNVA gained entry into five local churches, proving at least to themselves that their mission was not a futile one.

The CNVA also organized the San Francisco to Moscow Walk for Peace in 1960–1961. This represented a departure for the organization, because the action was not just a protest against nuclear weapons; it was also a plea for unilateral disarmament. This departure was reinforced two years later, when a similar walk from Montreal, Canada, to Washington, D.C., to Guantanamo, Cuba, demonstrated that the tactic now included liberation as well as demonstration. The walk was disrupted in Atlanta, Georgia, when the CNVA became embroiled in a civil rights struggle there.

From 1963 on, the CNVA actively opposed U.S. involvement in the Vietnam War. Using tax resistance campaigns, draft refusals, and weapons plants protests, the committee participated with a broad coalition of antiwar activists representing a variety of organizations. Its members also conducted teach-ins on college campuses, and three incidents of self-immolation involved members of the CNVA.

Partially because of the increasing radical representation among war protesters as the Vietnam War escalated, the CNVA merged with the WRL in 1967. The action was taken for several reasons, including the desire to remain convincingly in the camp of the political left rather than become aligned with the liberal antiwar protesters. Those behind the merger, including A. J. Muste, were convinced that the left would continue to provoke the government to abandon military tactics, while the liberals were more intent on persuading the government to adopt a more enlightened attitude in regard to military operations.

The CNVA's major accomplishment was to make popular the concept of nonviolent action. It always looked beyond protesting nuclear arms and war to include a concern for social justice, including civil rights. Thus, it was an important link between the peace movement and the emerging civil rights movement.

See also Muste, Abraham Johannes; SANE/FREEZE; War Resisters League.

References Wank, Solomon, ed., *Doves and Diplomats: Foreign Offices and Peace Movements in Europe and America in the Twentieth Century* (1978); Zaroulis, Nancy, and Gerald Sullivan, *Who Spoke Up? American Protest against the War in Vietnam 1963–1975* (1984).

Committee on the Cause and Cure of War

In 1925, Carrie Chapman Catt, encouraging women to use their new voting franchise to help put an end to all war, organized a Conference on the Cause and Cure of War. The conference was an outgrowth of work begun in 1924 when Catt, representing several women's groups, lobbied to promote a program for peace and disarmament. The conference met annually until 1939 as the Committee on the Cause and Cure of War. Catt served as chairwoman until her retirement in 1932. Originally designed to promote antiwar and pacifist solutions to world conflict, the committee shifted to collective security solutions in the mid-1930s as the threat of fascism became more and more apparent.

See also Catt, Carrie Chapman.

Reference Wittner, Lawrence S., *Rebels against War: The American Peace Movement 1941–1960* (1969).

Common Cause

Founded by John Gardner in 1970, Common Cause has been active as a nonpartisan lobbying group addressing a variety of issues, including nuclear arms, government accountability, and tax reform. The quarter million members of Common Cause have engaged in numerous campaigns directed at such issues as women's rights, closer monitoring of military spending, the MX missile program, and the Star Wars project, as well as the nuclear freeze movement. The organization makes most of its appeals through the pages of its widely circulated bimonthly publication, *Common Cause*.

Reference Day, Alan, ed., *Peace Movements of the World: An International Directory* (1986).

Common Heritage Institute

Founded in 1967, the Common Heritage Institute is a think tank located at Villanova University in Philadelphia. Since its inception, it has focused on four main issues that it believes are tied to the issue of lasting world peace: reversing the arms race, closing the gap between rich and poor nations, improving the effectiveness of the United Nations (U.N.), and determining how best to use the wealth of the world's oceans. Common Heritage holds nongovernmental organization status as a U.N. associate.

Since 1969, Common Heritage has held yearly conferences on issues revolving around the four areas cited. The first conference was titled On the Future of the United Nations. Subsequent conferences dealing with the U.N. included the 1978 conference, which considered proposals put forth by then-President Jimmy Carter to reform and restructure the peacekeeping organization. In 1983, the conference, cohosted by 27 participating organizations, was on Peace, Justice, and International Institutions. At that conference, bolder proposals that would transform the U.N. into a world federation with the necessary power and authority to enforce international law came under consideration. Common Heritage identified the stockpiling of nuclear weapons as the foremost threat to world peace as well as to human life. The organization has published a number of books, scholarly studies, and other educational materials in order to achieve its goals. Its newsletter, *Common Heritage*, provides an extensive bibliography on arms control and nuclear weapons. Common Heritage also conducts seminars, public lectures, luncheons for U.N. diplomats, and conferences.

Reference Meyer, Robert S., *Peace Organizations Past and Present* (1988).

Conference on Peace Research in History (CPRH)

In 1963, the American Historical Association (AHA) created an ad hoc committee to study the causes of peace. A year later the ad hoc committee became the Conference on Peace Research in History (CPRH). Members of the conference include diplomatic, political, military, and institutional historians as well as writers working in the peace and social justice movements. The primary goal of the membership is to make peace research relevant to scholarly disciplines as well as to policy makers and members of governments around the world. The CPRH is affiliated with the AHA, the Consortium on Peace Research Education and Development, and the United Nations (U.N.) as a nongovernmental organization. It is credited with putting peace research on the agenda of the AHA and numerous other professional organizations.

During its lifetime, the CPRH has sponsored many important conferences, including ones on Peace and Sovereignty, The Multinational Corporation as an Historical Phenomenon, and Peace Research and Its Impact on the Curriculum. In addition to publishing and distributing research papers, the CPRH publishes a newsletter and a quarterly journal, *Peace and Change*.

Reference Meyer, Robert S., *Peace Organizations Past and Present* (1988).

Conscientious Objectors (COs)

Conscientious objectors (COs) have been a part of U.S. history since the nation's founding, but those who professed their pacifism have rarely found a receptive au-

dience for their beliefs, least of all in times of war. COs have included persons unwilling to perform any work that might enable a war effort, those who refuse to pay taxes during times of war, those who protest allocations for military spending, and draft resisters. The so-called historic peace churches, including the Society of Friends and the Mennonites, have preached pacifism since their establishment in the United States, and most religious pacifists have been members of those churches. In the country's early wars—including during the Revolutionary War, the War of 1812, and the Civil War—COs were subject to having their property confiscated and, in some instances, subjected to physical abuse.

During World War I, COs found it particularly difficult to exercise their rights without recrimination. Government policy allowed only members of peace churches to secure CO status, but in all cases, alternative service was required. Others who claimed CO status or who were political opponents of the war were forcibly inducted into the service and then court-martialed. Some 500 individuals were court-martialed, most of whom were sentenced to military camps or prisons. A handful were actually sentenced to death, although all of those sentences were commuted. Those serving time in camps and prisons were harshly treated by their captors, and at least one young pacifist died as a result of his imprisonment. The Wilson administration's campaign to promote "100 percent Americanism" helped to persuade the majority of the public that anyone who opposed the war was a subversive. That attitude helped to create a situation in which the government was able to use the Espionage Act of 1917 and the Sedition Act of 1918 to effectively eliminate antiwar protest by prosecuting people for violation of one or the other measure. Using the Alien Act of 1918, the government deported thousands of people who were suspected of subversion, without benefit of trial. It was because of the wholesale suspension of constitutional rights that organizations like the Fellowship of Reconciliation (FOR) and the American Civil Liberties Union (ACLU) were founded.

During World War II, the FOR worked closely with government agencies in order to establish suitable civilian public service (CPS) camps for COs. Objectors serving in CPS camps performed a variety of services, from working in mental hospitals to participating in experiments in disease transmission. The Selective Service Act of 1940 exempted those who could demonstrate opposition to war based on religious training and belief. Individuals who failed the test for religious training and belief, along with those who refused to register for the draft, were given prison terms. The majority of imprisoned COs were members of the Jehovah's Witness Church, but approximately 1,000 others were either radical pacifists or African Americans who objected to a segregated armed forces and to discrmination at home.

The Vietnam War, more than any other war, caused significant numbers of opponents to resist. Because of the unpopularity of the Vietnam War, most COs had political rather than religious motives for claiming exemption. A coalition of antiwar groups helped many COs to prepare the necessary paperwork for exemption. After more than a decade of war, approximately 50,000 COs had fled the country in order to evade the draft. More than 100,000 young men burned their draft cards, and an estimated quarter million draft-eligible men never registered. Since the end of the Vietnam War, U.S. COs have registered their opposition primarily through campaigns to refuse payment of taxes and by refusing to register for the draft.

References Foner, Eric, and John Garraty, eds., *The Reader's Companion to American History* (1991); Wittner, Lawrence S., *Rebels against War: The American Peace Movement 1941–1960* (1969); Zaroulis, Nancy, and Gerald Sullivan, *Who Spoke Up? American Protest against the War in Vietnam 1963–1975* (1984).

Council for a Livable World (CLW)

Concerned because they had intimate knowledge of nuclear weapons' destructive nature, a group of scientists headed by nuclear physicist Leo Szilard founded the Council for a Livable World (CLW) in 1962. The CLW's goal was twofold: to educate Congress and the public and to advocate rational arms control policy. Like the Center for Defense Information (CDI), the CLW has grown into a respected source of information about weapons systems, military budgets, and appropriations. It has also helped to formulate legislation and to monitor appropriations committees, keeping a close check on weapons systems price tags from first proposals to final markups.

An affiliate of the CLW is its Peace PAC, which supports candidates for the House of Representatives who are sympathetic to CLW goals. Many members of Congress have come to rely on CLW seminars and position papers, which provide invaluable information on the technical, scientific, and strategic nature of weapons systems. As many as one-third of the Congress and associated staff persons attend briefings at any given time, and CLW speakers are noted for their off-the-record, straight-talking explanations of the potential dangers of weapons like the MX missile and technology in development.

In the past, the CLW has worked for mutual and verifiable weapons reductions and against the development of "star wars" technology and chemical weapons. It maintains a grass-roots network of lobbyists who can be pressed into service when the need arises. It also maintains a nuclear hotline providing up-to-the-minute information on critical issues before Congress.

Just as the Peace PAC supports the election of Representatives, the CLW supports Senate incumbents and candidates who are in favor of CLW goals. By its own estimate, the CLW has helped to elect 75 senators since its founding.

It provides more antinuclear campaign funds than any other PAC group in the country. At the same time, the CLW encourages members to choose which of the endorsed candidates they wish to support.

The CLW has achieved a good deal of success over the years. It proved influential in getting a Limited Nuclear Test Ban Treaty signed in 1963. It also succeeded in halting the antiballistic missile system (ABMS), in banning biological weapons, in defeating a proposal for major MX deployment, and in helping to bring about the Strategic Arms Limitation Talks (SALT I and II) by virtue of its active support for mediation. Assessing its impact on the whole issue of nuclear war, the CLW has clearly been responsible for slowing the proliferation of nuclear weapons.

See also Szilard, Leo.

Reference Meyer, Robert S., *Peace Organizations Past and Present* (1988).

Council for International Understanding (CIU)

The Council for International Understanding (CIU), formerly the Cathedral of Peace Institute, was founded by Moorhead Kennedy in 1981. Kennedy, a veteran foreign service officer who was released with other hostages after being held captive in Iran for 444 days, founded the Peace Institute as a center for the study of religion and international affairs. After affiliating with the Myrin Institute for Adult Education in 1983, the institute changed its name.

Kennedy's experience in Iran persuaded him that the inability of Americans to understand in a meaningful way the viewpoint of foreign governments and cultures constituted a serious flaw in our ability to negotiate political differences. The CIU's mandate is to serve as an educational resource for Americans on both the individual and group level, in order to ensure that obstacles to the implementation of an effective foreign policy are minimized.

The council is particularly sensitive to dispelling some widely held U.S. notions, for example, that the perspectives of other cultures are not markedly different from our own. The CIU is also concerned with issues of conceptual difficulty for Americans, such as the link between terrorism and religion. Under Kennedy's direction, the CIU views itself as more than a forum for the dissemination of information. Because of the mistakes that Kennedy believes the United States made in its dealing with Iran during the Iranian hostage crisis, the CIU educates with the expectation of helping to create change and to "influence our political leadership toward sounder foreign policy formulation." Inherent in any new foreign policy formulation would be a more realistic understanding of other cultures.

References Kennedy, Moorhead, *The Ayatollah in the Cathedral: Reflections of a Hostage* (1983); Meyer, Robert S., *Peace Organizations Past and Present* (1988).

Cousins, Norman (1915–1990)

As a young man, Norman Cousins wanted nothing more than to play professional baseball. Reading and writing rounded out the array of his other favorite pursuits. Cousins, born in Union City, New Jersey, pursued all three interests at Columbia University. An unfortunate accident during baseball practice at Columbia, in which Cousins and a teammate collided head-on while chasing a fly ball, put the young sportsman in the hospital for several weeks and ended his hopes for a baseball career.

After graduating from Columbia in 1933, Cousins first joined the staff of the *New York Post* before quickly moving to *Current History*, as its book reviewer. In 1940, he became executive editor of the *Saturday Review of Literature*. He very quickly began to change the tone of the *Saturday Review*, writing articles that linked literature to current events, running feature articles, and inaugurating a

Norman Cousins

series of special issues devoted to the analysis of culture and literature in specific regions. One special issue, the theme of which was morale, featured Eleanor Roosevelt as the editor.

Although Cousins vigorously supported World War II, he was an ardent advocate of nuclear controls, the United Nations (U.N.), and world government. It was Cousins who helped arrange for the postwar visit to the United States of some atomic bomb victims, the "Hiroshima Maidens," so that they could take advantage of U.S. medical care. Cousins was very active in the Citizens Committee for a Nuclear Test-Ban Treaty as its co-chairman. He was also president of the United World Federalists. He believed wholeheartedly that there was only "one way to achieve effective control of destructive atomic energy, and that is through centralized, world government."

Like many of his peace colleagues during the post–World War II era, Cousins had to wrestle with the problem, perceived or real, of Communist involvement in peace organizations. A hugely successful rally on behalf of nuclear disarmament sponsored by SANE at Madison Square Garden, and attended by people like Eleanor Roosevelt, should have placed SANE in an excellent position to exert positive grass-roots influence on the nuclear issue. Because of unfounded accusations leveled against the organization by Senator Thomas Dodd of Connecticut, who asserted that SANE membership was rife with Communists, Cousins and other SANE leaders felt compelled to purge the organization of such Communists as might be found. It was an unfortunate decision that caused influential peace advocates like Linus Pauling to resign their membership in SANE. It also vitiated whatever influence SANE might otherwise have enjoyed.

Cousins spent most of his literary career at the *Saturday Review*, except for a brief stint from 1971 to 1973, when the publishers attempted to radically change the publication's format. Within two years, it was on the verge of bankruptcy, and Cousins was asked to resume editorial control. Cousins brought the *Saturday Review* back to health in so dramatic a fashion that he was named the Magazine Publishers Association's Publisher of the Year.

After serving as chairman of the board of editors, Cousins retired from the *Saturday Review* as an editor emeritus in 1978. Shortly thereafter, he was invited by the University of California at Los Angeles to take an adjunct professorship in its department of psychiatry and biobehavorial sciences. Cousins spent nearly ten years at UCLA. When he died in December 1990 at the age of 75, Cousins was still living in California.

References *Current Biography* (1943); *New York Times Biographical Service* (December 1990).

Creative Initiative
See Beyond War.

Culbertson, Ely (1891–1955)

Ely Culbertson, the son of an American engineer father and a Russian mother, did not take up permanent residence in the United States until he was nearly 30 years old. Born in Ploesti, Romania, Culbertson was raised in southern Russia. His participation in revolutionary activity during the Russia Revolution almost cost him his life. When he was 17, he was arrested for crimes against the state and faced a death sentence. His parents were able to persuade authorities that Culbertson was a U.S. citizen, and he was spared. From then until age 30, Culbertson roamed the world, assuming a variety of disparate identities from construction worker in Winnipeg, Canada, to revolutionary in Mexico and Spain, to student at Yale and in Paris and Geneva, to stowaway, gambler, and alcoholic.

Culbertson possessed a keen intelligence, read avidly, and taught himself seven languages, but in 1921 he was still at loose ends, without a clear idea of what he should be doing with his life. He moved to New York and decided to rely on a skill that had earned him a peripatetic living at other times in his life — card playing. Very quickly, Culbertson became an expert at bridge. He married Josephine Murray Dillon, a bridge teacher, who would shortly become the most famous female bridge player of her day, and the two proceeded to invent personalities that they believed would enhance their fortunes on the professional bridge circuit.

Culbertson also founded *Bridge World* magazine, which enjoyed enormous success with both professional and casual bridge players. In 1930, the Culbertsons and their partners played in the first international bridge match against the best British foursome. The Americans won handily. Culbertson had written a book on the first successful bidding system for contract bridge (honor count), *Blue Book*, which became an instant best-seller as a consequence of the Americans' victory. Culbertson achieved even more fame when he succcessfully challenged the foremost auction-bridge authority in the United States to a match. The contest was front-page news for days, and Culbertson's victory established his reputation.

In 1937, Culbertson turned his attention from bridge to world events. The gathering storm clouds in Europe persuaded him to become a full-time advocate for peace, an activity to which he devoted the remainder of his life. He campaigned for international peace and world federation. He also proposed a system for controlling major weapons and limiting tactical weapons, a proposal that received serious consideration by Congress. After World War II, Culbertson lobbied for the United Nations (U.N.), and when the U.N. became a reality, he lobbied to provide it with adequate policing power. He also wrote two books on the peace issue: *Total Peace* (1943) and *Must We Fight Russia?* (1947). Culbertson died in Brattleboro, Vermont, on 27 December 1955.

Reference Starr, Harris E., *Dictionary of American Biography*, supp. 1 (1944).

D.C. Nine

On 22 March 1969, nine members of the radical Catholic left staged a raid on Dow Chemical offices in Washington, D.C. The nine members of the raid, most of whom were Catholic priests, included Mary Melville—who was also one of the participants in a raid on the Catonsville, Maryland, draft board. After breaking into Dow, the protesters hung up several photographs of Vietnamese children who had been horribly disfigured by Napalm B, which was manufactured by Dow and sold to the government. The protesters broke up furniture, poured blood over records found in the offices, and tossed documents out into the street. All nine were arrested, as they expected. Once they were incarcerated in the D.C. jail, the nine protesters commenced a hunger strike. They were released from jail after one week.

See also Berrigan Brothers; Catonsville Nine; Dow Chemical Company.

Reference Zaroulis, Nancy, and Gerald Sullivan, *Who Spoke Up? American Protest against the War in Vietnam 1963–1975* (1984).

Davis, Rennie

See Chicago Seven.

Day, Dorothy (1897–1980)

When Dorothy Day, the founder of the Catholic Worker movement, received the Laetare Medal from the University of Notre Dame in 1972, she was characterized as a woman who had spent her life "comforting the afflicted and afflicting the comforted." That statement described the essential Dorothy Day.

Day was born in Brooklyn, New York, and grew up in Oakland and Berkeley, California. She flirted briefly with organized religion as a young woman but rejected it in favor of a secular quest for social justice. While she was a student at the University of Illinois, Day joined the Socialist party and, after returning to New York with her family, she joined the Industrial Workers of the World. At various times she worked for *The Call*, the Socialist daily newspaper; the Anti-Conscription League; *The Masses*, a radical publication, and its successor, *The Liberator*. Day, a member of the radical suffragists' National Womens Party, was one of the women arrested, and subsequently imprisoned in Occoquan Work House, for picketing the White House in 1917. It was while she was participating in a hunger strike in Occoquan that Day began to look toward organized religion again. But it was not until her daughter was born in 1927 that she seriously rethought her bohemian lifestyle and joined the Catholic Church.

Day began writing for *Commonweal*, the church's most liberal publication. When she was introduced to Peter Maurins and his theories about the social relevance of Catholicism, her life course was set. She and Maurins began publishing *The Catholic Worker* on 1 May 1933. In their view, the goal of their direct-action approach to social ills was the creation of a communitarian society. In addition to ministering to the day-to-day needs of the poor, the homeless, and the jobless of New York City, Day also advocated peace. She opposed military conscription during World War II and was a vocal critic of the government's internment of Japanese Americans. Day also refused to pay taxes in some instances, because she did not want to pay for the war.

With the advent of the nuclear age and the Cold War, Day's protests shifted. She organized an annual protest against nuclear readiness in New York City. For a number of years in the late 1950s and early 1960s, a cell in the New York House of Detention was reserved for Day because of her refusal to participate in a state-mandated mock nuclear attacks requiring all citizens to seek shelter in designated areas.

Active even in her seventies, Day was arrested with Cesar Chavez during a United Farm Workers protest in 1973. She was stricken with heart disease shortly thereafter and had to curtail her activities markedly. Among the people who gave testimony to the enormous influence that Dorothy Day and the Catholic Workers had on their lives were the cleric and author Thomas Merton; the Berrigan brothers; anti-Vietnam activist Michael Harrington, Socialist author of *The Other America,* and the controversial educator Ivan Illich. Dorothy Day died on 28 November 1980.

See also Catholic Worker.

References Miller, W. D., *Dorothy Day* (1982); *New York Times* (30 November 1980); Wittner, Lawrence S., *Rebels against War: The American Peace Movement 1941–1960* (1969).

Debs, Eugene Victor (1855–1926)

Eugene Debs devoted most of his life to championing the cause of railroad workers in the United States. Debs, born in Terre Haute, Indiana, began working for the railroads as a teenager. He was a member of the Brotherhood of Locomotive Firemen (BLF) and edited its national publication, *The Locomotive Firemens Magazine.* It was Debs's dedication that moved BLF leaders to appoint him secretary-treasurer and to move the national headquarters to Terre Haute.

In 1893, Debs organized the American Railroad Union (ARU), which was designed to bring all railroad workers together under one banner. Originally opposed to using the strike as a bargaining tool, Debs changed his mind when the railroads adamantly refused to improve oppressive working conditions. Although Debs disagreed with the timing, the ARU voted to strike against the Pullman Sleeping Car Company in

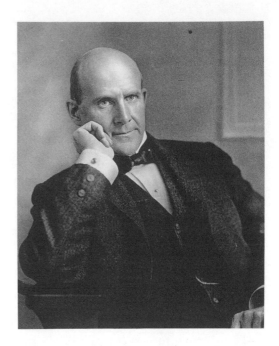

Eugene Debs

1894. Prompted by cutbacks in wages and rising prices instituted by the Pullman company in the midst of the depression of 1893, workers walked off their jobs and literally shut down rail traffic between Chicago and the West Coast. The walkout was dubbed the "Debs Rebellion" by Chicago newspapers. The federal government acted quickly to clamp down on the strike by issuing an injunction. Debs ignored it, was arrested, and eventually was indicted for violating the Sherman Antitrust Act of 1890. Although criminal charges against Debs were dropped, he was convicted on contempt charges and sent to prison.

Debs spent his six months in prison honing an appreciation for socialism as the political system that would best uphold the rights of working men and women. He converted what was left of the ARU into the Socialist Democratic Party of America; in 1900 its name was changed to the Socialist Party of America. As the party's nominee for the presidency in 1912, Debs was able to poll nearly

1 million votes—direct evidence of working people's discontent with both major political parties.

The Socialist party voted in 1917 to oppose U.S. entry into World War I, a vote that Debs endorsed. He remained silent for a short period but eventually felt compelled to speak out against the war, despite the probability that such an action would result in his arrest. Several prominent Socialist opponents of the war had already met a similar fate, including Kate O'Hare and Rose Padtor Stokes. In the spring of 1918, Debs gave an antiwar speech in Canton, Ohio, and in June he was arrested for violation of the Espionage Act. A jury of retired bankers and businessmen convicted Debs, who was sentenced to ten years in prison.

Not to be deterred, Debs ran a second presidential campaign from prison in 1920 and still managed to garner nearly 1 million votes in the election. By then, however, the 75-year-old Debs was ill, and efforts were made to have him pardoned. Woodrow Wilson refused to entertain the idea, but when Warren G. Harding was inaugurated, he did grant Debs a pardon, on Christmas Day 1921, both because of the aging Socialist's physical ailments and because Harding did not want to provide the labor movement with a martyr should Debs die in prison. Debs returned to Terre Haute, where he spent the remaining years of his life. He considered suing the federal government on the grounds that he had been stripped of his civil liberties, but he never recovered his health enough to pursue the idea. He died in Terre Haute on 20 October 1926.

Reference Ginger, Ray, *The Bending Cross: A Biography of Eugene Victor Debs* (1949).

Declaration of Conscience

On 3 July 1964, David Dellinger, A. J. Muste, Joan Baez, the Berrigan brothers, and Abraham Feinstein held a rally in Lafayette Square, across the street from the White House, to protest the Vietnam War. The rally was intended to publicize the Declaration of Conscience written by Dellinger, Muste, and Bayard Rustin. The declaration supported draft resistance as a "conscientious refusal to cooperate with the United States government in the prosecution of the war in Vietnam." It requested that people sign the declaration and by so doing "refuse to take part in the manufacture or transportation of military equipment or to work in the fields of military research and development." The Declaration of Conscience was one of two such statements issued in 1964.

See also Baez, Joan; Berrigan Brothers; Chicago Seven; Muste, Abraham Johannes.

Reference Zaroulis, Nancy, and Gerald Sullivan, *Who Spoke Up? American Protest against the War in Vietnam 1963–1975* (1984).

Dellinger, David

See Chicago Seven.

Dennett, Mary Coffin Ware
(1872–1947)

Like many of her generation, Mary Ware Dennett became a social activist early in life and remained an activist until her death at the age of 75. Born in Worcester, Massachusetts, Dennett graduated from Boston's Museum of Fine Arts School and then accepted a teaching position at the Drexel Institute in Philadelphia. At a time when most middle-class women did not work outside of the home, Dennett and her sister started their own business. The Boston Society of Arts and Crafts took note of the Ware sisters' crafts cooperative, and Dennett was soon elected director.

By then she was married to William Hartley Dennett. She spent the early years of her marriage raising her two surviving sons, but she very quickly was drawn into the women's suffrage movement. Her activities on behalf of the National American Woman Suffrage Association (NAWSA) placed strains on the Dennetts' marriage that they could not resolve. Dennett moved to New York with her two sons and was soon occupied with a number of social causes in addition to her suffrage work. She joined the Intercollegiate Socialist Society (ISS) and started working for the single-tax movement.

With the possibility of U.S. involvement in the world war that had already consumed Europe, Dennett, an avowed pacifist, became field secretary for the American Union against Militarism. She also campaigned for Woodrow Wilson's reelection when he promised to keep the United States out of the war. When Wilson had to break that pledge, Dennett resigned from the Democratic party and became one of the founders of the People's Council, a radical antiwar organization.

Dennett believed that one of the major causes of war, territorial expansion, was intertwined with the social problems caused by overpopulation. Thus, her efforts to bring about lasting world peace began to find stronger focus in the birth control movement. When Margaret Sanger, the founder of the American Birth Control League, went to Europe to escape prosecution under the Comstock Act, Dennett and two colleagues took over the work of the league and its reorganization. The Comstock Act prohibited the dissemination of birth control information through the mails by defining it as obscene. Dennett lobbied to have the law overturned. She spent the next 15 years working and acting as a spokesperson for planned parenthood, birth control, and, eventually, sex education for children. When the government prosecuted Dennett for publishing an essay on sex education, the American Civil Liberties Union (ACLU) took up her cause. In winning its case, the ACLU was able to set a major legal precedent when the courts excluded "serious instruction" on sex matters from the obscenity definition.

With advancing age, Dennett's activities began to focus again on more direct peace issues. She headed the World Federalist Association (WFA), an international peace organization, from 1941 to 1944. Failing health forced her to curtail activities thereafter, and she died in New York on 25 July 1947.

See also American Union against Militarism; World Federalist Association.

References James, Edward T., et al., eds., *Notable American Women, 1607–1950: A Biographical Dictionary* (1971); Kennedy, David M., *Birth Control in America: The Career of Margaret Sanger* (1970).

Detzer, Dorothy (1893–1981)

By the time she reached her mid-20s, Dorothy Detzer had internalized a fundamental belief in pacifism grounded in a secular humanism that rejected war as an acceptable means of settling conflicts. Her pacifist views had been developing for several years, but it was the experience of World War I that brought them to full flower. As a volunteer with the American Friends Service Committee (AFSC) relief mission in Vienna and the Soviet Union, Detzer observed firsthand the brutality of war on the lives of innocents, particularly the helpless children. Moreover, her twin brother, Don, had succumbed to poison gas during the war. For Detzer, then, pacifism was both a personal and a humanitarian choice.

Detzer was born in Fort Wayne, Indiana, and attended the Chicago School of Civics and Philanthropy. Detzer's mother and her mother's friends influenced the direction that her life followed. One of her mother's best friends was Alice Hamilton, a colleague of Jane Addams. Hamilton took Detzer to Chicago in 1905 to meet Addams and to visit Hull House. When the war began, Detzer went to work at Hull House as a counsellor to young women. After her return from the AFSC mission work in Europe, Detzer joined the Women's International League for Peace and Freedom (WILPF).

The WILPF most fully embraced the ideals that Detzer believed in, especially the relationship between peace and economic security. In 1924 she became the WILPF's national secretary and worked out of the organization's legislative office in Washington. When Detzer took over as national secretary, the main offices of the U.S. WILPF branch were located in Philadelphia. Detzer argued forcefully that the headquarters had to be relocated in Washington, because it was in the nation's capital that the true work for peace would be done. Although many WILPF members believed that peace education was the most important element of their work, the organization allowed Detzer to move the offices to Washington, where she and her coworkers could better monitor the legislative process. For the next two decades, Detzer worked tirelessly on behalf of peace.

The list of lobbying efforts carried out by Detzer during the 1920s and 1930s constitutes a description of the major work done by the U.S. peace movement advocates of the time. She lobbied for the League of Nations and the World Court. She directed major lobbying campaigns for disarmament and the Kellogg-Briand Pact. In addition, Detzer pigeonholed any available congressman to lobby on behalf of withdrawing the U.S. Marines from Nicaragua and Haiti and for liberalizing immigration laws so that conscientious objectors (COs) could become naturalized U.S. citizens. Thanks largely to Detzer's efforts in support of the League of Nations Anti-Slavery Convention in Africa, the WILPF was awarded the insignia of the Order of African Redemption. Detzer consistently supported and lobbied for congressional resolutions favoring the outlawing of war, for example, the Frazier Amendment, which would have made war unconstitutional. In addition, she supported efforts to broaden free trade agreements and was an avid supporter of the Tydings Resolution for a world economic conference.

As good a politician as she was a lobbyist, Detzer made every effort to broaden the WILPF's base of support by supporting other causes that she believed in, including civil rights, trade unionism, and farm issues. In 1946, Detzer resigned

Dorothy Detzer

from the WILPF in order to go to work for the United Nations (U.N.). Being offered a post at the U.N. was the culmination of a long career of fighting for peace. Detzer intended to begin her new job as soon as she received security clearance, but the clearance never came. Perhaps because of her prior association with Socialists and Communists such as Earl Browder and Norman Thomas, and with the Cold War just beginning, Detzer was considered too risky to be given security clearance.

Detzer then turned to work on her memoirs, which were published in 1948 as *Appointment on the Hill*, and moved toward a more private life and marriage at the age of 63 to Ludwell Denny, the editor-in-chief for the Scripps-Howard newspapers. She died in Monterey, California, on 21 January 1981.

See also Addams, Jane; Hamilton, Alice; Women's International League for Peace and Freedom.

References Detzer, Dorothy, *Appointment on the Hill* (1948); Josephson, Harold, ed., *Biographical Dictionary of Modern Peace Leaders* (1985); Wittner, Lawrence S., *Rebels against War: The American Peace Movement 1941–1960* (1969).

Dewey, John (1859–1952)

John Dewey was the most influential educator of the twentieth century and a true product of the Progressive Era. Dewey's beliefs in both the innate goodness of humankind and in the potential for education to change and ameliorate society's ills were unshakeable. They were the cornerstones of Dewey's personal philosophy and to a large extent determined his approach to social problems.

Dewey, born in Burlington, Vermont, graduated from the University of Vermont in 1879. He earned his Ph.D. at Johns Hopkins University in 1884 and began his long and illustrious career as an educational philosopher at the University of Michigan, where he taught from 1884 to 1888 and then again from 1889 to 1894. He spent the following ten years at the University of Chicago before moving on to Columbia University in 1905. He remained at Columbia as professor, and then as professor emeritus, until 1939. During that time he developed his philosophy of education that so influenced U.S. education. He also helped to found the American Association of University Professors and served as the organization's first president in 1915.

Dewey's road to peace activism began during World War I. Initially, he was not opposed to the war and even supported U.S. intervention. Later, however, like many whose hopes for a better world rested on the war's outcome, Dewey was disillusioned with the results. He came to view war as an irrational force in a world that required, above all, rationality in order to effect positive change. In Dewey's view, the League of Nations was nothing more than a league of governments. As such, he refused to support it and sought instead an alternative. He believed that in order to achieve lasting world peace, people had to understand first that international cooperation was in everyone's best interest. That understanding would come about through education. Dewey also joined the American Committee for the Outlawry of War, although he never believed that war would be eliminated through a legislative pronouncement. War would only be eliminated through a shared concept of its immorality.

Throughout the 1920s and 1930s, Dewey was a member of the Committee on Militarism, which objected to college ROTC programs and other issues. Convinced that military training ran counter to academic and individual freedom, Dewey argued against militarism in education. He also advocated transnational education, proposing that all allusions to war as a glorious endeavor be eliminated from textbooks and that a curriculum be developed in all fields that transcended national boundaries. It was Dewey's hope that such a program could be initiated in grammar schools, while children were still open to ideas unfettered by nationalistic bias.

Throughout his life, Dewey retained an optimistic belief in the fundamental goodness of people, notwithstanding his disappointment over the causes and initiation of a second world war, and he never strayed from the idea that education was the vehicle that could produce a lasting world peace. Dewey died in New York City on 1 June 1952.

References Howlett, Charles F., *Troubled Philosopher: John Dewey and the Struggle for World Peace* (1977); Wittner, Lawrence S., *Rebels against War: The American Peace Movement 1941–1960* (1969).

Dingman, Mary Agnes (1864–1961)

Mary Dingman began her career as a teacher, became a professional working with the YWCA, and finally shifted to working for international peace and disarmament. Born in Newark, New Jersey, Dingman graduated from Northfield Seminary (1895), New Palz Normal School (1899), and Columbia Teachers

College (1910). She taught for a brief time in Spring Valley and Brooklyn, New York, public schools and then at Dana Hall, a private girls school in Wellesley, Massachusetts. In 1914 she left teaching to become a traveling secretary for the YWCA, working with Florence Simms in the new social gospel movement then being adapted to the YWCA industrial education program. Simms had initiated the efforts to attract working women to the YWCA in 1910, and the continuation of this extension work occupied Dingman for several years.

In 1917, Dingman was sent to France to organize a program for women war workers. After the war, Dingman took over the YWCA work in France and Belgium, and by 1921 she had overseen the opening of more than 20 working women's clubs, with total membership of 10,000. She next served in London as the industrial secretary of the YWCA World Committee. In 1923 she went to the Far East to help organize the China National Committee. While there, Dingman served on a multinational Commission on Child Labor. When the YWCA transferred its world headquarters to Geneva, Switzerland, the transition marked a shift in Dingman's career as well. Fourteen women's peace organizations joined together as the Women's International Organization (WIO). The WIO then established a Peace and Disarmament Committee and elected Dingman its president in 1931 and initiated a program to focus world attention on the problem of disarmament. The Peace and Disarmament Committee represented some 45 million women who belonged to member organizations. One of the committee's early tasks involved presenting petitions with 8 million signatures to members of the World Disarmament Conference of 1932. Dingman attended a variety of peace and disarmament conferences. She resigned her YWCA position when she was reelected president of the Peace and Disarmament Committee in 1935.

While traveling in Italy in 1939, Dingman was arrested by Fascist authorities on unspecified charges. She had previously endorsed League of Nations sanctions against Italy because of its involvement in the Ethiopian War. She was released within 24 hours when the U.S. Department of State intervened on her behalf. After returning to the United States in 1940, Dingman resigned as president of the Peace and Disarmament Committee and concentrated on public lecturing. She lobbied for favorable congressional action on the United Nations (U.N.), and in 1948, Dingman was appointed a consultant for the International Union for Child Welfare. She served as the union's U.N.'s consultant until her retirement. Dingman died in Berea, Kentucky, on 21 March 1961.

Reference Garrity, John, ed., *Dictionary of American Biography*, supp. 7 (1981).

Dole, Charles Fletcher (1845–1927)

Charles Fletcher Dole's greatest contribution to the U.S. peace movement was the counsel he gave and the perserverance that he inspired in others, including Emily Greene Balch, who eventually was awarded the Nobel Peace Prize for her dedicated work on behalf of peace. Balch willingly credited Dole with providing the shining example that she followed during her long career.

Dole, born in Brewer, Maine, graduated from Harvard College and the Andover Theological Seminary. As a Unitarian minister influenced by New England transcendentalism, Dole's religion was one of practical application rather than abstract theology. His first appointment was to the Plymouth Church in Portland, Maine, where he served for two years. In 1876, he accepted a call to First Congregational (Unitarian) Church of Jamaica Plain, Massachusetts, where he remained for the next 40 years.

Dole could not abide violence of any sort and, therefore, was an uncompromising pacifist. His work as a peace advocate brought him into contact with many of the prominent peace workers in Boston, and for many years he was an active member of the American Peace Society (APS). Throughout his long career, Dole continued to work for peace, speaking out against U.S. intervention in Cuba, lobbying against using force in the Phillipines, and opposing military intervention to protect U.S. missionary outposts. Like many peace advocates, Dole was distressed when World War I began and steadfastly refused to endorse U.S. involvement. He was also an outspoken opponent of the naval buildup that had helped to influence the war.

Although he was not a particularly memorable speaker, Dole did write numerous articles and books, on both religion and on the search for peace, that influenced others to take up the cause. Dole died on 27 November 1927 in Jamaica Plain.

Reference Josephson, Harold, ed., *Biographical Dictionary of Modern Peace Leaders* (1985).

Douglas, Helen Gahagan (1900–1980)

Before entering politics as a candidate for the House of Representatives from California's 14th District in 1944, Helen Gahagan Douglas had achieved success as a playwright, an actress, an opera singer, a New Dealer, a staunch Democratic party activist, a wife, and a mother.

Douglas—born in Boonton, New Jersey—and her four siblings grew up in a conservative Republican family on Long Island. As a student at Barnard College, she found her first true calling and, despite her father's opposition, appeared in several successful Broadway productions between 1922 and 1928. A talented but untrained vocalist, Douglas gravitated toward opera and toured with several opera companies in Europe for the next two years.

Shortly after her return to Broadway, Douglas married actor Melvyn Douglas, and as they made their way from New York to California at the height of the

U.S. Congresswoman Helen Gahagan Douglas speaks at World Youth Rally in New York City.

Great Depression, Douglas came face to face with the poverty-stricken rural migrants. This experience was followed quickly by a firsthand look at Nazi Germany in 1937 when a concert tour took her to Salzburg. It had a profound effect on her. Thereafter, Douglas became a relief worker in Franklin Roosevelt's New Deal administration and served in a variety of agencies, primarily focusing on the plight of rural Americans. She became a highly visible member of the Democratic party and, as the war in Europe drew to a close, Douglas decided it was time to make the shift from an implementer of legislation to a lawmaker. She served three consecutive terms as an avowedly liberal congresswoman from California's 14th District. Her bid for a Senate seat in 1950 failed when her opponent, Congressman Richard Nixon, taking advantage of the supercharged politics of the McCarthy Era, succeeded in portraying her as soft on communism.

Her direct involvement in the peace movement came late in life and was a consequence both of her concern for the alarming intensification of the Cold War and the increasing U.S. involvement in Vietnam. In 1964, Douglas was a delegate for the Jane Addams Peace Association at the Soviet-American Women's Conference in Moscow. She also served as cochair of the Women's International League for Peace and Freedom (WILPF). A long bout with cancer finally claimed her in 1980, and, although she had become increasingly gloomy about the prospects for peace, she nevertheless continued to work toward that end until her death.

Reference Whitney, Sharon, and Tom Raynor, *Women in Politics* (1986).

Dow Chemical Company

As opposition to the Vietnam War intensified in 1966 and 1967, many antiwar activists began to view Dow Chemical Company as the embodiment of everything that was wrong with U.S. policy.

Dow Chemical produced a particularly horrendous chemical compound used in Vietnam. Napalm B, which had been developed by Harvard University scientists during World War II, was a petroleum jelly substance that burned when it reached temperatures of 1000°F. It also stuck to whatever it spattered on, including humans; thus, it was responsible for not only severe burns and disfigurements but also countless burn deaths.

Dow, which also made the body bags used to transport military personnel who were killed in action, was the only company that manufactured Napalm B for sale to the government. In 1966 alone, Dow produced 54,620 tons of Napalm B, more than had been used during the entire Korean War. The public became aware of napalm and its uses in Vietnam when the Women Strike for Peace (WSP) began to campaign against Dow in 1966. An early demonstration against the Dow plant in San Jose, California, resulted in the arrest of four strikers, variously referred to the in the press as the "housewife terrorists" and the "napalm ladies." The four were found guilty of attempting to obstruct a shipment of napalm. The protest and the resulting publicity began to bear fruit the following January, when *Ramparts* magazine and, more importantly for circulation, the *Ladies Home Journal* both ran prominent pieces on the destructive nature of napalm on human beings. *Ladies Home Journal* focused particularly on the numbers of children who had suffered the effects of napalm.

Dow Chemcial representatives on routine recruiting trips to college campuses suddenly found themselves the targets of antiwar activists—along with the usual targets like the CIA, the ROTC, and the draft. On 21 February 1967 the most intense demonstration against Dow took place on the campus of the University of Wisconsin at Madison. One hundred students staged a sit-in at offices used by Dow recruiters. Ultimately, 19 students were arrested. The following day, more than 200 students, angered over the arrests, blocked the chancellor in his office, refusing to budge until the chancellor agreed to post bail for the arrested students. In the fall of 1967, more than 20 demonstrations against Dow took place on college campuses—from Boston College to New York University to the University of Chicago and the University of California at Berkeley. Most of the protests were organized by Students for a Democratic Society (SDS), and the tactics employed during this round of protests were decidedly more confrontational than passive. Madison was again the site of the worst of the protests. In October, Madison police charged a building held by student activists. More than 300 students were barricading the doors; many were bloodied and battered by police trying to clear the building. For the first time on a U.S. college campus, police used tear gas against student demonstrators. Students called for a general strike. Although Dow eventually was banned from the campus, 13 students were expelled from the university, and three faculty members were fired for supporting the strike.

The president of Dow Chemical, H. P. Doan—who was also the grandson of the founder—expressed some concern over the bad publicity accruing to Dow. Nevertheless, Dow made it clear that the company would continue to manufacture napalm and sell it to the government and that the company would continue to recruit prospective employees on college campuses.

By 1968 the antiwar movement was occupied with other issues, and Dow became less of a focus for protest. Nevertheless, in 1969, two additional protests against Dow Chemical were staged. The first occured on 22 March 1969, when nine radical Catholics, most of whom were priests, entered the offices of the Dow Company in Washington, D.C. They wrecked office equipment, poured blood over records, posted photographs of Vietnamese children who had been napalmed, and threw documents out onto the street. The D.C. Nine, as they were known, were arrested for destruction of property and trespassing, among other charges. On 7 November 1969, the self-proclaimed Beaver 55, a group of eight members of the Catholic left, entered the Dow offices in Midland, Michigan, and erased data from magnetic tapes containing chemical and biological research. True to Dow President Doan's word, the company did not suspend napalm production.

Dow eventually became a topic of discussion at an International War Crimes Tribunal sponsored by the Bertrand Russell Peace Foundation. The tribunal condemned Dow's continued napalm production and characterized the compound as one of the "most vicious weapons ever used in warfare." Whether napalm deserves that title, Dow illustrated, in the eyes of many peace activists, an amoral corporate ethos that placed profit above lives.

See also Berrigan Brothers; D.C. Nine; Students for a Democratic Society.

References *New York Times* (22–23 February 1967, 23 March 1969, 8 November 1969); Zaroulis, Nancy, and Gerald Sullivan, *Who Spoke Up? American Protest against the War in Vietnam 1963–1975* (1984).

Du Bois, William Edward Burghardt (1868–1963)

W. E. B. Du Bois spent his entire adult life fighting the racism that helped to enslave nonwhites personally, politically, and economically, not only in the United States but around the world. He also participated in the campaign to realize world peace and argued that there was a fundamental relationship between colonialism or slavery and war.

Du Bois was born in Great Barrington, Massachusetts, and graduated from Fisk University in 1888. At Harvard University, Du Bois earned an M.A. (1891) and a Ph.D. (1895). His academic career as a professor of sociology took him from Wilberforce University to the University of Pennsylvania and finally to Atlanta

University, where he remained until his retirement in 1944.

In 1907, Du Bois was one of the founders of the National Association for the Advancement of Colored People (NAACP), which quickly became the premier civil rights organization dedicated to gaining equality for African Americans. He also served as editor of the NAACP journal, *The Crisis*, from 1910 to 1934. Even before the NAACP and *The Crisis*, Du Bois had published a short essay entitled "Credo," which was published in *The Independent* in 1904. "Credo" was a denunciation of war and militarism and a call for world peace, justice, and equality. The essay—which was well-received, widely read, and reprinted frequently—gained worldwide exposure.

Du Bois never forgave himself for succumbing to appeals made by Woodrow Wilson as the United States prepared to enter World War I. Although Du Bois supported U.S. participation at the time, he later admitted that he had made a mistake. During the interwar years he continued to press for disarmament and took every opportunity to discuss publicly his views on the relationship between racism, colonialism, and war. As World War II approached, Du Bois, mindful of his error in supporting World War I, refused to support the Allies for several months. However, even he could not remain neutral in the face of Nazi tyranny. As a participant in the planning conferences for the United Nations (U.N.), Du Bois fought to bring the twin issues of racism and colonialism to the attention of conference members.

Until his death, he lobbied for disarmament, especially with the advent of nuclear weapons. In 1949, Du Bois headed the Peace Information Center. During his tenure, the center initiated a campaign against the atomic bomb and succeeded in obtaining signatures of over 1 million Americans on the Stockholm Peace Pledge. He also took up several unpopular causes, including U.N. recognition of the Peoples Republic of China. Because of his

W. E. B. Du Bois

activities, the U.S. government indicted Du Bois in 1950, charging him with being an unregistered foreign agent. Although he was acquitted, the episode left Du Bois distressed and saddened. He spent the last part of his life in Ghana, where he died on 27 August 1963.

See also Stockholm Peace Pledge.

References Aptheker, Herbert, "W. E. B. Du Bois—A Man for Peace." *Political Affairs* (August 1982) 41: 31–35; Josephson, Harold, ed., *Biographical Dictionary of Modern Peace Leaders* (1985).

Dutton, Samuel Train (1849–1919)

Samuel Train Dutton was born in Hillsboro, New Hampshire. He enjoyed a long career as an educator and school administrator and also became a prominent figure in the world peace movement.

Dutton was appointed superintendent of schools in South Norwalk, Connecticut, soon after graduating from Yale University (1873). He became widely known for his theories regarding the role of schools in the community and the practical needs of the students who would be taking their place in that community. He also fiercely defended retention of the classics as a cornerstone of a good education when cost-conscious school board members threatened to eliminate that aspect of public school education. Dutton was invited to lecture at a number of colleges and universities. He lectured on pedagogy at Harvard (1895–1897), the University of Chicago (1897–1898), and Boston University (1898).

Dutton's interest in world peace grew out of his belief that wars were the result of ignorance. Only through education, he believed, could the world hope to eliminate war. In 1906, Dutton helped to found the New York Peace Society and served as its secretary. He was also a director of the American Peace Society (APS) and the World Peace Foundation. He helped to found the World Court League and was a member of the International Commission of Mediation of the Carnegie Foundation in 1913. Dutton also advocated exchange programs with foreign countries for both professors and students as a way to further promote peace through education.

Although he was gravely disappointed when World War I began, Dutton nevertheless chose to make his contribution where he believed it would be most helpful. He served as the secretary and vice-chairman of the executive committee of the American committee for Armenian and Syrian relief, later known as the Near East Relief. Dutton, the father of two adopted daughters, was the father-in-law of another prominent world peace advocate, the Reverend Frederick Lynch. Dutton died in Atlantic City, New Jersey, on 28 March 1919.

See also American Peace Society; Lynch, Frederick Henry; World Peace Foundation.

References *National Cyclopaedia of American Biography*, vol. 23 (1967); Patterson, David S., "An Interpretation of the American Peace Movement, 1898–1914." In *Peace Movements in America*, ed. Charles Chatfield (1973).

Easter Peace Walks

The Easter Peace Walks were held annually in New York City by U.S. peace groups in order to protest nuclear weapons and the arms race. The walks were held to coincide with the British Aldermaston, or Ban-the-Bomb marches. The annual walks, held in the late 1950s and early 1960s, were part of a concentrated effort by peace organizations to encourage the United States and the U.S.S.R. to enter into a mutual treaty to ban nuclear weapons. At one of the largest of peace walks, in 1963, approximately 70,000 people participated. Conflict arose when David Dellinger and A. J. Muste spoke to the rally about the growing conflict in Vietnam. One of the major sponsoring organizations of the peace walks, SANE, threatened to ban Dellinger and Muste from further participation for straying from the primary focus of the rally.

Reference Zaroulis, Nancy, and Gerald Sullivan, *Who Spoke Up? American Protest against the War in Vietnam 1963–1975* (1984).

Eastman, Crystal (1881–1928)

Crystal Eastman grew up believing that women could and should compete in every area of life and enjoy the same rights and freedoms taken for granted by men in U.S. society. As a consequence, she lived her life the way she wanted to and fought to change those things that stood in her way. Born in Canandaigua, New York, Eastman drew much of her strength and determination from her mother, Annis Bertha Ford Eastman, who had to take over family responsibilities from an ailing husband. Annis Eastman, a staunch advocate women's rights, succeeded her husband, Thomas Beecher, as principle pastor of Park Church in Elmira, and was the first woman to be ordained a Congre-

gationalist minister in New York state. She taught her three sons and her daughter to persevere in the face of adversity.

Crystal Eastman graduated from Vassar College in 1903, received an M.A. from Columbia in 1904, and graduated from New York University Law School in 1907. Eastman, nearly six feet tall, was a formidable presence, an excellent athlete, a gifted orator, and a tireless advocate for the rights of women, minorities, and workers. Her first job after law school was working for Paul Kellogg, investigating working conditions for the Russell Sage Foundation's Pittsburgh Survey. Her report, *Work Accidents and the Law*, became a seminal weapon in the fight to establish workman's compensation laws. Eastman—as Governor Charles Evans Hughes's first woman commissioner of New York State's Commission on Employer's Liability and Causes of Industrial Accidents, Unemployment, and Lack of Farm Labor—drafted the nation's first workman's compensation law.

In 1912 she joined forces with radical suffragists Alice Paul and Lucy Burns to found the Congressional Union for Woman Suffrage, which later became the National Woman's Party. She was in accord with Paul on the necessity of women's suffrage and an equal rights amendment to the Constitution.

In 1913, while a delegate to the Woman Suffrage Congress in Budapest, Eastman met some of the leading women peace advocates, including Rosika Schwimmer, Holland's Dr. Aletta Jacobs, and Britain's Emmeline Pethick-Lawrence. Eastman founded the New York Woman's Peace Party the following year and introduced Pethick-Lawrence to Jane Addams. In 1915, the three founded the Women's Peace Party, later renamed the Woman's International League for Peace and Freedom.

Crystal Eastman

Eastman also became executive director of the American Union against Militarism (AUAM), founded by Oswald Garrison Villard, Lillian Wald, and Norman Thomas, among others. Believing Woodrow Wilson's vow to keep the United States out of World War I, Eastman supported the Democrat in his first term. But as the Preparedness Campaign got underway, she threw her support to Charles Evans Hughes. In 1915, Eastman conducted a Truth about Preparedness Campaign, in which she emphasized the role of war profiteers in propagandizing for military increases and called for a nationalization of the war industry. When the United States did enter the war, Eastman declared that the peace movement had three major goals: to stop the war in Europe, to prepare for the peace following the war, and to defend against militarism.

Throughout the war, Eastman lectured and wrote on peace. Concerned because those who spoke out against the war were being stripped of their civil liberties, Eastman, along with her assistant, Roger Baldwin, and Norman Thomas, created a Civil Liberties Bureau (CLB) of the AUAM. When the AUAM was disbanded, the CLB became the American Civil Liberties Union (ACLU).

As the war progressed, Eastman was drawn more and more toward socialism. With her brother, Max Eastman, she founded *The Liberator*, which was intended to be a forum for both feminism and socialism. In the 1920s, Eastman and her second husband, British poet and pacifist Walter Fuller, moved to England, where he was music director for the British Broadcasting Corporation. She spent her time between the United States and Britain, vainly looking for employment in a postwar political climate decidedly unfriendly to someone who had openly embraced socialism and declared that the Russian Revolution was a positive event. She was blacklisted and earned only a modest living writing for those periodicals that still welcomed her, such as Alice Paul's *Equal Rights*. Eastman continued to travel frequently, speaking on behalf of peace, feminism, equal rights, and socialism. She died on 8 July 1928 at the age of 47.

See also American Civil Liberties Union.

References Cook, Blanche Weisen, *Crystal Eastman on Women and Revolution* (1978); Sochen, June, *Movers and Shakers: American Women Thinkers and Activists, 1900–1970* (1972); Sochen, June, *The New Woman: Feminism in Greenwich Village 1910–1920* (1972); Whitman, Alden, ed., *American Reformers* (1985).

Eastman, Max Forrester (1883–1969)

Max Eastman, born in Canandaigua, New York, credited two people with having the greatest influence on his life: his mother, Annis Ford Eastman, and his sister, Crystal Eastman. Annis Eastman, a staunch advocate of rights for women, succeeded the venerable Thomas Beecher as principle pastor of Park Church in Elmira, New York. She was the first woman to be ordained a Congregationalist minister in New York state. She taught her three sons and her daughter to persevere in the face of adversity, as she herself had had to do when her husband became ill. Her daughter, Crystal, learned well from her mother never to be daunted by circumstance and to pursue what she truly wanted, even if it was not a socially accepted pursuit for women.

Although Max Eastman described himself as something of a "Mama's boy" as a youngster, when he left home to attend Mercerburg Academy in Pennsylvania, he was well prepared to chart his own course. He graduated from Mercerburg with the highest grades in the history of the school and attended Williams College on scholarship, graduating in 1905. At Columbia University, Eastman was a protégé of John Dewey and, although he did not pursue a Ph.D., he had completed all the requirements. Eastman remained in Greenwich Village, steeping himself in poetry and radical politics. He founded the Men's League for Women's Suffrage in 1909 and became a proficient public speaker advocating equal rights for women. In 1911,

Max Eastman

Eastman was named editor of *The Masses*, which quickly became a forum for radical political ideas and avant garde artists and writers, including Stuart Davies, George Bellows, Sherwood Anderson, Amy Lowell, Floyd Dell, and William Carlos Williams.

Like many of his colleagues, including his sister Crystal, Eastman—and by extension, *The Masses*—opposed U.S. entry into World War I. So vigorous was Eastman in his opposition that in 1917 the federal government suppressed publication of *The Masses*. Eastman, along with six colleagues on the editorial board, was indicted under the Espionage Act for conspiracy to promote mutiny and for obstructing the draft. Two subsequent trials, both of which ended in hung juries, gave Eastman a national reputation as a radical.

In 1918, he and Crystal founded another radical journal, *The Liberator*, which they published and edited and which continued to condemn war and promote peace. In the years immediately after

World War I, he seemed to move even further left politically than he had been before the war. Gradually, he became disillusioned with communism, especially after Joseph Stalin took over the Russian government. His rejection of communism was so complete that in the 1950s he supported Senator Joseph McCarthy. His political shifts from radicalism to socialism to communism to conservatism—with turns often taken when everyone else seemed to be going the other way—seemed an affirmation of the intellectual independence with which he had been imbued as a child. Max Eastman died on 25 March 1969.

References Cook, Blanche Weisen, *Crystal Eastman on Women and Revolution* (1978); Whitman, Alden, ed., *American Reformers* (1985).

Eddy, George Sherwood (1871–1963)

Sherwood Eddy devoted his life to two Christian endeavors: the YMCA and the Student Volunteer Movement. An ardent believer in the Christian evangelical movement, Eddy became one of the most powerful American voices spreading the social gospel and bringing to mainstream U.S. churches a commitment to world peace. It was a career path that Eddy arrived at during his senior year in college.

Eddy graduated from Phillips Andover Academy and Yale University. At Yale he studied to become a civil engineer and fully intended to practice that profession; however, he became interested in the campus mission movement in his last year, and by graduation was totally committed to Christian mission work. Eddy spent several years furthering his studies at Union Theological Seminary and Princeton Theological Seminary before going to India to do mission work in 1896. For the next several years he worked in India and Asia. Eddy and fellow missionary John R. Mott conducted a series of mission campaigns that finally took them to China in 1914. After World War I began, Eddy worked through the YMCA with soldiers in Britain and, later, with Allied troops abroad.

Prior to the war, Eddy had not considered himself a pacifist. However, a combination of the war's disappointing outcome and the counseling of his secretary, Kirby Page, convinced him that pacifism was the only rational response to agression. Eddy and Page became a formidable team, researching and writing numerous books and articles on the subject of peace, as well as on other social and international issues, and speaking on college campuses throughout the country. Eddy also helped to organize the Fellowship for a Christian Social Order. In 1921 he founded and conducted the Sherwood Eddy Seminar. Ministers, educators, and public speakers were invited to travel to Europe each summer as part of the seminar in order to study and meet with political, religious, and scholarly leaders to whom Eddy had access. The seminars proved invaluable for assessing the contemporary world, as those who attended wrote widely read and respected position papers on a variety of international issues.

With the approach of World War II and the increasing evidence of Nazi atrocities Eddy, like many other committed pacifists, found it impossible not to support those alligned against Hitler. He embraced the concept of the "just war" while making it clear that war ultimately had to be abolished. In an increasingly nuclear-dominated world, Eddy continued to promote the necessity of abolishing war. Christians had a responsibility, he argued, to become advocates of internationalism if they truly sought world peace. Eddy died on 3 March 1963 in Jacksonville, Illinois, leaving behind him the legacy of a life spent on behalf of peace and justice.

References Josephson, Harold, ed., *Biographical Dictionary of Modern Peace Leaders* (1985); Wittner, Lawrence S., *Rebels against War: The American Peace Movement 1941–1960* (1969).

Educators for Social Responsibility (ESR)

Educators and parents in Cambridge, Massachusetts, who were seeking ways in which education could be used to help prevent nuclear war, founded Educators for Social Responsibility (ESR) in 1981.

Drawing members from among the parents, teachers, and administrators of elementary schools, high schools, and colleges, the ESR adopted the motto "educating for new ways of thinking in the nuclear age." The group was dedicated to exposing students to a variety of views regarding nuclear weapons development and the arms race and to developing students' critical thinking skills.

The ESR maintains a National Resource Center, which provides educational materials, teacher training, curriculum development, a newsletter, curricula updates, and information on state, regional, and national programs. Through a strong network of chapters across the country, the ESR works with school systems and parent-teacher groups to plan and introduce new programs. It conducts workshops, in-service training programs, and institutes that offer alternative views on nuclear arms issues and other social issues. It also sponsors programs and conferences and provides educational resource people for workshops in local communities. Its publications range from materials directed at all ages—from kindergarten students to adults—and include *Forum*, a journal of new ideas, programs, and resources related to nuclear education. In 1986, Executive Director Susan Alexander, in her progress report, encouraged financial support for "educating a generation for the challenge of peace" through the ESR's Fund for the Future.

Reference Meyer, Robert S., *Peace Organizations Past and Present* (1988).

Einstein, Albert (1879–1955)

Albert Einstein, a brilliant theoretical physicist, was born in Ulm, Germany. The son of middle-class Jewish parents, Einstein was a late reader and was considered a mediocre student. In those things in which he had an avid interest, however, Einstein demonstrated a decided lack of mediocrity. A geometry textbook, given to him as a gift at the age of 12, and his independent study of science, played major roles in his intellectual development.

Unable to find a university teaching job after his graduation from the Zurich Eidgenössiche Technische Hochschule (ETH) in 1900, Einstein secured a job at the Swiss Patent Office in Bern, Switzerland. As a patent clerk, little was required of him, but he benefited from the free time he had to pursue his own interests. In 1905, Einstein published a series of papers that helped to establish his credentials as a theoretician of stature. The papers explained his theories on light quanta, on the existence of atoms, and—most significantly—his theory of relativity, which ultimately came to be represented in his famous equation, $E=mc^2$, in 1907. Work done during that era earned for Einstein a Ph.D. from the University of Zurich in 1905. For the next ten years his reputation among physicists and mathematicians grew steadily, and in 1912 he won the Nobel Prize for physics. Einstein moved from the University of Zurich to the German University in Prague, the Prus-

sian Academy of Sciences, and the ETH, from which he had graduated 12 years earlier. In 1913 the Prussian Academy of Sciences invited Einstein to join the society and offered him the post of director of scientific research at the Kaiser Wilhelm Institute for Physics in Berlin. Einstein remained there until 1933. While at the Kaiser Wilhelm Institute, Einstein completed his work on relativity.

Einstein's public reputation as one of the most important theoreticians of his day enhanced his opportunities to speak out and work for some of the social causes in which he believed, especially pacifism, Zionism, and intellectual freedom. He maintained that scientific truth had no national boundaries and considered nationalism a potent threat to human progress and to peace. Einstein firmly believed that scientists had a moral responsibility to make known their position on issues that affected humankind. Einstein, an opponent of war, based on what he had seen during World War I, served on the board of directors of the German League for Human Rights (the leading pacifist organization in that country), the Women's International League for Peace and Freedom (WILPF), and War Resisters International. His solution to abolishing all war was for people to refuse to fight. In the 1920s his militancy was not welcome. He was vilified in Germany and was considered dangerously naïve in London, Paris, and Washington—even by other peace advocates, who believed that the problems were too complex to simply accept war resistance as an effective way of eliminating conflicts.

When the Nazis came into power, Einstein and his wife happened to be visiting the United States. He made an immediate decision not to return to Germany. He had had a previous agreement to spend part of each year at the newly formed Institute of Advanced Study at Princeton University. The position quickly became a full-time appointment.

With the discovery of nuclear fission in Germany in 1938, Einstein and other

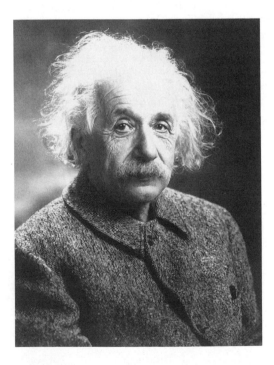

Albert Einstein

scientists were asked to write Franklin Delano Roosevelt, urging him to establish a U.S. nuclear development program in order not to be caught short if and when Germany succeeded in its quest. Einstein was never more than a part-time consultant on the Manhattan Project, and after the war he became a strong voice for controlling nuclear weapons and for world government. Just as he had continued to speak out against the Nazis before and during the war, Einstein did not allow political considerations to interfere with what he saw as his moral responsibility to the world. His long-held Socialist views and his belief in world government were grist for some of his critics' mills. For years, the FBI kept a file on Einstein, believed by many to be a Communist, although he was not. He was, however, a constant critic of the Cold War and of the arms race. He considered stockpiling atomic weapons just short of criminal on both sides. He also advocated making the United Nations (U.N.) into an organization truly accountable to the entire world and not just to the strongest nations.

Einstein's loyalty again came into question during the McCarthy Era, but once again he did not let criticism, even rabid McCarthyism, quiet his denunciation of nuclear weapons. In early 1955, Einstein and a group of international scientists issued a document known as the Einstein-Russell Appeal. The appeal criticized, in the sharpest possible language, the United States and the U.S.S.R.'s apparently heedless plunge toward nuclear annihilation. It was Einstein's last contribution to world peace. He died in Princeton, New Jersey, on 13 April 1955.

See also Einstein-Russell Appeal.

References *Dictionary of American Biography*, supp. 5 (1951–1955); Josephson, Harold, "Albert Einstein: The Search for World Order." In *Peace Heroes in Twentieth Century America*, ed. Charles DeBenedetti. (1988).

Einstein-Russell Appeal

Few voices willing or able to speak out against the arms race and the proliferation of nuclear weapons were heard in the early 1950s in the United States. Between 1950 and 1956 the peace movement seemed to consist of little more than a handful of isolated individuals, variously characterized as "crackpots," "misguided," or, more ominously, "un-American." The nation had settled into an increasingly tense Cold War with its new arch enemy, the Soviet Union. The chilling effect of the Cold War combined with the domestic political phenomenon of McCarthyism—a politically repressive bullying technique disguised as patriotism and promoted by its demagogic cheerleader, Senator Joseph McCarthy—created a diversion that peace advocates did not begin to address until mid-decade.

Finally, in July 1955, a group of scientists and philosophers issued an appeal to all nations that signaled a break in the Cold War silence. Known as the Einstein-Russell Appeal, the statement was addressed to "all the powerful governments in the world in the earnest hope that they might agree to allow their citizens to survive." The document was written by Albert Einstein and Bertrand Russell and was signed by Einstein, Percy Bridgeman, Hermann Muller, and Linus Pauling of the United States; Russell, Cecil Powell, and Joseph Rotblat of England; Frederick Joliot-Curie of France; Leopold Infeld of Poland; Hideki Yukawa of Japan; and Max Born of Germany. The signers appealed to governments not as members of particular nations but as members of the human race. The appeal conveyed the fear that mankind was at a grim crossroad in history and faced the appalling reality that, left unchallenged, political leaders might choose ultimate self-destruction through the policy of nuclear weapons development and stockpiling. "Shall we choose death," the statement asked rhetorically, "because we cannot forget our quarrels? We appeal as human beings to human beings: Remember your humanity and forget the rest."

By the time the Einstein-Russell Appeal was released, Albert Einstein had already died. The appeal constituted his final writings and his last thoughts on the Cold War. His harshest words were directed at "statesmen in responsible positions on both sides" who continued to support policies of military superiority as a tool of intimidation despite the clear knowledge that a misstep might doom millions. "Political passions, once they have been fanned into flames, exact their victims," were Einstein's last words. With the logjam of silence broken, other voices were heard. A week after the Einstein-Russell Appeal, 52 Nobel laureates meeting at conference in Switzerland also issued a statement urging the suspension of force as a "final resort of policy." Fifteen U.S. Nobel scientists were among the signers of this statement, including Linus Pauling. Scientists were once again accepting their responsibility to make clear the consequences of using weapons that they had helped to create.

References Pauling, Linus, *No More War!* (1958); Wittner, Lawrence S., *Rebels against War: The American Peace Movement 1941–1960* (1969).

Emergency Committee of Atomic Scientists (ECAS)

One of the most difficult issues for scientists in general, and atomic scientists in particular, to deal with in the years immediately following World War II was that of their moral obligation to mankind versus their intellectual obligation to science. Scientists working on nuclear projects of any sort had to make a decision on this issue. The largest group of scientists mobilized against a nuclear arms race was the Federation of American Scientists, whose 2,000 members in 1946 included those who were absorbed into the organization when it combined with the Federation of Atomic Scientists. The Federation of American Scientists' publication, the *Bulletin*, noted that the organization was accused of naïveté for not recognizing that a nuclear weapons program was necessary in the face of the potential threat posed by communism.

A tiny group of very prominent scientists—including Albert Einstein, Hans Bethe, Linus Pauling, and Leo Szilard—believed that the federation was not forceful enough in educating both the government and the public about the significant danger posed by a proliferation of nuclear weapons. They organized the Emergency Committee of Atomic Scientists (ECAS) in 1946; Einstein became its chairman. The committee immediately argued that a world authority to deal with these issues was necessary to human survival. It was a remarkable statement that could not easily be dismissed because of the stature of the scientists involved. Given the circumstances, the public was not ready to give its support to the committee, regardless of the scientists' credentials. For the public, and for many in government as well, the issue was not simply accepting or rejecting a weapons system. It involved the use of a type of energy that presumably had positive benefits as well as negative consequences. Most people also believed that the government was bound to do whatever was necessary to contain the spread of communism. Finally, the possibility of relinquishing independence and sovereignty in exchange for a world government had never been acceptable to Americans. It was, for example, the key issue that had kept the United States from joining the League of Nations after World War I. While the ECAS called for world government, very few were willing to give that call much credence. The ECAS was important, nevertheless, because it set out the nuclear issue in clear and concise terms with no ambiguity. The ECAS was shortlived; by 1950 it had ground to a halt. Internal dissension helped to speed along its demise. "How can we presume to rescue the American people from their uncertainties," Einstein asked rhetorically, "if we cannot agree among ourselves?"

See also Bethe, Hans; Einstein, Albert; Pauling, Linus; Szilard, Leo.

References Pauling, Linus, *No More War!* (1958); Wittner, Lawrence S., *Rebels against War: The American Peace Movement 1941–1960* (1969).

Federal Union, Inc.

Founded by Clarence K. Streit, the Federal Union, Inc. was established in 1943 to promote Streit's views on world federalism. Streit, a *New York Times* correspondent who regularly reported on the proceedings of the League of Nations in Geneva, was distressed over the league's failure to become the vibrant organization for world order that Woodrow Wilson envisioned, so he wrote a book entitled *Union Now*. The book, published in 1939, proposed a federal union of 15 democracies operating as a confederation to ensure world peace. *Union Now* achieved extraordinary popularity as U.S. readers eagerly sought viable alternatives to war as a method of resolving international conflict. Throughout World War II, Federal Union, Inc. helped to generate an avalanche of books and articles, all of which advocated the formation of some kind of world government.

Reference DeBenedetti, Charles, ed., *Peace Heroes in Twentieth Century America* (1988).

Feld, Bernard T. (1919–1993)

Explaining his fierce opposition to nuclear weapons and the arms buildup, Bernard Feld said in 1982, "I was involved in the original sin and I have spent a large part of my life atoning." A Brooklyn-born City College graduate who earned a Ph.D. in physics from Columbia University, Feld worked as an assistant to Enrico Fermi and Leo Szilard on the atomic bomb project during World War II. Working with Fermi and Szilard at the University of Chicago and at the Los Alamos proving grounds in New Mexico, Feld was an integral member of the team that finally succeeded in producing a working atomic bomb. After the United States dropped the weapons on Hiroshima and Nagasaki in 1945, Feld was appalled at the degree of destruction unleashed and horrified at the prospects for even bigger bombs in the future.

He quit the project and resigned from government research shortly thereafter, determined to help create a civilian nuclear agency. Feld eventually accepted a post as professor of physics at the Massachusetts Institute of Technology, where he remained until his retirement in 1990.

In the meantime, Feld was a leader of the Pugwash Conferences. Pugwash, a forum for scientists to keep the public alerted to the perils of nuclear war, was founded in 1957. Feld also was instrumental in creating the Federation of American Scientists, one of the first such groups intent on controlling nuclear weapons. He also served as president of the Albert Einstein Peace Foundation and was the editor of the *Bulletin of Atomic Scientists*, which printed the well-known "doomsday clock." (Using a theoretical clock where 12:00 would be the actual moment of nuclear war, the publishers determined how close the world was to 12:00 by assessing the level of political tension at any given time. For many years during the Cold War, the time hovered between 11:55 and 11:59.)

During the 1980s, Feld remained a vocal opponent of the Reagan administration's nuclear stockpiling policies. Feld's dozens of peace essays were compiled in a 1979 publication, *A Voice in the Wilderness*. Feld died at his home in Brooklyn on 19 February 1993.

See also Pugwash Conferences.
Reference *New York Times* (20 February 1993).

Fellowship of Reconciliation (FOR)

A British organization founded in 1914, the Fellowship of Reconciliation (FOR) was a religious pacifist organization. In

1915, A.J. Muste began meeting with other members of the international FOR in the United States to protest the United States's possible entry into the war. The FOR developed into one of the leading exponents of radical protestantism in the United States. Its members were recruited largely from the ranks of younger clergymen and from the ranks of religiously motivated professionals. Among its more prominent leaders were John Haynes Holmes, Harry Emerson Fosdick, John Nevin Sayre, and A.J. Muste. The War Resisters League (WRL), founded in 1923 by Jessie Wallace Hughan, was an outgrowth of the FOR and attracted political, humanitarian, and philosophical objectors to war. The WRL was the FOR's secular counterpart.

During World War I, the FOR offered counseling and advice to conscientious objectors (COs). In times of peace, it involved itself in a variety of social causes.

For example, during the depression of the 1930s, it was very active in the labor movement. It led strikes and helped workers to organize unions, despite the fact that labor unions did not necessarily exhibit a reciprocal interest in pacifism. Nevertheless, in 1932, fully 75 percent of the FOR's members indicated that they would cast their votes for the Socialist party candidate for president—a strong indication of the left-of-center attitudes held by its members.

With the growth of fascism in Europe and the possibility of another world war, the FOR and other pacifist organizations experienced sharp increases in membership. Between 1935 and 1941, the FOR grew from 4,271 members to 12,426. From August 1940 to August 1941 its membership increased by over 4,000. Once the war was a reality, much of the peace movement faded, while pacifist organizations like the FOR continued to

A Japanese-American child is being evacuated from the West Coast to an internment camp during World War II. The FOR opposed such camps, eventually bringing the case before the U.S. Supreme Court.

grow. During peacetime, pacifists were more often than not considered within the mainstream of U.S. ideals, but once war broke out, pacifists were isolated from the mainstream because of their insistence on nonviolent solutions. Pacifists could not be equivocal about their beliefs in wartime; therefore, they tended to join organizations in order to make a statement. Throughout the war, the FOR maintained numerous offices for counseling and advising COs and maintained branch offices in 125 out of 133 Civilian Public Service (CPS) camps established to provide a means of alternative service for COs. It found itself open to charges of un-American activity when, after Germany surrendered, it expressed fears regarding the consequences that might accompany Japan's forced, unconditional surrender. It had also opposed the internment of Japanese Americans during the war. The head of the FOR's youth group, Gordon Hirabayashi, was responsible for bringing the case before the Supreme Court. While the court eventually ruled that the United States Government had acted imprudently in removing Japanese-Americans on the West Coast to detention centers for the duration of the war, it took almost fifty years before the government was ordered to make some restitution for land and property confiscated and never returned to the rightful owners.

Not surprisingly, immediately following the war's end, the organization's membership declined markedly. Once again it expanded its activities to include other social causes, particularly civil rights, and was—along with the Congress of Racial Equality (CORE)—a cosponsor of the first freedom rides in April 1947, in what was characterized as a Journey of Reconciliation.

In the chilly atmosphere of the Cold War, the FOR came under repeated attack. Suspected of being a Communist front group, the FOR denied the charges and resented the constant demands to provide evidence of loyalty. A widely distributed pamphlet entitled "How Red is the Federal Council of Churches?" labeled the FOR a "radical-pacifist group using Christian terms to spread communist propaganda." In a 1950 radio show, popular actor Robert Montgomery called the FOR a "stooge" of the Communists. Notorious double agent Herbert Philbrick also attacked the organization in his column, which appeared in several major newspapers, including the *New York Post*. Such an accumulation of accusations caused FOR members problems in the community and, in some cases, loss of jobs. A librarian in Ohio with 35 years of service was fired because she was a member. Similarly, a college teacher in New Jersey was dismissed for failure to sign the state's loyalty oath, a request made of him because he belonged to the FOR. The organization weathered the accusations and continued to pursue its agenda of peace and reform.

In the late 1950s it joined with SANE to protest nuclear weapons atmospheric testing and eventually to protest nuclear weapons under any circumstances. Besides its participation in the nuclear freeze movement, the FOR took an early stand in the Vietnam conflict, objecting to the Gulf of Tonkin Resolution passed in 1964, which gave the president a free hand in waging war in Southeast Asia. In December 1964, the FOR was one of the major sponsors of a rally at Madison Square Garden intended to keep the Vietnam issue before the public. Throughout the war, the FOR was a prominent member of the opposition to U.S. policy. It continues to seek peaceful and nonviolent solutions as an alternative to war.

See also Muste, Abraham Johannes.
References DeBenedetti, Charles, ed., *Peace Heroes in Twentieth Century America* (1988); Wittner, Lawrence S., *Rebels against War: The American Peace Movement 1941–1960* (1969); Zaroulis, Nancy, and Gerald Sullivan, *Who Spoke Up? American Protest against the War in Vietnam 1963–1975* (1984).

Fonda, Jane (1937–)

Jane Fonda's career has been controversial, not so much because of the films she has appeared in but because of her activities as an antiwar activist during the Vietnam War. The daughter of Hollywood legend Henry Fonda, Jane spent the first ten years of her life in Los Angeles before her family relocated to Greenwich, Connecticut. She attended Vassar College briefly but left to study art in Paris. When she returned to the United States, Fonda began studying acting with Lee Strasberg at the Actor's Studio in New York.

Her name opened doors for her on Broadway and in Hollywood, but her early roles were largely forgettable. Two early films in which she was able to demonstrate her talent were *Barefoot in the Park* and *Cat Ballou*. In 1964 she married French director Roger Vadim, who attempted to turn her into an American Brigitte Bardot. Perhaps her most notable role from that period was as the title character in the futuristic fantasy *Barbarella*.

In the late 1960s, Fonda began to change her image. Opposed to the Vietnam War, she became a vocal advocate for U.S. withdrawal. With actor Donald Sutherland, she formed the Anti-War Troupe, which released several films, including *Free the Army* (1972) and *Introduction to the Enemy* (1974), documenting her infamous trip to Hanoi where she was photographed and filmed touring the countryside with her hosts, including North Vietnam government representatives and members of the military. A widely-circulated photograph showed Fonda sitting on an anti-aircraft gun emplacement. Labeled "Hanoi Jane" and branded a traitor by those who supported the war, Fonda's trip to North Vietnam did more to create antipathy toward her personally than any of her other antiwar activities. Much later, Fonda apologized for her trip to North Vietnam, but she has always maintained that her primary motive was to help, in some fashion, to bring the war to a close. When she resumed her Hollywood career in the mid-1970s, many of Fonda's films reflected her political and social beliefs, including *Coming Home* (1978), a film that focused on the plight of returning Vietnam veterans; *Julia* (1977); and *The China Syndrome* (1979). In 1973 she married her second husband, former student activist Tom Hayden, and the two toured the country, giving lectures on their political theory, which they called economic democracy.

Even in the late 1980s, Fonda had to answer her critics regarding her trip to Hanoi. While filming *Stanley and Iris* in Connecticut, Fonda addressed veterans groups and apologized not for her opposition to the war but for going to Hanoi to do so. In the 1980s she also became a spokeswoman for physical fitness, producing several best-selling exercise videos. In 1991, her marriage to Tom Hayden ended in divorce and Fonda married media mogul Ted Turner.

References *New York Times* (December 1991–January 1992); Uglow, Jennifer S., ed., *The Continuum Dictionary of Women's Biography* (1989).

Ford Peace Ship

Henry Ford is remembered primarily for his revolutionary automobile manufacturing process that used mass-produced interchangeable parts in the construction of his famous Model T. The introduction of the Model T paved the way for average people to own automobiles. Automobiles, in turn, helped to change the very fabric of U.S. society. Ford, a self-taught entrepreneur, was considered an automotive genius. The Ford Motor Company, which he founded, eventually became one of a handful of corporations that dominated automobile manufacturing and sales the world over.

Henry Ford was also something of an eccentric, who did not believe in history and who was an unabashed anti-Semite. It was this eccentricity that led to his involvement in the U.S. peace movement. Ford was persuaded by peace advocates,

Delegates aboard the Ford Peace Ship. Jane Addams, front row, second from left, was among them.

including Rosika Schwimmer and Louis Paul Lochner, that an independent mediation effort could convince belligerent European countries to submit to arbitration of their conflicts and thus end the First World War in Europe. At the same time, the peace advocates believed that a successful peace effort would circumvent the spread of war, and in particular, the United States would be spared involvement in the conflict. In November 1915, Ford announced that he was pledging his fortune to the cause of peace and would seek to facilitate neutral mediation. He also announced that he was chartering the neutral liner, *Oscar II*, which thereafter became known as the Ford Peace Ship, for that purpose.

Ford appointed Lochner his general secretary and charged him with organizing a conference of neutral governments that would act as a mediation board. On 4 December 1915, the Ford Peace Ship left Hoboken, New Jersey, with more than 160 peace advocates, students, and reporters. The voyage was anything but peaceful, as the reformers and their mission were treated with derision by the press, including the reporters who were on board the ship.

A six-nation Neutral Conference for Continuous Mediation was organized in 1916, with funding from Ford, but by the summer of 1916, his less-than-fervent support of the peace mission led him to abandon the ship and return home. Left so peremptorily, the reformers were confused and divided about how to proceed. Lochner continued to gather support for mediation. When he returned to the United States to report to Ford, Ford once again demonstrated his lack of commitment. He cut off his funding for the peace mission and for the conference, and it was forced to adjourn indefinitely.

See also Lochner, Louis Paul; Schwimmer, Rosika.

References James, Edward T., et al., eds., *Notable American Women, 1607–1950: A Biographical Dictionary* (1971); Josephson, Harold, ed., *Biographical Dictionary of Modern Peace Leaders* (1985); Knock, Thomas J., *To End All Wars: Woodrow Wilson and the Quest for World Order* (1992).

Fosdick, Harry Emerson (1878–1969)

As a young Baptist minister, Harry Emerson Fosdick wrote a book entitled *Challenge of the Present*, which was published in 1917. It was a well-reasoned, eloquent defense for taking up arms against the Axis powers. Fosdick, like many of his colleagues, considered World War I a just war, necessary because of the evil intent of Germany and its allies.

Fosdick, who was born in Buffalo, New York, was the pastor of First Baptist Church in Montclair, New Jersey, during the war. He had taken that post after graduating from Colgate University in 1900, Union Theological Seminary in 1904, and Columbia University in 1908. A year after *Challenge* appeared, Fosdick was invited by the prestigious First Presbyterian Church of New York to accept a position as assistant pastor. During his tenure at First Presbyterian Church, Fosdick found himself in conflict with congregation fundamentalists, who objected to what they characterized as the modernist wing, led by Fosdick. In part, the fundamentalists were reacting to Fosdick's gradual shift away from his support of World War I and toward a total recantation of his earlier position, a transition completed by 1923. Fosdick's reversal was heavily influenced by the writings of Kirby Page, who collaborated with Sherwood Eddy to produce a notable body of work on peace, pacifism, and Christian responsibility.

Fosdick himself was a dynamic speaker, able to command enormous respect as a leading spokesman for the peace movement. He was a strong supporter of the League of Nations and the World Court and advocated outlawing war. In 1934, Fosdick vowed that he would never support another war. By that time, his conflict with the fundamentalists had led him to resign from First Presbyterian Church. Very shortly thereafter, he was offered and accepted the leadership of Park Avenue Baptist Church, which ultimately led to the creation of New York City's Riverside Church. Fosdick remained there for two decades. During that time he continued to speak out against war and to work for peace. His insistence on bringing international issues to the pulpit created some conflict for him at Riverside Church. When, for example, in 1933, he spoke out against Nazi crimes to his parishioners, some of them expressed their extreme displeasure. They accused Fosdick of being too politically aggressive. Nevertheless, despite his critcism of the Nazis, Fosdick refused to endorse the war. His continued eloquence on the subject persuaded many Protestant churches to follow his lead in taking a stand against the war on the grounds that no war could be justified, no matter how just the cause seemed to be. Fosdick retired from Riverside Church in 1946. He also retired from Union Theological Seminary, where he had taught practical theology since 1915. He died in Bronxville, New York, on 5 October 1969.

References Josephson, Harold, ed., *Biographical Dictionary of Modern Peace Leaders* (1985); Van Doren, Charles, ed., *Webster's American Biographies* (1974); Wittner, Lawrence S., *Rebels against War: The American Peace Movement 1941–1960* (1969).

Fulbright, J. William (1905–)

As the chairman of the Senate Foreign Relations Committee during the Vietnam War, James William Fulbright gained national prominence for his outspoken criticism of U.S. foreign policy. His powerful position, coupled with the unusual phenomenon of the Foreign Relations Committee chairman's standing in opposition to a military action, gained both praise and condemnation for the Missouri native.

Fulbright was born in Sumner, Missouri, but grew up in Fayetteville, Arkansas, and considered Arkansas his home state. In 1925 he graduated from the University of Arkansas and spent the next three years at Oxford University as a Rhodes Scholar before returning home to study for his law degree at George Washington University. He worked for a brief time as a special attorney for the Department of Justice. In 1935, Fulbright joined the faculty at George Washington's School of Law but remained there only briefly before going home to Arkansas and the University of Arkansas Law School. From 1939 to 1941, Fulbright was president of the University of Arkansas.

Fulbright was drawn to politics and was elected to the House of Representatives in 1942. Two years later, Arkansas sent him to the U.S. Senate. Fulbright served the cause of peace immediately after World War II when he sponsored what became known as the Fulbright Act. With monies realized from the sale of surplus war goods abroad, an educational exchange program was established that later received permanent government funding. The prestigious Fulbright Scholars program has been expanded to include teachers, college professors, and research scholars as well as the originally designated college graduates, and it has helped to promote international understanding and cooperation since its inception.

Fulbright was by no means a pacifist, despite his concerns with education and peace. He led the floor fight on behalf of President Lyndon Johnson in 1964 to secure passage of the Gulf of Tonkin Resolution, which gave the president significant leaway in the military intervention in Vietnam. Fulbright's support was short-lived, however, as it became apparent to him that U.S. involvement in Vietnam far exceeded what had originally been intended. In a series of lectures in 1965, it was Fulbright who coined the phrase *arrogance of power* to describe U.S. policy in Vietnam. As the war continued to escalate, Fulbright became an increasingly vocal critic. In 1968 the Foreign Relations Committee held open hearings on the war, with Fulbright presiding. He remained a critic throughout the war, gaining the animosity of Johnson and his successor, President Richard M. Nixon. Advancing age persuaded Fulbright to step down after serving nearly four decades in Congress.

J. William Fulbright

References Fulbright, J. William, *The Arrogance of Power* (1966); Van Doren, Charles, ed., *Webster's American Biographies* (1974); Zaroulis, Nancy, and Gerald Sullivan, *Who Spoke Up? American Protest against the War in Vietnam 1963–1975* (1984).

Fund for Peace

Founded in 1967 by a coalition from the private, academic, and nonprofit sectors, the Fund for Peace is committed to human survival in a livable world. From the outset, the fund has used its resources to inform Congress and the public about a variety of issues, including the threat of nuclear war, increased military spending, human rights abuses by governments around the world, the economic disparity between industrial and developing nations, and violations of civil liberties.

In order to promote its message, the fund has launched several influential projects, including The Center for International Policy, directed by William

Goodfellow; The Center for Defense Information (CDI), directed by Admiral Gene R. La Rocque; The Center for National Security Studies, directed by Morton Halperin; and The Institute for the Study of World Politics, directed by Dr. Kenneth W. Thompson. Other projects sponsored by the fund include The Alternative Defense Project, an analysis of world security systems that provide an alternative to the concept of "star wars," and an International Conference on Accidental Nuclear War, the purpose of which was to provide information regarding potential causes of nuclear war and ways in which the risk of accidental war might be lessened.

Reference Meyer, Robert S., *Peace Organizations Past and Present* (1988).

Ginn, Edwin (1838–1914)

Edwin Ginn, founder of the World Peace Foundation, was born in Orland, Maine. Ginn graduated from Tufts University (Tufts College) in 1862 and immediately entered the publishing business. By 1868 he had founded Ginn & Co. and had published his first book, *Allen's Latin Grammar.* Ginn & Co. specialized in school and college textbooks and very quickly became the nation's premier academic publisher. While building a business and raising a family, Ginn also managed to return to Tufts to earn a Ph.D. in literature in 1902. It was Ginn's publishing colleague and friend, Edwin Doak Mead, who persuaded him of the importance of international peace through arbitration. As a consequence, much of Ginn's later life was spent championing the peace cause. Ginn founded and endowed the World Peace Foundation in 1910, naming Mead as its director. Ginn died in Winchester, Massachusetts, three weeks before his seventy-sixth birthday, on 21 January 1914.

See also Mead, Edwin Doak; World Peace Foundation.

References Patterson, David S., "An Interpretation of the American Peace Movement, 1898–1914." In *Peace Movements in America*, ed. Charles Chatfield (1973); *Who Was Who in America*, vol. 1 (1943).

Global Education Associates (GEA)

Using the double focus of research and education, Global Education Associates (GEA) of East Orange, New Jersey, was founded in 1973. Its goal was to create a multinational, multi-issue movement for world order incorporating social and economic justice, peace, and ecological balance. The organization has conducted more than 1,500 seminars worldwide toward advancing the attainment of these goals. It coordinates its efforts in association with four other affiliates: Genesis Farm, an organic farm and residence in Blairstown, New Jersey; the Ministry of Concern for Public Health, which monitors and studies levels of radiation; GEA of the Upper Midwest; and the Philippine Council for Global Education. Most of the work done by the five affiliated organizations is conducted through workshops and leadership seminars. Its publication, *Breakthrough*, is a forum for discussing weapons systems and alternative defense strategies, among other things.

See also Global Learning, Inc.

Reference Meyer, Robert S., *Peace Organizations Past and Present* (1988).

Global Learning, Inc.

An offshoot of Global Education Associates (GEA), Global Learning, Inc. seeks to develop a global perspective in elementary and secondary education in order to promote international understanding, cooperation, and, ultimately, world peace. Global Learning, founded in 1973, follows a three-step approach of legitimization, training for teachers, and community support. Its goal is to make education less parochial and isolated, and more global and interdependent, thus promoting understanding within the world community.

In order to have its goals recognized as legitimate alternatives to standard educational concepts, Global Learning has worked with the New Jersey State Department of Education, with county superintendents, and with professional education associations. Through a series of seminars, workshops, in-service programs, university courses, and conferences, Global Learning has, at the same time, pursued teacher education. Community support efforts have focused on civic and church-related community groups and hunger task forces.

Through its efforts, Global Learning has succeeded in forming a Consortium for Global Education, composed of both professional associations and individuals, which publishes a newsletter entitled *Leanings.* It has also published a series of manuals for both teachers and activists. Global Learning helped to develop the curriculum for a course on world history and culture that is a required addition to the New Jersey high school social studies program. Global Learning also developed a series of interactive computer games designed to enhance problem-solving skills and to promote collaborative solutions.

Reference Meyer, Robert S., *Peace Organizations Past and Present* (1988).

Global Perspectives in Education, Inc. (GPE)

Global Perspectives in Education, Inc. (GPE), founded in 1977, is a publishing company committed to international understanding and world peace that uses an instructional approach to spread its message. Since its inception, GPE has developed a number of curriculum enhancement guides that are used to supplement and complement standard curricula used from elementary school through high school, and including some college.

GPE is supported by funding from private corporations, foundations, government agencies, and individuals. Its publications help to promote the "critical thinking skills students will need for the challenge of the culturally diverse and independent world they will face as adults." The organization offers two subscription publications, *Access* and *Travel and Learning Abroad,* both of which inform readers about new materials as well as about upcoming conferences and activities, scholarships, international exchange programs, internship opportunities, and travel abroad.

Reference Meyer, Robert S., *Peace Organizations Past and Present* (1988).

Golden Rule

As part of a series of escalating nonviolent actions protesting the testing of nuclear weapons in the atmosphere, the Committee for Non-Violent Action (CNVA) sponsored an attempt to disrupt atmospheric testing in the Pacific in 1958. Captain Albert Bigelow, a former housing commissioner in the state of Massachusetts and an officer in the United States Navy who had served on three combat vessels during World War II, intended to bring his boat, the *Golden Rule,* into designated test site waters.

From the day that the United States had dropped an atomic bomb on Hiroshima, Bigelow had grown increasingly convinced of the total immorality of all war. In 1952, no longer able to serve in the navy with a clear conscience, Bigelow resigned his commission in the naval reserve. At the time of his resignation, he had one month to serve before he would have been eligible for his pension. Taking the consequences of Hiroshima to heart, Bigelow invited two of the so-called Hiroshima maidens to live with his family while they underwent the necessary surgery to correct injuries sustained in the bombing.

Bigelow's transformation from warrior to peace advocate was completed when he became a Quaker and embraced pacifism. He later recalled how despondent the members of the CNVA were when the government announced its intention to test nuclear weapons at Eniwetok Atoll in the Pacific. The idea to mount a protest that could not be ignored led to Bigelow and three other pacifists volunteering to sail the *Golden Rule* into test waters.

After notifying Dwight Eisenhower of their intentions, they set sail for Honolulu in the summer of 1958. Upon their arrival in Hawaii, the crew members were issued a temporary injunction by a federal court, which ordered them not to leave Honolulu for the Eniwetok Atoll. After careful consideration, Bigelow and his crew decided to push on with their mission, despite the injunction. As their craft was leaving Honolulu, the crew members were stopped, arrested, and placed on probation for violating the injunction.

Still undaunted, they once again tried to leave Honolulu for Eniwetok, and once again they were placed under arrest. This time the court sentenced the crew to 60 days in jail.

For the remainder of the test period, the crew members of the *Golden Rule* served out their sentences. In an unexpected development, another boat, owned by Earle and Barbara Reynolds, arrived in Honolulu just as the crew of the *Golden Rule* was standing trial. The Reynolds took up the cause and succeeded in sailing their boat, the *Phoenix*, into the designated test site waters.

See also Phoenix.

Reference Wittner, Lawrence S., *Rebels against War: The American Peace Movement 1941–1960* (1969).

Gregg, Richard (1885–1974)

Richard Gregg, one of the premier pacifist theorists of the twentieth century, gave up a career as a corporate lawyer in order to devote his life to developing a philosophy of nonviolence. Gregg, born in Colorado Springs, Colorado, graduated from Harvard College in 1907 and Harvard Law School in 1911. Gregg was well situated in a Boston law firm that specialized in industrial relations law when he happened upon an article about Gandhi. The article contained excerpts from Gandhi's writings that so impressed the young Quaker lawyer that he began studying everything Gandhi had written.

In 1925, Gregg resigned his position in the law firm and traveled to India. For the next four years, he learned firsthand about Gandhi and his theory of nonviolence. Part of that time was spent actually living in Gandhi's ashram. After his return to the United States, Gregg began writing and lecturing on nonviolence, and in 1934 he published *The Power of Non-Violence*, a ground-breaking exposition of the theory of nonviolence as a realistic and logical response to aggresion. Gregg provided for pacifists a way out of their theoretical quandary over whether nonviolence could be anything other than

a symbolic gesture to combat violence. In Gregg's view, nonviolence was powerful because it actually reflected strength rather than weakness. He characterized nonviolence as a type of "moral ju jitsu," capable of disarming an opponent by throwing him off guard and thus opening the way for negotiation and ultimate agreement.

Despite the enormous popularity of *The Power of Non-Violence*, pacifists did not readily turn to Gregg's solution when World War II presented them with the long-standing moral issue of resistance to evil. Even Gregg was pessimistic when confronted with nazism. Some time later, however, Martin Luther King, Jr. did embrace Gregg's views on pacifism and nonviolent resistance and employed them in the civil rights struggle. Gregg died on 27 January 1974, in Eugene, Oregon.

References Josephson, Harold, ed., *Biographical Dictionary of Modern Peace Leaders* (1985); Wittner, Lawrence S., *Rebels against War: The American Peace Movement 1941–1960* (1969).

Ground Zero

In 1981, Dr. Roger Molander, a former staff member of the White House National Security Council, organized Ground Zero in an effort to enlist grassroots support for seeking alternative solutions for promoting world peace and preventing nuclear war. Molander had served as chairman of the group preparing research for the SALT II negotiations. In 1982 a "Ground Zero Week" was organized. Nearly a million citizens across the country participated in educational workshops geared to inform the public about nuclear weapons. Since that first campaign, Ground Zero has made available a variety of materials that render nuclear information accessible to all citizens.

Working with such organizations as schools, churches, and service groups, Ground Zero initiated a "fuses and firebreaks" concept of instruction, focusing on the twin questions of how nuclear war could start and what measures might be adopted to prevent such an occurrence. Ground Zero identified six "firebreaks," intended to prevent nuclear war, as necessary for citizen groups and organizations to promote: (1) nuclear nonproliferation, (2) arms control, (3) improved conflict resolution, (4) control over the sale of conventional weapons, (5) improved superpower communication, and (6) improved U.S.–Soviet relations. More than 7,000 groups nationwide have participated in a role-playing game devised by Ground Zero entitled "Firebreaks War/Peace Game." In addition to a wide variety of media publications, Ground Zero published its basic primer, *Nuclear War: What's In It for You?*, which became a national best-seller.

Reference Wank, Solomon, ed., *Doves and Diplomats: Foreign Offices and Peace Movements in Europe and America in the Twentieth Century* (1978).

Gruening, Ernest (1887–1974)

When President Lyndon Baines Johnson asked for discretionary war-making

Senator Ernest Gruening

powers via the Gulf of Tonkin Resolution in 1964, Ernest Gruening was one of only two U.S. senators who voted to withhold that power. The Gulf of Tonkin Resolution was the vehicle with which Johnson greatly expanded the U.S. commitment in Vietnam, setting into motion a costly war that would become one of the most divisive in U.S. history. Gruening had already spent nearly 50 years in public service by 1964. The years had not worn down his commitment to peace, however, nor his resolve to oppose a war in Vietnam.

Gruening graduated from Harvard College and Harvard Medical School, intent on following his father into medicine. In the last year of medical school, influenced to some extent by the reform impulse that launched the Progressive era, Gruening's interests began to shift from medicine to journalsim and public service. After graduation, he took the first of several reporting jobs in Boston and New York. During World War I, he served first on the War Trade Board and then as a member of the military, in the U.S. Field Artillery. On his return to the United States, he took over as managing editor of *The Nation*. In 1924, when Senator Robert La Follette ran for president as the Progressive party candidate, Gruening directed his national publicity campaign. La Follette was defeated, and Gruening went on to Portland, Maine, where he became the founding editor of the *Evening News*.

As an early New Deal supporter, Gruening was named director of the Division of Territories and Island Possessions. A presidential appointment in 1939 made him governor of Alaska Territory. When Alaska attained statehood, Gruening became one of its first two U.S. senators in 1958. When Lyndon Johnson proceeded to step up U.S. involvement in Vietnam by virtue of the Gulf of Tonkin Resolution, Gruening did not hesitate to characterize Johnson's actions as duplicitous and in violation of the 1954 Geneva accords. Gruening continued to speak out against the war and attempted to block further funding. In 1968, Gruening was defeated in his quest for a third term, but he continued to lobby against the war. After rejoining *The Nation* as an editorial associate, Gruening spoke out frequently, particularly on college campuses. In 1972 he joined George McGovern's campaign for the presidency against Richard Nixon. Although disappointed in the outcome, Gruening continued to speak out against the war until his death on 26 June 1974, in Washington.

References Josephson, Harold, ed., *Biographical Dictionary of Modern Peace Leaders* (1985); *New York Times* (27 June 1974).

Hamilton, Alice (1869–1970)

Alice Hamilton was a quintessential example of a particular segment of U.S. society in the late nineteenth and early twentieth centuries: educated, middle-class women who chose careers over marriage and dedicated a significant portion of their lives to social and political progressive reform. Hamilton's father, a Princeton graduate who went into the wholesale grocery business, became a recluse after his business failed in 1885. Hamilton credited her mother with teaching her the importance of personal liberty.

Determined to support herself, Hamilton chose medicine over her family's objections and received her M.D. from the University of Michigan in 1893. Not wishing to go into patient treatment,

Dr. Alice Hamilton

Hamilton spent the next four years completing her internship and studying abroad. In 1897 she accepted a position as professor of pathology at the Women's Medical School of Northwestern University. Accepting the Northwestern position also allowed her to take up residency at Hull House, where she quickly became a member of the Hull House inner circle, which included Jane Addams, Florence Kelley, and Julia Lathrop. Working with such an illustrious group of reformers represented a great stride in Hamilton's transformation from a politically neutral observer to an advocate of increasingly radical reforms.

At the same time, professionally, Hamilton was becoming the foremost expert on industrial diseases and lead poisoning. As a member of the Illinois Commission on Occupational Diseases in 1910, she was appalled that the United States, in contrast to Germany and England, still largely ignored occupational diseases. In 1911, Hamilton accepted a position as U.S. Department of Labor special investigator. Her research presented compelling proof that helped persuade many employers to begin improving safety conditions for their workers.

Hamilton's work with Chicago's poor and underprivileged reinforced her growing concern for finding peaceful solutions to world problems in order to preserve resources that might otherwise be squandered on war. In 1915 she accompanied Jane Addams to the International Congress of Women at The Hague. She and Addams also visited war capitals in order to present women's peace proposals to leaders of beligerent nations. She also investigated the role of munitions manufacturers in the war and visited German-occupied Belgium. Shortly after the war ended, Hamilton attended the second international Congress of Women and saw firsthand the consequences of war-related famine in Germany.

The interwar years found Hamilton teaching at Harvard Medical School as an assistant professor in industrial medicine. In addition to her efforts to secure international peace, Hamilton continued to press for reform for women and children. By the time World War II came about, Hamilton, while still subscribing to pacifist beliefs, nevertheless became convinced that the United States had to take a stand against Hitler. Always an independent thinker, she opposed the Korean War, and—as late as 1963—signed a letter calling for an end to U.S. involvement in Vietnam. Although she managed to remain politically active well into her nineties, failing health finally caught up with Hamilton, who died in September 1970 at the age of 101.

References Josephson, Harold, ed., *Biographical Dictionary of Modern Peace Leaders* (1985); Sicherman, Barbara, et al., eds., *Notable American Women, The Modern Period: A Biographical Dictionary* (1980).

Harkness, Georgia Elma (1891–1974)

Characterized as the "most visible woman theologian in mid-century America," Georgia Harkness turned to pacifism after a tour of war-ravaged Europe in 1924. Distressed at the misery resulting from World War I, Harkness joined the Fellowship of Reconciliation (FOR) and became an active participant in the international ecumenical movement that, among other things, preached reconciliation and the peaceful resolution of world conflict.

Harkness had joined the Methodist Church at the age of 14, and her resolve to live a life dedicated to God's service was reinforced when, while a student at Cornell University, she became active in the Student Christian Association and the Student Volunteer Movement. Continuing her theological education, Harkness earned a Ph.D. in philosophy from Boston University in 1923. For the next 15 years she taught religion at Elmira College in New York and began a prolific writing career that ultimately resulted in 38 books on the topics of religion, theology, religious education, and faith.

Harkness did not abandon her pacifist views during World War II. Because of her reknown as a theologian she was able to attract public attention when she spoke out in favor of reconciliation. Her pacifism and theological liberalism remained at odds with a personal conservatism, however, and disagreements with the tactics of tax and draft resistance advocated by the FOR caused her to resign from that organization in 1951. By that time she had accepted a post at the Pacific School of Religion in Berkeley, where she remained until her retirement in 1961. Although Harkness supported U.N. intervention in Korea, she continued to call herself a pacifist and remained active in promoting international ecumenism through her work with the World Council of Churches. She was also an outspoken critic of the Vietnam War. Harkness suffered a fatal heart attack in 1974.

References *New York Times* (22 August 1974); Sicherman, Barbara, et al., eds., *Notable American Women, The Modern Period: A Biographical Dictionary* (1980).

Hayden, Tom (1939–)

Tom Hayden achieved national recognition as a defendant in the Chicago Seven trial in Chicago in 1969. Authorities charged him and his codefendants with inciting the riots that wracked Chicago during the Democratic party convention in 1968. Antiwar protesters had come to register their opposition to continuing U.S. involvement in Vietnam, and the nation watched with mounting horror as Chicago police, under the direction of then-mayor Richard Daley, clubbed into submission the mostly youthful demonstrators.

Born in Royal Oak, Michigan, Hayden became involved in the antiwar movement as a student at the University of

Tom Hayden in the Santa Monica headquarters of the Indochina Peace Campaign.

Michigan. A cofounder of Students for a Democratic Society (SDS) in 1961, Hayden served as the organization's president in 1962 and 1963. He also wrote the Port Huron Statement, a manifesto issued by SDS in 1962, which condemned the war in Vietnam and called on students nationwide to join in opposition. In 1963 Hayden joined the staff of the Student Non-Violent Coordinating Committee and helped to found the Economic Research and Action Project in 1964. Always seeking new ways to enlist antiwar supporters, Hayden also founded the Indochina Peace Campaign.

The trial of the Chicago Seven rivaled news of the war itself in the nation's newspapers. Despite the actions of the Chicago police, who were later condemned as instigators of the riots by an independent commission charged with investigating the episode, most Americans were persuaded that Hayden and his codefendants deserved to be placed on trial. The 1960s, by any measure, had been a decade of profound disruption. People were tired of protest, dissension, and demonstration. Nevertheless, Hayden was acquitted of the charges, a verdict that he hailed as a moral victory. He continued protesting

the war until it finally began to wind down in 1974 and ended in 1975.

In the early 1970s, Hayden's path crossed with that of antiwar activist and actress Jane Fonda. Hayden supported Fonda's ill-advised and much-publicized trip to Hanoi. The two later married, finally settling in California with Fonda's daughter, Vanessa, and their son, Troy. (The marriage ended in divorce after 15 years.) While Fonda resumed her movie career, Hayden moved into mainstream politics. He ran first for the U.S. Senate in California but was defeated in the primary in 1976. Thereafter, he plunged into state politics, immersing himself in issues that he believed important to the future of the state and country. In 1977 he founded and served as the chairman of the California Campaign for Economic Democracy. A staunch foe of nuclear energy, Hayden also served as chairman of the SolarCal Council from 1978 to 1982. The SolarCal Council supported research for alternative solar energy solutions to the state's energy needs. In 1982, Hayden was elected to the California state legislature. He was chairman of the Labor and Employment Commission and the Subcommittee on Higher Education.

References Hayden, Tom, *Tom Hayden: A Memoir* (1990); *Who's Who in America*, 46th ed. (1991).

Hennacy, Ammon (1893–1970)

Ammon Hennacy considered himself a "one-man revolution," but in fact, he was too much of an individualist to be a true revolutionary. Hennacy was born in Negley, Ohio, and briefly attended Hiram College, the University of Wisconsin, and Ohio State University. From a very early age, he was drawn to radical politics and moved from socialism, to communism, and then to the Wobblies. Hennacy sought out ways to express his opposition to various government policies, from refusing to pay income taxes to picketing IRS offices on April 15.

He was a pacifist who spent a year in solitary confinement for being a conscientious objector (CO) during World War I. After his release from prison, Hennacy and his common-law wife traveled from state to state until they had hiked through all 48 states. For a while they settled in Wisconsin, where they bought a farm, and Hennacy became a social worker in Milwaukee. After his wife and two daughters left in 1940, unable to live with his radicalism, he spent the next ten years working as a day laborer in the Southwest. In 1942, as commited as ever to pacifism, Hennacy notified the government that he would not register for the draft. He also refused to pay an income tax, because to do so would be to support the war effort.

Hennacy converted to Catholicism in 1952, mostly under the influence of Dorothy Day, whose work and writings he had long admired. After moving to New York, he began working at Day's Hospitality House on the Lower East Side and shortly thereafter began editing the newspaper *The Catholic Worker*. For the remainder of his life, Hennacy worked with the Catholic Worker Movement. Many of the movement's projects bore his stamp. For example, it was he who conceived of the civil defense drill protests in the 1950s as a way to protest nuclear weapons; Hennacy and other Catholic Workers were prepared to go to jail for not cooperating with civil defense requirements that everyone seek shelter during civil defense drills. Eventually, Hennacy moved to Salt Lake City, Utah, where he opened a Hospitality House. He died in Salt Lake City on 14 July 1970.

References Josephson, Harold, ed., *Biographical Dictionary of Modern Peace Leaders* (1985); Wittner, Lawrence S., *Rebels against War: The American Peace Movement 1941–1960* (1969).

High Technology Professionals for Peace (HTPFP)

High Technology Professionals for Peace (HTPFP) was one of many groups that organized in the early 1980s because of the perceived threat of the increasing possibility of nuclear war. The group was formed in 1981 by scientists, engineers, and other technical workers organized to oppose the threat of nuclear war. Their avowed mission is to provide information about the impact on society that various weapons systems did and could have, both by virtue of their existence and their potential use.

The organization conducts educational and scientific projects and promotes discussion of issues regarding the defense industry. An important service to its members is an informal advisory network that encourages and supports reconsideration of career decisions. It also distributes information to students on professional ethics and the arms industry. Part of the support system for professionals engaged in this dialogue is an employment agency for those seeking alternatives to weapons-related employment. Working with other peace groups, the HTPFP also provides an invaluable service by making available to legislators information and technical analyses of weapons systems and related considerations. Much of HTPFP's research and analysis is published in a newsletter entitled *Technology and Responsibility*.

Reference Meyer, Robert S., *Peace Organizations Past and Present* (1988).

Historic Peace Churches

The three oldest and largest of the so-called historic peace churches in the United States are the Society of Friends, the Mennonites, and the Brethren. All three came out of the same tradition of pacifism and nonviolence espoused by the Society of Friends in 1660: "We utterly deny all outward wars and strife, and fightings and outward weapons, for any end, or under any pretence whatever. This is our testimony to the whole world. The spirit of Christ, by which we are guided, is not changeable. . . . Therefore, we cannot learn war any more." By the mid-1930s, the Brethren claimed a U.S. membership of nearly 200,000; the Mennonites had 114, 337 members; and the Society of Friends had 93,697 members. Each of the churches had action groups, which have been involved to a lesser or greater extent in the peace movement throughout the twentieth century.

The American Friends Service Committee (AFSC) was and is probably the most proactive organization, while the Mennonite Central Committee (MCC) and the Brethren Service Committee attracted less attention. All three of the historic peace church action groups were extremely active in the immediate pre–World War II period, and during the war itself, in working with the Roosevelt administration and the military to hammer out alternative service for conscientious objectors (COs). The peace churches agreed to provide the entire funding for alternative service programs. The National Service Board for Religious Objectors (NSBRO), which represented the peace churches, opened a series of Civilian Public Service (CPS) camps in late 1940.

Consistent with their longtime commitment to pacifism, the peace churches rejected the war itself. The Brethren Church resolved that "the church's historic conviction that violence in the rela-tions of men is contrary to the spirit of Christ must be reaffirmed." The wartime policy of the Friends, as stated by Quaker historian Rufus Jones, said that "there must be amidst all the confusions of the hour a tried and undisturbed remnant of persons who will not become purveyors of coercion and violence, who are ready to stand alone, if it is necessary, for the way of peace and love among men."

Although the Mennonites had the best overall record of pacifism, with nearly three of every five young male Mennonites declaring their status as COs, there was, nevertheless, some erosion of strict pacifism within all three churches. For example, most Quaker colleges during the war years accepted military training programs, and fully three-fourths of all Quakers called to service refused to accept CO status. Like most pacifists confronted with the enormity of the threat from Hitler, the Nazis, and fascism, members of the historic peace churches—who in other times would have retained their strict adherence to pacifism—found themselves caught in a moral dilemma. Most of them found it impossible to sit out World War II.

The peace churches, in addition to their support of COs and alternative service programs, also devoted much of their efforts during the war to relief programs. The MCC provided hundreds of thousands of dollars in relief and assistance to war-torn areas in France, Poland, China, and England. The Brethren Service Committee sent relief workers to war-ravaged Europe. The Friends operated the Friends Ambulance Unit in China, provided relief in India and France, and assisted the United Nations Relief and Rehabilitation Administration in the Mediterranean.

All the action groups of the peace churches were active in efforts to eliminate nuclear weapons and to end the arms races in the 1950s, and when the Vietnam War escalated in the mid-1960s, they once again worked to protect the rights of COs and to halt the war.

References Jacob, Philip E., *The Origins of Civilian Public Service* (1946); Pickett, Clarence Evan, *For More Than Bread* (1953); Wittner, Lawrence S, *Rebels against War: The American Peace Movement 1941–1960* (1969).

Hoffman, Isador B. (1898–1981)

Isador Hoffman was a cofounder of the Jewish Peace Fellowship (JPL), organized in 1941 to provide a place of support and counsel for young Jewish pacifists who sought conscientious objector (CO) status. Over the next 40 years, the JPL became a widely respected Jewish representative to the world peace movement.

Hoffman was born in Philadelphia, Pennsylvania, and graduated from Columbia College and the Jewish Theological Seminary of America. As the Jewish chaplain to students at Columbia University from 1934 to 1967, Rabbi Hoffman earned a reputation as the foremost American Jewish pacifist. Hoffman spent several years in the Middle East and participated in conferences held by Jewish Palestinian Zionist intellectuals who sought a solution to the conflicts in that region of the world. Out of these conferences came the idea that a peaceful solution could be arrived at if Jews and Arabs were jointly empowered to share authority. With the advent of World War II and the holocaust that left six million Jews dead, Hoffman shifted his support to the State of Israel. He would again return to the idea of an Arab-Jewish reconciliation in the 1970s, but by then the distressing lack of Arab peacemakers, together with the militarization of the region, made reconciliation problematic.

Once the JPF came into existence, Hoffman threw himself into working for nonviolence and conscientious objection based on Jewish tradition. He was also the cofounder of the American Jewish Society for Service, an organization that provided Jewish men and women with an opportunity to make positive contributions by channeling idealism into specific outreach projects. Hoffman worked actively within several peace organizations, including SANE, FOR, and the National Interreligious Board for Conscientious Objectors. Even in retirement, Hoffman continued to work for peace. In 1981 he organized a group of retirement community members to protest the Trident submarine project that was underway at Groton Naval Station. In addition, he accepted numerous invitations to speak at high schools, colleges, and civic groups. Hoffman died in Danbury, Connecticut, on 27 January 1981.

See also Jewish Peace Fellowship.

Reference Josephson, Harold, ed., *Biographical Dictionary of Modern Peace Leaders* (1985).

Holmes, John Haynes (1879–1964)

A committed pacifist and social activist, John Haynes Holmes, like Richard Gregg, admired and was influenced by Gandhi's account of his nonviolent resistance to South African racism. Holmes's argument for pacifism, *New Wars For Old* (1916), preceded by almost 20 years similar views expressed by Gregg in *The Power of Non-Violence* (1934). Taken together, the two volumes constituted the most articulate exposition of U.S. pacifist theory. *New Wars For Old* established Holmes as one of the most important pacifist thinkers in the Western world.

Holmes, a Harvard-educated clergyman/writer/speaker, was born in Philadelphia, Pennsylvania. He belonged originally to the Unitarian Church and held pastorships at Third Religious Society Church in Dorchester, Massachusetts, and New York's Church of the Messiah. He was made full pastor at Church of the Messiah in 1912, but he severed all ties with Unitarianism after World War I, when, because of his pacifist stance and antiwar activities, he came under attack from the church. Thereafter, he helped to transform Church of the Messiah into the Community Church of New York, a nondenominational congregation that embraced oneness of the human spirit and the necessity for religion to serve people in a practical manner.

Holmes was also influenced in his philosophy by social gospel advocates, including Walter Rauschenbusch and Theodore Parker. Like many others of his generation, Holmes found that World War I helped to transform his belief system regarding pacifism. He became an active peace advocate and helped found the American Civil Liberties Union (ACLU) and the U.S. branch of the Fellowship of Reconciliation (FOR). He was also active in the American Union against Militarism. Following the war, Holmes took over as editor of *Unity*, a weekly publication, and contributed numerous articles on pacifism to other publications, including the *New Republic* and *The World Tomorrow*.

Holmes was extremely critical of the Versailles Treaty and the League of Nations, both of which he believed were dictated to and dominated by imperialistic powers. At the same time, he supported Salmon Levinson's Outlawry of War campaign, which called for a new international code and a new international world court to settle conflicts. In 1929, Holmes began a six-year stint as chairman of the War Resisters League (WRL). Despite the growing threat of fascism and the potential for war throughout the 1930s, Holmes refused to renounce pacifism. He opposed all U.S. military action abroad, even as he denounced Stalin and Hitler. In 1933, Holmes helped to organize the first large-scale protest against Hitlerism in the United States. When the United States entered World War II, Holmes once again stood by his pacifist philosophy, refusing to support the war effort in any way. Fearing that the United Nations (U.N.) was simply another version of the League of Nations, Holmes was leary of lending support to that organization.

From 1940 to 1950, Holmes served as chairman of the ACLU's board of directors. In the late 1940s he visited India and had the honor of meeting with Gandhi. His health was failing, however, and when he returned to the United States, Holmes was diagnosed with Parkinson's disease and chose to retire from public life. He returned to the Unitarian Church, persuaded that the Unitarians had finally come around to his position on world peace. Holmes died in New York City on 3 April 1964.

References DeBenedetti, Charles, ed., *Peace Heroes in Twentieth Century America* (1988); Josephson, Harold, ed., *Biographical Dictionary of Modern Peace Leaders* (1985); Wittner, Lawrence S., *Rebels against War: The American Peace Movement 1941–1960* (1969).

Holt, Hamilton (1872–1951)

Hamilton Holt, an educator and publisher, was born in Brooklyn, New York. After graduating from Yale University in 1894, he attended Columbia University for one year before taking a post with *The Independent*, a liberal weekly newspaper owned and published in New York by his grandfather, Henry C. Bowen. By 1913, Holt had taken over as editor and owner.

Holt's interest in the peace movement began in earnest at about the same time as he became a staff member on *The Independent*. He served on the executive committee for the first American Peace Conference, held in New York in 1907. He was a founder of the New York Peace Society and was active in the American Peace Society (APS), the World Peace Foundation, and the Church Peace Union. As the guest of various governments, Holt had an opportunity to visit the battlefronts of the Allied armies in 1918. After World War I ended, Holt was more than ever determined to help secure a means to avoid future wars, notably through the establishment of a world federation. He was a founder of the League to Enforce Peace and the League of Nations Non-Partisan Association.

Throughout the 1920s, Holt traveled to Europe on several occasions to attend the assemblies of the League of Nations. In the mid-1920s he was named president of Rollins College, a position he held until his retirement in 1949. During his tenure, Rollins's reputation as a respected institution of higher learning grew

Hamilton Holt

for the Advancement of the Colored Race, Netherlands-America Foundation, Italy-American Society, Friends of Poland, Armenian-American Society, and the Mexico Society of New York. He served as the executive director of the Woodrow Wilson Foundation and belonged to the United World Federalists and the American Society of International Law, as well as to a score of organizations that promoted labor, women's rights, and cultural and ethnic diversity. For his role in the world peace movement, Holt was honored by governments around the world, including those of Italy, Japan, France, Greece, and the Soviet Union. Holt died in Putnam, Connecticut, on 26 April 1951.

See also League to Enforce Peace; League of Nations.

References *National Cyclopaedia of American Biography*, vol. 40 (1967); Patterson, David S., "An Interpretation of the American Peace Movement, 1898–1914." In *Peace Movements in America*, ed. Charles Chatfield (1973).

immeasurably. Holt restructured the academic program at Rollins to bring together professors and students in an intellectually stimulating environment; he increased the endowment by $5 million; and he was responsible for the endowment of an Institute of Statesmanship, held annually at Rollins and attended by government leaders from around the world. Throughout his career at Rollins, Holt continued to promote world federation. He was a delegate to the United Nations Conference on International Organization in 1945, and in 1946, as a result of an anonymous donation of $25,000, Holt was able to sponsor the Rollins College Conference on World Government.

Like many of the reformers of his era, Holt's interests did not focus solely on the quest for peace. He helped to found a number of organizations that were intended to assist ethnic and cultural minorities of the day, including the Society

Holtzman, Elizabeth (1941–)

As a first-term congresswoman from New York's 16th Congressional District in 1973, Elizabeth Holtzman startled her colleagues by initiating a lawsuit against the Nixon administration, charging it with illegal and unconstitutional actions in the bombing of Cambodia. Although the Federal District Court agreed with Holtzman's contention that President Nixon had abused his presidential powers, its ruling was later overturned by the U.S. Court of Appeals. Nevertheless, Holtzman became the first person in the history of the United States to attempt to declare war unconstitutional.

"Liz" Holtzman, born in Brooklyn, New York, became the youngest woman elected to Congress when she defeated the powerful chairman of the House Judiciary Committee, Emanuel Celler. After graduating from Radcliffe College and Harvard Law School, Holtzman involved herself in New York City politics by working as an assistant to Mayor John V.

Lindsey. Through her attention to the people she was helping to serve, Holtzman built a substantial grass-roots following that helped her to unseat the long-entrenched Celler. The cornerstone of that and subsequent campaigns included Hotlzman's outspoken opposition to the Vietnam War and to massive military spending. Other concerns included health care, the Equal Rights Amendment, education, and the congressional senority system. As a member of the Judiciary Committee, Holtzman voted in favor of the Articles of Impeachment against President Nixon during the Watergate scandal. Her intense focus and serious demeanor caused some critics to charge that she was overzealous in her moral indictman of the president and his administration, but Holtzman has always acted on the premise that public accountability is the key to good government and has considered it her responsibility to be a watchdog as well as a lawmaker.

During her third term in Congress, Holtzman decided to run for the Senate. With very little special interest money to support her campaign, she failed to win the nomination and returned instead to New York City. Since then, Holtzman has remained active in New York politics. Although her integrity remains unquestioned, Holtzman's inability to develop a rapport with many segments of the voting population has prevented her from winning several important political campaigns, including one for mayor of New York and most recently for the U.S. Senate.

References Whitney, Sharon, and Tom Raynor, *Women in Politics*. (1986).

Hooper, Jessie Annette Jack (1865–1935)

Jessie Hooper in many ways typified women volunteers of the late nineteenth and early twentieth centuries. She was born in Winneshiek, Iowa, where she had an informal education, and left home only upon her marriage to Ben Hooper.

The couple moved to Oshkosh, Wisconsin, and Hooper immediately began to take an interest in her new community. She joined several civic and charitable organizations, including the Daughters of the American Revolution and the Benevolent Society of Oshkosh. She was instrumental in bringing the visiting nurses to Oshkosh and in establishing a tuberculosis sanitorium. She believed in women's suffrage, and for years she and her husband alternately chose the candidate for whom he would cast his vote in any given election. It was when she heard Susan B. Anthony speak at the World Columbian Exposition in Chicago in 1893 that she joined the Wisconsin Woman Suffrage Association and worked actively for suffrage. She also lobbied for a variety of reforms involving children's health and welfare. Carrie Chapman Catt, the president of the National American Woman Suffrage Association (NAWSA), impressed with Hooper's energy, enlisted her help in Washington. For several years, until suffrage was passed and ratified, Hooper spent several months each year on the road, traveling to various states on behalf of a suffrage amendment.

Hooper was the first president of the Wisconsin League of Women Voters (LWV), and the Democratic party nominated her to run against Robert La Follette for the senate in 1920. Although the campaign was doomed from its start, Hooper did manage to win the state's largest urban area, including the city of Milwaukee.

Although she had been a willing volunteer in support of the United States during World War I, Hooper worked to find peaceful solutions to world conflict. It was she who called together nine women's organizations in Buffalo, New York, to organize for peace. The group persuaded Carrie Chapman Catt to serve as chairwoman, and a national conference—the Conference on the Cause and Cure of War—was held in Washington, D.C. The conference met for the first time in January 1925 and was held annually thereafter as the Committee on the Cause and Cure of War. Until 1932, Hooper served as its recording secretary. She also traveled to Geneva, Switzerland, to deliver a petition containing hundreds of thousands of signatures, all asking for international disarmament. Her years of ceaseless activity finally caught up to Hooper. Failing health kept her from further peace work, and she died in Oshkosh on 8 May 1935.

References Starr, Harris E., ed., *Dictionary of American Biography*, supp. 1 (1944); Harper, Ida Husted, ed., *History of Woman Suffrage*, vols. 5 and 6 (1922).

Hughan, Jessie Wallace (1875–1955)

For four decades, Jessie Hughan devoted much of her time to organizing against war. Born in Brooklyn, New York, Hughan derived some of her independent thinking from her parents, both of whom advocated Henry George's single-tax plan. In addition, Hughan's mother, Margaret, was the president of the Brooklyn Women's Single Tax Club. Hughan graduated from Barnard College in 1894, where she was noted for her poetry and parodies. At Columbia University, where she earned both an M.A. and a Ph.D. in economics, Hughan became a convert to socialism, primarily as a result of her doctoral thesis research on the subject. Hughan had taught while studying at Columbia, and in 1907 she began a teaching career in the New York public schools that lasted until her retirement in 1945. She also ran, unsuccessfully, for a series of public offices, including alderman (1915), secretary of state (1918), lieutenant governor (1920), and U.S. senator (1924).

It was as a pacifist that she made her greatest contributions to peace. Following the outbreak of World War I in Europe, Hughan organized the Anti-Enlistment League for persons opposed to military service and for those who objected to other types of war support. Colleagues in this effort included the noted pacifists John Haynes Holmes and Tracy Mygatt; all of them grew increasingly alarmed as the United States drew nearer to declaring war. Hughan was also a charter member of the Fellowship of Reconciliation (FOR), founded in 1915.

Her efforts to resist war did not abate once peace was declared. In 1922, under the auspices of the FOR, Hughan organized the Committee for Enrollment against War, and in 1923 she formed the War Resisters League (WRL), which brought together representatives from the FOR, the Women's Peace Union, and the Women's Peace Society. She served as secretary of the WRL until 1945. The league supported conscientious objectors (COs) and eventually expanded to support efforts to secure social justice. In pursuit of her promotion of peaceful solutions to world conflicts, Hughan participated in league-sponsored parades. In 1938 she organized the United Pacifist Committee (UPC), whose focus was education. In 1940 she founded the Pacifist Teachers League. Reports of Nazi atrocities against the Jews prompted Hughan to campaign vociferously for an immediate armistice, arguing that millions of people were at risk. Her revulsion over the German government's actions did not shake her belief in pacifism as the ultimate weapon against war, however, and she continued to support COs and to oppose the Civilian Public Service (CPS) camps, where war objectors were assigned nonpaying jobs in lieu of military service. Throughout her teaching career, Hughan was pressured at various times by the school board to discontinue her antiwar activities. She refused to accede to the pressure, and she retired uneventfully from teaching in 1945. During the ten years prior to her death in 1955, Hughan continued to work actively on behalf of pacifism as the honorary secretary of the WRL.

See also Committee for Enrollment Against War; United Pacifist Committee; War Resisters League.

References Chatfield, Charles, *For Peace and Justice: Pacifism in America, 1914–1941* (1971); Sicherman, Barbara, et al., eds., *Notable American Women*,

The Modern Period: A Biographical Dictionary (1980); Wittner, Lawrence S., *Rebels against War: The American Peace Movement 1941–1960* (1969).

Hull, Hannah Clothier (1872–1958)

Hannah Clothier Hull, born in Sharon Hill, Pennsylvania, was the daughter of the founder of Strawbridge and Clothier Department Stores and grew up in the privileged world of Philadelphia society. She graduated from Swarthmore College in 1891. Because her family refused to allow her to take a job, she turned to voluntarism and worked in a Philadelphia settlement house. Although she did some graduate work in history at Bryn Mawr College in 1896, her marriage to William Hull in 1898 ended her formal education.

The Hulls met while both were engaged in volunteer social work. William Hull was a professor of history at Swarthmore. For over 40 years the Hulls were active in the peace movement. Hull attended the Second Hague Conference for International Peace in 1907 with her husband, beginning her decades-long efforts to promote pacifism. A concomitant interest in securing women's suffrage also occupied her.

Even after the United States entered World War I, Hull continued to espouse pacifism. From 1917 to 1920 she served as chairwoman of the Pennsylvania branch of the Women's Peace Party (WPP). She also did volunteer work with the American Friends Service Committee (AFSC) and was involved in the programs providing aid for French and Russia civilians as well as in programs that distributed food to children in Germany and Austria. For almost two decades, from 1928 to 1947, Hull was the vice-chairwoman of the AFSC board. The bulk of her time and effort, however, was spent promoting the Women's International League for Peace and Freedom (WILPF).

In 1922 Hull represented the WILPF at an emergency International Conference of Women at The Hague, which urged a reasonable settlement of reparations payments and a withdrawal of occupying forces from Germany. In 1924, Hull succeeded Jane Addams as the chairwoman of the U.S. branch of the WILPF when Addams took over as chairwoman of the international organization. Hull and Addams worked closely together and maintained a strong friendship until Addams's death in 1935. Hull served as chairwoman of the national board until 1938 and as president of the U.S. branch from 1933 to 1939. As a moving force in the WILPF, Hull joined a nationwide Peace Caravan organized by Mabel Vernon in 1931. The caravan crisscrossed the country, holding rallies and public demonstrations and gathering signatures for petitions on disarmament. Hull was a delegate to the World Disarmament Conference in Geneva in 1932, and in 1935 she helped to organize the People's Mandate to Governments to End War. This committee was instrumental in gathering 8 million signatures for a peace petition from people around the world.

Hull resigned her leadership position in the WILPF only after the death of her husband in 1939. After a prolonged period of mourning, Hull gradually returned to her work with the WILPF, the AFSC, and the Friends Peace Committee. Until her death in 1958, Hull remained active, attending every Philadelphia meeting of the peace groups and serving on the boards of numerous women's groups. The governor of Pennsylvania appointed her to the Pennsylvania Mother's Assistance Fund, and she also served, at Herbert Hoover's request, on the board of the National Committee on Food for the Five Small Democracies in 1940. Her commitment to peace and pacifism stood as a beacon to all.

References Chatfield, Charles, *For Peace and Justice: Pacifism in America, 1914–1941* (1971); Sicherman, Barbara, et al., eds., *Notable American Women, The Modern Period: A Biographical Dictionary* (1980).

Hutchins, Grace (1885–1969)

When Grace Hutchins joined the Socialist party as a protest against U.S. participation in World War I, it almost cost her a teaching job. It was not the first time that Hutchins had caused discomfort for upholding her beliefs, nor would it be the last.

Hutchins was born in Boston, Massachusetts, into one of Boston's socially elite families and graduated from Bryn Mawr College in 1907. While she was in college, Hutchins supported women's suffrage, a development that her parents found distressing—for reasons that are not altogether clear, because neither parent could be accused of turning a deaf ear to social issues. Her father, Edward, was a prominent attorney who founded the Legal Aid Society and incorporated the Boston Bar Association. Her mother devoted a great deal of energy to the Baldwinsville Hospital for Crippled Children and the Home for Aged Women. It was at Bryn Mawr that Hutchins determined to do missionary work. After graduation, she left for Wachung, China, where she served as teacher and then principle of St. Hilda's School for Chinese Girls from 1912 to 1916. On her return to the United States, Hutchins took a job at a social training school in New York City, the post that she nearly lost because of her Socialist affiliations.

Hutchins's lifelong concern for working class women and children began at about this time. She enrolled at the New York School of Philanthropy to study labor and worked for several months in a factory in order to fulfill course requirements. Hutchins also took courses at Columbia University Teacher's College. Hutchins, who was a pacifist, joined the Fellowship of Reconciliation (FOR), serving as business executive, press secretary, and contributing editor to the FOR publication *The World Tomorrow* at various times. Along with her friend and longtime companion, Anna Rochester, Hutchins traveled extensively on behalf of FOR and coauthored a book entitled *Jesus Christ and the World Today* (1922), which dealt with social issues and Christian response.

In 1927, Hutchins was arrested in Boston during a demonstration on behalf of Nicola Sacco and Bartolomeo Vanzetti, two Italian immigrants who were accused of robbing a shoe factory and murdering one of the guards. Hutchins continued to investigate and write about labor conditions throughout the 1920s and 1930s. Among her publications were *Labor and Silk* (1928) and *Women Who Work*, which went through three editions in 1933, 1934, and 1952. As a member of the Communist party, which she joined with Anna Rochester, Hutchins ran for public office in New York: alderman (1935), controller (1936), and lieutenant governor (1940); all these campaigns were unsuccessful. She remained an active member of the Communist party, at various times lending monetary support to Elizabeth Gurley Flynn and coming into conflict with Whitaker Chambers during the Alger Hiss trial. She died in New York on 15 July 1969.

References New York Times (16 July 1969); Sicherman, Barbara, et al., eds., *Notable American Women, The Modern Period: A Biographical Dictionary* (1980).

Institute for Peace and Justice

Founded in 1970 by Kathy and Jim McGinnis, the Institute for Peace and Justice began as a center for peace studies on the campus of Saint Louis University in St. Louis, Missouri. From its inception, the challenge of the institute has been found in the statement, "if you want peace, work for justice." Primarily an educational organization, the nonprofit institute was created to provide educational resources to individuals and organizations, religious and secular. The institute addresses a broad spectrum of issues, including economic justice, hunger, racism, sexism, peacemaking, the nuclear arms race, nonviolent conflict resolution, and Gandhian nonviolence.

IPJ advocates an action program that follows two paths: first, direct and immediate help for individuals who are victims of injustice and, second, a longer-range program directed at effecting the social change necessary to accomplish the institute's goals. To that end, the institute provides resource development aids, including books, filmstrips, videotapes, advisory services, newsletters, teaching and leadership training involving workshops, faculty in-service training, summer institutes, and seminary courses, and family camps. Elementary and secondary teachers are provided with curriculum and resource development assistance. Advice is also given on the college level. The institute has advised schools, college faculties, seminaries, campus hunger ministries, churches, religious leaders, individuals and families, justice and peace networks, and St. Louis–area peace and justice groups.

In addition to the resources mentioned, the institute also sponsors the Parenting for Peace and Justice Network (PPJN), which has affiliates in more than 150 cities in the United States, Canada, and several countries around the world. In 1983 the PPJN captured nationwide attention when several of its members appeared on the Phil Donahue interview show to discuss the arms race, television and children, and the Nestle boycott. The PPJN has made videotapes of this discussion available to those seeking information.

Reference Meyer, Robert S., *Peace Organizations Past and Present* (1988).

Institute for Space and Security Systems

Dr. Robert Bowman, a retired U.S. Air Force Lieutenant Colonel and the former director of so-called Star Wars research for the Air Force, was an unlikely candidate to found an organization dedicated to opposing the development of nuclear weapons. Nevertheless, in 1982, Bowman, alarmed at the Star Wars appropriations, founded the Institute for Space and Security Systems, with the primary goal of preventing nuclear war.

In the view of Bowman and his colleagues, an arms race in space would increase the danger that nuclear war would occur. Moreover, Bowman argued that the antiballistic missile (ABM) system proposed for Star Wars would be ineffectual in providing protection and would violate several treaties—including the ABM treaty. If both superpowers implemented such a system, he argued, either could launch an attack and destroy the enemy system without warning. The incentive to initiate a first strike would be so compelling as to make nuclear war an almost certain consequence as soon as both systems were in place. Bowman and his institute mounted a compelling argument that caught the attention of both the public and the press and helped to weaken support for the Star Wars system proposed by the Reagan administration.

A blunt spokesman for what he considered responsible technological development, Bowman stated unequivocally that "Star Wars has nothing to do with defense. It is a blatant attempt to regain absolute military superiority through development of new offensive weapons, disguised as defense." The institute succeeded in securing several important delays in the development of Star Wars, including getting Congress to restrict testing of antisatellite weapons against space targets, getting the Pentagon to delay the scheduled first test of advanced antisatellite systems, working with Soviet space experts to iron out details of a treaty that would benefit both sides, getting space weapons included in the umbrella arms talks between the United States and the U.S.S.R., and, finally, securing a moratorium on antisatellite testing against targets in space.

Bowman has testified many times before Congress on space and security measures. In addition, his institute publishes a newsletter, *Space and Security News*, a forum for research and position papers on the subject.

Reference Meyer, Robert S., *Peace Organizations Past and Present* (1988).

Institute on Global Conflict and Cooperation (IGCC)

The Institute on Global Conflict and Cooperation (IGCC) was one of several organizations founded in the early 1980s with the purpose of promoting world peace through research and study of the causes of war. In 1983 the University of California Board of Regents established this multicampus research group with two points of focus. The first called for investigating conflict situations that had the potential to develop into full-scale wars; the second involved considerating alternative forms of international cooperation to deal with crises threatening world peace.

The main IGCC administrative offices are located at the University of California at San Diego, with branch liaison offices at each of the university's regional campuses. When the regents funded the IGCC, it was with the idea that there were certain functions regarding international conflict situations to which a university was particularly well-suited to lend its expertise. With the IGCC, the University of California system was able to explore ideas as well as to teach in areas not generally covered in college curricula. The program not only investigates the causes of global conflict but also the ideas, institutions, and policies that could be employed to diffuse critical situations and then to resolve conflicts. The IGCC supports a wide range of programs, including research and education, fellowships, seminars, lectureships, libraries, and Peace Research Workshops. Proposals are submitted for IGCC approval from students, faculty, and staff in the University of California system. These individual projects are supplemented by larger projects intitiated by the central office.

Reference Meyer, Robert S., *Peace Organizations Past and Present* (1988).

International Association of Educators for World Peace (IAEWP)

Officially organized in 1969, the International Association of Educators for World Peace (IAEWP) was founded by Dr. Charles Mercieca of Alabama. The IAEWP, which has more than 15,000 members and chapters in 50 countries around the world, was founded on the premise that education and organized activity combined would act to open lines of communication, eliminate fear and mistrust, articulate the desire for peace, and provide models for peace.

The organization publishes a journal, *Peace Progress*, which prints articles and papers from contributors around the world. Of particular interest is a section in the journal that outlines the activities leading to peace in the previous year and a listing of current and upcoming peace meetings of organizations around the world. It also publishes a *World Newsletter.* The most recent World Congress of the IAEWP was held in China in 1990.

Reference Meyer, Robert S., *Peace Organizations Past and Present* (1988).

International Friendship League Pen Pals

Founded in 1934, the International Friendship League (IFL) operates on the profoundly simple premise that in a person-to-person relationship, individuals from different cultures and political systems can learn to appreciate and understand their respective differences. The IFL headquarters is located in Boston, Massachusetts, and serves as a clearinghouse for people who wish to correspond with individuals from other countries. Membership is open to everyone over the age of six. By the mid-1980s, approximately 1,600 pen pals were matched up each month. The IFl now operates in more than 129 countries, and although the predominant language of correspondence is English, there are actually very few language barriers that would prevent participation in the program. The league's slogan, "have a pen pal and see the world!" has successfully helped to promote peace and understanding among citizens from countries around the world since its inception. For the price of a postage stamp, the league continues to flourish.

References Meyer, Robert S., *Peace Organizations Past and Present* (1988).

International Peace Academy

Since its founding in New York City in 1970, the International Peace Academy has become a significant force in the research and study of international peacekeeping methods. United Nations (U.N.) Secretary-General Javier Perez de Cuellar noted that the "fortunate combination of theory and practice ... has made the

Academy ... a unique and exceptionally fruitful institution." The academy maintains a transnational board of directors and staff and is funded by contributions from both corporations and individuals. It focuses on three areas: conducting training seminars in peacekeeping and multilateral regulation; researching conflict studies and the role of mediators in conflicts; and building a body of information related to its basic training seminars and made available to those who have undergone training.

Peacekeeping seminars have been held annually in Vienna since 1970. In 1980, the academy conducted its first annual Seminar for United Nations Diplomats, and since 1981 it has held regular off-the-record meetings of military and diplomatic representatives of the U.N. and the U.N. Secretariat. The academy also sponsors a Task Force on Technology to review technological developments that might be useful in peacekeeping. The *Peacekeeper's Handbook* has become a text for training peacekeepers, and a second publication, *Coping with Conflict*, is a yearly review of the academy's activities.

Reference Meyer, Robert S., *Peace Organizations Past and Present* (1988).

International Peace Research Association (IPRA)

The International Peace Research Association (IPRA), founded in 1964, is the only worldwide organization composed of peace researchers. The IPRA conducts research in the causes of war and other types of violence and the conditions of peace. In order to promote this research, it sponsors national and international studies and teaching related to world peace, it promotes contact and cooperation between scholars and educators, and it encourages the dissemination of research information throughout the world. Membership in IPRA is limited to individual and independent scholars, scientific institutions, and scientific associations engaged in issues of peace and the causes of war.

Results of the voluminous research coming out of the IPRA are regularly shared with other organizations, including the United Nations (U.N.). Since its founding, IPRA headquarters have moved from the Netherlands to Norway, Finland, Japan, and the United States. In 1987 it moved into its permanent headquarters in Rio de Janeiro, Brazil.

Reference Meyer, Robert S., *Peace Organizations Past and Present* (1988).

International Physicians for the Prevention of Nuclear War (IPPNW)

In 1980, Dr. Bernard Lown of the United States and Dr. Yevgeny Chazov of the Soviet Union founded International Physicians for the Prevention of Nuclear War (IPPNW) in order to publicize the dangers of nuclear war. A federation of affiliate organizations in more than 40 countries, IPPNW is governed by an International Council, which sets policy, and an Executive Committee, responsible for implementing policy. Persuaded that physicians had a unique role to play in helping to secure world peace, Dr. Lown articulated that role in an open letter in 1985: "We doctors have a solemn obligation to protect life. We must, by virtue of our professional oaths and codes of ethics, speak out against threats to life. . . .

Since the medical facts about nuclear war indicate that it is the greatest of all threats to life and health, we are compelled to convey those facts to our patients—the peoples of the world."

Since its founding, the IPPNW has created an international medical movement including a global network of more than 135,000 physicians; opened communication with physicians in the Soviet Union; distributed facts about the perils and consequences of nuclear war, including a volume of essays by physicians from around the world entitled *Last Aid: The Medical Dimonesions of Nuclear War*; exchanged visits between U.S. and Soviet physicians; been instrumental in securing agreement from the Soviet Union to stop nuclear testing on the condition that the United States agree also; received the UNESCO Peace Education Prize in 1984; and received the 1985 Nobel Peace Prize. Both Dr. Lown and Dr. Chazov were invited by the Nobel Prize Committee to accept the Nobel Peace Prize on behalf of their organization. Because the physicians involved believe that there cannot be "any effective medical response to nuclear war," the IPPNW continues to press for immediate and mutual moratoriums on nuclear explosions.

Reference Meyer, Robert S., *Peace Organizations Past and Present* (1988).

Jane Addams Peace Association

In 1948 the Women's International League for Peace and Freedom (WILPF) incorporated the Jane Addams Peace Association, named appropriately in honor of WILPF founder Jane Addams. The purpose of the association, as stated in its literature, was and is "to promote understanding among the peoples of all nations and races so that war and strife may be avoided and a lasting peace enjoyed." The association is the education affiliate of WILPF. Headquartered in New York City, the association sponsors and finances all of the educational projects undertaken by WILPF.

Among the ongoing programs sponsored by the association is the Jane Addams Children's Book Award, presented annually since 1953 for the children's book that most effectively promotes the cause of peace, social justice, world community, and the equality of the sexes and all races. The International Seminars Program, begun in 1961, arranges meetings that provide women from different countries the opportunity to discuss mutual concerns related to world peace. The Living Memorial Fund (1967) receives memorials and gifts to fund educational materials distributed to schools, libraries, and other facilities. The fund has made it possible for the distribution of thousands of pieces of material on peace, including material for younger readers. The Committee on Education, established in 1976, is responsible for the development of curricula for peace studies. The curricula are made available to teachers, parents, and publications. The committee also reviews education material. In 1980 a Racism Task Force was established, which is reponsible for writing articles and conducting workshops on racism. Incidents of racism are reported to the Task Force through a nationwide monitoring system. The International Disarmament Fund was established in 1981 and publishes material related to disarmament negotiations. It also provides assistance to national and international seminars on disarmament.

In addition to the permanent programs, the association sponsors and funds many other activities, including the publication of a booklet entitled *Women's Budget*, which discusses social programs benefiting women and children that might be funded if the military budget were to be cut. As a testament to the success of the association, it was able to purchase a building in Washington, D.C., in 1987 that now houses the Washington office of the WILPF.

References Meyer, Robert S., *Peace Organizations Past and Present* (1988); Sicherman, Barbara, et al., eds. *Notable American Women, The Modern Period: A Biographical Dictionary* (1980).

Jefferson, Charles Edward (1860–1937)

As the newly appointed pastor of Broadway Tabernacle Church in New York City, Charles Edward Jefferson was able to present his liberal brand of theology in such a persuasive yet understated manner that he attracted to his sermons new parishioners from all over the city while at the same time retaining the allegience of the older and more conservative members of the church.

Jefferson, born in Cambridge, Ohio, spent two years as superintendent of the Worthington, Ohio, school system following his graduation from Ohio Wesleyan University in 1886. Intending to practice law, he entered Boston University Law School, but he very quickly came

Dr. Charles Edward Jefferson

under the influence of Phillips Brooks, the preacher at Trinity Church, and transferred to the divinity school in 1885. In 1887 he was ordained a minister of the Congregational Church and for the next decade served as the minister of a Chelsea, Massachusetts, parish. In 1897 he received his appointment to the Broadway Tabernacle Church in New York.

During his first trip to Europe, in 1895, Jefferson became a supporter of world peace movements and thereafter lectured and wrote extensively on world peace. Employing the same understated, conversational style that he used to deliver his sermons, Jefferson attracted large audiences for his peace advocacy lectures. His published essays include "Christianity and International Peace" (1915), "What the War Is Teaching" (1916), "Soldiers of the Prince" (1916), and "What the War Has Taught Us" (1919). Despite his hopes for world peace, once World War I began, Jefferson converted one floor of his church for use as a canteen for soldiers,

and after the war, returning servicemen knew that they could find a temporary stopping-off place in the parish rectory. He remained an active member of the Church Peace Union, to which he belonged, and continued to speak out in favor of peaceful solutions to world conflict. Jefferson died at Laurel Lake, New Hampshire, on 12 September 1937.

References National Cyclopaedia of American Biography, vol. I (1967); Patterson, David S., "An Interpretation of the American Peace Movement, 1898–1914." In *Peace Movements in America*, ed. Charles Chatfield (1973).

Jewish Peace Fellowship (JPF)

Concerned that the rights of Jewish conscientious objectors (COs) might be at risk, the Jewish Peace Fellowship (JPF) was founded in 1941 to provide support for those who could not, for religious reasons, participate in the world war. In the early years of its existence, the JPF worked independently to counsel COs. By building a network of religious leaders and Jewish organizations and by publishing newsletters, the JPF provided training for counselors and information and legal counsel for potential COs.

By 1966 the JPF had linked up with other groups, including the National Inter-Religious Service Board for Conscientious Objectors, the American Friends Service Committee (AFSC), and the Fellowship of Reconciliation (FOR) in order to expand and strengthen its base of operations and to meet the needs of a growing clientele as the Vietnam War began to escalate. An integral part of its program has been a long-standing commitment to disarmament and to an equitable Middle East policy that would both recognize the legitimacy of the state of Israel and the rights of the Palestinian people. The JPF is dedicated to nonviolent social change and has promoted that philosophy in the pages of its publication, *Shalom: The Jewish Peace Letter.*

Reference Meyer, Robert S., *Peace Organizations Past and Present* (1988).

Jobs with Peace Campaign

Jobs with Peace, founded in 1978, is an effort to redirect tax dollars from defense spending to local jobs and social programs, including education, public transportation, housing, and health care. Since its founding, Jobs with Peace has won the endorsement of more than 100 members of Congress, city councils across the country, labor unions, and community, religious, and peace organizations.

Jobs with Peace provides educational information for classroom use and for use by labor and community leaders. Among the programs it has launched to educate people is a unique high school curriculum in English, social studies, and science called *Crossroads*. It has also produced a slide show called *Jobs with Peace* and has published *Books, Not Bombs*, which demonstrates the effects of federal cuts in education and which was prepared jointly with the National Education Association. In yet another publication, *Federal Budget for Jobs, Peace, and Justice*, the organization drew up an alternative federal budget, showing the areas where redirected tax dollars would create new jobs, thus undercutting the fears of communities relying heavily on defense industry jobs. Jobs with Peace believes that judicious cuts in the military budget would not adversely affect the economy. The organization works jointly with other local and national groups, including labor, peace, low-income, and Third World groups.

Reference Meyer, Robert S., *Peace Organizations Past and Present* (1988).

John T. Connor Center For U.S./U.S.S.R. Reconciliation

The Connor Center was founded in 1983 as an ecumenical center concerned with establishing reconciliation among religious communities in the United States and the Soviet Union. Initially, activity focused on religious groups in Indiana and Illinois, but the goals of the Connor Center soon created a more national following. The Connor Center worked closely with other religious groups active in the peace movement that sought to forge links between U.S. and Soviet religious communities, for example the National Council of Churches.

In 1984, when the National Council of Churches sponsored a two-week trip to the Soviet Union for almost 200 lay persons and members of the clergy, the Connor Center sponsored the group's coleader. Similar religious exchanges between the two countries have been conducted since 1956. For local congregations, the Connor Center prepares materials illuminating religious life in the Soviet Union and generally answering whatever questions Americans might have about their Soviet counterparts. The center also translates documents in both English and Russian in order to ensure greater communication between all parties. The effort to keep information flowing extends to a monthly newsletter, occasional position papers, and materials for use by those who participate in U.S.–Soviet exchanges.

Reference Meyer, Robert S., *Peace Organizations Past and Present* (1988).

Jordan, Barbara C. (1936–)

Barbara Jordan achieved national recognition as a member of the House Judiciary Committee during the Watergate scandal that brought down the Nixon administration. In the course of the televised hearings, Jordan gained the public's respect. Speaking always with measured words delivered in a deep, riveting voice not unlike that of an evangelical preacher, it was Jordan more than almost any other single member of the committee who was able to convey to the country the serious constitutional nature of the charges and the gravity with which the Judiciary was duty-bound to address the issues. "My faith in the Constitution is whole, it is complete, it is total," she declared. "I am not going to sit here and be an idle spectator to the diminution, the subversion, the destruction of the Constitution."

Jordan was born in Houston, Texas, the daughter of Arlyne Jordan and Benjamin M. Jordan, a Baptist minister. Jordan graduated from Texas Southern University in 1956 and received a law degree from Boston University in 1959. She was engaged briefly in private practice in Houston before becoming the administrative assistant for the county judge of Harris County, a position she held until 1966.

Her entry into politics came in 1962, when she ran unsuccessfully for the Texas State Senate. In 1964 she tried again, and again she lost. In 1966, however, Jordan won a seat in the Texas Senate, helped out by a marked increase in the number of African-American registered voters. Her tenure in the Texas legislature was marked by several firsts, including her status as the first African American elected to the legislature since Reconstruction and the first woman president

Representative Barbara C. Jordan of Texas

pro tem of the Texas Senate. In 1972, Jordan was elected to the House of Representatives as a congresswoman from the 18th District of Texas and became the first African American woman elected from the South.

Jordan is perhaps the best-known and most-admired African American woman in the state of Texas. Her short career as a high-profile congresswoman positioned her to assume an expanded leadership role on the national level. Her friendship with Lyndon Baines Johnson, who had been her mentor in Texas politics, proved more than helpful. Her first congressional committee appointment was to the House Judiciary Committee. Public recognition of her integrity, her legislative ability, and her oratorical excellence came from several quarters. Beginning in 1974, the *World Almanac* named her one of the 25 most influential women in the United States for ten consecutive years, while the editors of the *Ladies Home Journal* selected her as one of the 100 most influential women in the country. *Time Magazine* named Jordan one of its Women of the Year for 1976. Her electrifying keynote address at the Democratic National Convention that year helped to solidify her stature as a national figure. At the same time that Jordan, a strict constitutionalist, was gaining a public reputation for integrity and intelligence, she was also inviting the derision of some of her colleagues in the Congressional Black Caucus as an "Uncle Tom." A firm believer that everyone, including African Americans, would benefit equally from strict constitutional interpretation, Jordan would not waver from that position. Her political résumé included aggressive opposition to the Vietnam War and opposition to military expenditures, particularly those earmarked for support of the war. She also supported environmental issues, as well as those measures that she believed would lead to social changes beneficial to the poor, the elderly, and other groups considered on the margins of society.

In 1978, after being diagnosed with a disease destined to gradually impair her mobility, Jordan chose not to seek reelection. Her decision generated a good deal of speculation at the time, because she had been such a highly visible and widely respected member of Congress. Confronted, however, with a formidable physical challenge, Jordan elected to cut short her public political career in favor of concentrating on alternative pursuits, about which she was equally passionate. Returning to her native Texas, Jordan accepted a professorship in the Lyndon B. Johnson School of Public Affairs at the University of Texas in 1979. Since 1982, she has held the Lyndon B. Johnson Centennial Chair in National Policy. Reflecting her interest in minority rights, in 1985 Jordan was appointed by the secretary-general of the United Nations (U.N.) to serve on an 11-member commission charged with investigating the role of transnational corporations in South Africa and Namibia. Although her career since leaving Congress has focused on her position as an academic, Jordan has always refused to say she would never return to public life. At the Democratic National Convention in 1992, Jordan was a key speaker on behalf of Bill Clinton's nomination. Although confined to a wheelchair, Jordan spoke with the passion, eloquence, and integrity that first brought her to public attention two decades earlier.

References Haskins, James, *Barbara Jordan* (1977); *New York Times* (13 February 1979); Stineman, Esther, *American Political Women: Contemporary and Historical Profiles* (1980); *Wall Street Journal* (6 February 1975).

Jordan, David Starr (1851–1913)

A man of remarkable talent and intellectual depth, David Starr Jordan distinguished himself throughout the world in at least three distinct fields: education, science, and international peace. He possessed a combination of talents, any one of which would have established any other single individual as successful beyond question.

Dr. David Starr Jordan

Born in Gainsville, New York, Jordan graduated from Cornell University in 1872 after having earned a B.S. and an M.S. in three and a half years. He leaned first toward botany, but took up ichthyology after coming under the influence of the reknowned Louis Agassiz. Jordan spent his early career teaching at a variety of colleges and high schools before taking a position with Indiana University in 1879. In the meantime, he had also earned his M.D. from Indiana Medical College in 1875 and a Ph.D. from Butler University in 1878. He was appointed president of Indiana University in 1885. For the next six years, Jordan worked to transform the curriculum and the structure of that university.

Jordan's stewardship at Indiana attracted the attention of Leland Stanford, who selected Jordan in 1891 to become president of the newly founded Leland Stanford Junior University (now Stanford University). Jordan's arrival in California heralded a new intellectual development in the West. Jordan remained president of Stanford until 1913, but in that short time, he made Stanford into a premier academic and intellectual institution that equaled in prestige the greatest universities in the country.

One consequence of his prodigious research as an ichthyologist was that he reached the conclusion early on that war, from a strictly biological point of view, was useless, destructive of the environment, and psychologically, physiologically, and economically pointless. As a result, he became a leading proponent of internationalism and of world peace. From 1909 to 1911, Jordan was the director of the World Peace Foundation, founded by publisher Edwin Ginn. When World War I began, Jordan intensified his efforts to promote internationalism. In 1915 he was the president of the World Peace Conference held in San Francisco and sponsored by the Carnegie Church Peace Endowment.

In addition to scores of scientific publications, Jordan wrote voluminously on the peace movement, including: *The Philosophy of Despair* (1902, reissued in 1907 as *The Philosophy of Hope); The Call of the Nation* (1910); *War and Waste* (1912, 1914); *War's Aftermath* (1914); *War and the Breed* (1915, 1922); *World Peace and the College Man* (1916); *Ways to Lasting Peace* (1916); *Alsace-Lorraine: A Study in Conquest, 1913* (1916); *Democracy and World Relations* (1918); *A Plan of Education to Develop International Justice and Friendship* (1925); and his autobiography, entitled *The Days of a Man* (1922). Jordan died in Palo Alto, California, on 19 September 1931.

References *National Cyclopaedia of American Biography*, vol. 22 (1967); Patterson, David S., "An Interpretation of the American Peace Movement, 1898–1914." In *Peace Movements in America*, ed. Charles Chatfield (1973).

Kellogg, Paul Underwood (1879–1958)

While still in his twenties, Paul Underwood Kellogg, already a journalist of some note, left the security of his job as editor of *Charities*, the New York Charity Organization publication, to launch an investigation of social conditions in Pittsburgh, Pennsylvania. The result, a six-volume study of everyday life and working conditions in Pittsburgh, was published as the *Pittsburgh Survey* and made Kellogg's reputation.

Kellogg, who was born in Kalamazoo, Michigan, embarked on a career in journalism immediately after graduating high school. After working for several years as a reporter for the *Kalamazoo Daily Telegraph*, he moved to New York in order to enroll at Columbia University. As a philanthropic studies major, Kellogg's education was financed by the New York Charity Organization, and it was this connection that brought him to *Charities* and eventually to the post of editor. Kellogg eventually returned to *Charities* after his Pittsburgh project was completed. *Charities* was renamed *Survey*, and Kellogg became its editor-in-chief in 1912. With his brother, Arthur Kellogg, as managing editor, *Survey* became on the national level what the *Pittsburgh Survey* had been in that city. When the *Pittsburgh Survey* was published (1910–1914), it became the foundation for ongoing efforts on the part of social reformers to enact a variety of social changes and reforms, including a shorter workday, better working and housing conditions, and workman's compensation legislation.

Kellogg continued to work for progressive reforms throughout his career as a journalist and editor. His expertise led President Franklin D. Roosevelt to call upon him to help frame the Social Security Act of 1935. Kellogg's lifelong commitment to social reform was not limited to his tenure as editor of the *Survey*, nor to his performance of public service when called upon. He was also deeply committed to world peace. He, like many of his liberal colleagues, had opposed the United States's entry into World War I, although once war had been declared, Kellogg had supported his country.

While doing volunteer work for the American Red Cross, Kellogg took the opportunity to study the effects of the war on Europe in 1917 and 1918. His concern about the treatment of those who resisted the war led him, along with Roger Baldwin, to help found the American Civil Liberties Union (ACLU). He was also a founder and president of the Foreign Policy Association, an organization that supported international cooperation in resolving world conflict. In the 1930s, Kellogg was in the forefront of those who opposed Francisco Franco and who campaigned for shipping arms to Spain. Even after his retirement from journalism, Kellogg continued to voice support for liberal and progressive causes and for world peace. He died in New York City on 1 November 1958.

See also American Civil Liberties Union; Foreign Policy Association.

References Chambers, Clark A., *Paul U. Kellogg and the Survey: Voices for Social Welfare and Social Justice* (1971); Whitman, Alden, ed., *American Reformers: An H. W. Wilson Biographical Dictionary* (1985).

Kellogg-Briand Treaty

Also known as the Pact of Paris, the Kellogg-Briand Treaty was signed in Paris on 27 August 1928. On the one hand, it represented the most ambitious attempt to outlaw war that the modern world had yet seen, and on the other hand, the Kellogg-Briand Treaty was only the culmination of a decade-long exercise in enacting totally ineffective peace treaties.

The Kellogg-Briand Treaty, so named because it was negotiated by U.S. Secretary of State Frank B. Kellogg and French Foreign Minister Aristide Briand, was signed by representatives of all the great powers, with the sole exception of the Soviet Union. After the fact, even the Soviets finally became signatories to the treaty. At the heart of the treaty was the simple, uncomplicated notion that war ought to be illegal. The treaty declared that the contracting parties "solemnly declare in the names of their respective people that they condemn recourse to war for the solution of international controversies, and renounce it as an instrument of national policy in their relations with one another." Notably, the treaty provided absolutely no penalties against those nations that resorted to force, and it excluded wars fought in "self-defense." Finally, at the behest of the British, the treaty did not apply to certain areas of the world threatened by civil disobedience. Thus, Egypt and India, both part of the British Empire, and both of which were chafing under British rule, were exempted from the solemn promise not to resort to violence. In the end, although the intentions of those who promoted the treaty—including U.S. peace organizations—were certainly altruistic, the treaty large loopholes and its lack of any means of enforcement guaranteed its failure.

See also Power Treaties.

References Link, Arthur S., et al., eds., *The American People: A History* (1981); Schlesinger, Arthur, Jr., *The Crises of the Old Order* (1957).

Kennedy, Robert F. (1925–1968)

After a five-year period following his brother John F. Kennedy's assassination, during which he shed most of his cold warrior beliefs, Robert Kennedy appeared to be on the threshhold of a new era in his life. Within hours of winning the California Democratic primary campaign on 5 June 1968, however, Kennedy was fatally wounded by a Syrian busboy, Sirhan Sirhan.

Robert Kennedy, born in Brookline, Massachusetts, was the third son of the powerful Kennedy family. He graduated from Harvard University in 1948. He had entered Harvard during World War II, but after the untimely death of his oldest brother, Joseph, who was killed in action, Robert decided to join the navy as a common seaman. He served as a crewman aboard the destroyer *U.S.S. Joseph P. Kennedy*, named for his brother.

Robert Kennedy went on to earn a law degree at the University of Virginia in 1951 and accepted a position at the Department of Justice in the Criminal Division. In 1953 he was appointed assistant counsel to the Hoover Commission and later served as assistant counsel to Senator Joseph McCarthy's Senate Permanent Subcommittee on Investigations. Rising to chief counsel and staff director, Kennedy moved on to the Senate Committee on Improper Activities in Labor and Management, where he also served as chief counsel. He gained national prominence during his investigation of the Teamster's Union and its presidents, Dave Beck and Jimmy Hoffa. Hoffa bitterly resented Kennedy, whom he considered an over-privileged rich kid who had never had to work a day in his life. It was a mutual dislike that persisted as long as both men were alive. Kennedy wrote a bestselling account of his investigation into the Teamster's Union entitled *The Enemy Within* (1960).

Throughout the 1950s, Kennedy also served as campaign manager for his brother John's House and Senate races. When John Kennedy decided to make a run for the presidency in 1960, Robert was his right hand and alter ego. After the election, the president-elect appointed Robert his attorney general, despite the latter's hesitation. As attorney general, it was Robert Kennedy who led the administration's way in areas like civil rights, enforcing federal voting laws, and reforming

Attorney General Robert F. Kennedy speaking to civil rights demonstrators in front of the Justice Department in Washington, D.C.

the criminal justice system. As the president's closest friend and advisor, Robert supported the administration wholeheartedly, including its decision to send advisors to Vietnam. Robert Kennedy was also a key participant in the Cuban Missile Crisis. At one point, the administration received conflicting notes from Soviet Premier Nikita Khrushchev, during what was perhaps the tensest moments in the crisis. When the administration was at a loss over how to interpret a second message—which was negative, although shortly before, a first message had been positive—it was Robert Kennedy who resolved the situation by advising that they ignore the second message and proceed as though the first message were still operative. Shortly thereafter, the crisis ended when Khrushchev ordered the return of Soviet freighters en route to Cuba.

A year later, John Kennedy was shot by Lee Harvey Oswald in Dallas, Texas, and Robert, for the first time in nearly two decades, had to chart his own political and personal course. In 1964 he ran for the Senate in the state of New York and won the seat. As a senator, Kennedy began to reevaluate many of his previous positions. He was among the earliest critics of President Lyndon Johnson's Vietnam policy. Gradually, he became associated with many of the leading social causes and leaders of the day, including Martin Luther King and the civil rights movement and Cesar Chavez and the Farmworkers Union. He also took up the cause of American Indians and Eskimos and became an advocate of the poor, the uneducated, and those who lived on a daily basis with discrimination and poverty.

His increasing outspokeness over Vietnam raised hopes among many that he would run for the Democratic nomination in 1968. Kennedy initially rejected the idea, not because he did not have the heart to engage in a campaign against Johnson, but because he truly believed that his candidacy would serve only to irrevocably split the Democratic party and thus pave the way for a Republican victory. He persisted, nevertheless, in efforts to persuade Johnson to seek a peaceful solution in Vietnam. When Senator Eugene McCarthy entered the Democratic primary and won over 40 percent of the vote in the New Hampshire primary, it sent a clear message to Kennedy that the Democratic party was already split over the peace issue. On 16 March 1968, Kennedy announced that he was entering the race. Despite the feeling of many people that Kennedy had held back until McCarthy had tested the waters, Kennedy's campaign over the next several months met with enthusiasm and success. He won every primary he entered, with the exception of Oregon. Less than a month after he began his campaign, on 2 April 1968, Johnson announced that he would not seek reelection.

Two days later, on 4 April 1968, Martin Luther King was shot dead in Memphis, Tennessee. Devastated by this latest tragedy, Kennedy, against the advice of his staff, decided to keep a speaking engagement with inner-city African Americans that had already been scheduled. Kennedy was perhaps the only white politician who could have made the terrible announcement that King was dead to the throngs of African Americans gathered to hear him speak and who could have made an appeal for peace and been heeded. One month later, Kennedy himself was dead, gunned down as he left a hotel ballroom in Los Angeles after delivering his California primary victory speech.

References Morris, Richard B., ed., *Encyclopedia of American History* (1976); Newfield, Jack, *Robert Kennedy: A Memoir* (1967); Zaroulis, Nancy, and Gerald Sullivan, *Who Spoke Up? American Protest against the War in Vietnam 1963–1975* (1984).

King, Martin Luther, Jr. (1929–1968)
When the Nobel Peace Prize Committee chose Martin Luther King, Jr. as its 1964 recipient, the committee chairman noted that King was "the first person in the Western world to have shown us that a struggle can be waged without violence.

He is the first to make the message of brotherly love a reality in the course of his struggle, and he has brought this message to all men, to all nations and races." In view of the tragic circumstances of King's death four years later, the chairman's words seem somewhat ironic, but only if King's life is ignored, for he truly was a man of peace and nonviolence.

Martin Luther King was born in Atlanta, Georgia, and was baptized Michael Luther King, Jr., after his father, a Baptist minister. When the youngster was six, two white playmates told him he could no longer play with them. It was his first experience with racism, and his mother had to explain it for him. His father provided a higher ideal for him by telling him about Martin Luther, the religious leader of the Reformation. From then on, father and son changed their names to Martin Luther King.

King graduated from Morehouse College and, following a family tradition, he announced his intention to become a minister. His father, grandfather, great-grandfather, brother, and uncle all were ministers, King would later point out. During his senior year at Morehouse, King was ordained and made assistant pastor of Ebenezer Baptist Church in Atlanta. It was the same church that his grandfather had founded and that his father served as pastor. By this time, King's skills as an orator had long been apparent, and he took the opportunity at Morehouse to develop them further. From Morehouse, King went to the predominently white Crozier Theological Seminary in Chester, Pennsylvania. It was at Crozier that King first became acquainted with the writings of Gandhi. He sensed immediately that Gandhi's nonviolence could be applied to different situations, specifically, to a movement to help African Americans. At his graduation from Crozier, King, who was the president of his senior class, delivered the valedictory speech. Armed with a fellowship from Crozier, King then went on to Boston University in 1951 to study for his Ph.D.

in theology. He used his time in Boston well, studying the leading theological ideas of the time and taking philosophy courses at Harvard. He also met and married Coretta Scott, who was studying voice at the New England Conservatory of Music.

By 1954, King was ready to accept a pastorship. Although he had numerous offers from both churches and colleges in the North, he was determined to return to the South, where, he believed, he could accomplish more for African Americans. When Dexter Avenue Baptist Church in Montgomery, Alabama, offered him a position, Coretta expressed reservations. She had grown up in that area and knew how unenlightened Montgomery was in racial matters. King nevertheless accepted the Dexter Avenue offer, and the couple moved to Montgomery in September 1954. The following year, events in Montgomery precipitated by an otherwise ordinary woman, helped to push King onto a national stage from which he would not step down for the remainder of his life.

Rosa Parks, a seamstress returning home from work after a long day, boarded a bus in Montgomery and refused to give up her seat to a white man who boarded after her. Her subsequent arrest for failing to obey segregation laws infuriated the African-American community. Church leaders organized what was supposed to be a one-day boycott of the Montgomery buses. They chose as their spokesman the young Dexter Avenue minister, both because of his powerful oratory and because he was too new in the city to have made any enemies. At the age of 27, King became chairman of the Montgomery Improvement Association, as the boycott group was called. From the outset, King made it clear that the protest was to be nonviolent: "Our actions must be guided by the deepest principles of the Christian faith. ... If you will protest courageously and yet with dignity and Christian love, future historians will say, 'There lived a great people—a black people—who injected new meaning and dignity into the veins of civilization.' This is our challenge and overwhelming responsibility." So successful was the boyott and so determined were the protesters that the boycott lasted not one day but more than a year. It ended only when the U.S. Supreme Court declared that segregation on buses was unconstitutional. By the end of the boycott, King had become the target of death threats and unwarranted arrests and had had a bomb thrown into his home.

The Montgomery Bus Boyott was not the first civil rights action undertaken in what is generally referred to as the modern civil rights movement. It was, however, the first action that garnered national attention and brought focus to the whole issue of segregation in the South. King very quickly became the leader of the Southern Christian Leadership Conference, the organization that coordinated most of the major civil rights actions. Responding to appeals from King, a series of nationally monitored protests, sit-ins, demonstrations, and marches took place throughout the South. King never asked others to do what he himself was unwilling to do, so in most instances he was in the front line of any action. As a consequence, he sustained numerous beatings and arrests. Yet, even when incarcerated, King did not let opportunity slip by. When white ministers cautioned African Americans about moving too quickly, King wrote his impassioned "Letter from Birmingham Jail." It was his answer to the white ministers and notice to the world that African Americans could wait no longer.

King never wavered from his insistence on nonviolent protest, and this brought him more support from white Americans than he might otherwise have enjoyed. It was not that King was being disingenuous, for nonviolence was fundamental to him. His position on nonviolence also opened doors for him. He traveled throughout the North, raising money, soliciting support, and making speeches to political leaders, labor leaders, and business leaders.

In 1963, King organized a March on Washington (MOW) that attracted 250,000 people, including 75,000 whites, to the nation's capital in order to urge that Congress pass civil rights legislation that was then pending. King delivered perhaps his best-known speech during that gathering. Standing on the steps of the Lincoln Memorial, King gave Americans his vision of a country where everyone was truly equal. His "I Have a Dream" speech was an emotional appeal to draw on what was best rather than to fear what was different. "Let freedom ring from every hill and every molehill of Mississippi. From every mountainside let freedom ring. And when we allow freedom to ring, when we let it ring in every village, from every hamlet, and in every state and every city, we will speed up that day when all of God's children . . . will be able to join hands and sing in the words of the old Negro spiritual: 'Free at last! Free at last! Thank God almighty, we are free at last!'" Over the next two years, Congress passed the Civil Rights Act of 1964 and the Voting Rights Act of 1965. Passage of the legislation did not signal a slowdown in King's activity. He continued to place himself in harm's way, because he believed he had no alternative.

In early 1964, King learned that he was being considered for the Nobel Peace Prize. He was certain that the prize would go to someone who was active in international peace issues. When he received word that he had indeed been chosen, King was incredulous. At 35, he was the youngest individual to receive the Nobel Peace Prize. He traveled to Oslo with other civil rights leaders because, in his view, he only represented what they had all been doing. The prize money awarded to King—approximately $54,000—was given to the civil rights movement.

King came away from Oslo with more than the peace prize. He also had an almost overwhelming understanding of what the rest of the world was expecting from him. When he returned, therefore, he felt strongly that he could no longer re-

Civil Rights leaders, including Martin Luther King, at the March on Washington, August 1963.

main silent on other issues, including the Vietnam War. He had to risk alienating politicians and others on whom he had relied in the past, in order to remain true to his own convictions. King did alienate some politicians and colleagues who thought that he should stick to the issue of civil rights. Criticism from quarters that previously had been supportive did not stop King. He also took on the issue of U.S. poverty and lobbied for federal assistance to the poor. King had planned a Poor People's March for 20 April 1968, in Washington, but on 4 April 1968, while lending support to striking sanitation workers in Memphis, Tennessee, Martin Luther King, Jr. was assassinated.

King had long before come to terms with the probability that his would be a short life. Delivering a sermon at Ebenezer Baptist Church a few months before the assassination, King had spoken about it, saying that he wanted no long eulogy. "Say that I was a drum major for justice. Say that I was a drum major for peace. That I was a drum major for righteousness. . . . I won't have any money to leave behind. . . . I just want to leave a committed life behind." Few American lives in the twentieth century were more committed than King's.

References Garrow, David J., *Bearing the Cross: Martin Luther King, Jr. and the Southern Leadership Conference* (1986); King, Martin Luther, Jr., *Why We Can't Wait* (1963); Lewis, David L., *King: A Critical Biography* (1978); *New York Times* (5, 6 April 1968).

Kirchwey, George Washington (1858–1942)

George Kirchwey was a noted lawyer and criminologist who dedicated much of his career to prison reform. He was born in Detroit, Michigan. After graduating from Yale University in 1879, Kirchwey studied for his law degree at Yale, New York University, and the University of Cincinnati (1908). He practiced law in Albany, New York, for 16 years. In addition, he was dean of the Albany Law School and a professor of law. From 1902 to 1916 he was Kent professor of law at Columbia University. His interest in prison reform stemmed from a stint as warden of Sing Sing (1915–1916), after which he accepted a post as head of the department of criminology at the New York School of Social Work.

Throughout his career, Kirchwey also worked to promote international peace, and from 1906 to 1921 he was a director of the American Society for International Law. In 1917 he was made president of the American Peace Society (APS). His retirement activity included writing several volumes on the law and contributing to the *Encyclopedia Britannica*. Kirchwey died in New York City on 3 March 1942.

References Patterson, David S., "An Interpretation of the American Peace Movement, 1898–1914." In *Peace Movements in America*, ed. Charles Chatfield. (1973); *Who Was Who in America*, vol. 2 (1972).

La Follette, Robert Marion (1855–1925)

Even before the guns of August stopped firing, signaling the end of World War I, Robert La Follette was marshaling support to limit the influence of what later became known as the military-industrial complex. La Follette objected to U.S. participation in the war not because he was a pacifist but because, in his view, the war was being promoted by industrialists and profiteers. La Follette's opinion was specific not only to World War I. His experiences in and out of politics had led him to the belief that giant corporations and special interests were more likely to be concerned about their own profit margin than they were about what was best for the country.

Senator Robert La Follette

La Follette was born in Primrose Township, Wisconsin. After graduating from the University of Wisconsin in 1879, he accepted a position as Dane County district attorney. He entered politics as a Republican and was elected to the U.S. House of Representatives in 1884. It took him nearly two decades to come to the conclusion that most conflicts were struggles between the masses, who wanted to retain control over their own lives, and the special interests, who wanted to exploit the masses. As a firm believer in progressivism, La Follette was certain that he could create a truly democratic society in Wisconsin if the voters would elect him governor. From 1901 to 1905 he served the state in that capacity. As governor he endeavored to pass laws that would tax and regulate railroad companies and that would give the people the power to nominate political candidates.

Looking out on the rest of the world from Wisconsin, La Follette saw similarities between the struggle to gain popular control at home and the failed Russian Revolution and the Filipino insurrection. He saw even sharper analogies with the Mexican Revolution and began to realize that the same corporations that exploited U.S. farmers, laborers, and consumers also sought to exploit underdeveloped countries. As a consequence, La Follette, who was elected to the U.S. Senate in 1905, bitterly opposed President Woodrow Wilson's intervention in Mexico in 1914 and 1916. In an effort to prevent the United States from becoming involved in World War I, La Follette, supported by Wilson's former secretary of state, William Jennings Bryan, proposed a war referendum bill in Congress that would have required a popular vote before the country could enter the war. La Follette also organized a Senate filibuster to

125

prevent consideration of a bill that intended to arm merchant ships. Although the filibuster blocked the bill, the measure was later enacted by executive order. During the war, La Follette was one of a handful of senators who fought against the suppression of civil liberties and defended the right of free speech, free assembley, and a free press. Opposed to the Versailles Peace Treaty as it was presented, La Follette attempted to incorporate reservations into the treaty, including an 80-percent reduction in arms spending, a prohibition against further territorial annexation, and an end to the exploitation of natural resources owned by weaker countries. None of his reservations were accepted. Until his death on 18 June 1925, La Follette continued to work for and advocate peace, which he insisted could be achieved if the profit motive were removed from preparing for and waging war.

See also Bryan, William Jennings.

References Josephson, Harold, ed., *Biographical Dictionary of Modern Peace Leaders* (1985); Knock, Thomas J., *To End All Wars: Woodrow Wilson and the Quest for World Order* (1992).

Lake Mohonk Peace Conferences

In 1895 peace activist Albert Smiley invited 35 prominent supporters of international arbitration to the first of what would become annual Lake Mohonk peace conferences. Smiley had used Lake Mohonk, the site of his Catskill Mountains resort in New York state, to host other conferences. In 1883, he initiated annual conferences on the status of Native American Indians, and in 1894 he hosted a conference on the status of African Americans. The peace conferences, which met annually for 22 years, had far-reaching effects. For one thing, they marked a departure from the ad hoc meetings that had previously characterized the U.S. peace movement. They also provided a common meeting place for all peace workers, particularly those from the Northeast and Midwest, where ideas could be exchanged and agendas set. The latter was probably most important, because the conferences became the catalyst for organizational plans that would coordinate activities and broaden the appeal of the peace movement. By 1905 the conferences reached their maximum capacity of 190 delegates. Among those who attended on a regular basis were the movers and shakers of the peace community, such as David Starr Jordan and Hamilton Holt.

See also Holt, Hamilton; Jordan, David Starr; Smiley, Albert Keith.

Reference Patterson, David S., *Toward a Warless World: The Travail of the American Peace Movement 1887–1914* (1976).

Lawyers Alliance for World Security

The membership of the Lawyers Alliance for World Security includes more than 7,000 lawyers, judges, law students, law librarians, and clerks in 57 chapters throughout the country. Founded in 1981 the alliance organized to educate both legal professionals and the general public regarding the dangers of nuclear war and to encourage conflict resolution through negotiations rather than war. Formerly the Lawyers Alliance for Nuclear Arms Control, the alliance changed its name to the Lawyers Alliance for World Security in 1990. In addition to educational projects conducted in local communities by the local chapters, the alliance has sponsored conferences between U.S. and Soviet lawyers at home and abroad. Many of the lawyers who belong to the alliance also are members of the Lawyers' Committee on Nuclear Policy, which takes a more legalistic approach to preventing nuclear war.

Reference Wank, Solomon, ed., *Doves and Diplomats: Foreign Offices and Peace Movements in Europe and America in the Twentieth Century* (1978).

Lawyers' Committee on Nuclear Policy

The Lawyers' Committee on Nuclear Policy was founded on the principle that nuclear war is a violation of both U.S. constitutional law and international law and is, therefore, contradictory to the "fundamental tenets of a democratic society." The committee's objectives include the establishment of an international consensus on the illegality of nuclear weapons, the elimination of foreign policies that rely on threats of nuclear war, an international program to eliminate nuclear weapons, and support for individuals using the legal system to challenge the concept of nuclear war and nuclear weapons. The committee provides legal assistance to individuals and organizations concerned with disarmament and has several programs set up to provide assistance and advice, depending on the particular goal of the individual or organization seeking its help. In addition, its members deliver lectures, participate in workshops, and in law school programs aimed at informing students and faculty. The committee participated in the 1982 International Symposium on the Legal and Moral Dimensions of Nuclear Weapons, which resulted in draft treaties presented to the United Nations (U.N.) special session on disarmament. Its 600 members include both practicing lawyers and academics.

League of Nations

As part of the post–World War I peace settlement in 1920, the Treaty of Versailles authorized the establishment of a worldwide peacekeeping body to be called the League of Nations. The league had its origins in Woodrow Wilson's Fourteen Points plan to bring about world peace.

Wilson had done everything within his power to keep the United States out of the war in order to take up the role of neutral mediator and bring to fruition his long-cherished plan for world peace. Although the resuming of German submarine warfare and other events conspired to bring the United States into the war, Wilson nevertheless resolved to make the league a key component of any peace set-

tlement. When, in 1919, he met at Versailles with other world leaders, he brought with him his Fourteen Points. What he did not anticipate was the resistance in the U.S. Senate to some aspects of the league plan. In particular, on the question of self-determination versus collective security, conservative members of the Senate, led by Henry Cabot Lodge, refused to budge. In spite of Wilson's monumental efforts to appeal directly to the public, the U.S. Senate never did ratify the Treaty of Versailles and the United States never became a member of the League of Nations. For this reason, as much as for any intrinsic problems with the league's organization, it was doomed to failure.

For a time, however, the League of Nations did struggle to operate according to its mandate. The league had four main bodies: the Council, the Assembly, the Secretariat, and the World Court. Neither the Assembly nor the Council could act without a unanimous vote, a flaw that also helped to bring about its demise. War was not outlawed, but there were provisions to prevent hostilities from breaking out before steps had been taken to resolve the conflict politically and diplomatically. Under the terms of the league covenant, there was no provision for arms control or for disarmament. The Council comprised one member each from each of the larger, more powerful nations and representatives from several smaller nations serving on a rotating basis. The Assembly comprised one representative from each member nation. Although the Assembly could bring up for discussion any issue that a member thought important, the Assembly itself could not pass legislation or make decisions. That function was reserved for the Council. Perhaps the most successful aspect of the league was its establishment of the World Court at The Hague. Disputes referred to the World Court were resolved according to international law. Despite the ultimate failure of the league, it served as a prototype for the future

United Nations (U.N.); thus, it was a significant advance in the search for world peace and for world order.

Reference Knock, Thomas J., *To End All Wars: Woodrow Wilson and the Quest for World Order* (1992).

League of Women Voters (LWV)

At the 1919 convention of the National American Woman Suffrage Association (NAWSA), Carrie Chapman Catt and other leaders of the NAWSA discussed the role that women had to play in both national and international politics once the Suffrage Amendment was ratified by the requisite number of states, as would shortly happen. Catt and her colleagues voted to establish the League of Women Voters (LWV) immediately in those states where women could already vote. Their purpose was twofold: (1) to encourage women voters to help with the ratification process and (2) to quickly put into place a political education forum for women that would help them to organize their new power.

For Catt, who had always translated votes for women into the power to change things for the better, a LWV was the logical organizational forum to pursue interests that most affected women's lives. Her intention initially was to refrain from taking any real leadership role in the new LWV, because she believed that it was time for younger women to become leaders. However, when the U.S. Congress and the American people rejected the League of Nations, in which she and its other supporters—both private and public figures—had placed so much hope for world peace, Catt felt obligated to mobilize women voters in the cause of world peace. At a 1921 meeting of the LWV, Catt proposed that women use their new political power to influence public opinion and put an end to war. Thus, from the very beginning, it was clear that the league's legislative agenda would not be confined to issues that traditionally were associated with women but would cover the entire spectrum of political issues.

League members considered all political issues relevant to the lives of women. The league's primary role became one of educating not just female voters but all citizens. International relations and peace have been primary issues throughout its long and illustrious history. When the league met in 1923 it made it clear to the public that the prevailing attitude of isolationism that developed in the aftermath of World War I was "neither wise nor possible for this nation." The league never shied away from pointing out the mistake that had been made in not joining and supporting the League of Nations. When the League of Nations stood helplessly by while Japan invaded Manchuria in 1931, the LWV noted that, with U.S. support, the League of Nations might have been better able to effectively oppose Japan's predatory actions.

Much of the LWV's efforts throughout the 1920s and 1930s were directed at promoting U.S. membership in the World Court. At the 1932 Disarmament Conference in Geneva, the LWV was able to supply pages and pages of petitions to the conference. The LWV also supported the Kellogg-Briand Pact, the essential element of which was a denunciation of war as an instrument of national policy. As plans for a United Nations (U.N.) were being developed at Dumbarton Oaks in 1944 and 1945, the LWV, fearing a repeat of public resistance to the League of Nations, launched an all-out campaign in support of the U.N. The most powerful LWV member at the time, First Lady Eleanor Roosevelt, went on to become an official member of the U.S. delegation charged with drawing up the U.N. Charter. The LWV has never wavered since then in its support for the U.N., for a U.S. foreign policy that improves the quality of life for people, and for a free world trade policy.

A Minnesota delegation poses with a petition supporting the world Court Proposal in front of the headquarters of the National League of Women Voters. This petition had 43,000 names and, unrolled, measured a mile in length.

Since World War II, the LWV has spent half its time and resources on international issues that the organization sees as directly related to world peace. The other half of its resources is given to national domestic issues. It has taken stands on the issue of nuclear weapons by proposing an arms control program that focuses on policy and spending decisions. It has also become widely known because of its Education Fund, which it founded in 1957 as a research and education organization. Since 1976 the LWV has sponsored the national presidential debates. Although the LWV now includes male members, its basic goals and aims—including education, discussion, and legislation—have remained unchanged since its founding in 1919.

See also Catt, Carrie Chapman; League of Nations.

References James, Edward T., et al., eds., *Notable American Women, 1607–1950: A Biographical Dictionary* (1971); Meyer, Robert S., *Peace Organizations Past and Present* (1988).

League to Enforce Peace

Organized in 1915 by William Harrison Short, the League to Enforce Peace had as its goal the establishment of a permanent League of Nations. Proponents of a League of Nations advocated international arbitration as a cornerstone of a successful permanent peace. The first president of the League to Enforce Peace was former president of the United States, William Howard Taft. It was Short, however, who raised $850,000 to finance the league's work and who served as its executive director and who ran day-to-day activities. When it appeared that the League of Nations had been safely established following World War I, Short considered the work of the League to Enforce Peace finished, and it disbanded in 1921.

See also Short, William Harrison.

References Patterson, David S., "An Interpretation of the American Peace Movement, 1898–1914." In *Peace Movements in America*, ed. Charles Chatfield (1973).

Levermore, Charles Herbert (1856–1927)

Charles Levermore had the distinction of winning the Edward Bok American Peace Award in 1924. Bok, editor of the *Ladies Home Journal* and a longtime peace advocate, put up $100,000 in prize money for the peace plan deemed to have the most merit by a jury that had to consider thousands of proposals.

Levermore, born in Mansfield, Connecticut, taught for many years on the college level. A graduate of Yale (1879), he earned his Ph.D. from Johns Hopkins, where he was a classmate of Woodrow Wilson, with whom he maintained a lifelong friendship. His dissertation, *Town Government in New Haven*, won the John Marshall Prize and was later published as *The Republic of New Haven*. Levermore taught briefly at Hopkins Grammar School and at the University of California. In 1888 he went to the Massachusetts Institute of Technology as an assistant professor, remaining there until 1893, when he gave up his full professorship to become principal of Adelphi Academy in Brooklyn, New York. Levermore was also instrumental in founding Adelphi College for women and served as its first president until 1912. Ill health forced him to curtail his activities, and he lived for a year in the South in order to speed his recovery. In 1913, he became director of the college and university bureau of the World Peace Foundation in Boston, Massachusetts. From 1915 to 1917 he served as acting director of the World Peace Foundation. For the next decade, he was secretary of the New York Peace Society, secretary of the World Court League, secretary of the League of Nations Union, and secretary of the American Association for International Conciliation. In January 1923, Levermore

helped to organize the League of Nations Non-Partisan Association; he served as its vice-president until his death.

Levermore received $50,000 from the American Peace Award. The remaining $50,000 was never awarded, because the rules of the contest stipulated that congressional approval of the peace plan had to precede the final installment of the award. Nevertheless, Levermore used his winnings to travel in Europe and the Far East, where he studied international relations. He was preparing for another trip to Asia when he died in Berkeley, California, on 20 October 1927.

References National Cyclopaedia of American Biography, vol. 6 (1967); Wittner, Lawrence S., *Rebels against War: The American Peace Movement 1941–1960* (1969).

Levinson, Salmon Oliver (1865–1941)

Salmon Levinson was born in Noblesville, Indiana, on 29 December 1865, a few short months after the Civil War ended. He attended the University of Chicago and then transferred to Yale University, graduating in 1888. He returned to Chicago to study law at the Chicago College of Law. After receiving his LL.B. in 1891, Levinson embarked on a successful career as a lawyer specializing in the financial reorganization of corporations. His talents and expertise in the field allowed him to live very well. By 1914 he had made a fortune. During that entire period of nearly a quarter century, Levinson never seemed especially interested in peace issues. Perhaps because of his total immersion in his career, he never exhibited anything other than passing interest in foreign policy. When war broke out in Europe, however, it was so shocking to him that he immediately began to devise a plan that would eliminate any future wars.

Levinson's long years as a lawyer naturally pointed him in the direction of crafting a legal deterrent to war. He came up with a straightforward plan: make war an internationally illegal act and impose sanctions against those who refuse to submit conflicts to arbitration and who chose war to settle their dispute. If all nations agreed to the plan, war would be outlawed and violators would be subject to retribution from the entire world. Levinson hoped that President Woodrow Wilson would incorporate his idea into the League of Nations Covenant. Consequently, he supported the league in its early stages. Once it was clear that his plan would not be included, Levinson took every opportunity to speak out against the league. He continued to refine his plan for the Outlawry of War, as it came to be known. His final version called for the use of force against so-called mad-dog states that refused to listen to reason. Even though the final version alienated some pacifists because it advocated a last-resort use of force, Levinson's plan received more across-the-board support than any other suggestions offered at the time. Among his supporters were John Haynes Holmes and John Dewey, two of the most respected of the peace leaders.

The closest that Levinson came to seeing his plan adopted was in 1927, when French Minister Aristide Briand incorporated part of the outlawing war concept in what eventually became the Kellogg-Briand Pact, which was signed by nearly every nation in the world. Unfortunately, because the pact did not contain an enforcement clause, it proved to be a hollow victory at best. Levinson made a remarkable effort to unite the peace movement behind a single concept. He died on 2 February 1941 in Chicago, just months before the United States entered World War II.

See also Dewey, John; Holmes, John Haynes; Kellogg-Briand Pact.

Reference Josephson, Harold, ed., *Biographical Dictionary of Modern Peace Leaders* (1985).

Libby, Frederick Joseph (1874–1970)

Born in Richmond, Maine, Frederick Libby graduated from Bowdoin College in 1894. He spent several years abroad—studying in Berlin, Heidelberg, Marburg, and Oxford—and then returned to the United States to enter Andover Theological Seminary. From 1905 to 1911, Libby served as pastor of the Magnolia, Massachusetts, Union Congregational Church. He resigned his pastorship to travel in China and Australia in 1911 and 1912 and then took a teaching position at Phillips Exeter Academy, where he remained until 1920. During World War I, Libby joined the Society of Friends and worked with the organization to provide relief and reconstruction. In 1921 he founded the National Council for the Prevention of War, and from 1921 to 1970 he served as its executive secretary.

Libby recognized the potential inherent in organizing women for the peace cause. In the 1930s he already believed that "women constitute the backbone of the peace movement in America," a view he shared with others in the peace movement as well as with some nervous

Frederick J. Libby

politicians who frequently expressed concern at the prospect of peace advocates mobilizing even more women. Libby died in Washington, D.C., on 26 June 1970.

References Josephson, Harold, ed., *Biographical Dictionary of Modern Peace Leaders* (1985); Wittner, Lawrence S., *Rebels against War: The American Peace Movement 1941–1960* (1969).

Lochner, Louis Paul (1887–1975)

Louis Lochner enjoyed two careers, both of which he excelled at. His later career, as a journalist, placed him at the center of history in the years surrounding World War II. Lochner was the bureau chief for the Associated Press in Berlin from 1928 to 1941, when circumstances dictated that he leave Germany. He returned as bureau chief after the war, from 1944 to 1946. In the interim, he was a radio commentator whose knowledge and familiarity with the Nazi ruling elite in Berlin made him an especially insightful analyst. Lochner, who won a Pulitzer Prize for distinguished foreign reporting in 1939, also took on short-term assignments for the U.S. Department of State and the United Nations (U.N.) Long before his Pulitzer Prize–winning reportage, Lochner had made a name for himself as one of the foremost peace advocates of the World War I era.

Born in Springfield, Illinois, Lochner graduated from the University of Wisconsin in 1909. It was during his Wisconsin days that he became interested in internationalism and the whole peace issue. He founded a national association of Cosmopolitan Clubs, whose purpose was to promote international friendship. Lochner served as the organization's first president. After graduating, Lochner accepted a position as the general secretary of the University of Wisconsin Alumni Association and became the leader of Corda Frates, an international student association. He also joined the Chicago branch of the American Peace Society (APS) and served as the its general secretary from 1914 to 1915 and as director of the APS's Central West Department. Lochner's work in the Peace Society brought him into contact with peace activists in both the United States and Europe. He helped to organize the Emergency Peace Federation, a consortium of peace groups, whose aim it was to persuade President Woodrow Wilson to act as mediator between the warring European factions and to promote the concept of a lasting peace. Lochner joined other peace groups with similar goals, including the American Union against Militarism, and continued to lobby Wilson. Although Wilson wanted to play the role of mediator, he believed that the time was not yet propitious for successful mediation and consistently declined peace activists' proposals.

In December 1915, Henry Ford, the auto magnate, sponsored a peace expedition and hired Lochner as the group's general secretary. Lochner was also placed in charge of coordinating the six-nation Neutral Conference for Continuous Mediation, which was organized in February 1916 in Stockholm, with funding from Ford. Ford, however, proved to be a peripatetic sponsor of peace. In the summer of 1916 he cut off funding for the conference and it was forced to adjourn. Lochner stayed on in Europe, hoping to conduct personal diplomacy between the warring factions. The following January he was able to report to Wilson that both sides were willing to accept mediation, and Wilson expressed his own encouragement. Nevertheless, when Lochner returned to Ford with his report, Ford again demonstrated his lack of commitment by abruptly ending his peace sponsorship and firing Lochner.

Disappointed, Lochner threw his efforts into helping to organize demonstrations and rallies. He served as the executive secretary of the People's Council for Democracy and Terms of Peace until 1919. His official service to the peace cause ended when he joined the Associated Press as a foreign correspondent in the early 1920s, but he never lost hope that the concept of internationalism would one day be adopted. Lochner died in Wiesbaden, Germany, on 8 January 1975.

See also Ford Peace Ship.

References Josephson, Harold, ed., *Biographical Dictionary of Modern Peace Leaders* (1985); Knock, Thomas J., *To End All Wars: Woodrow Wilson and the Quest for World Order* (1992).

Lockwood, Belva Ann Bennett (1830–1917)

Belva Ann Lockwood has the distinction of being the first woman nominated for the office of president of the United States—not once but twice—and of carrying out a creditable campaign with very little money or support. In 1884 and again in 1888, the Women's Equal Rights Party nominated Lockwood. At a time when most women in the United States still could not vote, Lockwood not only accepted the nomination but engaged in campaigns that helped to bring about wider awareness of women's growing desire to become true participants in U.S. democracy.

Born in Royalton, New York, Lockwood graduated from Genesee College in Lima, New York, in 1857, where she was trained to teach. Lockwood did teach for seven years. During the Civil War, she was also president of the Ladies Aid Society, a relief agency for those suffering hardship because of the war. After the war, she went to Washington to take over the Urban League Hall, a similar relief organization. Her work brought her in contact with working women and with the inequities they faced because of their sex. In 1870, Lockwood helped to secure a law giving female government employees equal pay with men. Her experience made it clear to her that the law could be used to effect change. She enrolled at the National University Law School, earned her degree in 1873, and was admitted to the bar in Washington, D.C. In 1876, Lockwood helped secure passage of a bill enabling female lawyers to be admitted to the bar of the U.S.

Belva Ann Lockwood

Supreme Court, and in 1879 she became the first woman so admitted.

Lockwood opened law offices in Washington. Her interests covered a wide range of issues, including Indian affairs, pensions, and women's rights. She was also keenly involved in peace organizations. As a member of the International Peace Bureau, Lockwood maintained a Branch Peace Bureau in Washington and edited its publication, *The Peacemaker.* Her work on behalf of peace organizations, particularly those concerned with solving conflict through arbitration, occupied a major portion of her life for 40 years. Lockwood was instrumental in preparing the first bill recommending the establishment of an international arbitration court, an idea that would emerge as mainstream when Woodrow Wilson proposed it as part of his Fourteen Points in peace discussions following World War I. Lockwood served as secretary of the Universal Peace Union (UPU) for nearly 40 years, balancing that duty with those of running her own law firm, which she maintained until her death on 19 May 1917. Lockwood is commonly credited as one of the major national peace advocates of the Progressive era.

References Josephson, Harold, ed., *Biographical Dictionary of Modern Peace Leaders* (1985); *National Cyclopaedia of American Biography* (1967).

Love, Alfred H. (1830–1913)

Alfred Love was the senior member of the A. H. Love & Co., Inc. firm, a Philadelphia woolen goods dealership begun by his father. A member of the liberal branch of the Society of Friends, Love stood by his pacifist beliefs when the Civil War started. He refused to supply woolen goods for use by the army, and as a consequence he was forced to dissolve his firm. He remained in the woolen commission business for over 60 years, however. Love had a number of interests that he pursued, including women's suffrage, abolition, prison reform, and the rights of Native Americans. His primary interest, however, was promoting peace.

In 1866 he helped to organize the Universal Peace Union (UPU) and served as its president until his death. During that time, Love was instrumental in forming more than 50 branches of the UPU. He was both an effective speaker on behalf of peace and a persuasive writer. For more than 40 years, Love edited several peace journals, including *The Bond of Peace*, *The Voice of Peace*, *The Peacemaker*, and *Court of Arbitration*. Love died in Philadelphia on 29 June 1913.

References *National Cyclopaedia of American Biography*, vol. 16 (1967); Patterson, David S., "An Interpretation of the American Peace Movement, 1898–1914." In *Peace Movements in America*, ed. Charles Chatfield (1973).

Lowenstein, Allard (1929–1980)

Describing Allard Lowenstein, Eleanor Roosevelt wrote, "He is a person of unusual ability and complete integrity. I think he will always fight crusades because injustice fills him with a sense of rebellion." Lowenstein did spend the better part of his life engaged in a variety of causes, from civil rights to peace.

He was born in Newark, New Jersey, but grew up in the suburbs of New York City. As a young child, Lowenstein took the side of the Loyalists in the Spanish Civil War and always insisted that the United States should have fought Hitler earlier than it did. He graduated from the University of North Carolina in 1949. While there, Lowenstein worked with university President Frank Graham in efforts to integrate the campus. When Graham was elected to the Senate, Lowenstein went along as his special assistant. In 1954, Lowenstein graduated from Yale Law School. He was also a student organizer for Adlai Stevenson's presidential bids. After serving two years in the army, he took a position at the United Nations (U.N.), as a consultant to the American Association. While there, he was able to meet his idol, Eleanor Roosevelt, and the two developed a very close working and personal relationship. Lowenstein also worked for Senator Hubert Humphrey as his foreign policy advisor. In 1959 he traveled to South Africa to investigate the conditions under apartheid. He delivered a scathing report to the United Nations Trusteeship Council and later wrote about the trip in a book entitled *Brutal Mandate* (1962).

Lowenstein continued down his wandering career path by teaching political science at Stanford University for a year and at the University of North Carolina for two years. In the early 1960s, Lowenstein became very much a part of the civil rights movement, organizing student volunteers for voter registration drives, organizing the Mississippi Freedom Vote, and advising Martin Luther King, Jr. and the Southern Christian Leadership Conference. By 1967, Lowenstein was teaching again, this time at the City University of New York. He had also begun to criticize President Lyndon Johnson and the Vietnam War unrelentingly. As 1968 approached, Lowenstein spent a great deal of energy organizing students to support an alternative candidate. The candidate turned out to be Eugene McCarthy, who entered the New Hampshire primary and, with the help of thousands of students mobilized by Lowenstein, walked away with 21 of New Hampshire's 24 Democratic electors. When Robert Kennedy entered the race, Lowenstein remained with McCarthy out of loyalty. Lowenstein considered Johnson's decision not to run again something of a personal victory for him and a vote for peace.

Lowenstein returned to New York, entered the race for the 5th Congressional District House seat in Nassau County, and won the nomination. At the Democratic Convention in Chicago, which turned into a riotous affair with Chicago police using unnecessary force on student demonstrators, Lowenstein tried to force an open convention. In the end, with no other alternative, he supported Humphrey for president. Lowenstein won his own congressional race and for two years served New York as a congressman. In Washington he continued to speak out against the war. His reelection bid was stymied when the Republican-controlled legislature gerrymandered Lowenstein's district, eliminating the Jewish and liberal "five towns" area, where most of his support was centered. He lost the election to Republican conservative Norman Lent.

Lowenstein practiced law in New York and took over the leadership of Americans for Democratic Action (ADA). On 14 March 1980, Allard Lowenstein was gunned down by Dennis Sweeney, a former student activist who had suffered a mental breakdown. Lowenstein had intended to run for office again; instead, like so many other casualties of the tumultuous Sixties, Lowenstein's promising future was ended abruptly.

References *Current Biography* (1971); Zaroulis, Nancy, and Gerald Sullivan, *Who Spoke Up? American Protest against the War in Vietnam 1963–1975* (1984).

Lynch, Frederick Henry (1867–1934)

A Congregational clergyman born in Peace Dale, Rhode Island, Frederick Henry Lynch was also an editor for several publications, including the *Yale Divinity Quarterly* and the *Christian Century*. Lynch attended Yale University (B.A., 1894; B.D., 1897) and served in churches in New England and New York. His role as both clergyman and editor led to his interest in the peace movement.

In 1909, Lynch married Maude Barrows Dutton, the adopted daughter of peace activist Samuel Train Dutton. Lynch served as secretary of the Church Peace Union from 1914 to 1926 and founded the World Alliance for International Friendship, serving as secretary for that organization as well. He was also a member of many other organizations. When World War I ended, Lynch spent every summer thereafter in various European countries, attending international conferences. A prolific and widely read author, Lynch's publications included *The Peace Problem (1911); Through Europe on the Eve of War* (1914); *The Last War* (1915); *The Christian in War Time* (1917); *One Great Society: A Book of Recollections* (1918); and *Mobilizing for Peace* (1924). Lynch died in New York on 19 December 1934.

References Patterson, David S., "An Interpretation of the American Peace Movement, 1898–1914." In *Peace Movements in America*, ed. Charles Chatfield (1973); *Who Was Who in America*, vol. 1 (1943).

McCarthy, Eugene
See Children's Crusade.

McCloy-Zorin Agreement for Disarmament Negotiations

Early in John F. Kennedy's administration, he and Soviet Premier Nikita Khrushchev agreed to have their envoys meet with the aim of producing an agreement for negotiating a disarmament treaty. Kennedy appointed John McCloy, and Valerian Zorin represented the Soviets. McCloy and Zorin met three times, in Washington, D.C., Moscow, and New York City. On 20 September 1961, McCloy and Zorin signed a Joint Statement of Agreed Principles for Disarmament Negotiations. The McClo-Zorin Agreement represented a significant step forward in stopping the arms race.

Both governments reported the agreement to the United Nations (U.N.) General Assembly, and the U.N. unanimously adopted the agreement as a foundation for future negotiations. With an agreement in principle signed by both sides, the way was cleared for drafting an actual disarmament treaty. With the assassination of Kennedy, however, treaty negotiations came to a standstill. After that, neither side seemed able to move away from a concept of national security based on military power. Efforts to secure an end to the arms race became another casualty of the Kennedy assassination.

Reference Meyer, Robert S., *Peace Organizations Past and Present* (1988).

Magnes, Judah Leon (1877–1948)

A lifelong pacifist, Magnes was born in Oakland, California. He graduated from Hebrew Union College and earned a Ph.D. from Heidelberg University in 1902. Never content to accept the status

quo, Magnes was a vocal opponent of the Spanish-American War as well as of his fellow rabbis, who were willing to support war. His first appointment as rabbi was with a small synagogue in Brooklyn, New York. After that, he went on to the more well-known Temple Emanu-El on New York's Fifth Avenue. When the United States entered World War I, Magnes reenforced his pacifism. Although he believed in the right of individuals to protect themselves (for example, he believed it was necessary for Jews to defend themselves against pogroms), the matter of nations waging war on each other was an entirely different story. In 1917, Magnes appeared at Madison Square Garden with other peace advocates—including Roger Baldwin, Eugene Debs, and Norman Thomas—in a huge antiwar rally. Not only did Magnes have to contend with war supporters in general, he also had to deal with other Jews who feared that his outspoken opposition to the war would reflect badly on their patriotism. Such criticism did not deter Magnes, and he continued speaking out against war at rallies in other cities. In November 1917 and February 1918, Magnes authored a series of articles that appeared in the *New York Post* and which were attributed to "Observer." In the articles, Magnes condemned the war and demanded a fair peace treaty.

Magnes was one of those who helped to establish the Civil Liberties Bureau (CLB) of the American Union against Militarism (AUAM) in 1918. The CLB, founded to help defend those whose civil liberties had been abridged because of their opposition to the war, was later renamed the American Civil Liberties Union (ACLU). Magnes was also involved in the Bureau of Legal Advice for Conscientious Objectors.

His move to Israel, where he spent the last half of his adult life, came soon after the war. He worked with Martin Buber and other unionists in Israel and was a cofounder of Ichud, which sought reconciliation between Jews and Arabs. In 1925, Magnes was named chancellor of Hebrew University. Although he maintained his pacifist stance, particularly in his efforts with Ichud, Hitlerism and the Nazi atrocities were simply too much, even for him. Although it was a reluctant decision, Magnes supported the Allies' action in World War II. He died soon after the war's conclusion, on 27 October 1948, in New York City.

See also American Civil Liberties Union; American Union against Militarism.

Reference Josephson, Harold, ed., *Biographical Dictionary of Modern Peace Leaders* (1985).

Marburg, Theodore (1862–1946)

Theodore Marburg, born in Baltimore, Maryland, entered his father's tobacco business in 1881, where he worked alongside his three brothers. For the next 19 years, the Marburg brothers nurtured the business, expanded it, and finally sold it to the American Tobacco Company in 1900. Thereafter, Marburg devoted his life to studying politics and political economy and to promoting international peace.

Marburg was a delegate to the American Peace Society (APS) conference in Chicago in 1909, and in 1910 he organized the Maryland Peace Society. During that year he also helped to organize the American Society for the Judicial Settlement of International Disputes, serving as its president from 1913 to 1916. When the Third National Peace Conference (NPC) was held in Baltimore in 1911, Marburg chaired the executive committee. His efforts on behalf of international peace were recognized in 1912, when President William H. Taft appointed Marburg U.S. minister to Belgium. During his service as minister, Marburg became convinced that Germany was a menace to the United States and, although he hoped for a peaceful

settlement of the war in Europe, he warned the country on more than one occasion to prepare itself to fight.

On his return to the United States in 1915, Marburg helped found the League to Enforce Peace. World War I convinced him more than ever that future peace depended on an alliance of nations, and he became an early supporter of the League of Nations Covenant. When the U.S. Senate refused to ratify the Treaty of Versailles, which contained the covenant, Marburg was crestfallen. In his view, refusal to ratify constituted a national blunder of monumental proportions. Throughout the 1920s he continued to press for internationalism and permanent peace. Marburg also made many literary contributions that were widely read, including *The War with Spain* (1898); *Expansion* (1900); *The Peace Movement Practical* (1910); *Salient Thoughts on Judicial Settlement* (1911); *Philosophy of the Third American Peace Conference* (1911); *League of Nations* (1917); and a two-volume work entitled *Development of the League of Nations Idea* (1932). Marburg died in Vancouver, British Columbia, on 3 March 1946.

See also League to Enforce Peace.

References National Cyclopaedia of American Biography, vol. 34 (1967); Patterson, David S., "An Interpretation of the American Peace Movement, 1898–1914." In *Peace Movements in America*, ed. Charles Chatfield (1973).

Martin, Anne Henrietta (1875–1951)

The first half of Anne Martin's adult life was spent working for women's suffrage and pursuing a political career. Born in Empire City, Nevada, Martin received intellectual encouragement from her father, a wealthy banker and politician, and moral support from a mother, who would have been happier had her daughter led a more conventional life.

Martin graduated from the University of Nevada in 1894 and went on to Stanford University, where she earned a second B.A. and an M.A. in history. During her college career, Martin became a champion tennis player. She also golfed, rode, and climbed mountains. Unfortunately, the late nineteenth century was not a time when women who excelled in sports could find an outlet for their talent. In 1897 she returned to the University of Nevada, founded its history department, and began an academic career. Officially, she remained head of the department until 1901, but in 1899 she left for Columbia University in New York—and, thereafter, for the universities of Leipzig and London—to study art.

In 1901 Martin's father died, and she returned briefly to the United States. After attempting to straighten out her father's estate and being rebuffed in favor of her brothers, Martin decided to return to Europe. Her family's insistence on letting the men handle the financial affairs turned her into an instant feminist. When she returned to England, Martin became a suffragette and worked with the militant Pankhursts. For participating in a demonstration in 1910, Martin was arrested. By then she had joined the Fabians and had begun to write under a pseudonym.

Martin returned to Nevada in 1911 and very quickly was elected president of the Nevada Equal Franchise Society. It was under her leadership that Nevada suffragists were able to wage a successful campaign to give women the vote in that state. In 1914, Martin transferred her energies to the national suffrage campaign, working at first with the conservative National American Woman Suffrage Association (NAWSA). She quickly realized that the traditional state-by-state method of obtaining suffrage would take decades to accomplish. Consequently, she turned to a younger, more radical group, the National Women's Party (NWP), whose founder, Alice Paul, had also worked in London with the Pankhursts and had brought back many of their tactics. Martin was named chairwoman of the NWP in 1916 and oversaw the political campaign to put pressure on the Democrats in the 12 full suffrage states. In 1917 she became vice-chairwoman and legislative chairwoman of the NWP.

Martin's experience as a political organizer and campaigner encouraged her to make a run for the U.S. Senate from the state of Nevada in 1918. Although her campaign in 1918 and a subsequent campaign for a Senate seat in 1920 were both unsuccessful, Martin helped mobilize women to use their votes to make a difference on issues in which women had a particular interest and on politics in general. Her campaign issues ran a gamut from support of the Sheppard-Towner bill to provide welfare for mothers and children to prohibition and environmental issues. Notably, she was also opposed to the League of Nations, because she believed the organization would simply continue to breed war.

After her 1920 defeat, Martin moved to Carmel, California. It was then that she became interested in the Women's International League for Peace and Freedom (WILPF) and began working for issues related to world peace. From 1926 to 1936, Martin served on the national board of the WILPF and was the western regional director from 1926 to 1931. She represented the WILPF at world conferences in Dublin (1926) and Prague (1929). Although much of her writing during this period was directed toward women, Martin was not one to hold her tongue when she believed women were making wrong choices. For example, when Carrie Chapman Catt influenced the League of Women Voters (LWV) to take on primarily an educational role, Martin criticized her loudly for not encouraging women to take direct political action and thereby tackle problems head-on. When she came to the conclusion that the WILPF was not acting forcefully enough to achieve its goals, Martin resigned and joined the People's Mandate to Governments to End War.

Martin was committed to seeing women achieve equality in all respects. She believed strongly that women had to take their unique position and perspective and apply it to public life. On 15 April 1951, Martin died in Carmel, California.

References Lunardini, Christine A., *From Equal Suffrage to Equal Rights: Alice Paul and the National Woman's Party 1910–1928* (1986); Sicherman, Barbara, et al., eds., *Notable American Women, The Modern Period: A Biographical Dictionary* (1980).

May 2 Movement

An offshoot of the Progressive Labor Movement, the May 2 Movement was founded in the Spring of 1964 at Yale University to protest U.S. involvement in Vietnam. Four hundred college students met on 2 May 1964 at the Cathedral of St. John the Divine in New York City. They demanded immediate withdrawal from Vietnam as well as cessation of military aid to the government of South Vietnam. Other groups represented in the May 2 Movement were the Young Socialist Alliance and the Socialist Workers Party. The rally marched to Times Square and then on to the United Nations (U.N.).

Reference Zaroulis, Nancy, and Gerald Sullivan, *Who Spoke Up? American Protest against the War in Vietnam 1963–1975* (1984).

Mead, Edwin Doak (1849–1937)

Although he was born in the rural New Hampshire town of Chesterfield, Edwin Mead expanded his horizons from early boyhood when he developed an avid interest in books and in learning. He remained in Chesterfield until young adulthood, however, clerking for one brother-in-law in his store and editing a small monthly magazine consisting mostly of stories, essays, and poetry. Another brother-in-law, William Dean Howells, had a profound influence on Mead's career and life when he secured for Mead a position with Ticknor & Fields, a Boston publishing firm. Mead worked there for the next nine years, learning about the publishing industry and developing contacts with prominent literary figures in Boston.

Mead's own career as an author was launched when he went to England to prepare for the Episcopal ministry. New England transcendentalism and English church teaching led him to leave the church, and he began concentrating instead on writing. His writing, and subsequently his lectures, covered a broad range of topics but focused predominantly on historical and religious tracts. When Edward Everett Hale retired as editor of the *New England Magazine* in 1890, his protégé, Mead, was promoted from assistant editor to editor. Mead remained with that magazine until 1901, involving himself in a wide variety of reform and educational movements, including women's suffrage. In 1898 he married Lucia True Ames. They were a well-matched couple, because both were dedicated to a principal interest—the search for a lasting peace.

A longtime advocate of the belief that nations could resolve conflict through arbitration, Mead was a delegate to international conferences throughout Europe, at which he represented the American Peace Society (APS). At the thirteenth annual International Peace Conference, which met in Boston in 1914, he served as the executive committee chairman. Mead was also responsible for persuading his friend, publisher Edwin Ginn, to take up the peace cause. Ginn eventually established a fund supporting the World Peace Foundation, and Mead became its director in 1910. Due largely to Mead's efforts, the World Peace Foundation became influential in the international peace movement. The United States's entry into World War I was a shattering experience for Mead and one from which he never fully recovered. He resigned as director of the World Peace Foundation in 1917, but he never abandoned his hope for a lasting peace and eventually continued the work. Edwin Mead died in Boston on 17 August 1937.

See also Ginn, Edwin; Mead, Lucia Ames; World Peace Foundation.

References *National Cyclopaedia of American Biography*, vol. 28 (1967); Patterson, David S., "An Interpretation of the American Peace Movement, 1898–1914." In *Peace Movements in America*, ed. Charles Chatfield (1973).

Mead, Lucia Ames (1856–1936)

Like her husband and fellow peace worker, Edwin Mead, Lucia Ames Mead was born in rural New Hampshire, in the town of Boscawen. She attended private schools and high school in Salem, Massachusetts. After her graduation, Lucia Ames studied music and eventually taught music to both children and adults in Boston. Her true passion, however, was pursuing peace, and she began to write and give lectures on international arbitration. She was a delegate to several international peace conferences and made frequent trips to Europe.

In 1898 she married Edwin Mead. They were in Switzerland attending the first international church conference on peace when World War I began. Lucia Mead participated in efforts to establish a League of Nations and was in Paris for the peace conference in 1919. In 1920 she, along with several other league promoters, embarked on a nationwide speaking tour in support of the League of Nations.

A tireless worker, Mead served as vice-chairwoman of the National Council for the Prevention of War, chairwoman of the arbitration committee of the National Council of Women, secretary of the U.S. branch of the League for Permanent Peace, and president of the American Peace Society (APS). Her reform interests ran to other issues as well. Along with her coworker and fellow Bostonian, Mary Ware Dennett, Mead was a champion of women's suffrage in Massachusetts. She was also a member of the National Association for the Advancement of Colored People (NAACP) and a benefactor of the Street School in Mintor, Georgia, a manual training school for African Americans. She was a director of the Twentieth Century Club in Boston, which she and her husband founded, and a member of the Old South Historical Society, the Japan Society of Boston, and the American Civil Liberties Union (ACLU). By the time of her death in Brookline, Massachusetts, on 1 November 1936, Mead had a long list of publications related to peace and other topics, including *Primer of the Peace Movement* (1907), *Patriotism and the New Internationalism* (1907), *Swords and Ploughshares* (1921), and *Law or War* (1928).

See also American Peace Society.

References National Cyclopaedia of American Biography, vol. 28 (1967); Patterson, David S., "An Interpretation of the American Peace Movement, 1898–1914." In *Peace Movements in America*, ed. Charles Chatfield (1973).

Miller, Orie Otis (1892–1977)

As president of the Miller-Hess Shoe Company, Orie Miller helped to build a successful business, but his heart was in his work as a mission and peace advocate. Miller was born in Middlebury, Indiana. He attended Purdue University for a brief time and then went to Goshen College, graduating in 1915. Miller—a member of the Mennonite Church, one of the historic peace churches—was a lifelong pacifist. His upbringing developed characteristics that would make him a successful businessman: he was practical, a good administrator, and also something of an autocrat, which often helped him to get things done in a timely fashion but which left some people with an uncomfortable feeling about him.

In 1919, Miller went to the Near East as a volunteer with one of his church's service missions. Very quickly he was made the Red Cross director in Beirut, and in 1920 he headed up a group of mission workers headed for the Soviet Union to provide relief to that revolution-torn country. As a consequence of Miller's efforts, the Mennonite Church established the Mennonite Central Committee (MCC).

The MCC became the organization primarily responsible for peace, relief work, and service in North America. Not surprisingly, Miller was chosen to serve as the MCC executive secretary-treasurer, a post that he held from 1935 to 1958. He was also the financial agent of the Mennonite Board of Education from 1922 to

1955 and the president of Mennonite Mutual Aid from 1945 to 1962. Most of Miller's work for peace advocacy was done through the MCC. He had been a member of the church's Peace Problems Committee, beginning in 1925. Consequently, he worked with representatives from the other historic peace churches on several projects. Of particular importance was their joint effort to propose a suitable alternative service program for conscientious objectors (COs). The program, the Civilian Public Service (CPS), became the standard alternative for individuals who felt morally bound to refrain from war participation. Several Mennonite CPS camps were organized, which Miller helped to run. In addition, he was one of the founders of the National Service Board for Religious Objectors (NSBRO). Although neither Miller nor his church was entirely satisfied with the alternative service program, because any assistance to the government could be interpreted as support for the war, they nevertheless accepted it as the best possible solution.

Miller retired from most public activity in the early 1960s. On 10 January 1977, he died in Lititz, Pennsylvania.

References Erb, B. Paul, *Orie O. Miller: The Story of a Man and an Era* (1969); Josephson, Harold, ed., *Biographical Dictionary of Modern Peace Leaders* (1985).

Mills, Charles Wright (1916–1962)

Charles Wright Mills was born in Waco, Texas. He graduated from the University of Texas in 1938 and earned his Ph.D. from the University of Wisconsin in 1942. A sociologist by profession, Mills taught at the University of Maryland until 1945. He was invited to join the faculty at Columbia University in 1945 and remained there until his death. As a sociologist, Mills focused on issues related to the emerging Cold War. He was part of a small group of academics who were asking hard, critical questions about Cold War policy and who therefore gained reputations as radicals, but Mills always insisted that his role was not that of an activist; he argued that he was merely doing what he believed was incumbent upon those in the social sciences: examining the central issue of the day.

In Mills's view, the military was in the process of expropriating a new role for itself, as a central figure among the new power elite. American society, Mills believed, had become increasingly bureaucratized, thereby generating a more passive middle and lower class. Moreover, an educated and informed public played an increasingly smaller role in decision making on the national level. The result was a new power elite that was increasingly more concentrated and increasingly less accountable. He saw a permanent war economy in which "militarism has become an end in itself," becoming the foundation for corporate wealth and power. Mills elaborated this theory in *The Causes of World War III*, which was published in 1958. The book marked a departure for Mills, who had previously insisted that he was not an activist, precisely because it was more polemical in style. In addition to defining the power elite, Mills addressed the question of peace in a nuclear age. The advent of nuclear weapons had simultaneously made war total and absurd. War had lost its value as an instrument of foreign policy. What was required, therefore, was a reorientation of both U.S. and Soviet foreign policy to accommodate the new reality. Mills's last book, *Listen Yankee*, published in 1960, examined U.S. foreign policy regarding the social revolutions occurring in Third World nations. The combination of these two books thrust Mills into the forefront of academic critics of U.S. foreign policy and the Cold War. He became one of the most widely read sociologists in the country, and his work served as a catalyst for many in the emerging New Left. Mills died on 20 March 1962 in Nyack, New York.

References Josephson, Harold, ed., *Biographical Dictionary of Modern Peace Leaders* (1985); Mills, C. Wright, *The Causes of World War III* (1958); Mills,

C. Wright, "Listen Yankee." *Harpers Magazine* (December 1960).

Mobilization for Survival

Mobilization for Survival was formed by a broad-based coalition of liberals and left-liberals who united to protest against the construction of nuclear power plants and to protest the nuclear arms race. The coalition, organized in 1978, was an umbrella organization intended to coordinate the civil actions of several existing antinuclear groups in order to maximize their efforts and to demonstrate the depth and breadth of the antinuclear movement.

Reference DeBenedetti, Charles, ed., *Peace Heroes in Twentieth Century America* (1988).

Moratorium/New Mobilization

The first mobilization against the Vietnam War took place on 15 April 1967 in New York and San Francisco. The gathering was originally called the Spring Mobilization to End the War in Vietnam. Those who participated in the moratorium represented a broad spectrum of organizations that united to register a common protest. Thousands of people of all ages, backgrounds, political affiliations, and occupations marched together to protest the war. The spirit of the mobilization carried over long after the actual event, providing an impetus to thousands to continue their opposition to the government and its reliance on military solutions.

By 1969 the first mobilization committee was replaced by a New Mobilization committee, which drew its leadership and direction from those who were angered by political persecution of the Black Panthers and the Chicago Seven and by the failure of Eugene McCarthy and his fellow antiwar supporters to capture the Democratic party. At the same time, in 1969, another coalition was formed, composed mainly of activists in peace organizations such as SANE and those who had been involved in the McCarthy campaign and in Senator Robert F. Kennedy's campaign to gain the Democratic nomination. The format of the moratorium, scheduled for October, was a one-day strike against business-as-usual, which would then expand each month until the war had been brought to a close. Moratorium leaders tended to work through accepted political channels. Consequently, it gained more public support than it otherwise might have. Organizers were careful to employ tactics that would keep the peace movement on board while not offending or alienating necessary political support. The New Mobilization and the Moratorium found themselves almost in competition as both groups organized massive marches and demonstrations scheduled to take place at the same time, November 1969. Ultimately, the leaders of the New Mobilization and the Moratorium agreed to cooperate in order to avoid possible violent confrontation and to avoid fracturing the peace movement irreparably. On 15 November 1969, approximately 500,000 war protesters converged on Washington, D.C. This massive show of support for peace was a testament to the ability of two sets of leaders, whose political interests were not necessarily compatible, to put aside apparent differences in order to present a united front. By April 1970 the coalition had already dissolved. Political interests, financing, and logistical support were no longer working to bring the leadership together. The New Mobilization was able to generate some activity after the Kent State and Jackson State shootings, but there were no massive demonstrations thereafter.

Reference Chatfield, Charles, ed., *Peace Movements in America* (1973).

Morrison, Charles Clayton (1874–1966)

In 1908, Charles Morrison bought a bankrupt church periodical called the *Christian Century* at a sheriff's sale. When he retired as its publisher in 1947, the

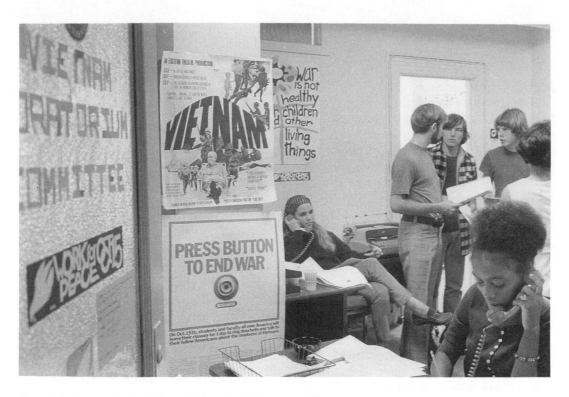

Peace Activists organize in Vietnam Moratorium Committee offices.

Christian Century was the most prestigious Protestant journal in the world. Had he achieved recognition for no other reason, Morrison's life and career would still have been worthy of notice. In 1927, Morrison wrote a book entitled *The Outlawry of War: A Constructive Policy for World Peace*, which helped to define a specific goal for an important segment of the peace movement in the United States and internationally as well.

Morrison, who was born in Harrison, Ohio, graduated from Drake University in 1898. He was a fellow in philosophy at the University of Chicago from 1902 to 1905 and began his career as an ordained minister of the Disciples of Christ. For the next six years, Morrison served as pastor in churches in Clarinda and Perry, Iowa, and Chicago and Springfield, Illinois. Morrison was an advocate of liberal theology, believing in the innate goodness of humans and in the potential for social reform to eradicate society's ills.

Although he was always critical of war, he was not necessarily a pacifist. He did, however, believe that in the years preceeding World War I, technology had so advanced that war was no longer thinkable. Nevertheless, Morrison supported President Woodrow Wilson when he asked for a declaration of war in 1917. Morrison believed that the circumstances forced upon Wilson by Germany left the president no choice. He continued to support Wilson and the Allies throughout the war and into the 1920s, including plans for a League of Nations. Gradually, as the consequences of the war became more and more disillusioning, Morrison, along with many other peace advocates who had supported the war, began to regret his earlier decision.

The Outlawry of War, dedicated to his fellow peace activist, Salmon O. Levinson, and with a forward by John Dewey, was Morrison's response to the folly of choosing war as a vehicle of foreign policy. Morrison wanted the outlawary of war to be considered solely on its own merits, without comparison with or discussion of other peace proposals. Endorsing Senator William Borah's resolution of 1923, which would have made war an international crime, Morrison advocated the establishment of an international court convened to adjudicate urgent problems. By this time, Morrison had already rejected the League of Nations and the Geneva Protocol of 1924 as woefully inadequate in their conception, because they relied on using war to curb war. Morrison offered the optimistic opinion that neither military nor economic sanctions would be necessary to enforce the edicts of an international court, arguing that "united public opinion of the world" would be sufficient to make nations comply with a peaceful solution to conflicts.

While critics complained that Morrison's assumptions were naïve at the very least, he never wavered in his belief. He continued to work for his cause and was one of the staunchest supporters of the negotiations leading up to the Kellogg-Briand Pact in 1928. Morrison was invited to the signing ceremony on 27 August and firmly believed that because of the pact, "international war was banished from civilization." Ironically, the lack of any real enforcement clauses in the Kellogg-Briand Pact sealed its fate as a meaningless weapon for eradicating war and provided clear proof that more than "united public opinion" would be necessary to truly succeed.

Through the *Christian Century*, Morrison continued to oppose any action that could lead to war, including German rearmament. He was equally opposed to President Franklin D. Roosevelt's actions after the war started in Europe, for example, he opposed the Lend Lease program to provide ships and materials necessary for Great Britain to defend itself. Morrison strove for a negotiated peace settlement up to the moment that Japan attacked Pearl Harbor. Although he insisted that a more conciliatory attitude toward Japan would have prevented war, Morrison finally had to accept the reality. Writing in the *Christian Century*, he characterized World War II as a "guilty necessity. . . . The war itself is the wages of our sin and injustice. It is a catostrophic tragedy . . . leaving us no choice save to decide on which side we shall fight."

Once the war ended, Morrison continued his opposition to policies that he believed threatened peace. He was mistrustful of the United Nations (U.N.), fearing that it would result in a new quest for empire that he believed would inevitably follow the war. He also spoke out against nuclear weapons and the Truman Doctrine on the grounds that they would do only harm. Morrison retired as editor of the *Christian Century* in 1947, although he continued to speak out against war. He died on 2 March 1966 in Chicago, Illinois.

References Josephson, Harold, ed., *Biographical Dictionary of Modern Peace Leaders* (1985); "Voice of the Century." *Newsweek* (23 June 1947); Wittner, Lawrence S., *Rebels against War: The American Peace Movement 1941–1960* (1969).

Morse, Wayne Lyman (1900–1974)

Although the United States had been a presence in Vietnam economically and, shortly thereafter, with limited ground forces, since 1954 when the French colonial forces fell at Dien Bien Phu, it was a full ten years later that the United States significantly escalated its commitment to the war. Wayne Morse and Alaska Senator Ernest Gruening were the only two senators who opposed deeper involvement in Vietnam by voting against the Gulf of Tonkin Resolution.

Wayne Morse was born in Madison, Wisconsin. He earned both a B.A. and an M.A. from the University of Wisconsin and then went on to earn law degrees from the University of Minnesota and Columbia University. A brilliant public speaker and debater, Morse taught debate at the University of Minnesota while attending law school. In 1929, the University of Oregon recruited him to teach at its law school. Morse developed something of a national reputation in both criminal justice and in industrial-labor relations. His skill as a negotiator led to an appointment to the National War Labor Board during World War II.

A lifelong Republican, Morse staged a successful run for the Senate in 1944. As a senator, his liberal leanings led him to support the United Nations (U.N.) Charter and the North Atlantic Treaty Organization. When he was disappointed in what he perceived as a Republican right turn in 1952, Morse declared himself an Independent. He also supported Adlai Stevenson for the presidency in 1952 and again in 1956. A year earlier, in 1955, Morse made an official switch to the Democratic party. Although he vigorously supported President Lyndon Baines Johnson's Great Society programs, Morse was not willing to support an escalation of the Vietnam War. On the floor of the Senate he expressed his concern about the United States' Third World image and about possible conflict with the Chinese. When a military escalation began in August 1964, after the Gulf of Tonkin Resolution, Morse publicly renounced U.S. policy regarding Vietnam, characterizing the conflict as an illegal and immoral war in direct defiance of U.N. principles. Morse never advocated an immediate and total U.S. withdrawal, however. Although he used more and more occasions to criticize U.S. policy, his remedy always focused on the cessation of bombing, limited combat along more secure coastal enclaves, and a negotiated settlement. Moreover, Morse stated several times that he would fully support U.S. intervention if Congress properly delcared war.

Despite this rather tepid approach to the war issue, Morse increasingly was viewed as a leading figure in the antiwar movement, especially because of his continued outspokenness during 1965 and 1966, well before antiwar sentiment so-lidified to any meaningful extent. Because of his position, he lent a great deal of credibility and respectability to the antiwar movement, which was undoubtedly his most important contribution. When the Tet Offensive in 1968 placed increased pressure on policy makers to justify a continuation of the war, and with a grueling reelection campaign facing him, Morse began to expend less energy on the war. He nevertheless lost his reelection bid to Republican Robert Packwood and lost again in 1972 when he ran against Mark Hatfield. Morse died on 22 July 1974 as he was preparing to wage another campaign to regain his lost Senate seat.

References Josephson, Harold, ed., *Biographical Dictionary of Modern Peace Leaders* (1985); *New York Times* (23, 24 July 1974).

Mott, John R. (1865–1955)

In recognition of his work in uniting "millions of young people in work for the Christian ideals of peace and tolerance among nations," the Nobel Peace Committee awarded John R. Mott the Nobel Peace Prize in 1946. Mott shared the award that year with longtime peace activist Emily Greene Balch.

Mott, a native of Potsville, Iowa, was in his first year at Cornell University when he had what can best be described as a conversion experience. Debating whether to become a lawyer or go back home after college to join his father's lumber business, Mott attended a lecture on 14 January 1886. The professor exhorted his students not to pursue worldly interests but to seek out the road leading to "the Kingdom of God." In Mott's view, the professor seemed to be speaking directly to him. Thereafter, Mott was determined to dedicate his life to Christian works. Several months later, while spending the summer as the Cornell YMCA representative to a student conference, Mott heard the evangelist Dwight Moody. Moody, a powerful speaker, persuaded not only Mott but 100 other young men to work in the foreign missions. In the meantime, Mott continued his work with the Cornell YWCA, became its president, increased its membership, and raised funds for a new building. By the time he graduated, Cornell's YWCA was the largest student YMCA in the world. Mott had found his career.

Over the next decade, Mott headed up the Intercollegiate YMCA and doubled its membership. He also integrated it with the Student Volunteer Movement for Foreign Missions. In 1895, with the funding of John D. Rockefeller and Cyrus McCormick, Mott founded the World's Student Christian Federation, which soon had affiliates in India, Japan, China, Australia, New Zealand, and Europe. Balancing his marriage and four children with his career, Mott continued working with Christian groups, particularly the YMCA, turning down college presidencies and an ambassadorial appointment by President Woodrow Wilson.

Although he abhorred war, Mott threw his support behind the Allies during World War I, offering the services of the national YMCA. After the war, he continued urging international Christian alliance and became known as the father of the World Council of Churches. During his long career, Motts's main goal was to promote the international understanding that would underscore world peace. During World War II his organizations worked with prisoners of war and refugees. In his Nobel address, Mott observed that the world needed leaders who were comprehending and vividly aware of the world situation, who were "thinkers, not mechanical workers"—people with a genuine vision that extended beyond the borders of a particular country. Moreover, Mott insisted, "spotless character" was a prerequisite for a true statesman who would follow principle in all circumstances. It was a vision of leadership that Mott adopted throughout his career and a challenge to leaders of the future. Mott died a few months before his ninetieth birthday, nine years after receiving his Nobel Peace Prize.

Reference Abrams, Irwin, *The Nobel Peace Prize and the Laureates: An Illustrated Biographical History 1901–1987* (1988).

Muste, Abraham Johannes (1885–1967)

It is a testament to A. J. Muste's reputation as an advocate of peace that in India he became known as "the American Gandhi" and that Martin Luther King, Jr. attributed to him "the emphasis on nonviolent direct action in the race relations field." Paradoxically, A. J. Muste was also responsible for founding of the American Workers Party in the 1930s, an organization that espoused radical Marxist revolution and which advocated violent change. He later described his embracing of radical Marxism as a "highly educational demonstration of the futility of compromise with a so-called lesser evil."

Muste, who was born in the Netherlands, immigrated with his family to Grand Rapids, Michigan, at the age of six. The Midwest at that time still harbored strong feelings about the martyred Abraham Lincoln and the Emancipation Proclamation, feelings which had a formative influence on the young Muste. He made the ideals of abolitionism and a belief in individual responsibility a part of his own being. After graduating from Hope College in Holland, Michigan, and teaching for a few years, Muste entered the Theological Seminary of the Dutch Reformed Church in New Jersey and later received a Bachelor of Divinity degree from Union Theological Seminary in 1913. As a theology student he also sat in on lecture courses by William James and John Dewey at Columbia University. His strict Calvinist upbringing gave way to a ministry of social needs and he soon joined the Fellowship of Reconciliation (FOR), an organization sponsored by the Quakers. As the United States drew closer to entering World War I, Muste moved closer to pacifism. He resigned from the FOR in 1917 and did volunteer work with the American Civil Liberties Union (ACLU), which he had helped to found.

From 1918 to 1933, Muste lived in Massachusetts and New York and spent his time working with labor union activities. He provided counseling in nonviolence to workers in the Lawrence textile strike in 1919 and negotiated a strike settlement. As general secretary of the Amalgamated Textile Workers of America, he became educational director at Brookwood Labor College in Katonah, New York. For several years he taught history and social problems at Brookwood. It was during his Brookwood years that Muste became involved in radical Marxism, but in 1936 he experienced a religious conversion, rejoined the FOR, and served as its executive secretary until 1953. Muste continued to advocate peace even after the United States entered World War II, but he worked with the Civilian Public Service (CPS) camp, sponsored by the historic peace churches such as the Quakers. As a volunteer Muste helped to find alternative service jobs for conscientious objectors (COs).

When the war ended, Muste worked with both domestic and international peace groups. In both he was an influential advocate of nonviolence in pursuit of social change. A staunch foe of nuclear arms, Muste and others refused to cooperate with civil defense drills and helped to organize protests. As chairman of the Committee for Non-Violent Action (CNVA), Muste tried to send a ship into a nuclear test zone in 1958 and, at the age of 75, was sentenced to nine days in jail for scaling a fence during a protest at a Nebraska missile site. Active until his death, Muste traveled to Hanoi, along with two other elderly clergymen, to meet with Ho Chi Minh and discuss the possibility of a settlement in the Vietnam War. A few weeks later, on 11 February 1967, A. J. Muste died.

See also American Civil Liberties Union; Committee for Non-Violent Action; Fellowship of Reconciliation.

References Hentoff, Nat, *Peace Agitator: The Story of A. J. Muste* (1963); Josephson, Harold, ed., *Biographical Dictionary of Modern Peace Leaders* (1985); Whitman, Alden, ed., *American Reformers: An H. W. Wilson Biographical Dictionary* (1985).

Mygatt, Tracy Dickinson (1885–1973)

Tracy Mygatt could easily have spent her life in genteel upper-class society, trading upon her heritage as a descendant of the country's first settlers. Instead, she spent her life embroiled in a variety of social causes and reform movements that came under the broad umbrella of the Progressive Era.

Mygatt, whose colonial forebears arrived in America in 1633, was born in Brooklyn, New York. A student at Bryn Mawr in the heyday of its activist president, M. Carey Thomas, Mygatt graduated in 1908, determined, as she said, to give her life over to the fight against social evils, including child labor. A committed pacifist with a deeply ingrained religiosity, Mygatt wrote a number of books, plays, and articles with religious themes. She had a lifelong commitment to the search for world peace, a democratic socialist economy, and international unity. Within two years of her graduation from Bryn Mawr, Mygatt was deeply involved in the settlement house movement. She understood fully the necessity for women to have safe, inexpensive, and reliable child care while they were at work, and in 1910 she founded the Chelsea Day Nursery. Her concern for the homeless in New York prompted her to demand of her Episcopal Church that it establish a program to feed and house needy people. Like many women, Mygatt favored women's suffrage and worked for it, organizing a Socialist Suffrage Brigade of the Christian Socialist League, of which she was a member. With her longtime companion and friend, Frances Witherspoon, Mygatt marched under the banner "Votes for Women/For Socialism and Peace."

Her commitment to peace was reinforced when World War I began. Characterizing the war as a "betrayal ... of humanity," Mygatt joined the Women's Peace Party (WPP), which was considered a militant antiwar group. She also worked actively with the People's Council, the American Union against Militarism, the Fellowship of Reconciliation (FOR), and, after the war, the War Resisters League (WRL). Mygatt was one of the founders of the Anti-Enlistment League in 1915, which sought to provide legal services for poor conscientious objectors (COs). The Anti-Enlistment League became the Bureau of Legal Advice in 1917, and was at least partially funded by the Civil Liberties Bureau (CLB), which became the American Civil Liberties Union (ACLU) in 1923. When the Bureau of Legal Advice merged into the ACLU, Mygatt turned her full attention to working with the WRL. Demanding the total renunciation of all wars, the WRL required its members to take a pledge renouncing war.

Mygatt always advocated peaceful resistance to war. In the 1930s she worked for a constitutional amendment to outlaw war and initiate disarmament. Looking toward international government as the best hope for peace, Mygatt helped to found and was the East Coast secretary of the Campaign for World Government (CWG). She was the CWG representative to the United Nations (U.N.) and argued strongly for making that organization a true vehicle for world federation and democracy. Mygatt believed that the alternative was to leave the door open for further use of nuclear weapons.

Mygatt did not allow advancing years to slow her down. She continued to lend support to the cause of peace and racial harmony and was an opponent of the Vietnam War. She died on Thanksgiving Day, 22 November 1973.

See also Campaign for World Government.

References Josephson, Harold, ed., *Biographical Dictionary of Modern Peace Leaders* (1985); Manahan, Nancy, "Future Old Maids and Pacifist Agitators: The Story of Tracy Mygatt and Frances Witherspoon." *Women's Studies Quarterly* 10 (Spring 1982).

National Campaign for a U.S. Peace Tax Fund

Founded by a group of concerned citizens in Ann Arbor, Michigan, in 1971, the National Campaign for a World Peace Tax Fund Bill changed its name to the National Campaign for a U.S. Peace Tax Fund in 1985. The purpose of the organization is to promote the introduction and passage of a tax bill that would allow any taxpayer who was conscientiously opposed to war of any sort to specifically designate that his or her taxes be used for nonmilitary programs. Ideally, the legislation would establish a trust fund, known as the U.S. Peace Tax Fund, which would receive the portion of a taxpayer's taxes that would otherwise go into military spending.

Supporters of the campaign have proposed a variety of projects that they believe would be appropriate recipients of the Peace Tax Fund, including a national academy of peace and conflict resolution, disarmament programs, peaceful resolution of international conflicts research, retraining workers to make the transition from military industries to nonmilitary work in socially acceptable programs, improvements in health and welfare, and international peace exchanges.

The World Peace Tax Fund Bill was introduced in Congress for the first time in 1972 by ten members of the House. In 1977, Senator Mark Hatfield introduced similar legislation in the Senate. The bill has been resubmitted in each succeeding Congress since then and has slowly gathered support. A variety of peace-oriented organizations, including the American Friends Service Committee (AFSC), Fellowship of Reconciliation (FOR), Pax Christi, and the Women's International League for Peace and Freedom (WILPF), have lobbied Congress and helped to publicize the peace tax idea.

Reference Wank, Solomon, ed., *Doves and Diplomats: Foreign Offices and Peace Movements in Europe and America in the Twentieth Century* (1978).

National Committee for a Sane Nuclear Policy
See SANE/FREEZE.

National Committee for an Effective Congress

The National Committee for an Effective Congress was founded in 1948 by a group of concerned Americans, most notably Eleanor Roosevelt. The committee was founded to counter the powerful vested interests that seemed to dominate U.S. politics. In particular, the group feared that big oil, big steel, the utilities giants, and Wall Street were exercising altogether too much influence in political affairs that affected both domestic and foreign policy. It was the committee that coined the term *radical right* when it took on Senator Joseph McCarthy in 1954. During the Civil Rights battles of the 1960s, the committee led the fight against the old guard Republicans and the so-called Dixiecrats, who were attempting to block any effective civil rights legislation. The committee focused part of its attack on the powerful and entrenched House Rules Committee, which had the ability to hold up proposed legislation almost indefinitely.

Although it was not founded as a peace organization, per se, the committee nevertheless took up the cause of peace when it became one of the first national organizations to take a stand against the Vietnam War. By 1972 the committee had broadened its range of concerns to include the military-industrial complex and the rapidly expanding military budget. The committee makes no pretense about its

151

liberal leanings and supports candidates for Congress who oppose, among other things, huge military budget increases, an escalation of the arms race, and military—as opposed to diplomatic—solutions to conflicts. In the four decades since its founding, the committee has become a respected political entity able to provide expert assistance to candidates in everything from polling to fund raising.

See also Roosevelt, Anna Eleanor.

Reference Meyer, Robert S., *Peace Organizations Past and Present* (1988).

National Council for the Prevention of War

Founded by Quaker pacifist Frederick J. Libby in 1921, the National Council for the Prevention of War had no individual members. Instead, it brought together pacifist groups with other peace advocates who were not necessarily pacifists. Member groups included the American Federation of Teachers, the YWCA, and the National Education Association. The council made concerted efforts to attract both farmers and labor groups to the cause of peace. Its monthly newsletter, *Peace Action*, much of which was directed at farmers and blue-collar workers, reached a circulation high of approximately 20,000. In addition, throughout the 1930s, the council's Washington headquarters sent out between one and two million pieces of literature annually. By 1935 the council was sending regular press releases to 600 publications nationwide and maintaining regular and reliable contact with newspapers in 300 congressional districts. The council also began broadcasting a regular radio program in 1935, frequently inviting congressmen and senators to deliver addresses, many of which were written by council staffers. In the mid-1930s, the council had 21 member organizations, operated on an annual budget of $100,000, and its regular congressional lobbyist was former congresswoman Jeannette Rankin.

See also Libby, Frederick Joseph.

Reference Wittner, Lawrence S., *Rebels against War: The American Peace Movement 1941–1960* (1969).

National Council of American-Soviet Friendship, Inc. (NCASF)

Since its founding in 1943, at the height of World War II, the National Council of American-Soviet Friendship, Inc. (NCASF) has strived to promote peace, particularly between the United States and the Soviet Union, to help bring about arms reductions on both sides, and to oppose the testing and use of nuclear weapons. The NCASF was one of the first organizations to oppose nuclear weapons following the bombing of Hiroshima and Nagasaki in 1945.

Besides producing educational material promoting its cause, the NCASF sponsors a cultural exchange between the two countries and friendship travel, wherein tours of the Soviet Union have been arranged with an emphasis on people-to-people contact in various Soviet cities. It also sponsored Camp Artek, an International Pioneer Camp on the Black Sea, to which U.S. youths have been invited each year since 1967. The key focus of the NCASF throughout the Cold War era involved efforts to promote détente between the two superpowers as a prerequisite to achieving world peace and lessening the threat of nuclear war.

Reference Meyer, Robert S., *Peace Organizations Past and Present* (1988).

National Impact Network

The National Impact Network, organized in Washington, D.C., in 1969, addresses three main priorities: halting the arms race, protecting human rights, and securing economic justice. Although its national office focuses on the Congress, state affiliates address state issues. Impact is an organization sponsored and supported by a broad spectrum of religious groups, including: the American Baptist Churches; the Catholic Committee on Urban Ministry; the Church of the Brethren; Church Women United; the Episcopal Church; the Episcopal Urban Caucus; the Evangelical Lutheran Church of America; the Friends Committee on National Legislation; the Jesuit Conference; the National Council of Churches; the Presbyterian Church, U.S.A.; the Reformed Church in America; the Union of American Hebrew Congregations; the Unitarian Universalist Association; the United Church of Christ; and the United Methodist Church.

Impact has several publications that keep its members informed. A monthly newsletter, *Update*, reports on the progress of peace-related issues in Congress. Another publication, *Hunger*, addresses such issues as global hunger and poverty, agricultural poverty, and food stamps. *Prepare* publishes reports on options for future legislative action regarding issues of concern. State affiliates also publish local versions of these publications.

Reference Meyer, Robert S., *Peace Organizations Past and Present* (1988).

National Mobilization for Survival (NMS)

The National Mobilization for Survival (NMS) began as a project of Survival Education in 1977. The NMS brought together both national and local groups already involved in activities ranging from lobbying for the complete elimination of nuclear weapons and a ban on nuclear power to calls for a reversal of the arms race and social justice. The NMS is instructional in nature. It provides a forum for local groups to become involved in national campaigns and brings together people working on a variety of issues from around the country. In addition, it helps to organize activities. The group considers communication its most important contribution to peace. By keeping affiliates and local groups informed of activites and campaigns in other communities as well as nationally, interested groups can combine efforts to increase the effectiveness of the campaigns. Its quarterly publication, *The Mobilizer*, keeps affiliates informed and acts as a forum for a peace actions. One of the ongoing campaigns included in the MFS national program is the Deadly Connection Campaign, an effort to provide educational material on the connection between military action and the nuclear arms race. The organization also conducts ongoing work on issues involving the Middle East, the former Soviet Union, apartheid, and the Rainbow Coalition.

Reference Meyer, Robert S., *Peace Organizations Past and Present* (1988).

National Peace with Justice Week (NPJW)

Originally initiated as a Peace Sunday, the National Peace with Justice Week (NPJW), under the direction of the National Council of Churches, became the largest religious forum for peace and justice. It is sponsored by more than 20 "inviting organizations," including Church Women United, the Baptist Peace Fellowship, the Lutheran Peace Fellowship, the National Association of Black Catholic Administrators, and the National Campus Ministry Association, as well as almost every religious denomination and organization in the country. The inviting organizations invite others to join in their coalition in support of NPJW.

The second annual NPJW, in 1984, brought together more than 20,000 local congregations and religious organizations nationwide. Each year NPJW provides a new packet of information and literature for distribution that emphasizes the constant theme of world peace and subsidiary issues such as working with the press, peace on the local and regional levels, organizing for peace, and youth activities.

Reference Meyer, Robert S., *Peace Organizations Past and Present* (1988).

Niebuhr, Reinhold (1892–1971)

Reinhold Niebuhr was the foremost U.S. theologian of the twentieth century. Born in Wright City, Missouri, Niebuhr attended Elmhurst College, Eden Theological Seminary, and Yale University. He began to develop his skills as a communicator and orator while still in college. He was an ordained minister of the Evangelical Synod of North America. Niebuhr served as pastor of Bethel Evangelical Church in Detroit, Michigan, from 1915 to 1928. It was while he was in Detroit that Niebuhr underwent a social awakening. He had supported World War I, believing—as did many of his colleagues in the clergy—that German aggression had to be stopped and that submarine warfare had forced the hand of a reluctant President Woodrow Wilson. Niebuhr's disillusionment with the results of the war developed along with his social awakening and resulted in a new social consciousness.

Niebuhr used his speaking skills to promote his new message and that, combined with a series of well-written articles, helped to bring him to the attention of pacifists such as John Nevin Sayre and Kirby Page. So impressed were they with Niebuhr that they agreed to support him financially if he would relocate in New York, teach at Union Theological Seminary, and coedit the pacifist journal *The World Tomorrow*. Niebuhr seized the opportunity to spread his liberal theology and his version of the social gospel. He, along with Sayre and Page, became active supporters of the Socialist Norman Thomas. Niebuhr was professor of ethics and theology at Union Theological Seminary from 1928 to 1960. In 1927, he wrote a book entitled *Does Civilization Need Religion?*, which was followed in 1932 by *Moral Man and Immoral Society: A Study in Ethics and Politics*. Both publications reexamined the assumptions that underlay Christian liberalism and the social gospel. In them, Niebuhr outlined the distinction between individual and social ethics as a way of understanding the role of religion and the responsibility of human beings and of nations. Individuals, Niebuhr argued, were motivated by ideals; indeed, ideals were a necessary precondition for men and women to act in an ethical manner. Nations, on the other hand, had to have a realistic understanding of the consequences of actions and the use of power. Although the ultimate value for individuals might be love,

for nations the ultimate value had to be justice in terms of the distribution of power.

Niebuhr served as chairman of the Fellowship of Reconciliation (FOR) in 1932 and 1933. Having reached the conclusion by 1934 that the working class, seeking a new social order, was justified in resorting to violence in the face of unrelenting intransigence, Niebuhr resigned his chairmanship. He still considered war between nations another matter entirely, but he could not preach total pacifism. As the 1930s drew to a close, and as events in Europe and in the Far East continued to cast shadows on the entire world, Niebuhr strayed further and further from pacifism. He opposed pacifist support for mandatory neutrality legislation in 1937, and after Neville Chamberlain's settlement in Munich, he broke with pacifism entirely. In 1941, Niebuhr began publishing *Christianity and Crises*, which directly challenged U.S. churches' support of pacifism and neutrality. Niebuhr's break with pacifism also signaled a more general renunciation of a nonviolent, noninterventionist approach to world affairs as the threats from Germany, Italy, and Japan became more and more obvious. Niebuhr believed that nonviolence was a useful social strategy only if considered in relative terms and not as an absolute religious conviction, regardless of circumstances. In *The Children of Light and the Children of Darkness*, published in 1944, Niebuhr contrasted what he considered the failure of liberal naïveté and the evil of totalitarianism. Following World War II, Niebuhr extended his analysis to the Cold War and greatly influenced the thinking of people like George Kennan, Dean Achison, and Hans Morgenthau, all of whom served in key government positions in the decades following the war. He supported Kennan's Containment Theory in the 1950s as an appropriate application of his philosophy to halt the spread of communism. At the same time, he opposed the nuclear arms race and the Vietnam War, because

Front and back views of the Nobel Prize Medal.

neither met the criteria of either his brand of Christian realism or "just war" pragmatism. Niebuhr died in Stockbridge, Massachusetts, on 1 June 1971.

References Josephson, Harold, ed., *Biographical Dictionary of Modern Peace Leaders* (1985); Wittner, Lawrence S., *Rebels against War: The American Peace Movement 1941–1960* (1969).

Nobel Peace Prize

Of the six Nobel prizes awarded annually, the Nobel Peace Prize is recognized worldwide as the most prestigious. It is the highest honor bestowed upon an individual or an organization and is awarded for furthering the cause of peace and fraternity among peoples of the world and among nations.

The Nobel prizes originate in Sweden and usually are awarded by Swedish juries at ceremonies in that country. The Nobel Peace Prize is administered and presented by the Nobel Peace Prize Selection Committee, which comprises members of the Norwegian Parliament and the Norwegian Nobel Institute. The award is presented concurrently with ceremonies in Stockholm on 10 December each year. The presentation is made in the presence of the King of Norway in the Great Hall of Oslo University and carries with it an honorarium that varies in value from year

to year. It is not mandatory that a Nobel Peace Prize be awarded each year. If the committee determines that no person or organization has made a significant contribution to world peace, it may decline to award the Nobel Peace Prize for that year. In the twentieth century, the following Americans have won Nobel Peace Prizes:

Theodore Roosevelt (1906)
Elihu Root (1912)
Woodrow Wilson (1919)
Charles G. Dawes (1925)
Frank B. Kellogg (1929)
Jane Addams (1931)*
Nicholas Murray Butler (1931)*
Cordell Hull (1945)
Emily Greene Balch (1946)**
John R. Mott (1946)**
American Friends Service Committee
  (1947)
Ralph J. Bunche (1950)
George C. Marshall (1953)
Linus C. Pauling (1962)
Martin Luther King, Jr. (1964)
Norman E. Borlaug (1970)
Henry A. Kissinger (1973)

*cowinners
**cowinners

Reference Abrams, Irwin, *The Nobel Peace Prize and the Laureates: An Illustrated Biographical History 1901–1987* (1988).

Nuclear Freeze Movement

In 1980, Randall Forsberg, the director of the Institute for Defence and Disarmament Studies, issued an appeal to the United States and the Soviet Union calling for an immediate halt to all testing, production, and deployment of nuclear weapons. Forsberg's appeal had its origins in a similar proposal made some 20 years earlier by the U.S. representative to the Geneva Disarmament Convention, Adrian Fisher. By 1981, Forsberg's appeal resulted in the establishment of a nuclear freeze campaign.

Central to the idea of a nuclear freeze campaign was the concept that war, in the age of nuclear weapons, could no longer be considered a viable instrument of foreign policy. In addition to the cessation of nuclear weapons production and testing, the freeze movement advocated a halt to military intervention in other countries by both the United States and the Soviet Union, a reduction of nuclear stockpiles, and a conversion of military-industry production to peaceful civilian production projects. The freeze campaign succeeded in influencing the outcome of referendums calling for a nuclear freeze in ten states in 1981 and 1982, all of which were approved by the voters. In 1982, the House of Representatives also passed a resolution calling for a nuclear freeze. A similar Senate resolution was tabled in 1983, but more than 20 state legislatures adopted nuclear freeze resolutions, as have hundreds of local councils.

Although the Nuclear Freeze Movement has been criticized for promoting an overly simplistic solution, it nevertheless struck a chord in citizens throughout the country who embraced and supported the campaign. Proof of widespread support for the idea of a nuclear freeze was demonstrated when nearly a million people turned out in New York's Central Park in support of the nuclear freeze campaign rally in 1982. More than 1,100 individual chapters were organized across the country and the campaign helped to organize or support rallies, workshops, seminars, and lobbying efforts. The Freeze Voter, a political action committee, was organized to lend support to candidates who were in favor of a nuclear freeze. By 1986—in addition to supporting legislation aimed at establishing a comprehensive nuclear test ban treaty, halting missile testing, and cancelling the MX program and other weapons systems—the campaign sponsored a conference entitled Common Sense Defense Budget, which concluded that real security depended not only on arms control but also on the development of a quality educational system, a productive civilian economy, and a program to rebuild the nation's infrastructure.

The Nuclear Freeze Movement maintains close ties with a variety of other peace organizations and has conducted polls claiming support for the idea of nuclear freeze by more than 80 percent of the population. Whether the Nuclear Freeze Movement actually had the support of that large a proportion of the American public, it was undeniably one of the most successful grass-roots organizations in the U.S. peace movement.

References Kaltefleiter, Werner, and Robert L. Pfaltzgraff, eds., *The Peace Movement in Europe and the United States* (1985); Meyer, Robert S., *Peace Organizations Past and Present* (1988); Schell, Jonathan, *The Fate of the Earth* (1982).

Nuclear Nonproliferation Treaty

Following ratification of the Nuclear Test Ban Treaty, the 18-nation Disarmament Conference in Geneva negotiated for more than four years before reaching agreement on the Nuclear Nonproliferation Treaty. Signed on 1 July 1968 by the United States, the U.S.S.R., and 60 other countries, ratification was delayed because of the Soviet invasion of Czechoslovakia on 20 and 21 August. Finally, on 13 March 1969, the Senate ratified the treaty by a vote of 83 to 15. As with the Nuclear Test Ban Treaty, neither France nor China were signatories. The treaty prohibited the spread of nuclear weapons. Nations signing the treaty agreed not to transfer weapons to nonnuclear states, and nonnuclear states agreed not to accept nuclear devices. The treaty also provided for safeguard procedures and insured nondiscriminatory access to nuclear energy for peaceful uses.

See also Nuclear Test Ban Treaty.

References Link, Arthur S., et al., eds., *The American People: A History* (1981); Morris, Richard B., ed., *Encyclopedia of American History*, Bicentennial Edition (1976).

Nuclear Test Ban Treaty

Efforts to enact a nuclear test ban treaty began in 1947 with the establishment of the United Nations (U.N.) Commission for Conventional Armaments. From the beginning, movement on the issue was deadeningly slow. The Korean War and the Cold War both conspired to prevent any progress whatsoever. In 1952 the U.N. Commission for Conventional Weapons combined with the U.N. Atomic Energy Commission to form the U.N. Disarmament Commission. Over the next decade, talks were conducted both in the U.N. General Assembly and outside, among individual governments. In 1954 the Disarmament Commission established a five-nation subcommitte to hold private negotiations. The five nations were the United States, the U.S.S.R., Great Britain, France, and Canada. In this context, discussions included a nuclear test ban as a prerequisite for the suspension of nuclear weapons production. In the meantime, both the United States and the U.S.S.R. continued to test nuclear weapons in the atmosphere.

The United States detonated weapons at the Bikini Atoll in 1954. Stunned at the amount of damage sustained by ships taking part in the tests (21 ships, including a World War II carrier, the U.S.S. *Saratoga*, were inadvertently sunk by the blasts), scientists were further shaken by the damage sustained by a Japanese fishing boat, the *Fukuryu Maru*. Of the 23 men aboard the fishing vessel, which was fully 1,000 miles away from Bikini, one man died from radiation exposure and the others all suffered serious injury. The incident helped to move the nuclear weapons talks along, but it was still another nine years before agreement could be reached.

In 1958, President Dwight D. Eisenhower announced that the United States would observe a period of test suspension, despite the fact that the Soviets had recently performed weapons tests. In 1961, however, the suspension was lifted, and in 1962 the United States once again conducted atmospheric tests in the Pacific. A summit meeting held in 1963 prompted President John F. Kennedy to appeal to Soviet Premier Nikita Khrushchev to agree to a ban. After several more months of negotiation, a Limited Nuclear Test Ban Treaty was signed in Moscow on 5 August 1963. The treaty prohibited atmospheric testing of nuclear weapons, testing in outer space, and testing underwater. Underground tests were exempted from the treaty. The treaty was ratified by the U.S. Senate on 24 September 1963 by a vote of 80 to 19. By that time, 99 nations had signed the treaty, which went into effect on 10 October 1963. The two major nations that refused to sign the treaty were France and China.

References Link, Arthur S., et al., eds., *The American People: A History* (1981); Morris, Richard B., ed., *Encyclopedia of American History*, Bicentennial Edition (1976).

Omaha Action

In 1959 the Committee for Non-Violent Action (CNVA) sponsored a campaign called Omaha Action. The name derived from the city of Omaha, Nebraska, where Mead ICBM base, a military installation, was located. Peace advocate A. J. Muste, then 75 years old, was one of the creators of the campaign and a prime participant as well. The purpose for initiating Omaha Action was described in a CNVA media release: "At the Omaha ICBM base—and wherever nuclear war preperations go on—great suffering and nameless torture are being prepared for countless men, women, and children in our own country and in other lands. We do not want to see our own people so afflicted. We do not believe we have the right . . . to afflict other people."

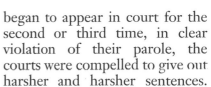

At Mead, protesters holding signs objecting to the missile race and to nuclear arms in general, held a week-long vigil. Authorities responded by imposing a media blackout and by influencing community leaders to refuse meeting rooms or speaking engagements for CNVA purposes. The CNVA was also prohibited from speaking with workers at Mead ICBM base or with other military and government personnel. Muste and his colleagues were forced to step up the confrontation and decided to take more direct action. Having alerted the media that the protesters were about to engage in a new tactic, townspeople, Legionnaires, and television crews gathered outside the gates of Mead. Muste and two others proceeded to climb the base's chain link fence. As soon as they dropped to the ground on the other side, authorities arrested the three trespassers. Initially, the demonstrators were given suspended sentences; however, as the fence climbing became a daily activity, and as protesters began to appear in court for the second or third time, in clear violation of their parole, the courts were compelled to give out harsher and harsher sentences. Ultimately, protesters in the Omaha Action found themselves serving six-month sentences for trepassing on government property.

Omaha Action received a great deal of press coverage in peace publications such as *Christian Century* (29 July 1959), *Mennonite* (11 August 1959), and *Visible Witness* (4 August 1959), as well as sporadic coverage in the local and national press. While the immediate effects of Omaha Action might have seemed minimal at best, it did serve to heighten awareness of the whole nuclear weapons issue. In addition, it was an opportunity for Muste to appeal to Soviet scientists to take similar steps. Writing to the president of the Soviet Academy of Sciences, Alexandr Nesmeyanov, Muste noted that the "Omaha Action is an example of a type of activity to which peace workers here often resort, namely an appeal to our own government to take unilateral action, to stop making H-bombs or missiles, whether or not the Soviet Union does the same. We wish that in your country some of your peace workers would similarly demand unilateral action on the part of your government."

See also Committee for Non-Violent Action; Muste, Abraham Johannes.

Reference Wittner, Lawrence S., *Rebels against War: The American Peace Movement 1941–1960* (1969).

Oxford Oath

The Oxford Oath was pledge taken by many antimilitarists and pacifists to refuse service in the armed forces or participation in wars. The Oxford Oath became popular in the 1920s, when the general disillusionment regarding World War I and its consequences was at its height. It was particularly popular among students on campuses across the country, and efforts by college administrators to prohibit students from becoming swearers to the oath were generally not well received. On one occasion, 3,500 students at the City College of New York booed the college president when he tried to prevent a reading of the Oxford Oath at a student rally. As the peace movement shifted its emphasis from pacifism to an emphasis on collective security in the immediate pre–World War II years, students systematically began to repudiate the Oxford Oath. Some former advocates of the oath, who subsequently served in the military, were persuaded by their own service experience and—perhaps more importantly—by their belief in the necessity of fighting nazism and fascism. "We all see things a little more clearly now," one former Oxford Oath–taker wrote in the pages of the *Saturday Evening Post*.

References Kahn, E. J., Jr., "A Soldier's Slant on Compulsory Military Training." *Saturday Evening Post* (19 May 1945); Wittner, Lawrence S., *Rebels against War: The American Peace Movement 1941–1960* (1969).

Page, Kirby (1890–1957)

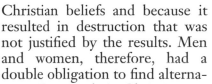

For three decades, from about 1920 to 1950, Kirby Page was the United States's leading pacifist publicist. An ordained minister of the Disciples of Christ, Page devoted his life to the quest for world peace.

Page was born in Fred, Texas. After graduating from Drake University in 1915, he did graduate work at the University of Chicago and Columbia University. His first and last parish, Ridgewood Heights Church of Christ, was located in Brooklyn, New York, but Page was there for less than three years when, in 1921, he accepted an offer from Sherwood Eddy, the head of the national YMCA, to become Eddy's private secretary and collaborator. Page also served as editor of *The World Tomorrow* from 1926 to 1934.

It was as an author and lecturer that Page was most able to influence the cause of pacifism and world peace. As a Drake University student, while he was preparing for the ministry, Page was greatly influenced by Walter Rauschenbusch and the idea of the social gospel. Originally intending to go into overseas mission work, Page was active in the YMCA and Student Volunteer Movement. While at the University of Chicago, he met Eddy, who he later agreed to work for as secretary and collaborator. When World War I began, Page accompanied Eddy to Europe with a group of student volunteers. Page helped provide services to German prisoners of war and used the opportunity to proselytize for pacifism. In Page's view, the ultimate goal was to abolish all war, but he recognized that in order to abolish war there had to be alternative solutions for settling disputes between nations. Page unequivocally believed that war was an unacceptable means of conflict resolution both because it was antithetical to Christian beliefs and because it resulted in destruction that was not justified by the results. Men and women, therefore, had a double obligation to find alternatives to war. It was their Christian responsibility and it was their civic duty. Page wrote a number of popular books on this theme, starting with *The Sword and the Cross*, which he wrote during the war. This was followed by *War* (1923), *The Abolition of War* (coauthored with Sherwood Eddy in 1924), *National Defense* (1931), and *Must We Go to War?* (1937).

Page's concerns with social ills, which had developed more fully while he served his Brooklyn parish, also steered him toward democratic socialism and drew him, along with many of his colleagues, to Norman Thomas. His dual mission of pressing for pacifism while grappling with social issues was a constant throughout his career. A cautious supporter of U.S. membership in the League of Nations, Page was nevertheless conflicted about the league, because it did not advocate abolishing war. With the rise of facism on the 1930s, Page became increasingly active in the peace movement. He wrote numerous books, articles, and pamphlets on the issue, and—because they were generally very inexpensive—his writings reached a wide readership. He was also influential in organizing and financing the Emergency Peace Campaign (EPC) in 1936 and 1937. The EPC's goals were to influence U.S. foreign policy makers to embrace international cooperation, strict neutrality, and mediation between European nations. Page's influence among peace movement activists in the 1920s and 1930s was significant. He continued writing and lecturing until he was unable to do either. His final writing dealt with the emerging Cold War, and his analysis of the political conflicts that were fueling it remained consistent with his earlier writings. Page died in La Habra, California, on 16 December 1957.

See also Eddy, George Sherwood.

References Josephson, Harold, ed., *Biographical Dictionary of Modern Peace Leaders* (1985); Wittner, Lawrence S., *Rebels against War: The American Peace Movement 1941–1960* (1969).

Paine, Robert Treat (1835–1910)

Robert Treat Paine, a descendent of Thomas Paine (*Common Sense*, 1776), and Robert Treat Paine, a signer of the Declaration of Independence and member of the first Continental Congress, was born in Boston, Massachusetts. After graduating from Harvard (1855) and attending Harvard Law School, Paine entered into a law practice in Boston in 1859. Judicious investments over the next 11 years made it possible for him to retire from law in 1870 and to devote his life to philanthropic and charitable works. Paine was particularly involved in helping to establish organizations that provided welfare for the needy and which employed a remarkably progressive philosophy that advocated both immediate help and ultimate independence for those who found themselves in dire straits. He also endowed the Robert Treat Paine Association, a private charity, and the Workingman's Building Association, whose goal it was to provide low-income housing for the working class. In addition to his charitable work, Paine was also an advocate of internationalism and of arbitration to ensure permanent peace.

Paine was president of the American Peace Society (APS) from 1891 until his death in 1910. He also was a member of the international arbitration conference at Lake Mohonk, New York, in 1895 and attended the annual conferences thereafter. Paine traveled to Washington, D.C., on several occasions in an effort to persuade President William McKinley and his secretary of state to negotiate an Anglo-American arbitration treaty. Paine remained active well into his 70s and made the opening address of the second Annual Peace Conference in Chicago in 1909. He died in Waltham, Massachusetts, on 11 August 1910.

References *The National Cyclopaedia of American Biography*, vol. 26; Patterson, David S., "An Interpretation of the American Peace Movement, 1898–1914." In *Peace Movements in America*, ed. Charles Chatfield (1973).

Parenting for Peace and Justice Network
See Institute for Peace and Justice.

Park, Alice Locke (1861–1961)

Alice Locke Park's life spanned both a century and a continent. She was born on 3 February 1861 in Boston, Massachusetts, and died on 17 October 1961 in Palo Alto, California. For most of her life, Park was active in a variety of reform and peace organizations, and she influenced the passage of several pieces of legislation on issues about which she cared deeply. These included the California Equal Child Guardianship Law, passed in 1913, and the California Bird and Arbor Day Law, passed in 1909.

Park was educated at the Rhode Island Normal School, from which she graduated in 1879 with a teaching certificate. She worked as a teacher, a lobbyist, a journalist, and a reformer. Through all of these pursuits ran her fundamental belief in the correctness of pacifism as an appropriate response to violence of any sort. Although her belief in pacifism long preceded her involvement in an organized peace movement, it was not until the Spanish-American War in 1898 that Park turned into a peace activist. Her convictions were forged by a dual heritage of Unitarianism and Quakerism along with experience in the women's suffrage movement that helped to inspire a belief in the power of organization to affect one's goals. Her major contributions to the peace movement came between 1898 and 1935, years spent traveling, speaking, writing, and organizing for peace.

As a delegate, spokesperson, and member of the Advisory Board for the

Women's Peace Society, Park traveled widely. She was also on the board of directors of the Women's International League for Peace and Freedom (WILPF). She represented both groups at international peace congresses in 1913 at The Hague; in 1924 in Washington, D.C.; in 1926 in Dublin, Ireland; in 1927 in Duisburg, Germany; and in 1927 in York, England. Park worked arduously to stave off U.S. entry into World War I. Her disappointment when the country did enter the war in 1917 was compounded by her disappointment in the Unitarian Church's refusal to oppose that step. Subsequently, she resigned from the church and turned to socialism.

Throughout the war, Park traveled about with her son, Carlton, speaking out on behalf of conscientious objectors (COs). Because she was not a wealthy woman, Park accepted subsidies from philanthropic patrons, most notably Mrs. J. Sargeant Cram of the Peace House in New York City. In addition, Park received support from several organizations. Her work as an international correspondent for the Federated Syndicate Press, a pro-labor press, enabled her to establish a sort of clearing house for pro-pacifist news stories, pamphlets, speeches, and articles at her Palo Alto home. She continued to mail out this material, as well as her own journalistic articles, to more than 550 newspaper and journal editors around the world, for nearly 70 years.

As with many of her endeavors, Park's work as a pacifist led to a variety of other reform issues as well. For example, her pacifism extended to all forms of violence, not just war. As a member of the American Humane Society, Park wrote a series of articles objecting to violence against children, specifically the practice of whipping school children to enforce behavior. Her most famous article written during the World War I era was one called "Disarm Christmas" (1914), in which she took to task the tradition of giving children weapons, both real and toy, as Christmas presents. Similarly, her

work with COs led to a concern for the rights of prisoners, prison reform, and, ultimately, to the organization of a state-wide network for prisoner relief in California. Although her advancing years sharply curtailed Park's activity by the late 1930s, she never stopped writing and distributing information regarding her various causes; she remained as active as her approaching 100 years allowed.

References *Alice Locke Park Papers*, Huntington Library, Pasadena, CA; Flexner, Eleanor, *Century of Struggle: The Women's Rights Movement in the United States* (1975); Josephson, Harold, ed., *Biographical Dictionary of Modern Peace Leaders* (1985).

Pauling, Linus (1901–1994)

Very few people make such outstanding contributions in their field to warrant a Nobel Prize. Linus Pauling won two Nobel Prizes in two completely different fields. Pauling, who was born in Portland, Oregon, was awarded the Nobel Prize for Chemistry in 1954 and the Nobel Peace Prize in 1962.

Pauling graduated from Oregon State College in 1922 and earned a Ph.D. in chemistry from the California Institute of Technology in 1925. In 1927, after completing two fellowships, he rejoined Caltech as a member of the faculty. Always interested in the theoretical aspects of chemistry, Pauling focused his research on atomic chemistry and quantum mechanics theory. He was instrumental in developing resonance theory, which was extremely useful in explaining the molecular structure of certain substances. In 1939 he wrote what was to become the classic in its field, *The Nature of the Chemical Bond and the Structure of Molecules and Crystals.*

With the approach of World War II, Pauling had no qualms about lending his extensive talents to military research and development. From 1942 to 1945 he worked for the National Defense Research Commission in the explosives division. He was also a consultant in medical research for the Office of Scientific Research and

Development and served on the Research Board for National Security. Because of his contributions to the war effort, President Harry S Truman awarded Pauling the Presidential Medal of Merit in 1948.

Pauling's primary focus at the time was still on research in chemistry. He and a colleague were awarded a $300,000 grant to investigate the effects of polio on human nerve cells. The grant allowed him to pull together years of research on molecular structure that resulted in a stunning breakthrough in 1951. Pauling and Robert Corey discovered the structure of several types of protein molecules, for the first time accurately defining the atomic structure of molecules. This knowledge-advancing discovery led to the Nobel Prize in Chemistry. One consequence of his research was that Pauling became acutely aware of the destructive effects of radiation on molucular structure. He, along with many other scientists, was shocked when he heard that atomic bombs had been dropped on Hiroshima and Nagasaki.

After World War II he became increasingly convinced of the tremendous potential for harm to the human race posed by nuclear weapons testing and development. He was a member of the militant Emergency Committee of Atomic Scientists (ECAS), whose membership included Albert Einstein, Leo Szilard, and Hans Bethe. Pauling became a staunch advocate of multilateral disarmament and an end to atmospheric nuclear testing. His book *No More War*, published in 1958, was a plea for disarmament. That same year, Pauling presented to the United Nations (U.N.) a petition signed by more than 11,000 scientists, which urged an immediate halt to nuclear testing. The Cold War notwithstanding, Pauling filed suit against the Defense Department and the Atomic Energy Commission (AEC) in an effort to obtain an injunction that would halt nuclear testing. The suit ultimately failed, but Pauling remained undaunted in his efforts to prevent nuclear catastrophe. In 1961 he spoke to the Soviet Union, via Radio Liberty, urging a halt to nuclear weapons production.

It is hardly surprising that Pauling endured attacks from Senator Joseph McCarthy, who accused the scientist of being a Communist. As late as 1960, Pauling was undergoing Senate investigation in an effort to coerce him into revealing names of persons who had assisted him in circulating his petition for nuclear disarmament. Moreover, he was one of the members of SANE (Committee for a Sane Nuclear Policy) who resigned from the organization when Senator Thomas Dodd's accusation that it contained Communists resulted in an attempted internal purge. What distressed Pauling and others was that SANE had just held an enormously successful rally at Madison Square Garden that had given rise to speculation that it could become a politically powerful instrument on behalf of peace. Rather than use the occasion of Dodd's attack on the organization to criticize nuclear policy, SANE leaders felt compelled to prove that it was not a Communist-front organization. Because of this, its effectiveness was mostly destroyed.

On 10 October 1963, the Nobel Prize Committee announced that Pauling had won the Nobel Peace Prize. He was the first person to have won two different Nobel Prizes. When asked to comment on which prize held more meaning for him, Pauling named the Peace Prize, "perhaps because I feel so strongly about the need for peace and an end to human suffering from war," he said.

Pauling resigned his chairmanship of the Caltech chemistry department in 1963 in order to accept a position with the Center for the Study of Democratic Institutions. In that position, he was better able to pursue his work on behalf of peace and nuclear disarmament. When the Vietnam War reached serious proportions in 1965, Pauling was one of those who lent his support to the antiwar movement, sponsoring a number of marches and speaking out against U.S. policy.

See also Bethe, Hans; Einstein, Albert; Emergency Committee of Atomic Scientists; Szilard, Leo.

References Current Biography (1964); Wittner, Lawrence S., *Rebels against War: The American Peace Movement 1941–1960* (1969); Zaroulis, Nancy, and Gerald Sullivan, *Who Spoke Up? American Protest against the War in Vietnam 1963–1975* (1984).

Peabody, George Foster (1852–1938)

George Foster Peabody, a successful businessman who believed in government ownership of the railroads and a single-tax system, was something of an anomoly. A Southerner, born before the Civil War, he donated much of his fortune to providing equal educational opportunities for African Americans. Peabody was also a pacifist, who had looked on as Union soldiers destroyed his hometown of Columbus, Georgia, during the Civil War. The war impoverished his family, forcing them to move north to Brooklyn, New York, in search of a new beginning. Peabody was educated in private schools until the age of 14. Thereafter, he was self-taught; he spent hours and hours in the Brooklyn YMCA library. A combination of intelligence, ambition, and the desire to succeed helped to ensure his future in business despite his lack of a formal education. Although he began his business career as an errand boy, he very quickly mastered the intricacies of Wall Street as an investment banker. By 1906 he had amassed enough of a fortune to retire and spend the remainder of his life engaged in public service and in philanthropic activities. He was also a well-known activist on behalf of pacifism and world peace.

Peabody's belief in pacifism, grounded as it was in his own experiences during the Civil War, was nurtured and refined by his public service experiences and his philanthropic endeavors. He believed firmly that the greedy aggression of nation states was responsible for promoting war, which, he argued, was not only inhuman but was also undemocratic. He publicly opposed the Spanish-American War as "wicked" and a "tawdry excuse for imperialistic greed."

Peabody attended the Eighth Annual Lake Mohonk International Peace Conference on Arbitration in 1902 and thereafter became a regular attendee. By 1905 he was donating significant sums of money to the American Peace Society in order to fund the publication of poetry and pamphlets paying tribute to pacifism. Peabody was also a staunch supporter of the Democratic party and of Democratic President Woodrow Wilson. In 1914, Wilson appointed Peabody as first deputy chairman of the New York Federal Reserve Bank; however, when Wilson authorized the U.S. Marines' attack on Vera Cruz, Mexico, in 1914, Peabody registered his opposition. He also opposed General John Pershing's foray into Mexico in 1915 in pursuit of Pancho Villa.

In January 1917, Peabody was elected chairman of the American Neutral Conference Committee, which supported Wilson's efforts to maintain neutrality regarding World War I. When Wilson asked for a declaration of war against Germany, Peabody was torn between his belief in pacifism and his support of Wilson. He ultimately decided that Wilson had little choice but to ask for war when faced with the resumption of German submarine warfare. Peabody withdrew his support from the Emergency Peace Federation, which he had helped to organize, believing that in a time of war, all citizens had to remain loyal to their nation. In the 1920s, Peabody endorsed the League of Nations. Like many of his colleagues in the peace movement, he was not hopeful at the results of the war, but he was hopeful that a League of Nations might encourage international cooperation. He died on 4 March 1938 in Warm Springs, Georgia.

See also Emergency Peace Federation.

References Josephson, Harold, ed., *Biographical Dictionary of Modern Peace Leaders* (1985); Ware, Louise, *George Foster Peabody: Banker, Philanthropist, Publicist* (1951).

Peace Churches
See Historic Peace Churches.

Peace Corps
For thousands of young Americans, the answer to President John F. Kennedy's challenge to "ask not what your country can do for you; ask what you can do for your country" was the Peace Corps. Kennedy established the Peace Corps program on 1 March 1961. From the start, the Peace Corps was given autonomy. Because much of the program's success has always depended on how it is perceived by developing nations, it was important that the Peace Corps remain independent. When they are abroad, volunteers are considered individuals—not an arm of U.S. foreign policy. The response of the nation's youth to the Peace Corps program demonstrated that idealism still flourished. As defined by the U.S. Congress, the Peace Corps has three goals: to help people in underdeveloped countries by supplying trained personnel; to generate among the people being served a better understanding of Americans; and to give Americans a better understanding of people of other cultures.

Kennedy appointed his brother-in-law, Sargent Shriver, to head up the Peace Corps project. Shriver and his aides developed the structure for selecting, training, and administering the Peace Corps, and within five months, by 1 September 1961, the first volunteers had begun work in their assigned countries. Although the majority of volunteers were college-age men and women, the Peace Corps attracted people of all ages. They volunteered for a two-year tour of duty, but it was not unusual for volunteers to extend their service time when the two years was up. At its most active, in 1966, the Peace Corps had more than 15,000 trained volunteers in the field, and since its inception, more than 100,000 volunteers have served in developing nations around the world.

Volunteers work on a variety of projects ranging from education to rural and urban development, health and nutrition, small business development, fish and game development, and animal husbandry. Host nations request volunteers to assist with specific proposed projects. Volunteers receive thorough training in the culture and language of their host country before they take to the field. The benefits generated by the Peace Corps for both the United States and for host countries that have been served by the volunteers is significant, although they are hard to measure. It is difficult to calculate the effect of paved roads and wells dug in thousands of rural communities. In many cases, the far more important benefit may be the cultural exchange. Americans, dedicated to helping people in underdeveloped countries improve their lives, often left these people with new impressions of America. At the same time, Peace Corps workers brought back with them a much better understanding of the people they had spent time working with.

Many former Peace Corps volunteers have gone on to government service in the State Department, Foreign Service, the Agency for International Development, and the U.S. Congress. Senator Paul Tsongas, a candidate for the Democratic party presidential nomination in 1992 and a former Peace Corps volunteer to Ethiopia, noted that "it produces a steady stream of people who understand the Third World." In offering his opinion about the value of the Peace Corps, Ambassador to Kenya William C. Harrop testified to the State Department that "there is no—I repeat no—U.S. overseas program that yields as much return for the taxpayer's dollar as the Peace Corps."

References Link, Arthur S., et al., eds., *The American People: A History* (1981); Meyer, Robert S., *Peace Organizations Past and Present* (1988).

Peace PAC
Beginning in 1962, the Council for a Livable World (CLW) acted, in part, as a PAC committee dedicated to electing

Peace Corps volunteers and local villagers sink a water well in the Bihar Region of India, 1967.

pro-peace candidates to the U.S. Senate. The CLW's successes prompted its governing board to establish Peace PAC for the Prevention of Nuclear War in 1982. Peace PAC was organized in order to elect pro-peace candidates to the House of Representatives. The CLW sufficiently funded Peace PAC so that all contributions could be applied directly to the support of peace candidates.

Peace PAC submits potential candidates to a selection analysis to ensure that funding will go to the candidates most likely to succeed. Party affiliation is not a criteria for selection, and recommendations are considered from both Peace PAC contributors and cooperating organizations. In order to receive Peace PAC funding, a candidate must be viable as either a challenger or an incumbent, and he or she must demonstrate an ability to mount a serious campaign. Peace PAC seeks out candidates who have demonstrated leadership on arms control and re-

sponsible military spending. Candidates must support measures leading to nuclear weapons freezes, a reduction in the number of weapons, and an end to the arms race. Candidates qualified to receive support are selected by the board of directors, which is made up of a broad spectrum of scientific and political experts.

Between 1982 and 1984 the number of people supporting Peace PAC legislative efforts grew from 6,000 to more than 15,000, and in January 1985, Peace PAC reported that four of its candidates had won their congressional seats. The successful candidates included Les Aucoin of Oregon, George Brown of California, Bruce Morrison of Connecticut, and Frances Farley of Utah. As a follow-up to their election efforts, Peace PAC provides legislators with information on upcoming votes and advice on weapons systems and military policy. A network of supporters stands ready to lobby individual congresspersons when the occasion arises, and a record of votes on legislation pertaining to nuclear arms is regularly distributed to supporters, peace groups, and the media. A Nuclear Arms Control Hotline is maintained and provides recommended grass-roots action to activists.

See also Council for a Livable World.

Reference Meyer, Robert S., *Peace Organizations Past and Present* (1988).

People to People International

People to People is a nonprofit voluntary organization made up of private citizens who want to advance international friendship in order to advance world peace. People to People operates outside of governments, establishing contacts between peoples of different countries. People to People's worldwide network of nearly 160 chapters is supported entirely by contributions and by the dues of its members.

When People to People was begun in 1956, it represented a different concept in pursuing world peace. President Dwight D. Eisenhower invited 35 business leaders to the White House on 11 September 1956 to urge them "to take advantage of the assumption that all people want peace, ... the problem is for people to get together and to leap governments, if necessary, to work out not one method, but thousands of methods by which people can gradually learn a little bit more about each other." The novelty of Eisenhower's challenge was that, although people had always been free to pursue foreign friendships, they had always done so without government urging. In this instance, the president of the United States was urging private citizens to reach out to other private citizens around the world. By the end of his term in office, Eisenhower came to realize that People to People would always remain under some shadow of suspicion as long as the government was administering the program. He requested that Joyce Hall, founder of the Hallmark Company and a longtime friend, take over the program. Hall took over, provided generous financial support, and oversaw People to People's growth from a relatively small local group to an international network.

People to People helps to sponsor individuals and groups traveling to other countries to meet their counterparts, and it brings visitors to the United States. Approximately 2,000 professionals (such as doctors, lawyers, and teachers) travel back and forth, participating in prearranged conferences, meetings, and briefings. People to People also arranges similar exchange programs for high school students. It conducts a classroom-to-classroom exchange, where special projects are prepared in one classroom and exchanged with students in a classroom in another country. It also maintains a pen pal program, a magazine exchange, and—on the community level—it arranges exchanges of people who are invited to private homes.

Reference Meyer, Robert S., Peace Organizations, Past and Present (1988).

People's Council on America
See Dennett, Mary Coffin Ware.

Phoenix

In 1954, Earle Reynolds, his wife Barbara, their children, and a guest from Hiroshima sailed their boat, the *Phoenix*, into Honolulu. The timing of their arrival was both coincidental and fortuitous for the Reynolds family and for members of the antinuclear movement. A short time prior to their arrival, U.S. federal authorities had arrested the crew of the vessel *Golden Rule*, after its repeated attempts to sail into designated nuclear test site waters in the Pacific. Intrigued by the notoriety attached to the *Golden Rule*, the Reynoldses attended the trial of its crew. Reynolds, an anthropologist formerly employed by the Atomic Energy Commission (AEC) in Japan as part of the team studying fallout from Hiroshima and Nagasaki, conducted his own investigation of the issues dealt with at the trial, including the issues of fallout and radiation hazards posed by nuclear testing in the atmosphere. The Reynoldses concluded that the crew of the *Golden Rule* were right to be concerned. They wrote to newspapers, the head of the AEC, and to President Dwight Eisenhower but received only polite responses. Eventually, the Reynoldses came to the conclusion that they had to act on their newfound convictions. On 1 July 1958, Reynolds radioed the Coast Guard that the *Phoenix* had entered the designated test site area. Responding quickly, the Coast Guard apprehended Reynolds's boat and arrested the crew.

Public response was equally swift on behalf of Reynolds family and provided some measure of the extent to which there was uneasiness about, if not outright opposition to, nuclear weapons development. Picket lines went up at Atomic Energy Offices across the United States as well as at other federal offices. While he was free on bail, Reynolds undertook a major speaking tour, covering 58 cities, and gave countless interviews for magazines and newspapers. So great was the uproar that an Atomic Energy official indicated on television that the government suspected a Communist plot behind the efforts to disrupt the atomic weapons testing. No evidence was presented to support such a theory. Reynolds was tried eventually and received a short prison sentence, but his protest gave the antinuclear movement a needed boost, coming as it did on the heels of the McCarthy Era, when dissent in general was viewed with a jaundiced eye.

See also Golden Rule.

Reference Wittner, Lawrence S., *Rebels against War: The American Peace Movement 1941–1960* (1969).

Physicians for Social Responsibility (PSR)

Physicians for Social Responsibility (PSR) was founded in 1961 by a group of U.S. physicians who were concerned about the potential negative impact on health caused by atmospheric nuclear weapons testing as well as by nuclear war itself. Unfortunately, the initial good intentions of PSR's founders were not sufficient to sustain the organization without strong, focused leadership. However, the organization has been credited with providing some of the impetus leading to the Nuclear Test Ban Treaty of 1963.

By 1978 the organization existed in name only. That year, Dr. Helen Caldicott, who had recently returned to the United States as a permanent resident from her native Australia, organized a meeting of PSR in her living room. The initial meeting consisted of 12 members. Caldicott was exactly the type of leader necessary to make PSR into an effective and thriving group. Caldicott, a pediatrician whose specialization was working with children who had cystic fibrosis, had long been committed to antinuclear activism. She ran an advertisement in the *New England Journal of Medicine* soliciting membership in PSR. Coincidentally, the most threatening U.S. nuclear accident occured at the same time, when the nuclear power plant at Three-Mile Island near Harrisburg, Pennsylvania, only a hundred miles from Philadelphia, sustained a near meltdown and had to be shut down. Membership in PSR increased immediately by 500. Over the next several years, membership continued to grow at the rate of about 250 new members per week. Working to reach both fellow physicians and the general public, PSR raised consciousness regarding the futility of the arms race. By 1981, PSR had persuaded the American Medical Association to pass a resolution calling on its member organizations to undertake a focused education program aimed at physicians and the public. Caldicott argued that the issue had to be a primary one for physicians because the Hippocratic Oath demands that "the life and well-being of all people on the planet are in our hands. This cause . . . is the ultimate form of preventive medicine."

By the late 1980s, almost 90 percent of all Americans agreed with PSR that there would be no winners in a nuclear war. Despite this recognition by the public, official policy throughout the 1980s remained committed to the biggest arms buildup in U.S. history. As a result, PSR issued a stern warning outlining the devastating effects that even a limited nuclear war would have on all mankind. The warning stated frankly that there was no possible effective medical response to a nuclear war, there was no civil defense against a nuclear war, recovery from such a war would be impossible, and there would be no winners in a nuclear war. The organization concluded that there could be no cure for nuclear war, only prevention.

The spokesperson for PSR continued to be Helen Caldicott, who also became its president. Ironically, as the organization grew in both size and influence, it also, of necessity, became more conservative, simply because its membership was much more diverse than that of the original small group. Caldicott's style of emotional involvement in her mission proved to be uncomfortable to a larger and larger proportion of the members. Internal criticism of her leadership style finally reached the point where Caldicott resigned as president in 1983 rather than try to change either her manner of expression or her beliefs. Today, PSR remains a national, nonprofit, nonpartisan organization with more than 30,000 members from a wide variety of medical specialties. It is primarily an educational forum for research on the effects of nuclear weapons and for the dissemination of information on the dangers posed by nuclear weapons and testing.

See also Caldicott, Helen.

References Current Biography (1983); DeBenedetti, Charles, ed., *Peace Heroes in Twentieth Century America* (1988); Meyer, Robert S., *Peace Organizations Past and Present* (1988).

Pickett, Clarence Evan (1884–1965)

From 1929 until his retirement in 1950, Clarence Pickett was the heart and soul of the American Friends Service Committee (AFSC). It was in large part due to Pickett's efforts that the AFSC, along with the Friends Service Council of London, was awarded the Nobel Peace Prize for its relief efforts in 1947.

Pickett was born in Cissna Park, Illinois. When he was two years old, the family moved to Glen Elder, Kansas, a Quaker community where Pickett was imbued with Quaker beliefs in community service and pacifism that he made a part of his life. He graduated from Penn College in Oscaloosa, Iowa, in 1910 and then went on to Hartford Theological Seminary. In 1913 he accepted a post as pastor of the Toronto Friends Meeting and remained there until 1917. He returned to Oscaloosa to become pastor of the Oscaloosa Friends Meeting, a position he held until 1919. While he was at Oscaloosa, Pickett counseled young men who sought conscientious objector (CO) status during World War I. His work with COs was not entirely approved of by everyone in Oscaloosa, and for a time Pickett had to endure vandals who painted yellow crosses on his house. From 1919 to 1922 he was secretary of the Young Friends Organization of America.

In 1922, Pickett went east to attend Harvard Divinity School. That year, he was also appointed professor of biblical literature at Earlham College in Richmond, Indiana, where he taught until 1929. At Earlham, Pickett taught one of the more popular classes in his department, a course called "Modern Social Problems in the Light of the Teachings of Jesus."

The AFSC invited him in 1929 to become its executive secretary, a post he held until 1950. In 1929 the AFSC had an annual budget of $100,000 and worked primarily on social service issues, race questions, and peace education projects. For the first several years of his tenure, Pickett and the AFSC were occupied with domestic concerns, including worker training, homestead subsistence projects, food and clothing relief, food projects for destitute miners in the Appalachian coal mines, and handicrafts teaching. President Franklin Delano Roosevelt appointed Pickett to head up a federal homesteading project in 1933 and 1934, and the AFSC developed its own homesteading project for 50 mining families from 1936 to 1939, called Penn-Craft. Pickett also served as chairman of the Emergency Peace Committee in 1931 and did some traveling in Europe on its behalf. As a consequence, he had an opportunity to see first-hand the growing refugee problem developing as a result of nazism.

Pickett had already begun to shift the AFSC's focus to international peace concerns. He served once again as chairman of the Emergency Peace Committee from 1936 to 1937. Over the next several years the AFSC was involved in food relief to both sides in the Spanish Civil War as well as in a work retraining program for Spanish refugees. It created an AFSC refugee relief center for Jews and others fleeing Nazi Europe during World War II. Relief efforts were restrained due to the war and the blocade of ships to Germany, but the AFSC was able to provide relief to Vichy France until 1942. When Quaker relief workers were detained there, the relief program was suspended.

During World War II, the AFSC, working with Mennonite and Brethren agencies, helped to provide alternative services for COs and got provisions for them into the 1940 Draft Act. The AFSC ran several CO camps for alternative service. It was also active in helping Japanese Americans interned in U.S. camps.

Immediately after the war, the AFSC had several hundred relief workers providing food and clothing in Europe and Asia. By this time its annual budget for foreign service had expanded to $7 million. The AFSC worked closely with the United Nations (U.N.) relief agencies, in some cases lending personnel and services to U.N. projects. Pickett was asked by the U.N. to take over as interim mayor of Jerusalem in 1948, when the British were leaving the Palestine mandate. He declined but continued to assist in relief work in the Gaza Strip.

Pickett retired from the AFSC in 1950, but it was only a partial retirement, for he remained quite active for several years. From 1950 to 1956 he was a member of the Quaker team at the U.N. Assembly. President Harry S Truman appointed him to his Commission on Immigration in 1952. In those years the pacifist movement had dwindled to what seemed like a few isolated pacifists. It made Pickett question whether they had "been mistaken in believing that a world without war is possible." Nevertheless, he continued to work toward that end. In 1957, Pickett, along with Norman Cousins, helped to organize SANE, the antinuclear organization. He was also chosen by President John F. Kennedy to serve on the Peace Corps Advisory Council, an appointment that did not deter him from picketing the White House to protest the arms race. Pickett always believed more in the efficacy of individual action than in mass action, and although he never refrained from organizing large-scale efforts, his own life was a testament to one person doing what he believed. On a trip to Boise, Idaho, Pickett died on 17 March 1965.

See also American Friends Service Committee; SANE.

References Jones, Mary Hoxie, *Swords into Ploughshares* (1937); Josephson, Harold, ed., *Biographical Dictionary of Modern Peace Leaders* (1985); Wittner, Lawrence S., *Rebels against War: The American Peace Movement 1941–1960* (1969).

Planetary Citizens

In 1972, noted peace activist Norman Cousins, former editor of the *Saturday Review*, and Dr. U Thant, former secretary-general of the United Nations (U.N.), organized Planetary Citizens. The purpose of the organization is to provide people with a global perspective on world affairs in the belief that such a perspective is necessary before true and enduring peace can be achieved.

Planetary Citizens advocates a stronger U.N. for the purpose of attaining human rights for all peoples, to end divisions separating people, and to end all wars among people. The president of Planetary Citizens, Donald Keys, helped to build the organization into one that registers hundreds of thousands of people, from more than 60 different countries, as citizens of the world. Planetary Citizens provides training, intern programs, information networks, public information, and a planetary passport—symbolic of a fundamental belief in a one-world concept of survival and peace. In the 1980s, Donald Keys called together experts on peace-making, military strategy, disarmament, and surveillance. Out of this meeting grew the Independent Commission on World Security, which was mandated to study two issues: problems created by mutual insecurity and the possibilities for mutual security. The commission's report advocated a three-tiered strategy for achieving world security. The first tier, characterized as transnational security, was necessary in a world not yet ready for true mutual security but capable of initiating policies that could lessen the threat of war. The second tier, an unarmed world, posited a situation where disarmament could take place in a mutually agreed upon fashion, assuming that effective global peacekeeping could be achieved. Finally, the third tier was a secure world, in which people everywhere could feel secure that their basic human rights were defined and guaranteed. The commission also suggested four key tasks that had to be addressed: transforming the arms system, building trust and openness, building a peace structure, and building a global community. The commission's report, entitled *Transition to World Security*, was released in 1987. At its release, Donald Keyes noted that "governments, but even more, people, need a vision and a goal. They need to see that peace is practicably realizable."

See also Cousins, Norman.

Reference Meyer, Robert S., *Peace Organizations Past and Present* (1988).

Port Huron Statement

In December 1961, Students for a Democratic Society (SDS) commissioned Tom Hayden to write a manifesto delineating the SDS's goals and defining the manner in which desired social changes could be made. In June 1962, Hayden met with several other SDS members at the Port Huron camp owned by the United Automobile Workers. The resulting document became known as the Port Huron Statement. It set two preeminent goals: to work to end the Cold War and to improve and increase democracy at home. The Port Huron Statement advocated a participatory democracy in which leadership would be decentralized and in which there would be an emphasis on rule by consensus.

See also Hayden, Tom.

Reference Zaroulis, Nancy, and Gerald Sullivan, *Who Spoke Up? American Protest against the War in Vietnam 1963–1975* (1984).

Power Treaties

In the 1920s several treaties were enacted that gave the illusion of a secure peace, but that lacked any effective measures to punish treaty violators. In effect, the treaties relied solely on good will at a time when suspicion and mistrust were still characteristic of many governments, despite the Treaty of Versailles that had officially ended World War I.

Efforts to secure a lasting world peace seemed to be moving ahead as never before. Even though the United States was not a member of the League of Nations, U.S. politicans and statesmen engaged in a series of international conferences throughout the decade, most of which were aimed at reducing arms and eliminating war as an acceptable method for settling conflicts. In reality, all of the treaties negotiated and signed during the decade rested on a foundation totally unsuitable for supporting the burden of peace. In the aftermath of World War I, Americans wanted nothing less than to be left alone, free of their age-old phobia of so-called entangling alliances.

George Washington, who warned the fledgling United States not to be drawn into European affairs, undoubtedly would have been flattered had he foreseen how seriously generations of Americans would heed his warning. Disillusioned by the consequences of war, Americans and their political representatives reverted to isolationism, refusing even to join the League of Nations. The farthest most people were willing to go was to draw the line at upholding the Monroe Doctrine and defending the Panama Canal Zone from interference. The country's resistence to accepting its new position in the world only made sense, however, if U.S. economic and political interests were not so far-flung. Both President Warren Harding and President Calvin Coolidge would have preferred to observe isolationism and refrain from any active participation in, or even acknowledgement of, world affairs. With U.S. industrial and economic institutions maintaining a presence around the world, however, no one could ignore what happened outside of U.S. borders. The solution, by majority consent, was to participate in world conferences in an effort to avoid war and to reduce arms—but with the strict understanding that the United States would not assume any obligation outside of the western hemisphere. Given this limitation, it is not surprising that some of the most stunning negotiations undertaken by U.S. statesmen in the early twentieth century should also have been some of the shallowest and least likely to be taken seriously.

The first series of treaties came about as a result of the Washington Conference. By 1921, the United States was on the brink of a naval race with both Great Britain and Japan. Japan had already become embittered toward the United States when the United States parked part of its large fleet in the Pacific in 1919. Jingoism on both sides fueled talk of war in both the U.S. and Japanese press. The last thing Americans wanted was another war, and very few were interested in engaging in a naval race. Senator William E. Borah proposed that the president invite both Great Britain and Japan to Washington to negotiate an end to arms escalation. There was sympathy in Great Britain for a similar conference, because the British were in no position economically to engage in a large spending program. In the end, Great Britain, Japan, France, and Italy, all designated as important naval powers, agreed to meet in Washington. In addition, China, the Netherlands, Belgium, and Portugal—all of which had interests in the Far East— also attended the conference. Negotiations resulted in five separate treaties:

1. The Five-Power Treaty. An agreement by the United States, Great Britain, Japan, France, and Italy to reduce their total naval tonnage according to a ratio arrived at by the negotiators, of roughly 5:3:3:1:1. The United States, Great Britain, and Japan also agreed not to further fortify existing possessions in the western Pacific.
2. The Four-Power Treaty. The United States, Japan, Britain, and France agreed to nullification of the Anglo-Japanese Alliance and further agreed to mutually respect Pacific possessions and to submit to joint conference any issue that could disrupt the peace.
3. The Nine-Power Treaty. Guaranteed the integrity of China and the preservation of the Open Door Policy.
4. The Shantung Province Treaty. China and Japan agreed that Shantung Province, taken by the Japanese from Germany during World War II, would revert back to China.
5. The Wartime Prohibition Treaty. The use of submarines to destroy international commerce was prohibited

during wartime, and the use of poison gas was outlawed.

When Harding presented the treaties to the Senate for ratification, the Senate did so rather quickly but with one major reservation. The Senate declared that the Four-Power Treaty did not obligate the United States to enter into any alliance nor did it obligate the nation to join in any mutual defense. As a consequence, the Washington Conference, the first successful disarmament conference in modern history, was largely ineffectual. The United States would cooperate whenever possible, but it would assume no obligation to enforce peace. Within 20 years of signing the various treaties, the only pledge that remained unbroken was the prohibition against the use of poison gas. The treaties did forestall war in the Pacific for another decade, however.

Throughout the 1920s, peace advocates continued to lobby for U.S. membership in the League of Nations. Secretary of States Charles Evans Hughes also commenced a campaign to get the United States into the Permanent Court of International Justice, also known as the World Court. Still unwilling to accept responsibility for helping to maintain the peace, U.S. isolationists in the Congress, led by Senator William Borah, managed to block Hughes's efforts. Insisting again that the United States would do everything it could to cooperate with the League of Nations and the World Court, the isolationists would not budge in their refusal to make any commitment whatsoever. The final abrogation of responsibility was evidenced in the Kellogg-Briand Treaty, which outlawed war as a viable means of settling conflict, except insofar as a signatory nation could take advantage of any of the several enormous loopholes that made the treaty virtually worthless. Like the earlier Washington Conference treaties, the Kellogg-Briand Treaty was destined to be broken sooner rather than later, and with barely a murmur from the document's well-meaning signers.

See also Kellogg-Briand Treaty.

References Link, Arthur S., et al., eds., *The American People: A History* (1981); Perkins, Dexter, *Charles Evans Hughes and American Democratic Statesmanship* (1953); Schlesinger, Arthur, Jr., *The Crises of the Old Order* (1957).

Presbyterian Peace Fellowship

During World War II, the Presbyterian Church, U.S.A. organized a Council of Presbyterian Conscientious Objectors in order to support and validate Presbyterian conscientious objectors. The council eventually changed its name to the Presbyterian Peace Fellowship. When the Presbyterian Church, U.S.A. joined with the Presbyterian Church United States, the Peace Fellowship, and the many peace efforts pursued by local congregations, became part of the Presbyterian Peacemaking Program.

See also Presbyterian Peacemaking Program.

Reference Meyer, Robert S., *Peace Organizations Past and Present* (1988).

Presbyterian Peacemaking Program

When the United Presbyterian Church, U.S.A., and the Presbyterian Church, United States agreed to merge in 1983 as the Presbyterian Church, U.S.A., the One Hundred Ninety-Fifth General Assembly urged all local congregations to integrate peacemaking efforts into the mission of the local churches. A "Commitment to Peacemaking" statement issued by the General Assembly outlined the multifocal program that the Presbyterian Church was advocating. Included in the program's goals were social, racial, and economic justice; support of human rights and economic justice in areas of concern around the world; an end to the arms race; reversal of nuclear stockpiling policies and militarism; and a reduction of tension among nations. In order to assist local churches in carrying out these peacemaking efforts, the Presbyterian Church made available a publication entitled *Peacemaking: the Believer's Calling*. It also published a series of pamphlets and brochures as well as a guide for implementing the Commitment to Peacemaking. One of the more helpful publications in this series, *Peacemaking Skills*, outlined progressively expanding peacemaking skills from Peacemaking in the Self to Peacemaking in the Community, and Peacemaking in the International Arena.

See also Presbyterian Peace Fellowship.

Reference Meyer, Robert S., *Peace Organizations Past and Present* (1988).

Promoting Enduring Peace (PEP)

Promoting Enduring Peace (PEP) grew from a simple idea pursued by a truly dedicated believer in peace and nonviolence. Dr. James Davis, a Quaker physician, believed that a grass-roots citizens' peace organization could fill a need in the peace community by providing information to ordinary citizens. His grass-roots movement began simply with Dr. Davis collecting appropriate articles and mailing them to people free of charge. Davis began his campaign for peace in 1952. By the time the United States became heavily involved in Vietnam, his grass-roots movement had grown to the extent that millions of pieces of literature were being sent out to classrooms, workshops, and other forums. The organization mails out articles on a quarterly basis, still free of charge, but accompanied by order forms for other pieces of literature that PEP publishes, including information on stopping the arms race, the nuclear weapons crisis, and increases in military spending. Among the recipients of PEP's annual Gandhi Peace Prize have been Eleanor Roosevelt, Norman Thomas, Linus Pauling, Dorothy Day, and Dr. Helen Caldicott. A variety of countries, including the former Soviet Union, have hosted PEP's international peace seminars. The organization works closely with other peace organizations, including the American Friends Service Committee (AFSC), the Women's International League for Peace and Freedom (WILPF), and Mobilization for Survival.

Reference Meyer, Robert S., *Peace Organizations Past and Present* (1988).

Psychologists for Social Responsibility (PSR)

In the early 1980s a number of professional groups sought to form associations of members of their profession for the purpose of opposing the arms race and the stockpiling of nuclear weapons. Psychologists for Social Responsibility (PSR), founded in 1982, was one of those associations. Intended as an instructive, educational organization, PSR outlined its goals and purpose in early publications. Members of PSR, committed to promoting peaceful solutions to world conflicts, would: combine high-exposure public forums with private, idea-development meetings; establish contact with psychologists internationally; use psychological principles to wage a campaign aimed at alerting the public to the dangers of nuclear war and the dangers of disbelieving or ignoring that danger; publish articles calling for a durable peace; encourage research on the issue and make their findings available to public and government figures; and maintain opposition to nuclear war. A five-year review of PSR's performance revealed to members that in almost every instance, the strategy defined in the early months of existence had been followed.

Reference Meyer, Robert S., *Peace Organizations Past and Present* (1988).

Pugwash Conferences

Among the many consequences of the Cold War intensification in the first decade after World War II ended, was a rending of the international scientific community, which was split along East-West lines according to political affiliations. Political and military leaders on both sides of the divide enjoyed a period of muscle flexing and saber rattling, at the foundation of which was the initiation of a massive weapons buildup and development, which took place without cautionary predictions and warnings from the scientific community. McCarthyism in the West and political repression in the East helped to mute otherwise vocal opponents of the arms race and the deployment of nuclear weapons. Nevertheless, the level of alarm building up among those most closely associated with nuclear weapons and the profound danger they posed for humankind, ensured that the scientific community would take the necessary risks to make their its known.

The first break in the silence came with the Einstein-Russell Appeal in July 1955. Once the appeal—signed by prominent members of the scientific community and issued to the "powerful governments" in the world, warning them of the grave dangers of nuclear proliferation and the daily increasing risk at which they were placing the human race in the name of nationalism—became public, scientists, philosophers, and Nobel laureates from around the world joined the demand for restraint. In July 1957 the first of a series of conferences, the Pugwash Conference of Scientists on World Affairs, was held in Pugwash, Nova Scotia. The meetings, known simply as the Pugwash Conferences, brought together scientists from East and West in an effort to bridge the gap that had been created and to rebuild an international scientific community that would once again act responsibly in helping to bring about peace and international cooperation.

Most of the Pugwash Conferences dealt with mundane technical problems that, although important to the success of the goals sought, seemed rather tame and dry to most observers. The first meeting in 1957, however, contained more than enough drama. For the first time in many years, scientists from East and West, previously forbidden contact with one another, were seated at the same table. An anecdote about an exchange between a Soviet and an American scientist at the first conference demonstrates the impasse that the scientific community had been in for the previous few years. "If this meeting had been held five years ago," the Soviet scientist observed, "Senator McCarthy would have accused you of being disloyal and you might have lost your job." The American to whom he spoke agreed but pointed out in return, "If it had been held four years ago, Stalin would have had you shot." The first Pugwash Conference and the series of events that surrounded it signaled the reassertion of the peace movement in the age of nuclear weapons.

See also Einstein-Russell Appeal.

References Pauling, Linus, *No More War!* (1958); Wittner, Lawrence S., *Rebels against War: The American Peace Movement 1941–1960* (1969).

Randolph, Asa Philip
(1889–1979)

A. Philip Randolph took the tenets of pacifism and applied them to his own pursuits: civil rights and ending segregation in the armed forces and in the workplace.

Randolph, a labor organizer and trade union leader, was born in Crescent City, Florida. His formal education consisted of sporadic studies at the City College of New York. When he became coeditor of *The Messenger* in 1917, Randolph's college education came to an end. Randolph opposed U.S. involvement in World War I. As a Socialist, he did not believe that engaging in or supporting a war to protect capitalism was in any way useful. He editorialized in the pages of *The Messenger*, characterizing the war as imperialistic and urging African Americans, as well as other Americans, to refrain from participating. He remained with *The Messenger* until 1928, while he became increasingly involved with trade unionism and organizing.

From 1925 to 1968, Randolph organized and served in a variety of offices for the Brotherhood of Sleeping Car Porters (BSCP), one of the few African-American unions. He continued working as a labor organizer and a trade unionist during the 1920s and the 1930s. Much of that time was spent in conflict with the Pullman Railroad Company, which fought against having to recognize the Brotherhood of Pullman Car Porters union. Most U.S. unions at the time had difficulty getting management to recognize them as legitimate bargaining agents for the employees of the company in question. Ultimately, Randolph succeeded in gaining recognition for the BSCP.

In 1936 he was chosen president of the National Negro Congress (NNC), a co-alition of African-American organizations intent on pursuing civil rights and economic opportunity. He remained NNC president until 1940. By then, his focus had become desegregation of the armed forces and race discrimination in companies that were awarded government contracts and in various government agencies. With World War II already underway in Europe and likely to engage the United States before long, Randolph organized a massive March on Washington (MOW) in 1941, urging thousands of African Americans to come to Washington, D.C., to participate. The purpose of the MOW was to persuade President Franklin D. Roosevelt to sign an executive order that would prohibit racial discrimination in the government and in any industry that might benefit from government defense contracts. Randolph emphasized that the MOW was a peaceful protest. Roosevelt recognized how damaging a massive protest could be and issued Executive Order 8802 on 25 June 1941. The order forbade discrimination in defense hiring on account of color. At the same time, Roosevelt established the Fair Employment Practices Committee (FEPC), which would act as watchdog committee investigating industries that were awarded government contracts and that practiced racial discrimination. The FEPC was the first federal agency established to protect the rights of African Americans since the Freedmen's Bureau. In 1943, Roosevelt gave the FEPC real teeth by assigning it the authority to enforce Executive Order 8802.

Randolph also supported conscientious objectors (COs) to the war and continued to advocate desegregation of the armed forces. In 1948, President Harry S Truman issued the executive order that ended segregation in the military. It was a victory for which Randolph could claim a great deal of credit.

Randolph's focus again shifted somewhat in the 1950s and 1960s. As the ranking African-American trade unionist, Randolph turned his attention to combating racism in the AFL–CIO. He did not always succeed in pursuading conservative craft unions to end racial discrimination, but he did convince labor leaders to support federal civil rights and other social welfare legislation.

Randolph's advancing years made it necessary for him to curtail his activity. Nevertheless, he—along with Martin Luther King, Jr.—was a prime organizer of the 1963 MOW. Consequently, Randolph helped to shape the civil rights movement of the 1960s and 1970s and to influence the course followed by civil rights activists. He and King shared a belief in Gandhian nonviolence, which the mainstream U.S. civil rights movement held as fundamental. Randolph spent his life finding ways to eliminate racial discrimination and to secure economic justice. Although he was not a nonviolence theoretician, he was one of its most ablest practitioners. Randolph died on 16 May 1979 at the age of 90 in New York City.

References Franklin, John Hope, and August Meier, eds., *Black Leaders of the Twentieth Century* (1982); Link, Arthur S., et al., eds., *The American People: A History* (1981); Josephson, Harold, ed., *Biographical Dictionary of Modern Peace Leaders* (1985).

Rankin, Jeannette Pickering (1880–1973)

Jeannette Rankin holds the distinction of being the only member of Congress to vote against the United States's entry into both World War I and World War II. She was born in Montana, the oldest of seven children. Her parents were ambitious for their children and urged them all to take advantage of the newly formed society of the frontier West. So encouraged, four of the Rankin daughters had professional careers. Jeannette Rankin graduated from

the University of Montana in 1902 and briefly pursued a career as a teacher. In 1908 she discovered the settlement house movement and moved east to enroll at the New York School of Philanthropy (now Columbia University School of Social Work). Her teachers included Louis D. Brandeis, Florence Kelley, and Booker T. Washington. Eager to apply social theory to practical situations, Rankin was soon convinced that institutional and social reform had to precede efforts to change individual lives.

She volunteered to work for women's suffrage in Washington state in 1910. When women in Washington won the vote that year, Rankin used her experience as a springboard and became field secretary of the National American Woman Suffrage Association (NAWSA). She organized in 15 states, including her home state of Montana. A women's suffrage referendum in Montana successfully passed in 1914. With the way now open for her, Rankin announced her candidacy for Congress on the Republican ticket. Promising to represent the special constituency of women and children, Rankin, in 1916, became the first woman elected to the U.S. Congress.

During her first week in office, in the spring of 1917, Woodrow Wilson asked Congress for a declaration of war. Rankin, a pacifist, did not make her decision lightly. She was besieged by women from the suffrage movement, including Carrie Chapman Catt, who urged her not to give women a bad name by voting against the war. Their fear was that women would be discredited as politicians and that the suffrage movement would be harmed. The only suffragist to counsel Rankin to vote her conscience was Alice Paul, the head of the militant Women's Party. Even her brother Wellington, who had been her campaign manager, urged her to support Wilson's request for a declaration of war. In the end, Rankin could not in good conscience vote for the declaration and she, along with 56 of her male colleagues, opposed the war.

Representative Jeannette Pickering Rankin of Montana

As her first term drew to a close, Rankin became persuaded that the unpopularity of her vote against war precluded reelection. In a surprising move, she announced her candidacy for the U.S. Senate. Even more surprisingly, she lost the Republican nomination by less than five percent of the total vote. Her pacifism had by then become the central focus of her life. During the 1920s she worked with Jane Addams and Florence Kelley in the Women's International League for Peace and Freedom (WILPF), serving on its executive board. She also lobbied for the Women's Peace Union and served as executive secretary for the National Council for the Prevention of War. Rankin moved to Georgia in 1924 because she believed the South was more receptive to peace issues, owing to the tragedies experienced by southerners during the Civil War. She founded the Georgia Peace Society in 1928, but in 1934 an American Legion branch in Athens, Georgia, accused Rankin of un-Americanism and claimed that the Peace Society was really a Communist front. Although the society continued to operate until the eve of World War II, funding eventually dried up, and Rankin was forced to close the society down.

With another world war looming, Rankin returned to Montana and again decided to run for a congressional seat, this time as a Republican peace candidate from the western district. An intense campaign followed, and once again Rankin became the "congresswoman from Montana." Ironically, she was soon faced with the issue of voting on a declaration of war. On 8 December 1941, again voting her conscience, Rankin became the lone member of Congress to vote against war. This time, the authorities had to protect her from an angry mob. Moreover, her vote sullied her reputation even among peace advocates. At the end of her term, Rankin retired to private life.

Between 1946 and 1971, Rankin traveled to India seven times in order to gather material for a book on peace. She discussed nonviolence with Gandhi and met with Prime Minister Nehru. On one trip she drove across India, stopping at every village to speak with the residents.

In 1968, Rankin once again became an activist on behalf of peace. She led a women's March on Washington (MOW) to protest the Vietnam War. Marching at the head of a group that called itself the Jeannette Rankin Brigade, Rankin had become a symbol for all of those who believed that women had a special stake in seeking peaceful solutions to conflicts. At the age of 88, Rankin once again considered running for Congress, but illness prevented her from doing so. She did continue to lobby for peace, and while on a speaking tour in California, on 18 May 1973, Jeannette Rankin died. Her polit-ical integrity and courage in maintaining her principles regardless of personal consequences had become an inspiration to a new generation of peace advocates.

See also Women's International League for Peace and Freedom.

References Giles, K. S., *Flight of the Dove* (1980); Josephson, Hannah, *Jeannette Rankin, First Lady in Congress: A Biography* (1974); Josephson, Harold, ed., *Biographical Dictionary of Modern Peace Leaders* (1985).

Reynolds, Barbara and Earle
See Phoenix.

Roosevelt, Anna Eleanor (1884–1962)

Eleanor Roosevelt learned very early in childhood that being born into a wealthy and socially prominent family provided no guarantees of personal happiness. At best, her immediate family was dysfunctional. Young Anna Eleanor never lived up to her mother's standard of beauty and charisma. Her father, Elliot Roosevelt, was a chronic alcoholic, who captured his daughter's allegiance and reverence but was incapable of providing her with the emotional support she needed. When she was seven, her parents divorced. A year later, her mother died, and in 1894 her father died. Thus, the future first lady was certainly in danger of living a life of unhappiness and unfulfillment.

It was her good fortune that Eleanor Roosevelt's grandmother, with whom she lived after her mother's death, sent her to the Allenwood School in England in 1895. At Allenwood she learned all of the important life lessons that helped to shape her character and her interests for the remainder of her life. Under the tutelage of the influential Marie Souvestre, she developed intellectually and socially. Allenwood, she later said, provided "the happiest years of my life . . . whatever I have become since had its seeds in those three years of contact with a liberal mind and a strong personality."

When she returned to the United States, she plunged into the social pur-

First Lady Eleanor Roosevelt gives her views on the U.N. Charter.

suits expected of the niece of President Theodore Roosevelt. At the same time, she began to take up the reform interests that would become so vital a part of her life. She joined the National Consumers League and did volunteer work for the Rivington Street Settlement House, which gave her an enduring understanding of and sympathy for the overwhelming difficulties with which the poor and the dispossessed face life. In 1905, Roosevelt married her cousin, Franklin Delano Roosevelt. For the next four decades, she became a mother, a political wife, and an activist for a variety of social causes, including civil rights and women's rights. In addition, from 1932 to 1945 she was first lady and fulfilled all the duties and responsibilities of that office. Moreover, Roosevelt changed the American public's perception of the first lady. She was not afraid to appear political, to advocate causes, or to make her opinion known. On issues like civil rights, she was far ahead of almost every other public official in the nation, including her husband. After her husband's death in 1945, she maintained a public profile. With World War II winding down, she was particularly interested in the then-developing United Nations (U.N.). President Harry S Truman appointed Roosevelt a member of the U.S. delegation to the U.N., and it was primarily through her efforts—lobbying other U.N. delegates, using her reputation and the force of her personality—that the U.N. Charter included a declaration of human rights accepted as inalienable by all civilized standards of mankind.

For the remainder of her life, world peace was a focus of Roosevelt's activities. In the intolerant postwar atmosphere, Roosevelt's liberal leanings often drew criticism from hard-line anti-Communists, who did not hesitate to label her "pink." In addition, although she consistently argued on behalf of world cooperation, she never agreed with her liberal colleagues who were willing to absolve the Soviet Union from any blame in the Cold War. She was one of the founders of Americans for Democratic Action (ADA), which advocated social activism at home and containment of communism abroad. At the same time, she was a foe of Senator Joseph McCarthy and used her newspaper column to condemn the witchhunts conducted during that era.

Eleanor Roosevelt remained an activist until her death. She constantly sought out and befriended young people involved in social activism. Her last official public office was serving as chairwoman of President John F. Kennedy's Commission on the Status of Women. When she died on 7 November 1962, the world lost one of the most illustrious women and one of the most influential reformers of the twentieth century.

See also Americans for Democratic Action.

References Lash, Joseph, *Eleanor: The Years Alone* (1972); Lash, Joseph, *Eleanor and Franklin* (1971); Roosevelt, Eleanor, *The Autobiography of Eleanor Roosevelt* (1958); Roosevelt, Eleanor, *This I Remember* (1949); Roosevelt, Eleanor, *This Is My Story* (1937).

Root, Elihu (1845–1937)

In a lifetime that spanned 92 years, Elihu Root distinguished himself in at least three distinct areas: as one of the ablest corporate lawyers in the nation, as a U.S. Senator and a Cabinet-level government

appointee, and as statesman who consistently strove to achieve world peace.

Root, who was born in Clinton, New York, graduated from Hamilton College in 1864 and, after teaching for one year at the Rome (New York) Academy, studied law at the University of the City of New York, graduating in 1867. For the next 30 years, Root devoted himself to his career as a corporate lawyer. He represented clients from the country's most prominent corporations and at various times was personal counsel to powerful people, including Jay Gould, Charles Dana, Thomas Fortune Ryan, and Chester A. Arthur.

On 1 August 1899, President William McKinley appointed Root secretary of war. In that capacity, he virtually redesigned the United States Army. As part of his program, Root established the Army War College in Washington, D.C., and created or reorganized special service schools, including schools at each base for army officers to receive elementary instruction in military theory and practice. As secretary of war, Root's greatest achievement was his creation of a Philippine policy for the United States. Root, in essence, wrote a document making it possible to create a republican form of government in the Philippines, with the added caveat that implementation of the plan had to conform in the fullest to the customs, habits, and even the prejudices of the native Filipinos.

In 1904, Root resigned as secretary of war, intent on resuming his private practice, but an urgent call from President Theodore Roosevelt brought him back into government, this time as secretary of state in 1905. Root's initial concern as secretary of state was primarily with Latin America. In words that would be echoed by Woodrow Wilson during World War I, Root declared that Americans, in their relations with Latin America, "wish for no victories but those of peace; for no territory except our own; for no sovereignty except sovreignty over ourselves." Root designed a general treaty of peace between Costa Rica, Guatemala, Honduras, Nicaragua, and El Salvador. He also helped to create the first formal international tribunal in the world by establishing the Central America Court of Justice. In 1907, Root directed the U.S. delegation to the second Hague convention to press for establishment of a permanent court of justice. Although the plan failed, after the conference Root began to work on securing agreements with individual countries that would adopt the principles of compulsary arbitration. Before he left the State Department, Root had enacted 21 agreements between the United States and reciprocating countries. Again contributing to the cause of international peace, Root signed a treaty with Canada in 1909 that created a permanent Canadian-American joint high commission for the settlement of future controversies.

On 27 January 1909, Root resigned as secretary of state after his election as senator from New York. As a senator, Root championed enforcement of the Hay-Pauncefote Treaty when Congress passed legislation giving the United States favorable shipping rates through the Panama Canal. Favorable rates were a violation of the Hay-Pauncefote Treaty, and in Root's view, such an abrogation would prove to the world that the United States was "false to all the principles that we have asserted to the world." Root became a staunch ally of Woodrow Wilson over this issue.

In 1910, Root became a member of The Hague Permanent Court of Arbitration. He chose not to run for reelection and retired from the Senate in 1915. As the United States entered the war, Root exhorted his Republican brethren to support Woodrow Wilson, and Wilson appointed Root as his personal emissary to Russia in 1917. When the Senate was considering the Treaty of Versailles, Root wrote three of the reservations to the treaty that ultimately doomed both the treaty and U.S. participation in the League of Nations. When Wilson rejected the reservations, Root threw his support to Warren G. Harding for president, because Harding favored an "association of nations." In 1920, Root accepted an invitation from the League of Nations to serve on a panel of jurists charged with creating a Permanent Court of International Justice. Root was generally considered the prime architect of the court, which was established at The Hague in 1921. For the remainder of his life, Root fought to gain accession to the Permanent Court of International Justice for the United States. When he was again invited to sit on a panel to redesign the court, in 1928, in view of its first years of experience, Root came up with the Root Formula, which would have allowed U.S. accession to the court without jeopardizing U.S. interests. The plan was endorsed by the League of Nations and by the Hoover administration, but the Senate chose to postpone its consideration indefinitely.

Elihu Root received numerous awards in recognition of his monumental commitment to world peace, including the Woodrow Wilson Foundation Medal for his part in establishing the Permanent Court of International Justice. The greatest recognition of his commitment, however, came in 1912, when the Nobel Peace Prize Committee awarded him the Nobel Peace Prize for his service in the cause of international peace. Root was an activist on behalf of a variety of causes for his entire life. He was president of the Carnegie Endowment for International Peace for 15 years (1910–1925), and a longtime supporter of philanthropic and civic causes as well. In 1924, he was chosen as chairman of a peace prize contest initiated by Edward Bok, which solicited ideas for preventing future wars between the United States and other countries. Although he was never a gifted orator, Root, by all accounts, possessed a brilliant analytic mind and an ability to solve even the most complex problem. He died in New York City on 7 February 1937.

References *National Cyclopaedia of American Biography*, vol. 26 (1967); Patterson, David S., "An Interpretation of the American Peace Movement, 1898–1914." In *Peace Movements in America*, ed. Charles Chatfield (1973).

SALT Talks
See Strategic Arms Limitation Talks.

San Francisco to Moscow Walk
The San Francisco to Moscow Walk, a major campaign of the Committee for Non-Violent Action (CNVA) in December 1960, marked the first departure from CNVA's previous concentration on opposing nuclear weapons to a focus that included lobbying for unilateral disarmament. Eleven radical pacifist members of CNVA left San Francisco in December 1960 on the start of a 6,000-mile walk. The route covered the United States, from the West Coast to the East Coast, and then resumed in Europe. A series of rallies accompanied the marchers as they proceeded across the United States. After going through England, France, West Germany, and East Germany, the marchers arrived at Moscow on 31 October 1961.

As each team of marchers arrived at a destination point along the way, it was replaced by another team, which then resumed the march. Most of those who arrived in Moscow had hiked for over 1,000 miles. As the march continued, publicity surrounding it grew. Consequently, local residents often joined the marchers to demonstrate their support for the official team. In this way, literally thousands of people participated in the march. Although the march did not accomplish the goal of unilateral disarmament, it did draw attention to the issue, increased CNVA enrollment, and emphasized the importance of civil liberties in general and free speech in particular. The CNVA was lauded in many quarters for carrying the issue of disarmament not only to the U.S. government, which many peace organizations had done in the past, but in taking the message to Moscow as well. The fact that there was more than one culprit in the arms race was not often acknowledged by those seeking disarmament.

See also Committee for Non-Violent Action.
Reference Wank, Solomon, ed., *Doves and Diplomats: Foreign Offices and Peace Movements in Europe and America in the Twentieth Century* (1978).

SANE/FREEZE
Formally organized as the National Committee for a Sane Nuclear Policy, SANE was founded in 1957 by Norman Cousins, Linus Pauling, Homer Jack, and Clarence Pickett. SANE was a response to public concern about nuclear weapons testing in Nevada and concern that such tests were harmful to the earth's atmosphere as well as to people. The organization garnered national attention when it ran a political advertisement in the *New York Times* on 15 November 1957 calling for a end to the nuclear arms buildup and the Cold War. The response was overwhelming, and by the summer of 1958, 130 chapters of SANE had been established nationwide.

The creation of SANE was the first foray in a battle for an end to above-ground nuclear weapons testing. Ultimately, SANE's efforts, along with those of other organizations, resulted in the Limited Test Ban Treaty of 1967. Operating in an era still jittery, despite the demise and condemnation of McCarthyism, SANE exercised an exclusionary policy regarding membership and activities. Initially, SANE did not approve of direct-action civil disobedience advocated by groups like the Committee for Non-Violent Action (CNVA), nor would it accept as members anyone who was affiliated with either the Communist or Socialist parties. With the escalation of fighting in Vietnam and the escalation in the arms race, SANE became less exclusionary regarding the types of activities it pursued. It was one of the first groups to oppose U.S. presence in Vietnam and the Vietnam War. It also continued its opposition to nuclear weapons. Leading a citizen's campaign against the building of antiballistic missiles (ABMs), SANE again experienced success, as both superpowers backed off from planned ABM expansion. When the Reagan administration proposed mobile deployment of MX missiles in the early 1980s, SANE played a leading role in blocking that effort. SANE had over 150,000 members and was, therefore, the largest single organization dedicated to reversing the arms race and opposing nuclear weapons development. SANE actively campaigned for political candidates who opposed nuclear weapons and the arms buildup.

In 1987, SANE merged with another antinuclear organization with which it had worked closely over the years, the Nuclear Weapons Freeze Campaign, adding Freeze's 1,800 nationwide chapters to SANE's membership. Renamed SANE/FREEZE, it became the largest peace group in U.S. history. The first president of SANE/FREEZE was the Rev. William Sloan Coffin, Jr., the former Yale chaplain whose antiwar activities brought him to public attention during the Vietnam War. SANE/FREEZE publishes a quarterly magazine, *SANE World/FREEZE Focus*, which keeps its members and chapters abreast of all current activities.

See also Coffin, William Sloan; Cousins, Norman; Nuclear Freeze Campaign; Pauling, Linus; Pickett, Clarence.

Reference Zaroulis, Nancy, and Gerald Sullivan, *Who Spoke Up? American Protest against the War in Vietnam 1963–1975* (1984).

Sayre, John Nevin (1884–1977)

For much of his life, John Nevin Sayre was a moving force in the Fellowship of Reconciliation (FOR), the organization of which he was a charter member. Sayre was born in South Bethlehem, Pennsylvania.

He graduated with a B.A. from Princeton University in 1907 and then went on to Episcopal Theological Seminary, Union Theological Seminary, and the University of Marburg, Germany. While he was at Union Theological Seminary, Sayre was influenced by some of his teachers who preached pacifism, including Henry Sloan Coffin, George William Knox, and George Coe. His own reading of the gospels also led him to the conclusion that pacifism was a logical response to conflict. So strongly did he believe in this that not even family ties or personal friendships could make him refrain from speaking out against violence and wars when he thought that his support of pacifism was appropriate.

His brother, Francis Sayre, was the son-in-law of President Woodrow Wilson, yet when Secretary of State William Jennings Bryan resigned from the administration, John Sayre felt compelled to publicly support Bryan and to oppose Wilson's policies regarding the war in Europe and U.S. preparedness. Sayre, at that point, was an instructor at Princeton University, a post he had resumed in 1914 after spending a year at Boone University in Wuchang, China. In 1915 he took a position as minister of Christ Church in Suffern, New York, and in 1919 he resumed teaching, this time at the Brookwood School in Katonah, New York.

In 1919, Sayre became the executive secretary of the FOR, a position he held intermittently over the next two and a half decades. He also served as chairman of the U.S. FOR from 1935 to 1938 and as chairman of the international FOR until 1955. Indeed, it was through Sayre's efforts that the International FOR, which operated as the missionary branch and foreign office, was created. Sayre was also responsible for creating the FOR branch in India, for strengthening the branch in South America, and for reviving the branch in Japan following World War II.

By many accounts, there were few pacifists more active than John Sayre in the 1920s and 1930s. He traveled to Nicaragua under the most primitive conditions to promote peace negotiations with the United States; he founded the Committee on Militarism in Education, which opposed compulsory military training in schools and which was a spearhead organization of the American Civil Liberties Union (ACLU); and he raised serious questions about the efficacy of the Washington and London disarmament conferences in 1922 and 1930. Sayre was also one of the few pacifists who objected to imposing a boycott on Japan, predicting in 1937 that such action would be a sure precursor to war with Japan. In 1938, he was one of the organizers of the World Economic Cooperation Conference, which attempted to reorder economic relationships between nations. Sayre also led a delegation that called on President Franklin D. Roosevelt to ask for an intergovernmental peace conference.

In addition to his other commitments, Sayre was president of the National Peace Conference (NPC) from 1935 to 1938, an organization of nearly 40 different nongovernmental groups, whose purpose was to promote peaceful solutions to conflict. In 1936 he became one of the staunchest members of the Emergency Peace Campaign (EPC), which established a No-Foreign-War policy that advocated strict neutrality, lower tariffs, and an international peacekeeping body. Just as he had opposed boycotting Japan, Sayre also opposed a boycott of German goods, arguing that such a stand would only provoke more tension. Neither Japan's attack on Pearl Harbor nor Hitler's atrocities in Europe caused Sayre to pull back from his pacifist beliefs. Indeed, in the case of Japan, Sayre believed that the United States was partially responsible for forcing Japan into a corner. In any case, he continued to support conscientious objectors (COs) throughout the war and defended pacifism. As a consequence, the FOR was stronger in terms of its membership, its resources, and its prestige in 1945 than it had been in 1939. Although the increased status may have

reflected a sharpened effort to protect the rights of dissenters rather than indicating an increase in the incidence of pacifism in the population, it nevertheless allowed the FOR to engage in campaigns around the world on behalf of both pacifism and economic justice. Well into his sixties, Sayre continue to travel, promoting the FOR and his own fundamental belief in pacifism. Despite earth-shattering events, which caused concern that war would always remain an option of foreign policy, Sayre never allowed himself to become discouraged. He died on 14 September 1977 in South Nyack, New York.

See also Fellowship of Reconciliation.

References Josephson, Harold, ed., *Biographical Dictionary of Modern Peace Leaders* (1985); Knock, Thomas J., *To End All Wars: Woodrow Wilson and the Quest for World Order* (1992); *New York Times* (15 September 1977); Wittner, Lawrence S., *Rebels against War: The American Peace Movement 1941–1960* (1969).

Schwimmer, Rosika (1877–1948)

Described as a tireless optimist who had quick intelligence, persuasiveness, and warmth, Rosika Schwimmer, perhaps more than any other individual, gave focus to the peace movement in the United States and Europe in the early twentieth century. Schwimmer was born in Budapest, Hungary, and spent her early adult years organizing female white-collar workers in Hungary after she had to delay a career as a journalist because of her father's death. She wrote political articles for newspapers in Germany and Hungary, where she gained a reputation as a women's rights advocate. Meeting U.S. suffragist Carrie Chapman Catt in 1904 inspired Schwimmer to work for women's suffrage in Hungary. She also continued to travel throughout Europe, lecturing on a variety of topics, including suffrage, child welfare, and marriage.

With the outbreak of World War I, Schwimmer drafted an appeal to neutral nations for continuous mediation designed to end the conflict. When Schwimmer came to the United States to appeal to

Woodrow Wilson, he refused to commit to a course of mediation. Thereafter, Schwimmer toured the country, speaking out on behalf of peace. Her advocacy sparked Jane Addams, and together they founded the Women's Peace Party (WPP). Schwimmer and Addams attended The Hague Congress of Women in 1915, and after adopting Schwimmer's proposal to sound out world leaders on a plan for neutral mediation, they organized delegations to meet with government officials in both the belligerent and neutral nations. Their conclusion was that world leaders would indeed welcome neutral mediation.

With Wilson's refusal to create a conference of neutrals, Schwimmer decided to create an unofficial one. It was she who persuaded Henry Ford to fund a private peace conference. Ford chartered a ship, called it the Ford Peace Ship, and accompanied a delegation to Stockholm for the Ford Neutral Conference on 8 February 1916. The failure of the Ford mission created dissension in the ranks of peace movement leaders.

When Hungary declared itself a republic in October 1918, Schwimmer was appointed minister to Switzerland, the first woman to hold a high diplomatic rank in modern times. A series of coups in Hungary, beginning in 1919, placed Schwimmer's life in danger because of her political views. With her personal safety in jeopardy, Schwimmer was forced to emigrate to the United States in 1921. In the "Red scare" environment in the United States following the end of the war, Schwimmer was accused of being a German spy or a Bolshevik agent. American Jews blamed her for Henry Ford's anti-Semitic campaign, arguing that she had somehow swindled Ford with the peace ship idea. Her plans to earn a living writing and lecturing foundered because of the criticism, but friends and family continued to support her. When she applied for citizenship in 1928, her application was denied on the grounds that, as a pacifist, she would refuse to bear arms in the country's defense. It was a ludicrous

ruling; nevertheless, it was upheld by the Supreme Court in 1929. The two dissenting justices in that decision, Oliver Wendell Holmes and Louis D. Brandeis, characterized Schwimmer as a "woman of superior character and intelligence, obviously more than ordinarily desirable as a citizen." Public support had turned in her favor once again, but Schwimmer refused to reapply for citizenship even after the Supreme Court reversed itself on the issue in 1946. Undaunted, she remained in the United States as a resident alien and continued to work for peace. She proposed various ideas to promote peace, including world citizenship, and a world constitutional convention. For the last ten years of her life, Schwimmer concentrated on a Campaign for World Government (CWG), which she began in 1937 with Lola Maverick Lloyd.

In 1948, Rosika Schwimmer was nominated for the Nobel Peace Prize. She died, however, on 3 August 1948, before the Nobel Peace Prize Committee chose its recipient. The committee announced that no suitable "living candidate" had been found, and the Peace Prize was not awarded that year.

See also Women's Peace Party.

References James, Edward T., et al., eds., *Notable American Women, 1607–1950: A Biographical Dictionary* (1971); *New York Times* (4 August 1948).

Scott, James Brown (1866–1943)

James Brown Scott was born in Ontario, Canada. A noted lawyer and educator, Scott earned a B.A. and an M.A. from Harvard University (1890, 1891). He remained at Harvard as a Parker Fellow, studying international law, and in 1894 he attended the universities of Berlin, Paris, and Heidelberg. The University of Heidelberg awarded him his law degree in 1894. Returning to the United States, Scott went to Los Angeles to practice law. In 1896 he organized a school of law and served as its dean for three years; the school would later became the law department of the University of Southern California. Scott literally worked his way back to the East Coast—as dean of the law school of the University of Illinois (1899–1903), as professor of law at Columbia University (1903–1905), and as professor of international law at George Washington University (1905–1907).

Scott's reputation brought him to the attention of Theodore Roosevelt, and Scott entered government service in 1906. Roosevelt sent him to The Hague Peace Conference in 1907. As a special advisor in the State Department, Scott served as a member of the State and Neutrality Board from 1914 to 1917. In 1910 he accepted an invitation from the Carnegie Endowment for International Peace to serve as director of the international law division. Scott believed in the necessity of establishing a world court to settle international disputes and worked toward that end. Six months before the outbreak of war in Europe, Scott, with the approval of Secretary of State Elihu Root, sought to establish an international tribunal consisting of the United States, Germany, Austria-Hungary, France, Great Britain, Italy, Japan, Russia, and the Netherlands. The coalition would have served as an arbitration tribunal to which all nations could turn to resolve disputes. Fighting began before any action could be taken.

With international law apparently in ruin because of the war, a major postwar task involved reinstituting the principles, rules of procedure, precedents, and the formulas that applied in particular ethnic and cultural circumstances. Under Scott's direction, the Carnegie Endowment published the results of gathering together these former principles, in a series of volumes, including *A Survey of International Relations between the United States and Germany, August 1, 1914–April 6, 1917* (1918); *The Armed Neutralities of 1780 and 1800* (1918); *The Treaties of 1785, 1799, and 1828 between the United States and Prussia* (1918); *James Madison's Notes on Debates in the Federal Convention of 1787 and Their Relation to a More Perfect Society of Nations* (1918); and *President Wilson's Foreign Policy* (1918).

James Brown Scott

Scott also wrote numerous volumes on international law, including *Peace through Justice* in 1917. He was an advisor to the U.S. delegation at the Paris Peace Talks in 1919 and at the Washington Arms Limitation Conference held 1921–1922. He was also a member of the international committee of jurists established by the League of Nations' Council in 1924.

References National Cyclopaedia of American Biography, vol. C (1967); Patterson, David S., "An Interpretation of the American Peace Movement, 1898–1914." In *Peace Movements in America*, ed. Charles Chatfield (1973).

Scudder, Vida (1861–1954)

At the age of 23, Vida Scudder, while doing postgraduate work at Oxford University, attended the very last lecture delivered by John Ruskin. It left her, for the first time, with a self-awareness of the tremendous privilege she enjoyed as a member of a wealthy family. This new awareness filled her with a social radicalism from which there was no turning back. Scudder was born in Madura, India.

When her father, a missionary, drowned the following year, Vida and her mother returned to the family home in Auburndale, Massachusetts. Her extended family of grandparents, aunts, and uncles provided Scudder with an idyllic childhood filled with travel and intellectual stimulation. Perhaps because of her father's tragic death, Scudder did not separate from her mother until 1920, when her mother died, except for one brief interlude. In 1880, Scudder enrolled at Smith College. After returning from her Oxford studies in 1885, Scudder acccepted a teaching position at Wellesley College.

In 1887, still concerned that she was not adequately fulfilling the responsibilities that she now perceived went hand-in-hand with her privilege, Scudder began making plans for a settlement house, the foundation for what would become the College Settlement Association. In 1889 the first settlement house was opened on Rivington Street in New York City. Three years later, Dennison House in Boston's South End opened.

One consequence of Scudder's work in the settlement houses was an interest in the plight of working women. Scudder and her close associate, Helena Dudley, involved themselves in that issue to the point that they were both elected to the Boston Central Labor Union as delegates. Scudder's frenzied pace of teaching, working in the settlement houses and raising funds to keep them going, and dealing with the conflicts between the Wellesley administration and her radical politics took a toll on her health; in 1901 she was forced to stop all activity for two years. Even then, Scudder could not totally disengage herself from her work. When she returned to Boston, after taking off two years to travel in Europe, she returned with new ideas for assisting immigrants and for furthering the cause of working women. She also helped to organize the Women's Trade Union League.

An ongoing concern for Scudder was reconciling her Christianity with her so-cialism. In 1911 she founded the Episcopal Church Socialist League, the goal of which was to apply Christian principles to social problems. As a result of her Socialist connections, Scudder was asked to speak at the 1912 Lawrence, Massachusetts, textile strike. Once again, she found herself at odds with Wellesley College. She was asked to suspend the course she taught at Wellesley that had brought her acclaim, "Social Ideals in English Literature."

When World War I began, Scudder supported President Woodrow Wilson's course of action. By the early 1920s, however, she had moved toward pacifism, and she joined the Fellowship of Reconciliation (FOR) in 1923. That summer, she delivered a series of lectures in Prague on peace and pacifism that were sponsored by the Women's International League for Peace and Freedom (WILPF). By the mid-1930s, Scudder's pacifism was firm; she did not waver from absolute pacifism.

After her retirement from Wellesley in 1928, she devoted her life to writing, particularly on the subject of Christianity and social problems, and to the causes she had supported over her lifetime. An intensely spiritual person, Scudder was able to integrate her activism and her spirituality quite effectively. She maintained a home with a former student and intimate friend, Florence Converse, an editor at the *Atlantic Monthly*, for many years. Scudder wrote prolifically, producing 16 volumes ranging from works on English literature to Christian ethics. She died suddenly on 9 October 1954 in Wellesley, Massachusetts.

References Garrity, John, ed., *Dictionary of American Biography*, supp. 5 (1980); Sicherman, Barbara, et al., eds., *Notable American Women, The Modern Period: A Biographical Dictionary* (1980).

Self-Immolation

During the Vietnam War, eight Americans resorted to self-immolation as an extreme form of protest. Following the example of Buddhist monks in Vietnam, these antiwar protesters literally burned themselves alive.

In March 1965, Alice Herz—a German-born, naturalized U.S. citizen, who had fled the Nazis in the 1930s—left a note explaining her actions. The 82-year-old Quaker, who had spent years working for peace as a member of the International League for Peace and Freedom and the Women Strike for Peace (WSP), said, "I did it to protest the arms race all over the world. I wanted to burn myself like the monks in Vietnam did." Several months later, in November 1965, another Quaker, Norman R. Morrison, took the same extreme step in front of the Pentagon. Roger La Platt, a 21-year-old student and former Trappist seminarian, left a message saying, "I am a Catholic Worker. I'm against war, all wars. I did this as a religious act." The other five Americans who performed self-immolation were Hiroko Hayashi, a 36-year-old old Japanese-American Buddhist from San Diego (12 October, 1967); Florence Beaumont, 55, a housewife from La Puente, California (15 October, 1967); Erik Thoen, 27, a student of Zen Buddhism from Sunnyvale, California (4 December, 1967); Ronald W. Brazee, 16, a high school student from Auburn, New York (19 March 1967); and George Winne, 23, a San Diego State University student (12 May, 1970).

Most Americans were horrified and stunned by these actions and could not comprehend them. Herz and Morrison were accorded hero status in North Vietnam. Their likenesses appeared on postage stamps and billboards, and the North Vietnam Women's Union predicted that their deaths heralded "an even greater and irresistable storm among the American people."

Reference Zaroulis, Nancy, and Gerald Sullivan, *Who Spoke Up? American Protest against the War in Vietnam 1963–1975* (1984).

Sewall, May Wright (1844–1920)

Born in Milwaukee, Wisconsin, May Wright Sewall graduated from North-western University in 1866. Two years later she earned her M.A. from Northwestern. Sewall spent her early career as a teacher and an administrator. She and her husband opened a school for girls that focused on training its students in the classics in order to prepare them for college. After her husband died in 1895, Sewall continued running the school on her own. In addition to her dual responsibility as teacher and administrator, Sewall found time to participate actively in a broad range of reform activities. She has been credited with helping to establish more important organizations than any other woman in the United States, including the National Woman Suffrage Association, the National Council of Women, the International Council of Women, the World's Congress of Representative Women, the General Federation of Women's Clubs, and the American Association of University Women. Most of her interests revolved around the support and promotion of women's rights, including suffrage. She also had an abiding interest in establishing a permanent peace and believed heartily in the idea of international arbitration as a means of settling disputes.

Sewall's inclusion in the inner circles of almost every important women's organization of her era gave her a cachet that she easily transferred to her work for peace. At various times she served as chairwoman of the International Council of the Committee on Peace and Arbitration, as delegate to numerous national and international peace conferences, as organizer and president of the International Conference of Women Workers for International Peace, and as organizer of the International Conference of Women Workers for Permanent Peace at the 1915 San Francisco World's Fair. Sewall was a persuasive speaker and addressed committees of both the Indiana state legislature and the U.S. Senate. For years, she was a regular contributor to the Indianapolis *Times* and an occasional contributor to several national newspapers. As an author, she wrote the chapter on

May Wright Sewall

Indiana for *The History of Woman's Suffrage*. She also wrote a volume entitled *Women, World War, and Permanent Peace* in 1915. Sewall died in Indianapolis on 22 July 1920.

References Josephson, Harold, ed., *Biographical Dictionary of Modern Peace Leaders* (1985); *National Cyclopaedia of American Biography*, vol. 19 (1967); Patterson, David S., "An Interpretation of the American Peace Movement, 1898–1914." In *Peace Movements in America*, ed. Charles Chatfield (1973).

Short, William Harrison (1868–1935)

William Harrison Short was born in College Springs, Iowa. Short graduated from Yale Theological Seminary in 1897 and served as minister in Congregational congregations in Wisconsin and Minnesota. He gave up the ministry when Andrew Carnegie persuaded him to work full time for the peace movement. Short's interest in the peace movement had brought him into contact with Carnegie, and he accepted the post of secretary of the New York Peace Society in 1910. Short was on the 1914–1915 committee that drafted concrete proposals for a league of nations, and in 1915 he helped organize the League to Enforce Peace, which William Howard Taft served as its first president. Short also raised $850,000 to maintain the league's work, served as the organization's executive director, and ran its day-to-day activities until 1921. By then, with the League of Nations apparently established, the work of the League to Enforce Peace came to an end.

From there, Short went on to head the Woodrow Wilson Foundation. Before resigning from that organization, he established branches in cities throughout the country. He next signed on to a general committee on the limitation of armaments that was cochaired by Samual Gompers and Oscar Straus. The committee stayed in session through the meeting of the Washington Naval Arms Limitation Conference of 1921–1922. Short spent a brief time as director of the Twentieth Century Fund before becoming director of the League of Nations Association in 1923. He also edited the *League of Nations Herald* until 1925.

Thereafter, Short's career took an unexpected turn when he became director of the Motion Picture Research Council in 1927 to study the influence of movies on children. The remainder of his active career was spent in that position. Short died in Philadelphia on 10 January 1935.

References *National Cyclopaedia of American Biography*, vol. 26 (1967); Patterson, David S., "An Interpretation of the American Peace Movement, 1898–1914." In *Peace Movements in America*, ed. Charles Chatfield (1973).

Slayden, James Luther (1853–1920)

James Slayden was elected to the U.S. Congress in 1896 and remained there until 1918, when Woodrow Wilson opposed his renomination and Slayden was persuaded to stand down. During his years in Congress, Slayden built his reputation as an intense promoter of international arbitration and permanent peace.

Born in Graves County, Kentucky, Slayden spent his early years on his father's tobacco plantation. He dropped out of Washington and Lee University because of poor eyesight and moved to Texas, where he spent three years ranching before starting a cotton export business.

His career in Congress paralleled his career as a peace activist. He was chairman of the U.S. branch of the Interparliamentary Union and a delegate to international peace conferences. Andrew Carnegie appointed Slayden as one of the original trustees of the Carnegie Endowment for International Peace, and he was a member—and from 1917 to 1920 was the president—of the American Peace Society (APS). He was a member of the Society for the Judicial Settlement of International Disputes, the American Society of International Law, and the World Court League. He also served on the council of direction for the Association of International Conciliation.

Throughout World War I, Slayden was such a vocal opponent of Woodrow

The Quaker Worship for Peace in Vietnam demonstration at the White House, 7 July 1969.

Wilson's policies that he incurred the president's wrath. In the face of presidential opposition to his renomination for Congress in 1918, Slayden decided to retire entirely from public life. He died in San Antonio, Texas, on 24 February 1924.

References *National Cyclopaedia of American Biography*, vol. 19 (1967); Patterson, David S., "An Interpretation of the American Peace Movement, 1898–1914." In *Peace Movements in America*, ed. Charles Chatfield (1973).

Smiley, Albert Keith (1828–1907)

Albert Smiley practiced the tenets of his Quaker religious upbringing in much of what he did, although he was not a strict pacifist.

He was born in Vassalborough, Maine, and graduated from Havorford College in 1849, where he taught until 1853, when he left to establish a school in Philadel-

phia with his twin brother, Alfred. The school focused on English and the classics and achieved moderate success. Nevertheless, Smiley left after four years to return to Vassalborough. From there, he went to Providence, Rhode Island, where he served as the principle of the Moses R. Brown Friends School. He remained there for the next 19 years.

In 1869, Smiley had purchased 300 acres on Lake Mohonk in the Catskill Mountains of New York. The property, intended as a resort, eventually boasted a 350-room hotel. Smiley's interest in world peace and the potentially effective use of international arbitration as a means of preventing wars led him to establish the Lake Mohonk International Arbitration Conferences in 1895. The conferences, which met annually for 22 years, attracted the luminaries of the peace movement and became a force in shaping public opinion about peace and the concept of arbitration. Smiley died at his winter home in Redlands, California, on 2 December 1912. The peace conferences, even without Smiley at the helm, continued for several more years.

See also Lake Mohonk Peace Conferences.

References *National Cyclopaedia of American Biography*, vol. 15; Patterson, David S., "An Interpretation of the American Peace Movement, 1898–1914." In *Peace Movements in America*, ed. Charles Chatfield (1973).

Society of Friends

The Society of Friends, whose members are usually known by the name Quakers, was founded in England in 1650. One of the principal tenets of Quaker religious philosophy is strict adherence to pacifism. The Society of Friends is the largest and best known of the many small pacifist Christian sects.

See also Historic Peace Churches.

Spock, Benjamin McLane (1903–1991)

The publication in 1946 of Dr. Benjamin Spock's *The Common Sense Book of Baby and Child Care* (later called simply *Baby and Child Care*) ushered in a new era in child rearing and immediately made the name Dr. Spock synonomous with baby care. Thus, when Spock became a social activist as a member of the Committee for a Sane Nuclear Policy (SANE) and as an opponent of the Vietnam War, his was a highly visible activism.

Benjamin Spock was born in New Haven, Connecticut. He attended Philips Academy in Andover, Massachusetts, and graduated from Yale University in 1925. In 1929, Spock earned an M.D. from Columbia University. He served residencies in both pediatrics and psychiatry in New York and completed six years of extensive psychiatric training at the New York Psychoanalytic Institute in 1940. He also maintained a private practice in pediatrics and taught pediatrics at Cornell University's Medical College.

Donald Porter Geddes of Pocket Books persuaded Spock to write a book on pediatrics. While serving a tour of active duty as a U.S. Navy psychiatrist, Spock completed the book that was to revolutionize attitudes toward child care. *Baby and Child Care* told the postwar parents of the baby boomers to trust their own instincts when it came to child care, to treat each child individually, and to exercise permissiveness rather than the harsh disciplinarianism of previous generations. In addition, Spock's advice to parents was published in a regular monthly column in the *Ladies Home Journal* from 1954 to 1963. After 1963 the column appeared in the pages of *Redbook*. Spock became *the* expert to whom parents automatically turned when faced with a child rearing problem. In later years, Spock came under criticism from feminists, who believed that he had placed too much emphasis on the responsibility of mothers to stay home and raise their children, and from conservatives, who believed that his endorsement of permissiveness led to a generation of undisciplined youngsters who experimented with drugs and protested too readily. Spock addressed some of the is-

Dr. Benjamin Spock

sues raised by feminists in later editions of *Baby and Child Care* by speaking to the responsibility of fathers in raising chldren. Those who criticized his permissiveness also objected to his antiwar activity, and many were probably influenced by politics more than by child care theory.

Spock was one of the founders of SANE and served as its cochairman for many years. As a SANE leader, he helped to intiate, in 1964, one of the earliest petitions urging the government to "work for a neutralized North and South Vietnam protected by international guarantees." Thereafter, he was a constant and vocal critic of Vietnam policy. In 1968, Spock—along with William Sloane Coffin, Marcus Raskin, Mitchell Goodman, and Michael Ferber—was indicted by the government for conspiracy to "counsel, aid, and abet young men to violate the draft laws." The indictment listed four specific acts committed by the accused: circulating a Call to Resist Illegitimate Authority, holding a press conference publicizing the call, announcing the events of a Stop the Draft Week, and accepting draft cards from potential draftees and presenting the cards to a member of the Department of Justice. With the exception of Marcus

Raskin, all of the defendants were found guilty, fined, and sentenced to two years in prison. The verdict was reversed on appeal in 1969 by the U.S. Court of Appeals. Although he had retired in 1967, Spock continued to write and to speak out against the war. His revised *Baby and Child Care* was published in 1970, shortly after publication of *Decent and Indecent* (1969), his assessment of and expression of concern for the fate of young adults. Dr. Spock died in 1991.

See also Call to Resist Illegitimate Authority; Coffin, William Sloan; SANE/FREEZE.

References Foner, Eric, and John Garraty, eds., *The Reader's Companion to American History* (1991); Van Doren, Charles, ed., *Webster's American Biographies* (1974); Zaroulis, Nancy, and Gerald Sullivan, *Who Spoke Up? American Protest against the War in Vietnam 1963–1975* (1984).

Stockholm Peace Pledge

In 1949 and 1950 many hundreds of millions of people around the world signed a document known as the "Stockholm Peace Pledge." In part, the pledge demanded the "outlawing of the atomic weapons as instruments of agression and mass murder. ... [and] strict international control to enforce this measure." The pledge also stated that any government "which first uses atomic weapons against any other country whatsoever will be committing a crime against humanity," and it called on "all men and women of good will throughout the world to sign this appeal."

According to some sources, the number of Americans who signed this pledge totaled a little over 1.3 million, and the number of signers worldwide was over 250 million. Others—for example W. E. B. Du Bois, then the head of the Peace Information Center—contended that the number of U.S. signers exceeded 2 million. Whatever the number, the Peace Pledge received notoriety not because it was signed by so many individuals but because it was a part of the so-called Communist "Peace" Campaign. As the Cold War intensified in the years immediately following World War II, the Soviet Union undertook a massive "peace" offensive. The purpose of the offensive was not really to secure peace. It was, rather, an effort to impede military efforts by the United States and other Western countries. Hearings held by the House Committee on Un-American Activities (HUAC) from 1949 to 1951 revealed that the Communist party employed a variety of front groups to accomplish its goal. It is also clear that the vast majority of people who signed the Stockholm Peace Pledge did so because it embodied principles that they supported. To these people, the Stockholm Peace Pledge was a straightforward declaration of their opposition to the use of nuclear weapons by any country.

In the Cold War atmosphere, the announcement that the Communist party had initiated the Stockholm Peace Pledge was a disturbing revelation, because most pacifist organizations were very wary of the Communists and made an effort to avoid them. As the Fellowship of Reconciliation (FOR) noted at the time, "communist-inspired 'peace' campaigns are not genuine" because their true purpose is in building up the Communist Party and not "pacifism or peace."

References Aptheker, Herbert, "W. E. B. Du Bois—A Man for Peace." *Political Affairs* 41 (August 1982); U.S. Congress, House Committee on Un-American Activities. *Report on the Communist "Peace" Offensive: A Campaign to Disarm and Defeat the United States.* 82nd Cong., 1st Sess., 1951; Wittner, Lawrence S., *Rebels against War: The American Peace Movement 1941–1960* (1969).

Strategic Arms Limitation Talks (SALT)

In 1970, with the Vietnam War not yet ended, and the country still at odds over the government's policy, President Richard M. Nixon began to negotiate an opportunity to visit the Soviet Union. Nixon hoped that a trip to Moscow—characterized by Secretary of State Henry Kissinger as a "point of near obsession"—would confound the peace demonstrators at home and help persuade the North Vietnamese to sign a peace treaty. Nixon was convinced that by demonstrating to the North Vietnamese that Soviet leaders considered them expendable when larger matters were concerned, the North Vietnamese would be forced to come to terms. In the summer of 1971, Nixon announced that he would be visiting China. Four weeks later, Moscow tendered an invitation and agreed to include talks on the limitation of strategic arms on their agenda.

Nixon visited Moscow in May 1972. It was a clear indication that both the Americans and the Soviets were willing to make an effort to lessen tensions between the two countries. Soviet Premier Leonid Brezhnev had his own reasons for agreeing to the talks, not the least of which was that the Soviets were in dire need of diverting some of their defense spending to increasing output of agricultural and consumer goods. The initial SALT talks, called SALT I, resulted in the signing of an agreement that provided for a severe limitation on the placement of ABMs and a freeze on the deployment of intercontinental ballistic missiles (ICBMs) by each side. The agreement was to last for five years and did not deal with improvements in quality. SALT I also allowed the Soviets to buy large quantities of U.S. wheat, the sale of which drove up domestic wheat prices.

In June 1973, Brezhnev came to Washington. Nixon and Brezhnev pledged never to engage in a nuclear attack and agreed to arrange a new round of talks, popularly called SALT II. SALT II was particularly promising, because the agenda included discussions of a halt to the construction of offensive nuclear weapons. For Nixon, the foremost advocate of the president as foreign policy maker, this was a major accomplishment. It was also the end of Nixon's efficacy in securing détente with the Soviet Union, because for the remainder of his time in office, he was embroiled in the Watergate scandal.

When Gerald Ford succeeded Nixon in the White House in 1975, SALT II negotiations faltered amid a renewed

mistrust between the two superpowers and continued technological innovations in weaponry that had the effect of constantly changing the playing field. Both powers did participate in the signing of a European Security Treaty in July 1975, along with 31 other nations, but no real movement on the issue of nuclear weapons took place. After Jimmy Carter became president, Carter and his secretary of state, Cyrus Vance, continued the SALT II negotiations. On 18 June 1979, Carter and Brezhnev signed the SALT II treaty in Vienna. SALT II would have set a limit on long-range missiles that each country could possess and it provided for a decrease in these missiles by 1981. Before the Senate could ratify the new treaty, however, the Soviets invaded Afghanistan in December 1979. Congress had been poised to act favorably on the SALT II treaty when it was signed, but with the invasion, Carter had to admit to new reservations regarding Soviet intentions, and the mood of the Senate changed as well. Consideration of ratification was suspended in the Senate and, in almost a complete turnabout of events, Congress added new funds to the military budget. The talk was no longer about détente but rather about a renewed Cold War.

References Schell, Jonathan, *The Time of Illusion* (1976); Szulc, Tad, *The Illusion of Peace* (1977); Link, Arthur S., et al., eds., *The American People: A History* (1981).

Strikes for Peace

The first nationwide strike for peace, or antiwar strike, did not occur until 1934. Approximately 25,000 students on campuses across the country participated in the strikes. In April 1934, 500 Vassar students in caps and gowns, led by the college president, paraded through the streets of Poughkeepsie, New York, chanting "no more battleships, we want schools." The following year, on 12 April 1935, 60,000 college students nationwide participated. In New York City alone,

10,000 students went on strike. At Columbia, 3,000 students listened to Roger Baldwin, Reinhold Niebuhr, and James Wechsler, while another 2,000 students heard history professor Harry Corman urge them to spread the antiwar gospel. The largest nationwide strike took place in 1937, when 500,000 students participated in a strike sponsored and coordinated by the United Student Peace Committee. Antiwar strikes at that time were generally very limited in scope and duration. Most consisted of students leaving classes for an hour before resuming their schedules. Students found very little sympathy among faculty and administrators of the colleges and universities involved. Quite frequently, the administration would respond quickly and very forcibly against strikers. Students at the University of California at Berkeley, for example, were arrested for handing out strike notices in 1935. Consequently, many strike organizations called their actions "peace assemblies," which found more favor among university administrators.

Once World War II began in earnest and once the United States became involved, most student strikes were suspended. In fact, as a group, students responsed to the war very positively. Those who had previously taken the Oxford Oath soon renounced their pledge never to engage in war. With the exception of conscientious objectors (COs), there was very little interest in the peace movement until well after the war ended.

In the late 1950s a student peace movement again began to emerge. Groups like the Fellowship of Reconciliation (FOR) and the Student Peace Union (SPU) helped to lay down the ground rules for future student protests by insisting on nonviolent civil disobedience as the acceptable tactic.

In the Vietnam era, student strikes were markedly different than earlier versions. For one thing, the student movement in the 1960s was primarily student-led as opposed to being led by an older generation of peace activists. Student strikers also had more willing supporters among the faculty, if not in the administration, than did students in the 1930s through the 1950s. Frequently, student strikes in the 1960s were planned by both students and sympathetic faculty. Finally, the strikes themselves were different in nature than the one-hour strikes of earlier decades. Time and again in the 1960s, student protesters took over college buildings, usually administration buildings, thus making normal activity on campus difficult at best. Student peace strikes in the 1960s occurred on both public and private campuses. It was not at all unusual to hear on the news that another college campus had been closed down by student protesters.

The culmination of the student strikes for peace occurred in 1970 on the campus of Kent State University in Ohio. The Governor of Ohio, James Rhodes, urged by the administration at Kent State, called out the Ohio National Guard to help maintain peace on the campus. Strikes at Kent State and other colleges around the country had been called in response to U.S. military attacks on Cambodia. The outcry at this apparent widening of the Vietnam War in the face of sustained calls for an end to hostilities touched a raw nerve in the United States. With emotions running high, it was only a matter of time before tragedy struck, as it did on the Kent State campus. National Guardsmen, most of whom were no older than the students, opened fire across an open field at a group of striking students. Four students were killed and several others were injured. Ironically, two of the fatally shot students were not participating in the strike. Almost at the same time, several students in Jackson, Mississippi, were shot by Mississippi State Police during a strike at Jackson State College. This round of strikes and the ensuing deaths signaled the end of campus peace strikes for all intents and purposes. The Vietnam War continued to wind down slowly, but nothing that happened after May 1970 galvanized students in the same way as evens that had motivated them to mount massive strikes in the previous half decade.

References Petersen, Patti McGill, "Student Organizations and the Antiwar Movement in America 1900–1960." In *Peace Movements in America*, ed. Charles Chatfield (1973); Wittner, Lawrence S., *Rebels against War: The American Peace Movement 1941–1960* (1969).

Student Peace Union (SPU)

Founded in 1959, the Student Peace Union (SPU) was a campus-based, issue-oriented organization. The SPU addressed both campus issues and national political issues. Initially, the SPU focused on nuclear testing and nuclear disarmament. Later, it expanded its interests to include questions of foreign policy. It was one of the earliest groups to express concern over the expanding Vietnam conflict.

The SPU was confined primarily to campuses. Although is gained its greatest support in the Midwest, SPU chapters sprang up on campuses across the country. Even so, its appeal to mainstream students remained marginal. At the height of its popularity, the SPU had chapters at only about 100 college campuses, and its national membership never exceeded 3,500. The SPU's impact far outweighed its size, however. It was established at a time when many college students were beginning to take a renewed interest in politics and in peace issues following the apparent apathy of the 1950s.

The SPU's leadership was an amalgamation of students concerned with peace issues and pacifists who had long been associated with the Fellowship of Reconciliation (FOR) and the American Friends Service Committee (AFSC). It also drew heavily on support from members of the Young People's Socialist League. In its approach to world peace issues, the SPU adopted a stance critical of both U.S. and Soviet foreign policies. In so doing, it was able to attract students not ordinarily receptive to organizations critical of the United States. Among its major activities were several peace protest marches on Washington. In particular, the 1962 March on Washington (MOW) attracted several thousand supporters and was the largest political demonstration held in the nation's capital since the 1930s.

By 1964 campus activism was moving along two paths: support for Students for a Democratic Society (SDS) and for the civil rights movement led by Martin Luther King, Jr. Although there remained a core of students committed to nuclear disarmament, with both the antiwar movement and the civil rights movement building up steam, the SPU dissolved itself. Despite its short-lived existence, the SPU created an extremely important transition between the nonactivism of the 1950s and the emergence of a New Left in the 1960s. It was instrumental in demonstrating that campus-based student groups could be a powerful force in focusing public attention on important national issues.

See also Students for a Democratic Society.

References Altbach, Philip G., *Student Politics in America: A Historical Analysis* (1974); Isserman, Maurice, *If I Had a Hammer . . . The Death of the Old Left and the Birth of the New Left* (1987); Vicker, George, *The Formation of the New Left: The Early Years* (1975).

Students for a Democratic Society (SDS)

Students for a Democratic Society (SDS) can be traced all the way back to the Intercollegiate Socialist Society (ISS), founded in 1905 by Upton Sinclair, Clarence Darrow, John Reed, Jack London, Norman Thomas, Edna St. Vincent Millay, and Walter Lippman. The ISS languished during World War I and was revitalized in 1921 as the League for Industrial Democracy (LID). The student arm of the LID was called the Student League for Industrial Democracy (SLID). Isolationist in nature, SLID remained active during the 1930s around the issues of domestic policy and opposition to entanglement in foreign affairs. It fell into disrepair with the advent of World War II. After the war, SLID revived in 1945, this time with a

Students for a Democratic Society members march against the ROTC and the war in Vietnam.

decidedly anti-Communist element. In 1960, SLID changed its name to Students for a Democratic Society. It also received a $10,000 grant from the United Auto Workers and hired a full-time field secretary, Al Haber, a graduate student at the University of Michigan, and Tom Hayden, also a University of Michigan student. Hayden was sent to Atlanta to join the civil rights movements and to keep SDS posted on civil rights activities. Hayden's reports were circulated on campuses nationwide. He was also the author of the Port Huron Statement, the SDS manifesto published in June 1962. In June 1963, SDS's most ambitious program was initiated: the Economic Research Action Project (ERAP), which was established to go into poor urban neighborhoods and organize residents to improve their economic and living environment.

When SDS invited iconoclastic journalist I. F. Stone to speak, it resulted in a propitious meeting on 7 April 1964 that helped to launch the antiwar movement. Stone spoke on the growing Vietnam conflict and the United States's involvement in that conflict. Stone urged SDS to participate in a forthcoming March on Washington (MOW) to protest the war. When SDS added the march to its agenda, it was also solidifying the then-disparate opposition to the war and claiming a central role in an organized antiwar movement. Thereafter, SDS remained in the thick of protest. When the so-called Chicago Seven came to trial following the Democratic Convention riots in Chicago in 1968, Tom Hayden was a principle defendant. At the height of the antiwar movement, the SDS radical fringe, calling itself the Weathermen, resorted to violent actions against the government and the military.

See also Port Huron Statement.

References Hayden, Tom, *A Memoir* (1990); Zaroulis, Nancy, and Gerald Sullivan, *Who Spoke Up? American Protest against the War in Vietnam 1963–1975* (1984).

Szilard, Leo (1898–1964)

The life and career of Leo Szilard stands as a prime example of the profound ambivalence experienced by many of the scientists who helped to develop nuclear weapons.

Szilard was born in Budapest, Austria-Hungary, and was educated at the King Joseph Institute of Technology in Budapest and the Institute of Technology in Berlin. He earned a Ph.D. in physics from the University of Berlin in 1922. Szilard had big visions, even as a very young man. Working as a physicist in Berlin in the early 1920s, he observed the disarray in which post–World War I Germany existed and developed plans for an organization that would take over when the government collapsed, as he believed it soon would. Whatever career he had envisioned for himself was aborted when Hitler came to power and Szilard became an émigré from Nazi Germany.

He left Germany very quickly after Hitler came to power and in 1933 helped organize a committee in England to provide assistance to refugee scientists. Once nuclear fission was discovered in 1939, bringing the idea of a chain reaction closer to reality, Szilard immediately grasped its military and political implications and began to worry about the moral responsibility that had now been placed at the feet of the scientific community. For Szilard, the moral issues would remain a constant for the rest of his life, leading him to become an activist for peace as well as a scientist.

At the same time, Szilard knew full well that Germany could as easily develop atomic weapons. Szilard was one of the scientists who helped to alert President Franklin Roosevelt to that possibility. As a consequence, Roosevelt appointed a commission to investigate the scientists' concerns, and out of that investigation the Manhattan Project was born. Because of the pioneering work he did on the uranium-graphite reactor, Szilard was a member of the top-secret Manhattan Project. Nevertheless, the intensity with which he drove himself in order to beat the Germans evaporated once Germany was defeated and Japan was on the ropes. Because of his deep concern over scientists' responsibility regarding the use and control of the weapon they had developed, Szilard sought to halt the use of the bomb in Japan or at least to warn the Japanese of an imminent attack before the bomb was dropped. Szilard and the other scientists who took this stand believed that using the bomb against Japanese cities would be immoral, and they feared that such an act would jeopardize international control of atomic energy.

After the war, Szilard turned to control of atomic energy and led the scientists who helped to secure passage of the McMahon Act, which established an atomic energy commission under civilian rather than military control. In an effort to make clear all their concerns, Szilard joined with other prominent scientists, including Albert Einstein and Linus Pauling, in the Emergency Committee of Atomic Scientists (ECAS). Beginning in 1946 the committee issued a series of startling statements deploring the state of relations between the United States and the Soviet Union and continued weapons research and development. Szilard left physics after the war and became a biologist, preferring to use his abilities in life-affirming research, but his political commitment grew even more urgent as the Cold War and the arms race both provided confirmation that what he had feared was coming to pass. He worked incessantly for disarmament and political resolution of conflict. In 1957, Szilard initiated the idea of direct meetings between Western and Eastern scientists. The result was a series of conferences, the Pugwash Conferences of Scientists on World Affairs, held in Pugwash, Nova Scotia. The Pugwash Conferences helped to bring together scientists, previously prohibited from meeting by their respective governments, to discuss not only nuclear weapons but world affairs in general.

In the meantime, Szilard wrote a series of satirical political fantasies on war and peace entitled *The Voice of the Dolphins*, published in 1961. *The Voice of the Dolphins* became popular, was translated into six languages, and helped to make Szilard a popular choice as a speaker at colleges and universities across the country. It was during a 1962 speaking tour that Szilard developed the idea for creating an organization called the Council for a Livable World (CLW), which would support candidates for the U.S. Senate who expressed a belief in peace issues. Szilard never stopped searching for a plan that would break the great power deadlock in the arms race that he believed was leading ultimately to mass "murder and suicide." His passion and concern for the fate of the world in a nuclear age made him a symbol of the committed, conflicted, ambivalent scientists who struggled to strike a balance between progress and responsibility. Leo Szilard died on 30 May 1964 in La Jolla, California.

See also Bethe, Hans; Einstein, Albert; Emergency Committee of Atomic Scientists; and Pauling, Linus.

References Josephson, Harold, ed., *Biographical Dictionary of Modern Peace Leaders* (1985); Wittner, Lawrence S., *Rebels against War: The American Peace Movement 1941–1960* (1969).

Teach-In

The teach-in originated during the Vietnam War as a form of protest. Patterned after the sit-ins so successfully employed during the civil rights movement a decade earlier, the first teach-in was held in April 1965. Teach-ins combined protest with education and in some cases were treated by participants as an occasion of festivity. Usually, classes were suspended during teach-ins by participating faculty members, who characterized their activity as "work moratoriums." The day-long discussion and analysis of U.S. policy in Vietnam and the conduct of the war often included ideas and suggestions about how students might influence events through their own actions.

The first teach-in was organized by 49 faculty members at the University of Michigan at Ann Arbor. Because of opposition from the university administration and from some members of the state legislature, who objected to state funds being used to support antiwar activity, the teach-in was scheduled to begin after the close of the day's classes. The event might not have had the support of so many faculty had not the president of the university offered the opinion that leaders like Secretary of Defense Robert McNamara, a "competent" leader, ought to be trusted regarding Vietnam. Even so, most faculty members were surprised to see some 3,000 students in attendance. The teach-in lasted until 8:00 A.M. the following morning and went on despite two separate bomb threats that forced officials to clear the buildings and turn the students out in sub-freezing weather while the threatened bombs were sought.

Over the course of the next several months, teach-ins became a popular way to protest Vietnam activity and were held on campuses throughout the country. Al-

though most teach-in sponsors were careful to clarify that the idea was to educate students, regardless of the opinions they came away with, the information provided very often turned students against Johnson administration policy. It was a measure of the influence exerted by the teach-ins that the Johnson administration tried to counter the growing trend by sending out a "truth team" to conduct seminars similar to teach-ins, but carrying the administration's message. The team, headed by Thomas Conlon of the Agency for International Development, toured several campuses. Its reception by students and faculty alike was chilly, if not outright hostile. After three weeks, the Washington team returned to Washington and no further forays were made on behalf of the administration.

The most ambitious teach-in was held on 15 and 16 May, 1965 when 122 colleges and universities were tied in by a special radio hookup to hear what was the most intensive discussion of U.S. policy to date. This teach-in was organized by the Inter-University Committee for a Public Hearing on Vietnam, which had grown directly out of the spring teach-ins. More than 100,000 students and an unknown number of private citizens heard a day-long debate between people like Arthur Schlesinger, Jr., Walt Rowstow, and Zbigniew Brzezinski taking the side of the administration against antiwar activists, including Hans Morgenthau and Bernard Fall. Teach-ins continued on college campuses but never reached the scope of the nationwide teach-in. Overall, teach-ins proved to be a useful educational process for those opposed to the Vietnam War. They provided students with focused, intense instruction intended to help them come to their own conclusions about the war.

References Zaroulis, Nancy, and Gerald Sullivan, *Who Spoke Up? American Protest against the War in Vietnam 1963–1975* (1984).

Thomas, Evan Welling (1890–1974)

Although his brother, Norman Thomas, was better known to most people, primarily because Norman was the head of the Socialist Party in America, Evan Thomas dedicated much of his life to the peace movement as well.

Born in Marion, Ohio, Evan chose to attend Princeton University, as had Norman seven years before him. During World War I, the brothers were on different sides, in a sense, with Norman lending cautious support to Woodrow Wilson's decision to enter the war and Evan remaining adamantly opposed to the war. Evan was one of a handful of pacifists who refused to accept any kind of service under military authority. As a consequence, he spent 18 months in Leavenworth Prison. He and his colleagues refused to obey prison regulations as a testament of their total opposition to anything having to do with the military, and they spent much of their prison time in solitary confinement. Even when he was chained to the bars of his cell and forced to stand for up to ten hours daily, Thomas would not succumb to military authority. His experiences during the war only deepened his commitment to pacifism.

After the war Thomas decided to pursue a career in medicine in order to demonstrate the constructive nature of pacifism. He graduated from New York University Medical School in 1933, thereafter joining the faculty as professor of clinical medicine, a post he held until 1948. As one of the nation's leading experts on syphilis and its treatment, Thomas was also a consultant to various medical organizations. From 1964 on he was director of the Children's Evaluation Unit of the Institutes for Achievement of Human Potential.

As World War II approached, Thomas became increasingly concerned with articulating a theory of pacifism that would both explain and define his own philosophy as it had evolved over the previous 20 years. In 1942 he wrote *The Positive Faith of Pasivism.* In it, Thomas argued that the war could not be attributed solely to the willful acts of a few dictators. In his view, the culture of war itself created the dictators. In other words, as long as war was acceptable as a last resort in settling conflict, there would always be men who would determine to amass the power to win such a war in order to realize their goals. The world had little choice, Thomas believed, but to seek to overcome evil with good. In order to do this, Thomas argued, one could not totally rely on politics, because politics stressed organization, and organization too often suppressed freedom and promoted corruption. Preferable was an acceptance of a democracy that included economic collectivism. Such a system would naturally support nonviolent resistance to tyranny. Part of that resistance would include the prohibition on military conscription, for without conscription, war and tyranny could not persist.

Perhaps because of nazism's degree of tyranny and the uncertainty that it produced in the ranks of pacifists, Thomas himself came to a point in his life where he was no longer certain about his own theory. He had been chairman of the War Resisters League (WRL) during the war, but by 1951, when he resigned, he was having second thoughts about the necessity of organization. Nevertheless, he could not resolve in his own mind how to encourage necessary organzation without "killing the humanity within us." Thomas never stopped struggling with these dilemmas until his death on 19 May 1974.

See also Thomas, Norman Mattoon.

References Josephson, Harold, ed., *Biographical Dictionary of Modern Peace Leaders* (1985); Thomas, Evan W., *The Radical "No"—Correspondence and Writing of Evan Thomas on War*, ed. Charles Chatfield (1974).

Thomas, Norman Mattoon (1884–1968)

Norman Thomas, frequently referred to as the "conscience of America," dedicated his life to the causes in which he believed.

Born in Marion, Ohio, Thomas attended Bucknell University and graduated from Princeton University in 1905. Following in his father's footsteps, Thomas became a Presbyterian minister and graduated from Union Theological Seminary. He married Frances Violet Stewart, whose own wealth allowed Thomas to pursue the joint causes of socialism, civil liberties, civil rights, and peace. In 1910 he was appointed pastor of East Harlem Presbyterian Church, a position he held until giving up the ministry in 1918.

In 1916, Thomas, a pacifist, joined the Fellowship of Reconciliation (FOR), an organization founded to help conscientious objectors (COs). He later founded and edited the FOR publication *The World Tomorrow*. Thomas also joined the American Union against Militarism, and in 1917 he, along with Crystal Eastman and Roger Baldwin, established the Civil Liberties Bureau (CLB) to help protest government violations of antiwar protestors' civil liberties. The CLB became the American Civil Liberties Union (ACLU) in 1921.

Thomas believed that socialism would ultimately triumph over capitalism and was politically active as a member of the Socialist party. Although he never won political office, he used the candidate's platform to spread the Socialist message. He ran on the Socialist ticket for mayor of New York in 1925 and 1929. He ran for the New York state senate in 1926, for New York City Board of Aldermen in 1927, and for borough president of Manhattan in 1931. In addition, he ran on the Socialist ticket for president every four years from 1928 through 1948. As a Socialist candidate, Thomas never equalled the votes that Eugene Debs was able to garner running on the same ticket in the pre–World War I years. Nevertheless, at the height of the Great Depression, with capitalism in question, he did poll over 800,000 votes. By 1936, Americans had turned to the New Deal as their best hope for economic recovery, and socialism, thereafter, never regained even its limited appeal.

Norman Mattoon Thomas

In 1938, with events in Europe nearing the breaking point, Thomas founded the Keep American Out of War Committee. Although he was no longer a strict pacifist, as he had been during World War I, he still believed that if the United States fought in another war, it would no longer be democratic. In his view democracy was at stake, and this belief prompted Thomas to allign himself with the America First Committee. He disassociated himself with America First after Charles Lindbergh gave a speech for the movement that many believed revealed anti-Semitism. Nevertheless, Thomas continued to hold fast to his position until the bombing of Pearl Harbor. The new situation caused him to lend what he called "critical support" to the war. He focused his attention once again on the preservation of civil liberties and was particularly critical of the government's decision to inter Japanese Americans. Thomas was also one of the first Americans to urge that the United

States serve as an asylum for refugees of Nazi crimes, but his importations fell on deaf ears throughout the 1930s. Polls taken in 1938 and 1939 revealed that less than eight percent of Americans were willing to admit Hitler's victims into the country. "I learned first hand how many Americans preferred to fight," Thomas said, "for the rights of Jews in Europe than to give them asylum in America." He was also one of the first to speak out against using atomic weapons on Japan.

Unlike many of his fellow Socialists, pacifists, and civil libertarians, Thomas did not believe that he had to be an apologist for the excesses and evils of communism. He had viewed communism first-hand in Spain and the Soviet Union in 1937 and found little reason to give his support to a political system capable of such oppression. He led the effort in 1940 to remove Communists from leadership roles in the ACLU. Always an independent thinker, Thomas refused to defend Communists' rights to hold sensitive government positions or teaching positions during the McCarthy era, but at the same time he did defend their civil liberties.

During World War II, Thomas abandoned his long-held belief that permanent peace would never be achieved until there was a world federation of Socialist states. As a consequence of the war, Thomas became convinced that peace would only be maintained if there were an international organization with adequate powers to enforce peace. He never stopped working for that goal, but he also never stopped being critical of the United States when it engaged in actions that he believed were counterproductive for a democratic state. Some of his later speeches were directed against the United States's involvement in Vietnam.

In the course of his lifetime, Thomas wrote hundreds of articles and 21 books, all of which dealt with democracy, socialism, peace, and civil rights and civil liberties. He died on 19 December 1968 in Huntington, New York.

See also Thomas, Evan Welling.
References Chatfield, Charles, "Norman Thomas: Harmony of Word and Deed." In *Peace Heroes in Twentieth Century America*, ed. Charles DeBenedetti (1988); Garrity, John, ed., *Dictionary of American Biography*, supp. 8 (1981); Wittner, Lawrence S., *Rebels against War: The American Peace Movement 1941–1960* (1969).

Trueblood, Benjamin Franklin (1847–1916)

When Benjamin Trueblood took over as the general secretary of the American Peace Society (APS) in 1892, the APS—the oldest peace organization in the country—had a membership of 400. By the time Trueblood retired, the APS membership list had grown to 8,000. In part, this was a reflection of the nation's growing concern with seeking alternative solutions to solving international disputes, but it also reflected Trueblood's dedication to the cause of peace and to the APS's success.

Trueblood, who was born in Salem, Indiana, graduated from Earlham College in Richmond, Indiana, in 1869. He taught English literature for a short time before moving into administration, first as the president of Wilmington College in Ohio and then as president of Penn College in Oskaloosa, Iowa, where he remained for 11 years. Trueblood was a devout Quaker, and there was little in his life—particularly in his work for a permanent peace—that was not influenced by his religious beliefs. He was foreign secretary of the Christian Arbitration and Peace Society from 1890 to 1891, and in 1892 the APS invited him to take over as general secretary. Under his stewardship, the APS grew not only in membership, but its publication, *Advocate of Peace*, also increased its circulation from 1,500 to 11,500 and in the process became an influential peace movement forum. The APS achieved a more national character when the headquarters were moved from Boston to Washington in 1911.

Trueblood also served as the chairman of the Joint Executive Committee of

Peace Societies at the World Columbian Exposition in Chicago and was an active participant at the Lake Mohonk Peace Conferences from their inception in 1895. It was Trueblood who first proposed that the Lake Mohonk conference discuss the possibility of establishing an international court of arbitration to which all nations could turn for resolution of disputes.

Trueblood attended every important international peace congress during his career and wrote numerous books, essays and pamphlets promoting the idea of arbitration, including *The Federation of the World* (1899). He served as general secretary of the APS until 1915 and was honorary secretary until his death. He died in Newton Highlands, Massachusetts, on 26 October 1916.

References *National Cyclopaedia of American Biography*, vol. 18 (1967); Patterson, David S., "An Interpretation of the American Peace Movement, 1898–1914." In *Peace Movements in America*, ed. Charles Chatfield (1973).

Union of Concerned Scientists (UCS)

The Union of Concerned Scientists (UCS), founded in 1969, began as a group of Massachusetts Institute of Technology students and professors who were interested in seeing a more humane application of scientific and technical knowledge. Since then it has evolved into a national organization including both scientists and nonscientists. The UCS has had a dual goal: an environmentally safe energy program and freedom from the threat of nuclear war.

An organization that advocates action, the UCS has been influential in several key developments related to nuclear energy. A UCS report to the Senate in 1974, in which the Atomic Energy Commission (AEC) was taken to task for allowing political and economic considerations to determine policy, resulted in a division of competing interests in the AEC. Two federal agencies—the Nuclear Regulatory Agency, concerned with regulating the industry, and the Energy Research and Development Administration, concerned with promoting nuclear power—were established to remove any conflict of interest. The following year, the UCS issued a critique of a study on nuclear reactors put out by the AEC. The critique prompted reevaluation of the AEC report, and eventually the Nuclear Regulatory Agency completely disavowed the report's findings.

Efforts to curb nuclear weapons proliferation date back to 1969, when the UCS sponsored teach-ins nationwide, which focused on the danger presented by a proposed antiballistic missile (ABM) system. The teach-ins helped to foster public support for an ABM treaty between the United States and the Soviet Union in 1972. Since then, the UCS gathered thousands of signatures for a Declaration on the Nuclear Arms Race, calling for the United States to halt production of nuclear arms; it opposed the MX missile as unnecessary and raised the possibility that the missile would initiate a new escalation in the arms race; and it was heavily involved in efforts to curtail the so-called Star Wars technology that threated to turn space into an extension of a weapons' system. Continued teach-ins and seminars on the dangers of nuclear war have helped to alert the public to the problem. In 1982 the UCS initiated a No-First-Use campaign on 300 campuses across the country. Among the supporters of this campaign have been 46 Nobel laureates in science and medicine and more than 500 members of the National Academy of Sciences. Another focus of the UCS has been the problems associated with nuclear waste and its disposal. A large part of the UCS's education program has been aimed at the general public, because the UCS believes that without public support for antinuclear war measures, no constructive changes will take place.

Reference Meyer, Robert S., *Peace Organizations, Past and Present* (1988).

Unitarian Universalist Peace Network (UUPN)

Carrying on a long and honored tradition as activists in social and political causes that has marked the Unitarian Universalist Church for decades, six Unitarian organizations banded together in 1985 in order to create a peace network. Dedicated to eradicating nuclear war, to ending the arms race, and to promoting world peace, the Unitarian Universalist Peace Network (UUPN) includes members of the Unitarian Universalist Association, the Peace Fellowship, United

Nations (U.N.) Office, the Women's Federation, the Service Committee, and the International Association of Religious Freedom.

The UUPN outlined a five-point plan to accomplish its ends: (1) an effective Rapid Action Alert Network, for contacting elected officials on various issues and for contacting members of the Unitarian Universalist Church; (2) a renewal of efforts to solicit contributions for the Fund for Peace grants program; (3) the establishment of programs to assist colleagues in developing effective peace programs, conferences, seminars, and workshops; (4) a system of distributing information, printed and visual resources, and action alert information to the publications of sponsoring organizations; and (5) strong participation in interfaith and international peace programs. A publication entitled *The Peace Activator* is a forum for ideas and information coming out of the UUPN, and an official *Issue/Action Briefing Packet* has been made available to interested groups. The UUPN operates in the belief that sharing news about its activities and its peace-oriented religious education and worship materials will help to create "a network of positive action for peace."

See also Unitarian Universalist Service Committee.

Reference Meyer, Robert S., *Peace Organizations Past and Present* (1988).

Unitarian Universalist Service Committee (UUSC)

The Unitarian Universalist Service Committee (UUSC), the service arm of the Unitarian Universalist Church, was organized in 1939 as a response to the growth of fascism in Europe. Its headquarters are in Boston, Massachusetts. The UUSC's original focus was working with refugees, and its efforts saved many from death camps and thousands more from starvation. After World War II, the UUSC branched out, working in a number of world trouble spots, including Central

America, India, the Caribbean, and Africa. In the United States the UUSC has worked extensively with American Indians and in urban slums. Its primary focus remains in Third World countries, however, and the organization continues to work toward eliminating poverty and militarism and toward fostering health care and human rights.

See also Unitarian Universalist Peace Network.

Reference Meyer, Robert S., *Peace Organizations Past and Present* (1988).

United Church of Christ

In unison with many other organized churches in the United States, the United Church of Christ in 1981 appointed a Peace Theology Development Team that was charged with preparing a position paper on peace and the relationship of the church to peace as an issue. Using the findings of the position paper, the General Synod in 1983 declared that the United Church of Christ was a "just peace church."

Just peace, according to the drafters of the position paper, was based on the concept of biblical peace as expressed by the Hebrew word *shalom*. Shalom, the writers determined, was "a communal well-being in which God's creation is justly ordered." A just peace, they further determined, was the "interrelation of friendship, justice, and common security from violence." Using these definitions, the General Synod placed the United Church of Christ in direct opposition to war. The synod also issued a Proposal for Action, requesting all members to organize for peace locally, regionally, and nationally. Four components of the action proposal were specified: spiritual development, education, political advocacy, and community witness. The proposal contained several central ideas, including the belief that peace was possible; that nonviolent conflict is normal and reflects diversity; that violence has to be at least minimized and, if possible, eliminated; that war has to be eliminated; and that the state is responsible for developing justice and minimizing violence. Having recognized that peacemaking was a central mission of the church, the Executive Council established a Peace Fund in order to ensure continuation of the peace ministry within the church. A monthly publication entitled *Courage in the Struggle for Justice and Peace* began publication in 1986 and provides information on peace activities in local congregations and conferences.

Reference Meyer, Robert S., *Peace Organizations Past and Present* (1988).

United Methodist Church

In 1980 the governing council of the United Methodist Church agreed to initiate a special program emphasizing peace and justice. The program, placed under the aegis of the Board of Church and Society, was a broad-based effort to design, promote, and provide resource materials. The defined purpose of the program was fourfold: (1) to make peacemaking a prominent feature of the church, (2) to create a structure that would give force and substance to the effort, (3) to bring together those committed to peace in a fellowship of God, and (4) to build on and expand peace efforts of the past.

In order to assist local congregations in fulfilling this program, the board made available a variety of educational materials that focused on the interrelated issues of faith and peace, including disarmament, democracy and freedom, support for the United Nations (U.N.), world trade and economic development, military conscription, and peace research, education, and action. The Methodist Church, not considered one of the historic "peace churches," nevertheless has a history of peace activism, including its 1940 declaration that the church would not officially "endorse, support, or participate in [World War II]." The Peace and Justice Program was originally mandated to last through 1984. Support for continuation of the program by many conferences within the church prompted the Council

of Bishops to approve a two-year antinuclear weapons program. The program's aims were to make clear the bishops' position on what they considered a nuclear arms race crisis, to promote full discussion of the issues involved—including alternatives to current defense buildup policies—and to urge participation by all Methodists in peace activism. The two-year program produced a publication entitled *In Defense of Creation: The Nuclear Crisis and a Just Peace*, which included discussion of the policy of deterrence, the effects of a nuclear war on humans, a plea for an ethic of reciprocity and mutual security, and a call for all Christian churches to work for peace.

Reference Meyer, Robert S., *Peace Organizations Past and Present* (1988).

United Nations (U.N.)

The United States, learning from mistakes made with the League of Nations, was determined to create a truly effective world body following World War II. President Franklin Delano Roosevelt and British Prime Minister Winston Churchill signed a document called the Atlantic Charter on 14 August 1941, which, in part, included a resolution calling for the establishment of a world organization mandated to keep the peace. Even before the war ended, Roosevelt and members of his administration met to discuss the shape that such a body would take. Like Roosevelt, Secretary of State Cordell Hull proceeded cautiously in order not to antagonize the public by appearing to move too swiftly. Even so, before government delegates met at Dumbarton Oaks, an estate near Washington, D.C., in 1944, Roosevelt and Hull already knew what they wanted the organization to look like.

After consulting with the Allies and further discussing the issue with Joseph Stalin and Winston Churchill at Yalta, Roosevelt consented to proceed. The United Nations (U.N.) was formally organized at the War Memorial Opera

House in San Francisco in 1945. At that time, delegates from 50 countries drew up the U.N. Charter, and the following year the organization formally convened. The U.N.'s current world headquarters are in New York City.

The U.N. Charter's preamble clearly defines the goals and concerns of the participating nations. Former First Lady Eleanor Roosevelt played an instrumental role in the adoption of several key human rights measures included in the charter. Among other things, the U.N., as set out in the charter preamble, is dedicated to: saving succeeding generations from the scourge of war; reaffirming faith in fundamental human rights, including the equal rights of men and women; establishing world order with justice and respect for the terms of treaties and other areas of international law; practicing tolerance and living together in peace; uniting to maintain international peace and security; accepting the principle of peaceful resolution to problems except where peaceful resolution is no longer possible; and employing international machinery to ensure the economic and social advancement of all people.

The U.N. Charter also sets forth four fundamental purposes: (1) maintaining international peace and security, using effective collective measures for the prevention and removal of threats to peace in order to bring about peaceful resolution to conflicts; (2) developing friendly relations among all nations, based on respect for equal rights and self-determination; (3) achieving international cooperation in solving international problems concerning economic, social, cultural, or humanitarian issues, and promoting respect for human rights; and (4) acting as the center for harmonizing the efforts of nations in attaining these ends. The charter also sets forth rights and responsibilities of member nations, including the right of equal sovereignty and the responsibility to fulfill all obligations of membership, including the obligation to settle disputes peacefully, to refrain from threats of force, to assist in any U.N. action, and to refrain from assisting any nation against whom sanctions have been imposed.

Structurally, the U.N. operates with six main bodies, each of which has a specific function to perform. They are: (1) the General Assembly, made up of representatives from each member nation, which controls finances, makes nonbinding recommendations, and oversees other U.N. organs; (2) the Security Council, charged with maintaining peace, which has 15 members—five of whom are permanent members (China, France, the U.S., the U.S.S.R., and Great Britain) with the power to veto any proposal—and whose proposals require nine votes for passage; (3) the Economic and Social Council (UNESCO), which coordinates the U.N.'s economic and social work; (4) the Trusteeship Council, composed of the five permanent members of the Security Council and charged with overseeing trust territories; (5) the International Court of Justice, or World Court, which has 15 judges who serve for nine-year terms and who hear cases referred by states involved; and (6) the Secretariat, which administers the programs and policies established by other U.N. organs. The Secretariat is headed by the secretary-general, who is elected by the General Assembly for a five-year term. Much of the success of the U.N. mission depends on the skill and political acumen of the secretary-general. The U.N. has been fortunate to have had a diverse and skilled group of secretaries-general, including Dag Hammarskjöld, U Thant, Javier Perez de Cuellar, and Boutras Boutras-Ghalli, all of whom held that post during the most perilous of times.

The U.N. also has a number of other specialized bodies, which deal with a variety of concerns, including relief, economics, communications, world health, aviation, labor, agriculture, freedom of the seas, education, science, culture, and space.

As the U.N. Department of Public Information has pointed out in a booklet entitled *United Nations Today–1984*, "the critical value of peacemaking and peace-keeping efforts would be instantly evident if they were to cease." Although it would be difficult to argue that the U.N. has not had a positive influence on world events, nevertheless, it is also true that the principles established for it frequently have been ignored. Its ability to maintain peace has been seriously questioned. In the final analysis, however, its effectiveness depends on the political will of the member nations. There is a direct correlation between the extent to which member nations act in an obstructionist way and the success of the U.N.'s mission.

Almost since its founding, various organizations have sought to reform or amend the Charter of the U.N. in order to give it more authority to enforce its resolutions. To this end, groups such as World Citizens Assembly (WCA), which characterizes the U.N. as the "best hope for mankind," have long engaged in lobbying efforts. Now, as it approaches its fiftieth anniversary, there are some signs that member nations are more willing to allow the U.N. to take on the role of peacekeeper in the manner intended when the charter was written. With the collapse of the Soviet Union, the breakup of the Eastern Bloc, and the lagging world economy, the remaining superpower—the United States—is more inclined to work in concert with the U.N. rather than to act unilaterally, as it has in the past. Changing world politics and this shift in attitude have rekindled hope that the U.N. will emerge stronger and with a clearer sense of its mandate and purpose.

References Lash, Joseph, *Eleanor: The Years Alone* (1972); Link, Arthur S., et al., eds., *The American People: A History* (1981); Meyer, Robert S. *Peace Organizations Past and Present* (1988).

United Nations Association of the United States of America (UNA–USA)

The United Nations Association of the United States of America (UNA–USA) is probably the oldest national United Na-

tions (U.N.) support organization in existence. Its roots go all the way back to 1923 and the League of Nations Non-Partisan Association, which, in 1945, changed its name to the American Association for the U.N. Two decades later, it allied with the National Committee for UN Day, founded in 1949, and became the U.N. Association of the United States of America.

In addition to being the oldest organization of its kind, it is also the largest private, nonpartisan group in the United States that concerns itself with international affairs. There are approximately 60 similar organizations throughout the world, each of which is dedicated to helping the U.N. successfully carry out the mandate embodied in its charter. The UNA–USA now consists of a network of 175 chapters nationwide and more than 130 affiliated national organizations. The organization draws its participants primarily from business, academia, the professions, and labor and includes many individuals who have held high-level government and U.N. posts.

The UNA–USA is, first and foremost, an information organization. It publishes the highly regarded *The Interdependent*. It briefs members of Congress on issues related to the U.N., allowing them to make better decisions. In addition, the UNA–USA briefs editors from hundreds of publications. It also analyzes the U.N. agenda, works with hundreds of organizations to keep their members apprised of international issues, prepares resource materials for thousands of students who attend mock U.N. conferences each year, analyzes U.S. foreign policy in terms of its impact on the U.N., and recommends what action the government should take. The UNA–USA is also a participant, with the 60 other international organizations, in the World Federation of U.N. Associations. In all instances, the UNA–USA's goal is to increase the public's awareness of global issues, to encourage multilateral approaches to international problems where appropriate, to build support for favorable U.S. policy on international issues, and to strengthen the U.N.

The UNA–USA was one of 25 cosponsors of the International Bicentennial Symposium on Strengthening the United Nations, held in Philadelphia in 1987.

Reference Meyer, Robert S., *Peace Organizations Past and Present* (1988).

United Pacifist Committee (UPC)

The United Pacifist Committee (UPC) was organized in 1938 by Jessie Wallace Hughan noted pacifist and Socialist. Increasingly dismayed by events in Europe, and hopeful of influencing a peaceful resolution, Hughans organized the UPC by bringing together a coalition of pacifist organizations. The UPC was founded to support conscientious objectors (COs) and to implement and coordinate a peace education program.

See also Hughan, Jessie Wallace.

Reference Sicherman, Barbara, et al., eds., *Notable American Women, The Modern Period: A Biographical Dictionary* (1980).

U.S. Committee against Nuclear War

The U.S. Committee against Nuclear War, founded in 1982 and dedicated to lobbying for a halt to the arms race, numbered approximately 30,000 members by 1985. The committee raised funds to petition Congress and to support congressmen and senators who were agreement with the organization. It claimed success in mobilizing a grass-roots campaign that resulted in House approval of the Nuclear Freeze Resolution in May 1983. The committee also supported a campaign to slow down deployment of MX missiles in Europe, and in the 1984 political campaign it supported 60 candidates for the Congress and the Senate. Nearly 50 of the candidates backed by the committee won their contests. The committee also rallied opposition support for the Star Wars technology development on the grounds that it constituted a major escalation in the arms race. The com-

mittee dissolved with the break-up of the Soviet Union.

Reference Meyer, Robert S., *Peace Organizations Past and Present* (1988).

U.S./U.S.S.R. Church Relations Committee of the National Council of Churches

The Church Relations Committee (CRC) was an organization activated by the National Council of Churches of Christ in the U.S.A. (usually referred to as the National Council of Churches or the NCC) in 1956, following the first exchange of NCC delegates between the United States and the Soviet Union. The purpose in creating the CRC was to develop long-range understanding and dialogue between people in both countries and, therefore, to help create favorable conditions for ending the Cold War and the arms race. Exchanges between the countries were originally scheduled for ten-year intervals, but with the worsening of relations, the exchange schedule was accelerated.

Church leaders in both countries issued a joint statement of disarmament entitled "Choose Life" in 1979. At the same time, annual meetings held in Geneva, Switzerland, commenced. At the 1985 Summit Conference in Geneva, a joint vigil was held in order to impress upon leaders of both nations their constituents' desire for peace. The CRC has succeeded in conducting its exchange programs even during the worst years of U.S./Soviet relations, when the threat of nuclear war was greatest. The largest exchange to take place under the auspices of the CRC program was in 1984, when 266 Americans visited Moscow, Zagorsk, and Leningrad before splitting into smaller groups and continuing on to a number of smaller cities and towns. The most striking impression that exchange delegates had was that the Soviet people, because of their direct experiences with the ravages of war—particularly those of World War II—were much more passionate about maintaining peace than Americans seemed to be. Delegates on both sides, however, seemed willing to confront the difficult questions associated with their nation's policies in the search for peace.

Reference Meyer, Robert S., *Peace Organizations Past and Present* (1988).

United World Federalists
See World Federalist Association (WFA).

Van Kirk, Walter William (1891–1956)

Walter Van Kirk's contribution to peace came in the form of his opposition to war and in his ability to act as conciliator between various factions in the peace movement.

Van Kirk, who was born in Cleveland, Ohio, graduated from Ohio Wesleyan University in 1917 and from the Boston University School of Theology in 1920. His career as a Methodist minister was spent in Massachusetts. Between 1919 and 1925 he served as pastor in Methodist churches in Dorchester, Needham Heights, and Lynn, Massachusetts. In 1925, Van Kirk accepted a post as secretary of the Department of International Justice and Good Will, Federal Council of Churches of Christ in America, a position he held for the next 25 years.

Van Kirk managed to reach a wide audience through his writings and through a weekly radio broadcast, *Religion in the News*, which was aired by NBC from 1936 to 1949. Although he was not strictly a pacifist, Van Kirk wrote in 1934 that pacifism was proliferating in the church as it had not done for centuries. He used his radio broadcasts to encourage pacifism as a viable alternative to war. In a more specific fashion, he also made known his opposition to naval appropriations in the 1930s.

His growing reputation as a commentator, writer, and administrator gained him enough support in 1935 to be named director of the National Peace Conference (NPC), a coalition that included approximately 30 peace organizations. The internationalists, like James Shotwell and Newton D. Baker, were attracted to Van Kirk's openness and ability to listen to and evaluate all sides fairly. When the NPC split over the issue of mandatory arms embargoes, Van Kirk, in his capacity as director, called for a world conference on economic relations in the hopes of repairing some of the injustices done by World War I and perhaps of preventing similar situations in the future. Because Van Kirk believed that inequitable economic systems helped to create war situations, he also believed that if nations could reach some agreement on economic relationships, then arms embargoes would not be an issue. When the NPC sponsored a Conference on World Economic Cooperation, Van Kirk took the opportunity to accuse Western powers of helping to destroy German democracy and called for economic "appeasement" and political security. This particular view was not terribly popular as Hitler became increasingly tyrannical.

Van Kirk supported the United Nations (U.N.) and served as one of the U.S. delegates in San Francisco in 1945. Although he continued to urge that the United States rely less on defensive military efforts and more on collective security, Van Kirk's beliefs regarding armed force seemed less certain in the years following World War II. He was more likely to support force on some level when the "enemy" was a Communist country, as he did by supporting U.S. involvement in the Korean War and by supporting a mutual defense pact in the Middle East to protect against Arab, Israeli, or Soviet aggression. Van Kirk's reputation as one of the foremost protestant authorities on international affairs received further reinforcement when he was appointed executive director of the Department of International Affairs of the National Council of Churches of Christ in the United States of America, a postion that he held from 1950 until his death on 6 July 1956 in Mount Vernon, New York.

References Josephson, Harold, ed., *Biographical Dictionary of Modern Peace Leaders* (1985); *New York Times* (8 July 1956).

Vernon, Mabel (1883–1975)

Mabel Vernon devoted her adult life to the pursuit of equality for women and peace for everyone.

Vernon's large and active family included five brothers and a sister plus another four half brothers and a half sister, all of whom lived in Wilmington, Delaware. Her father was the publisher and editor of the *Wilmington Daily Republican* and could afford to send his children to the best schools. After graduating from the Wilmington Friends School in 1901, Vernon left for Northampton, Massachusetts, to enroll in Smith College. Her Smith career was short-lived, however, and Vernon returned to Wilmington Friends after one month to study German. In 1903 she entered Swarthmore College, graduating in 1906 with an A.B. One of Vernon's college schoolmates was Alice Paul, who would later found the National Women's Party (NWP) and help to mount a successful campaign for passage of the Nineteenth Amendment. After leaving Swarthmore, Vernon began a teaching career. She accepted a position at Radnor High School in Wayne, Pennsylvania, where she taught German and Latin, but her heart was not in teaching.

Already an advocate of women's suffrage, Vernon attended the 1912 convention of the Philadelphia National Woman Suffrage Association, where she served as an usher. Alice Paul, her friend from Swarthmore, had recently returned from spending several years in England, where she had worked with the militant Pankhursts. Paul had been imprisoned at Hallowell Jail and had undergone forced feeding by the Hallowell authorities, all of which had taken a toll on her. Vernon would later recall how shocked she was on first seeing Paul again, for the athletic young woman she remembered was now gaunt and pale. Paul persuaded Vernon to give up her teaching job and, in exchange for a small salary, work for suffrage full time.

Vernon became the first national suffrage organizer for the militant suffragists. One of her first assignments was in Nevada, where she worked with Anne Martin to organize that state for suffrage. Vernon also coordinated the first cross-country suffrage tour, from the West Coast to Washington, for women bearing petitions with thousands of names to be delivered to President Woodrow Wilson. On 4 July 1916, Vernon was one of a small group of women who vocally disrupted a speech Wilson was delivering. A year later, Vernon was among the first group of suffragists picketing the White House to be arrested and incarcerated. After her release from prison, her effective speaking manner and stage presence made her a natural to tour the country in order to bring the suffrage message to the rest of the country. Vernon also campaigned during the ratification phase of the Nineteenth Amendment.

She spent over seven years working for equality before the Nineteenth Amendment was finally ratified in 1920. During that time, she had also managed to serve as campaign manager for Anne Martin's two unsuccessful Senate bids in 1918 and 1920 in Nevada. Stepping away from politics thereafter seemed appropriate, and for a time Vernon was the acting supervisor for the Swarthmore Chatauqua. In 1923 she took a year off to earn an M.A. in political science at Columbia University. By that time, the NWP had resolved to try securing an Equal Rights Amendment to the Constitution, and Vernon once again rejoined her former colleagues in quest of the new goal.

During this time, Vernon's interest in seeking peaceful solutions to world conflict began to increase. She joined the Women's International League for Peace and Freedom (WILPF) and ultimately curtailed all other activity in favor of doing peace work. In 1931, drawing on her experience as a suffrage organizer, Vernon organized a Peace Caravan in order to collect signatures on a petition to be presented at the 1932 World Disarmament Conference in Geneva, Switzerland. In subsequent years, Vernon represented

Mabel Vernon, National Executive Secretary of the National Women's Party (left), and Mary Moss Wellborn, national organizer, pose before leaving Washington to open headqarters in New York City to support Herbert Hoover's 1923 presidential campaign.

the United States at WILPF conferences in Zurich (1934) and Geneva (1935). She also served as campaign director for the WILPF's People's Mandate to End War. That led to her interest in Latin America, specifically, and Vernon served as director of the People's Mandate Committee for Inter-American Peace and Cooperation. Between 1950 and 1955 she was the chairperson for the People's Mandate. Her work in Latin America brought her the Diploma de Honor from the Ecuadorean Red Cross and the Ecuadorean Al Merito award. Failing health in her later years forced Vernon to retire in 1955. She died on 2 September 1975 in Washington, D.C.

See also Women's International League for Peace and Freedom.

References Irwin, Inez Haynes, *Up Hill with Banners Flying* (1964); Sicherman, Barbara, et al., eds., *Notable American Women, The Modern Period: A Biographical Dictionary* (1980); Stevens, Doris, *Jailed for Freedom* (1920).

Villard, Fanny Garrison (1844–1928)

Fanny Garrison Villard was an extraordinarily energetic woman who dedicated much of her life to improving the world she lived in. She worked tirelessly for a wide range of philanthropic causes. She was a staunch advocate of women's suffrage. Above all, she was a lifelong pacifist, as was her father, and she refused in all instances throughout her long life to compromise her pacifist principles.

Fanny Garison Villard grew up in New England and was one of seven children. Her father was the militant abolitionist William Lloyd Garrison. From him, Fanny learned to embrace progressive ideas, particularly those concerning abolitionism and women's rights. In 1886 she married a German immigrant, Henry Villard, who was the Washington correspondent for the Chicago *Tribune*. Henry Villard soon gave up newspaper work to go into finance. Eventually, he became president of the Northern Pacific Railroad. He was also an original partner in the Edison General Electric Company.

The Villards traveled throughout the country and, as their fortune grew, their interest in philanthropic causes also grew.

Fanny Villard was continuously involved in causes, from the National Association for the Advancement of Colored People (NAACP), to the Consumer's League, the Women's Exchange, the Working Women's Protection Association, and the Diet Kitchen in New York, which distributed food and medicine to needy children in the city. As the mother of four children, she had a particular interest in the welfare of poor children. She also campaigned actively for women's suffrage in New York, and in 1915 she led a march of 1,500 women up Fifth Avenue in support of a suffrage referendum.

With the outbreak of World War I, her fear that the United States might get involved prompted Villard to focus solely on issues of peace. As she did in her suffrage work, Villard spoke anywhere at any time on behalf of peace. She organized marches, rallies, conventions, parades, and petitions to the president. She urged absolute neutrality. In 1915, Villard, Jane Addams, and Rosika Schwimmer helped organize the Women's Peace Party (WPP). When the WPP voted to justify U.S. entry into the war if it came about because of an act of agression, Villard resigned. She refused to bend her principles in order to accommodate pragmatism. For the duration of the war, Villard focused her efforts on relief programs for refugees and support for conscientious objectors (COs). In 1919 she founded the Women's Peace League in New York, which was dedicated to promoting peaceful solutions for world conflicts. Villard died in Dobbs Ferry, New York, on 5 July 1928.

See also Women's Peace Society.

References *New York Times* (6 July 1928); Whitman, Alden, ed., *American Reformers: An H. W. Wilson Biographical Dictionary* (1985).

Villard, Oswald Garrison (1872–1949)

Oswald Garrison Villard was one of the most outspoken critics of U.S. participation in World War I. The son of Fanny Garrison Villard and the grandson of abolitionist William Lloyd Garrison, Oswald Villard was born in Germany on 13 March 1872 while his family was staying temporarily in Wiesbaden. Villard graduated from Harvard in 1893 and spent time in Europe traveling with his father. Upon his return to the United States, Villard took a position as an assistant to Harvard historian Albert Bushnell Hart. Eventually, he earned an M.A. from Harvard.

Although he enjoyed the work, academics seemed too passive for Villard's tastes, and he chose to go into journalism instead, undoubtedly influenced by the fact that his father owned *The New York Evening Post* and *The Nation*. After a short apprenticeship, Villard joined the *Evening Post* in 1897, which was then under the stewardship of Editor-in-Chief Edwin Godkin. It was an opportune time for Villard to be associated with the *Evening Post*, because the newspaper's opposition to the Spanish-American War in 1898 reinforced Villard's tendency to nonconformism. In 1909, Villard helped to organize a conference on African Americans to help celebrate the centennial of Abraham Lincoln's birth. As a consequence of the conference, Villard, W. E. B. DuBois, and others founded the National Association for the Advancement of Colored People (NAACP).

Villard's commitment to equal rights extended to equal rights for women. In 1911 he was one of the few men who marched in a suffrage parade in New York; he was rewarded for his support by becoming the target of spectators' taunts. Incidents like that did not deter him in the least. He was fundamentally convinced that the United States owed its greatness to the diversity of its people and that diversity was necessary to a flourishing democracy. When Woodrow Wilson was elected president, Villard held out hope that the advocate of progressivism would support the kind of diversity that Villard believed was indispensable. As chairman

Oswald Garrison Villard

of the NAACP, Villard proposed that a National Race Commission, with Jane Addams as chairwoman, be established in order to examine the condition of African Americans. Wilson hinted that he would support such an endeavor, but in the end he feared that the loss of his southern conservative constituency would be too detrimental. Villard then took to the stump, traveling around the country, speaking on behalf of a race commission and charging that Wilson had capitulated to racism. It was the opening salvo in a battle over Wilson's policies, both domestic and foreign.

When war began in Europe, Villard immediately began lobbying to keep the United States out of the conflict. Convinced that Wilson was not committed to keeping the country out of the war, primarily because of Wilson's intervention in Mexican politics from 1913 to 1916, Villard supported Charles Evans Hughes in 1916. During the war, Villard protested loudly against the abuse of civil liberties demonstrated in the treatment of antiwar advocates, such as Eugene Debs, and conscientious objectors (COs). He viewed the Treaty of Versailles as a "covenant with death," pointing out the harsh retribution imposed on the losers. Villard was convinced that the treaty contained the foundations for a future war. Villard was also critical of the Palmer Raids, which resulted in the arrests of aliens and radicals in 1919 and 1920, and he spoke out in favor of the Russian Revolution. His high-visibility criticisms once again made Villard the target of an unreceptive public. On occasion, he resorted to police protection to shield him from angry crowds. His outspokenness also cost him *The New York Evening Post*, which lost money as circulation dropped. He held on to *The Nation*, which became a forum for both his opinions and for liberal ideas. In the 1920s and 1930s circulation of *The Nation* rose from 7,000 to 40,000.

Throughout the 1920s and 1930s, Villard's sharp critiques were aimed at domestic issues rather than foreign policy issues, but as World War II approached, he once again advocated nonintervention. Although he condemned Hitler in no uncertain terms, he reiterated that the responsibility for Hitler's rise lay in the harsh peace terms that emerged from the Treaty of Versailles. Villard continued pressing his viewpoint even when others began to accept interventionism. Embittered by what he believed was an abandonment of reform, Villard joined the America First Committee, despite the fact that many of its members were diametrically opposed to Villard's reform views. The debate was finally put to rest on 7 December 1941 with the bombing of Pearl Harbor. Thereafter, Villard retired to his country home and concentrated on writing. He died in New York after suffering a fatal stroke on 1 October 1949.

References Humes, D.J., *Oswald Garrison Villard: Liberal of the 1920s* (1960); Whitman, Alden, ed., *American Reformers: An H. W. Wilson Biographical Dictionary* (1985); Wreszin, Michael, *Oswald Garrison Villard: Pacifist at War* (1965).

Volunteers for Peace (VFP)

Volunteers for Peace (VFP), located in Vermont, is a nonprofit, nondenominational organization founded in 1981 that operates a series of international camps. It coordinates workcamps in the United States and abroad, with field organizers providing consultation and placement services for camp volunteers and hosts. Members volunteer their time, energy, talents, and resources to promote world peace through a program of community service and travel. The organization does not advocate any particular doctrine, believing that the shared experiences of participants and their willingness to live and work together for the benefit of humanity will promote world peace.

Reference Meyer, Robert S., *Peace Organizations Past and Present* (1988).

Wald, Lillian (1867–1940)

Lillian Wald is best remembered for her enormous contribution to the founding and development of public health nursing as a profession, for her work as a social worker and a social reformer, and for her founding of the Henry Street Settlement on New York City's Lower East Side. She is less remembered for her equally ardent support of the peace movement and her own commitment to pacifism.

Wald was born in Cincinnati, Ohio. She was, in her own words, a spoiled child, by which she meant not that she was self-centered or lacked empathy for those less fortunate than she, but rather that she had had an idyllic childhood, free from want and strife, in an environment of love and support. At 16, Wald applied for admission to Vassar College, but because of her age she was turned down. Between the ages of 16 and 21, Wald lived a life that others might envy. As an upper-middle-class member of Cincinnati society, gifted with looks, health, and intelligence, Wald led an active social life. She could have chosen to continue this easy existence, but by 21 she was looking for more meaning in her life than she had yet found.

In 1899, Wald enrolled at New York Hospital's nurses training school. Still dissatisfied after working for one year as a nurse, Wald enrolled in the Women's Medical College in New York. While at Women's, Wald accepted an invitation to organize nursing classes for immigrant families on the Lower East Side. Her experience proved to be crucial and a turning point in her life. She left medical school, moved to the East Side with a friend, and determined to make the neighborhood her own and to make a positive contribution. Sponsored and funded by banker/philanthropist Jacob Schiff and his mother-in-law, Mrs. Solomon Loeb, Wald established a Nurses' Settlement on Henry Street in New York.

Starting with 11 nurses, including a leader in the nursing profession, Lavinia L. Dock, Wald's settlement house soon housed 92 nurses, who made approximately 200,000 calls per year on people too untutored or too indigent to avail themselves of other medical treatment. So successful was the settlement house that similar organizations appeared across the country and became the foundation for the Public Health Nursing movement. Wald helped to establish the first public school nursing program in the United States, and she was largely responsible for the establishment of a department of nursing and health at Columbia University Teacher's College in 1910.

In 1912, Wald was chosen as the first president of the National Organization for Public Health Nursing, another organization that she helped to found. Her efforts on behalf of her fellow neighborhood residents literally changed lives. As the Henry Street Settlement House expanded both its physical plant and its community activities, more and more adults and children became its beneficiaries. Scholarships were established to keep talented youngsters in school until age 16. Wald campaigned for tuberculosis eradication, better housing, better parks and playgrounds, and ungraded public school classes for retarded children. She, along with Florence Kelley, the director of the National Consumers League, helped to found the National Child Labor Committee. The list of people with whom Wald worked over the years and who considered her a friend included Jane Addams, Eleanor Roosevelt, Alfred E. Smith, Frances Perkins, Henry Morgenthau, and Sidney Hillman. Although

Lillian Wald

international cooperation. Wald also worked closely with the Women's International League for Peace and Freedom (WILPF), formerly the Women's Peace Party (WPP). She represented the WILPF at several international conferences and lobbied to promote its program, including efforts to get the United States into the League of Nations.

Until her death, Wald also worked continuously for disarmament, although her ability to remain active decreased dramatically after 1920, when she had to deal with health problems. Wald died in Westport, Connecticut, on 1 September 1940.

See also American Union against Militarism; Women's International League for Peace and Freedom.

References Duffas, Robert L., *Lillian Wald: Neighbor and Crusader* (1938); James, Edward T., et al., eds., *Notable American Women, 1607–1950: A Biographical Dictionary* (1971); Josephson, Harold, ed., *Biographical Dictionary of Modern Peace Leaders* (1985).

Wald had never heard of the settlement house movement before she became involved in Henry Street, her work soon brought her into contact with Addams, who became a particularly close associate, both in social reform work and in the peace movement.

In 1912, Wald opposed Theodore Roosevelt's bid for the presidency because she objected to his Panama Canal policy and to his desire to beef up the U.S. Navy with the addition of two more battleships. As a pacifist, Wald adamantly opposed the United States's entry into World War I. Shortly after the war started in Europe, Wald organized a parade of women to protest the fighting. More than 12,000 women marched up Fifth Avenue in New York on 29 August 1914 in response to Wald's appeal. In 1915, Wald and several colleagues founded the American Union against Militarism (AUAM). The organization's goal was to mobilize public support against miltarism and to work toward

War Resisters League (WRL)

An outgrowth of the Antiestablishment League (founded in 1915 to protest the war and to support conscientious objectors [COs]), the War Resisters League (WRL) was organized in 1923 as the U.S. branch of War Resisters International. The WRL brought together representatives of the Fellowship of Reconcilitation (FOR), the Women's Peace Union, and the Women's Peace Society. Jessie Wallace Hughan, a noted pacifist and Socialist, was the moving force behind the league's organization and served as its secretary until 1945. The WRL offered to support pacifists and COs who had no religious ties. Members of the WRL advocated nonviolent civil disobedience. In 1937, 12,000 people signed a WRL pledge stating: "War is a crime against humanity. We therefore are determined not to support any kind of war and to strive for the removal of all causes of war."

Following World War II, in 1947, the WRL sponsored the first draft card burning as a protest against peacetime conscription. More than 400 potential draftees participated in the protest. After passage of the Selective Service Act of 1948, the WRL, in concert with other peace groups, founded the Central Committee for Conscientious Objectors (CCCO). The WRL publication, *Liberation*, began appearing in 1956. It was a forum for social issues such as disarmament and civil rights and a primer for direct-action protest tactics. The WPL launched a campaign to protest nuclear bomb shelters in the 1950s and 1960s. In August 1963, then-Executive Secretary Bayard Rustin helped to organize the March on Washington (MOW). The WRL, a participating organization in the Times Square Vigil that began in October 1963 to protest the war in Vietnam, was influential in the anti-Vietnam protests of the 1960s and 1970s by organizing marches, rallies, and draft card burnings and by encouraging tax resistance and civil disobedience. Its concern with disarmament prompted the Continental Walk for Disarmament and Social Justice in 1976 and the Mobilization for Survival in 1977.

The WRL continues to organize activities geared toward eliminating the causes of war throughout the world. The organization's publication, *The Nonviolent Activist*, is published eight times yearly and contains news of WRL activities in both national and international forums.

See also Hughan, Jessie Wallace; Mobilization for Survival.

References Meyer, Robert S., *Peace Organizations Past and Present* (1988); Sicherman, Barbara, et al., eds., *Notable American Women, The Modern Period: A Biographical Dictionary* (1980); Wittner, Lawrence S., *Rebels against War: The American Peace Movement 1941–1960* (1969); Zaroulis, Nancy, and Gerald Sullivan, *Who Spoke Up? American Protest against the War in Vietnam 1963–1975* (1984).

Washington Naval Disarmament Conference

See Power Treaties.

Wechsler, James (1915–1983)

James Wechsler, a prominent journalist and author, was also renowned for his longtime advocacy of peace. Born in New York City, Wechsler graduated from Columbia University in 1935. He became identified with the peace issue during the wave of pacifism and peace advocacy that swept the country in the mid-1930s. As the undergraduate editor of the Columbia *Spectator*, Wechsler used his position to promote the cause of peace. He was one of the signers of the Oxford Oath at a student rally held at Columbia University in conjunction with the national student strike held on 12 April 1935. Wechsler, along with Roger Baldwin of the American Civil Liberties Union (ACLU) and theologian Reinhold Niebuhr addressed the 3,000-student audience, encouraging those who opposed war to sign the Oxford Oath, which was a pledge to refuse to serve in the armed forces under any circumstances. After graduating from Columbia, Wechsler began his journalism career with *The Nation*, taking a job as assistant editor, then labor editor, and finally Washington bureau chief. He remained with *The Nation* until 1947, when he left to take an editorial position with the *New York Post*. He remained with the *Post* until his death, first as editor and then as a regular political columnist.

Besides his activist work in the peace movement, Wechsler made a lasting contribution in a number of books on peace that he wrote over the years. *Revolt on the Campus* (1935) was followed by a series of books, including: *War: Our Heritage* (1937); *War Propaganda and the United States* (1940); *Labor Baron* (1944); *Age of Suspicion* (1954); *Reflections of an Angry Middle Aged Editor* (1960); and *In a Darkness* (1972).

Despite his desire for peace, Wechsler was not a pacifist. By the time World War II became a reality, he had resolved his conflict between a desire for peace and his perception that Hitler and fascism represented an unacceptable threat. He served in the United States Army during the conflict. He also sided with the peace activists in the Cold War era who believed that communism was a threat and had to be contained. Wechsler was a supporter of President Harry S Truman and the Marshall Plan as well as of George Kennan's Containment Theory. Even so, like many activists of the era, Wechsler had to contend with charges made by Senator Joseph McCarthy that he harbored Communist sympathies. Wechsler testifed before the McCarthy committee, acknowledging that as a student he had briefly been associated with the Communist party but that he was very quickly disillusioned and had since had an adversarial relationship with the Communists. McCarthy portrayed Wechsler as a typical Communist sympathizer who renounced the party in order to make people believe that he was no longer a part of it. It was a ridiculous charge and typical of McCarthy's tactics.

Wechsler was the recipient of several prestigious awards in recognition of his peace activism, including the Americans for Democratic Action's (ADA) Roosevelt Award in 1962, the ACLU Lasker Award in 1968, and the Fortune Society's Karl Messinger Award in 1978. Wechsler died on 11 September 1983 in New York City.

References *Who Was Who in America* (1972); Wittner, Lawrence S., *Rebels against War: The American Peace Movement 1941–1960* (1969).

West, Daniel (1893–1971)

Daniel West was born in Preble County, Ohio. He prepared for a career as a public school teacher at Manchester College, where he earned a B.A. in education in 1917. He then went on to Cornell University, graduating with an M.A. in 1920. West did teach in the public school system, as he had planned, but he was really drawn to work in the Church of the Brethren, one of the historic peace churches.

Between Manchester College and Cornell University, West had served in the military. His pacifism and long association with the Church of the Brethren caused him to accept only noncombatant service. After leaving Cornell, West began working with young people, as a teacher and youth leader for the church. His focus as a youth leader was to make his young charges aware of the peace tradition that was fundamental to their church. Eventually, his efforts led to the formation of a church organization called 20,000 Dunkers for Peace. Those who joined were required to make a commitment not to take part in any war. His peace group appealed particularly to those who sought a moral equivalent of war. From 1930 to 1936, West was director of youth work in the Church of the Brethren. West also toured college campuses, speaking on behalf of the Emergency Peace Campaign (EPC) in 1936. In 1938 he took over as the national staff leader in peace education, a post he held until 1959.

One of West's most innovative relief ideas involved sending heifers to areas where there was an urgent need to provide milk for children. He conceived the idea while doing relief work in Spain during the Spanish Civil War. West's idea was first implemented when heifers were exported to Puerto Rico in 1944. The Heifer Project soon became an international effort sponsored in part by the United Nations Relief and Rehabilitation Agency. The Heifer Project worked with the assistance of thousands of so-called sea-going cowboys, who donated their time and lifestock to see that the heifers reached their destination. The Heifer Project remained active for years, with West serving as its consultant. Over time, the focus shifted from postwar reconstruction to Third World development. West was honored on the twenty-fifth anniversary of the Heifer Project for his innovative approach to relief assistance and for his years of dedicated service to the project. He died on 7 January 1971 in Goshen, Indiana.

Reference Josephson, Harold, ed., *Biographical Dictionary of Modern Peace Leaders* (1985).

Wilson, Thomas Woodrow (1856–1924)

Thomas Woodrow Wilson was born in Staunton, Virginia. As a young man, he used to daydream about being elected U.S. Senator from Virginia and serving his state and country with honor. Although his interest in politics never abated, his life seemed to take a direction other than the one he had envisioned.

Wilson graduated from Princeton University in 1879 and then studied law at the University of Virginia. After passing the bar, he went into private practice in Atlanta, Georgia, for a short time. He soon found that practicing law did not provide the satisfaction that he had hope for. In 1883, Wilson entered graduate school at Johns Hopkins to earn a Ph.D. He completed his doctoral thesis in 1885. The thesis, *Congressional Government*, became a standard textbook on government and helped to establish Wilson as the expert in the field. He began a teaching career that took him from Bryn Mawr (1885–1888), to Wesleyan (1888–1890), and finally back to his alma mater, Princeton. At Princeton, his academic career was outstanding. Within two years, Wilson was selected as the first nonclerical president of the university. By the time he resigned in 1910, Wilson was considered one of the top two university presidents in the country; the other top president was Charles Eliot of Harvard University.

In 1910 local Democratic party officials in New Jersey tapped Wilson to be a candidate for governor of New Jersey. The Democrats had two criteria for their choice: first, the candidate had to have a reputation as a progressive, in order to appeal to the electorate of the time; and second, the candidate had to be someone easily manipulated to serve the real purpose of the machine. Wilson fulfilled half of the requirements. To the chagrin of the Democratic bosses, they discovered too late that Wilson could not be manipulated. His career in politics has been described as meteoric, and indeed, within three years of becoming a candidate for governor of New Jersey, the erudite academic took the oath of office as president of the United States.

Wilson's record as president was a commendable one. In his first term, he reformed the tariff (Underwood Tariff Act), modernized the banking system (Federal Reserve Act), reformed trade by establishing the Federal Trade Commission, and oversaw passage of the Clayton Antitrust Act. Increasingly, however, the war in Europe became a serious concern for him. Wilson was not a pacifist, but he wanted nothing more than to keep the United States out of the war. In part, Wilson had ambitions to act as a neutral mediator in helping to resolve the European conflict. As early as 1916, he had begun putting together a list of items that he deemed necessary for a lasting peace. By 1917, the war in Europe and the German resumption of submarine warfare left Wilson with little choice other than to ask for a declaration of war. Throughout the short but bitter period in which U.S. troops were involved in the fighting, Wilson continued to lobby for a just peace following the conflict.

Germany surrendered in November 1918, and Wilson left for Europe to participate in treaty negotiations in Versailles, France. Wilson's Fourteen Points became the basis for the treaty. The cornerstone of his proposal was the establishment of a League of Nations, which would become a world body, all the members of which would act in concert to maintain peace. It was a laudable and necessary set of conditions. Unfortunately, the bitterness of other Allies, notably France and Great Britain, forced Wilson to compromise on key issues. The result was that the Treaty of Versailles did little more than create a situation in Europe in which future war was almost inevitable. Moreover, the "politics as usual" resolution of imposing untenable reparations payments on Germany and carving up Europe to suit the Allies' desire for revenge, fatally injured Wilson's chances for getting the U.S. Senate even to ratify the treaty. Although he fought mightily for ratification when he returned to the United States, the Senate refused to endorse a proposal that, in its eyes, would cause the United States to relinquish sovereignty. It proved to be a mortal defeat for Wilson. Never able to revel in winning the Nobel Peace Prize in 1919, Wilson suffered a stroke in September of that year, leaving him incapacitated. He never fully recovered and died on 3 February 1924 in Washington, D.C. Although the League of Nations ultimately broke down, it was Wilson's legacy to the world, and it was reborn more successfully in the United Nations (U.N.).

References Knock, Thomas J., *To End All Wars: Woodrow Wilson and the Quest for World Order* (1992); Link, Arthur S., et al., eds., *The American People: A History* (1981).

Wisconsin Institute for the Study of War, Peace, and Global Cooperation

In its own words, the mission of the Wisconsin Institute is to "encourage and legitimize research and teaching on the roots of organized violence, on security issues, and on the factors necessary for a just global peace." A consortium of 21 institutions of higher education in Wisconsin combined to found the Wisconsin Institute in 1985. In addition to pooling resources to coordinate mutually beneficial programs, the consortium is also able to pursue common sources of funding. Employing a range of activities—providing curricular assistance to participating institutions; organizing conferences, symposia, and workshops; soliciting funds from private and public foundations; distributing research grants and providing release time for faculty and staff as well as funding for graduate students and undergraduates; and providing consultation and professional services to primary and secondary schools—the Wisconsin Institute enables scholars, teachers, and students alike to expand their understanding of war, peace, and justice.

Reference Meyer, Robert S., *Peace Organizations Past and Present* (1988).

Wise, Stephen Samuel (1874–1949)

An internationalist and an advocate of cooperative arbitration rather than war to settle disputes between nations, Stephen Wise nevertheless found himself supporting both World War I and World War II.

Wise was born in Erlau, Hungary. After immigrating to the United States he enrolled at Columbia University, graduating with a B.A. in 1892 and a Ph.D. in 1901. In 1893, Wise was ordained a rabbi, and until 1900 he was the rabbi of B'nai Jeshurun in New York. In 1900, Wise took a post in Portland Oregon, serving as rabbi of Beth Israel until 1906. He then returned to New York, where he became rabbi at The Free Synagogue, a position he held until his death in 1949.

Wise's move toward pacifism came relatively late in life. His first pronouncements in favor of pacifism came with Woodrow Wilson's Mexican policy and the border dispute between the United States and Mexico in 1914. His admiration for Wilson grew significantly when Wilson agreed to place the dispute in the hands of mediators. Wise joined with his friend, John Haynes Holmes, in speaking out against World War I when the conflict began in Europe. He was also a founder of the Anti-Preparedness Committee, which later became the American Union against Militarism. Wilson's preparedness program in 1916 almost caused Wise to disavow his support for the president, but his pacifism, unlike Holmes's, was neither unconditional nor absolute. When Wilson finally asked for a declaration of war after Germany resumed submarine warfare, Wise proclaimed to his congregation that he would stand with the president, who, he said, had no choice but to go to war. This stand infuriated many of Wise's peace colleagues.

Postwar doubts about the wisdom of supporting the war caused Wise to resume his relationship with his peace colleagues in the 1920s and 1930s. Even in the early 1930s, Wise could still vow that he would never again renounce his pacifism and support war. With the rise of Hitler, however, remaining a pacifist became unbearable for Wise. Although he continued—right up to the attack on Pearl Harbor—to hope that the United States would not be drawn into the war, from 1939 on Wise supported U.S. aid to the European allies. Continued opposition to the war by pacifists frustrated President Franklin Roosevelt. At one point, he called upon Wise to speak with Holmes in order to try persuading Holmes to drop his opposition. Although it was not a request that Wise could fulfill, he himself did proclaim his support for the war, convinced once again that the actions of ambitious tyrants could not always be resolved by peaceful methods.

Wise was an ardent supporter of the United Nations (U.N.) following the war. He died on 19 April 1949 in New York.

See also American Union against Militarism.

References Josephson, Harold, ed., *Biographical Dictionary of Modern Peace Leaders* (1985); Knock, Thomas J., *To End All Wars: Woodrow Wilson and the Quest for World Order* (1992); Wittner, Lawrence S., *Rebels against War: The American Peace Movement 1941–1960* (1969).

Rabbi Stephen Samuel Wise

Witherspoon, Frances (1887–1973)

As a child, Frances Witherspoon learned to hate war from her father, Samuel Andrew Witherspoon, a prominent Mississippi attorney and U.S. congressman, who made clear his opposition to the Spanish-American War and his disdain for both Theodore Roosevelt's foreign policy and Woodrow Wilson's Mexican policy. She agreed wholeheartedly with her father's opinions and assesments, and was equally outspoken among her peers and friends.

Frances Witherspoon, who was born in Meridian, Mississippi, arrived at Bryn Mawr College as an experienced political activist. In the years immediately after her graduation from Bryn Mawr in 1908, Witherspoon worked as a volunteer in a variety of organizations promoting women's suffrage, peace, and social change. With her Bryn Mawr classmate

and lifelong companion Tracy Mygatt, Witherspoon was a tireless public speaker on behalf of suffrage and peace.

Witherspoon's father died in 1915, and although she was already well embarked on a career as an agent of change, the distraught Witherspoon rededicated her life to peace and social change as a tribute to her beloved faher. As she and Mygatt continued their suffrage work and their joint writing projects—which included books, plays, articles, book reviews, and letters—Witherspoon also focused more pointedly on peace. In 1915 she accepted a post as assistant secretary of the Women's Peace Party (WPP). Disappointed when the party continued to support Wilson when he armed merchant ships, Witherspoon resigned from the WPP and threw herself into antiwar work. She supported rights for conscientious objectors (COs) and worked to keep them out of Bellevue Hospital in New York. (It was the practice at the time to send COs to Bellevue for "mental observation.") Witherspoon was one of the founders of the Bureau of

Legal Advice, a precursor of the American Civil Liberties Union (ACLU). In addition to counseling COs during the war, Witherspoon advocated improving conditions in military camps for COs, who were frequently treated badly.

When the war was over and the country very quickly fell into the grip of a "Red scare," Witherspoon was again in the forefront of those who sought to protect the rights of political prisoners who were threatened with deportation or with incarceration. Many so-called radicals had already received prison terms of 20 and 30 years. When the ACLU was founded in 1921, the Bureau of Legal Advice was one of many small organizations that became subsumed under the ACLU. After that, Witherspoon worked with the Fellowship of Reconciliation (FOR), the Women's International League for Peace and Freedom (WILPF), the War Resisters League (WRL), and SANE. The WRL was organized primarily by Witherspoon, Mygatt, and Jessie Hughan, and much of Witherspoon's work was undertaken on behalf of that organization.

Witherspoon remained an activist throughout her life. Even as late as 1968 she worked for peace, organizing Bryn Mawr alumni to protest the Vietnam War. It is a measure of her success at mobilizing support that she was able to run full-page advertisements in the *New York Times* and the *Philadelphia Bulletin* protesting the war. Not surprisingly, Witherspoon abhorred the Cold War unleashing of a nuclear arms race and the advent of antiballistic missiles (ABMs). Despite her distress at these developments, she always remained optimistic that her vision of a world free of war would prevail in the end. Witherspoon died in Philadelphia on 16 December 1973.

See also Mygatt, Tracy Dickinson.

References Josephson, Harold, ed., *Biographical Dictionary of Modern Peace Leaders* (1985); Manahan, Nancy, "Future Old Maids and Pacifist Agitators: The Story of Tracy Mygatt and Frances Witherspoon." *Women's Studies Quarterly* 10 (Spring 1982).

Women's International League for Peace and Freedom (WILPF)

The Women's Peace Party (WPP) was founded in 1915 by Jane Addams and Crystal Eastman as an outgrowth of an International Congress of Women held at The Hague in 1915. In 1919, at the Second Women's Peace Conference, women from 16 countries voted to continue the party permanently as the Women's International League for Peace and Freedom (WILPF). The party's slogan, from the beginning, has been "Listen to the Women for a Change."

Dedicated to searching for peaceful solutions to world conflict, the WILPF continued to lobby and meet throughout the 1920s and 1930s. By 1937, the organization had a permanent staff of 11 people, with 120 branches nationwide and 13,000 members. It was through the lobbying efforts of the WILPF that the Nye Committee was organized to investigate charges that munitions manufacturers had conspired to start World War I for their own gain. The WILPF successfully lobbied senators Norris, Gerald Nye, and even Secretary of State Cordell Hull into pursuing an investigation, although Hull later expressed regret over endorsing the Nye Committee. Moreover, the WILPF was allowed to choose the chief investigator for the committee. The choice was Steven Rauschenbush, by reputation a zealot and a radical, who was largely responsible for initiating the committee's more sensational revelations, although most proved to be unfounded.

As the totalitarian and fascist governments in Europe and the Far East began to exert themselves, the WILPF, like many other organizations, began to shift its focus from pacifism to collective security. Although the organization was reluctant to abandon pacifist principles in favor of war, there seemed to be little choice. Those who viewed fascism as a threat to peace came to the conclusion that the first order of business had to be the defeat of the fascist governments.

Once they were ended, the WILPF threw its full weight behind the idea of a collective security organization and urged support for the United Nations (U.N.).

The WILPF had as its goals in 1963: achieving a complete nuclear test ban treaty, economic planning for disarmament, nonviolent direct action for human rights, and support of the U.N. On 7 April 1964, protesting the Vietnam War, the WILPF sent 250 of its members to Washington to lobby government officials. The WILPF members issued a seven-point program that included a protest against the brutality of war, honorable withdrawal of U.S. forces, a call for stopping the use of napalm and defoliants in Vietnam, an end to a war that in its view could not be won, a cessation of support—both military and financial—of an unelected South Vietnam government, a negotiated settlement and a reopening of the Geneva Conference, and a forecast that the United States would "lose moral leadership in the eyes of the world if [it continued] a senseless war."

In the post-Vietnam era, the WILPF has been engaged in a number of campaigns, including Feed the Cities not the Pentagon Campaign (1976); Nuclear Weapons Freeze Campaign (1979); Conference on Racism (1979); Stop the Arms Race Campaign (1980); March for Jobs, Peace, and Freedom (1983); Listen to Women for a Change (1983); Campaign for Comprehensive Test Ban (1984); International Cruise Missile Alert (1985); and Campaign to Stop 'Star Wars' (1987). The educational affiliate of the WILPF is the Jane Addams Peace Association, which, among other things, has provided curriculum materials for peace education. With 130 branches across the United States and in 26 foreign countries, the WILPF "enables women to find their voice and increase their power."

See also Addams, Jane; Eastman, Crystal.

References Meyer, Robert S., *Peace Organizations Past and Present* (1988); Wittner, Lawrence S., *Rebels against War: The American Peace Movement 1941–1960* (1969).

Women's Peace Party (WPP)
See Women's International League for Peace and Freedom (WILPF).

Women's Peace Society
Founded in 1919 by Fanny Garrison Villard, the Women's Peace Society was Villard's response to those in the peace movement who allowed pragmatism to outweigh principled idealism. Villard was a pacifist who believed that the United States should not be drawn into war, regardless of the provocation. She believed totally in passive resistance to agressive behavior. Although Villard, along with Jane Addams and Rosika Schwimmer, had been instrumental in helping to establish the Women's Peace Party (WPP), Villard resigned as an executive board member and head of the New York City branch when, in 1916, the WPP voted to consider U.S. entry into World War I justified if it came about in response to an act of aggression. The Women's Peace Society, headquartered in New York City, was composed of individuals who believed in total disarmament, mediation of international disputes, free trade between nations, and absolute passive resistance to aggression. Villard firmly believed that to do anything less was hypocritical. Villard remained president of the Women's Peace Society until her death in 1928.

See also Villard, Fanny Garrison.

References James, Edward T., et al., eds., *Notable American Women, 1607–1950: A Biographical Dictionary* (1971); Whitman, Alden, ed., *American Reformers: An H. W. Wilson Biographical Dictionary* (1985).

Women Strike for Peace (WSP)
The Women Strike for Peace (WSP), founded in 1961 by Bella Abzug, had as its goal a general and complete passage of a nuclear test ban treaty. A self-described grass-roots organization, its membership was open to everyone. That nonexclusionary aspect made it a target for the House Un-American Activities Committee (HUAC) in December 1962. The

HUAC could find nothing un-American about the organization. Many WSP members characterized themselves as ordinary "housewives." They were forthcoming in participating in direct-action protest, but, unlike some of their younger counterparts, WSP members made it a point to dress well during their protests, which made it more difficult to classify them as anything other than concerned citizens. The WSP picketed the White House, the United Nations (U.N.), and the Congress. It was the first anti-Vietnam group to march on the Pentagon, and it helped to initiate the Times Square Vigils in October 1963. As the Vietnam War wound down, so did the WSP. Many of the women active in the WSP shifted their focus to the nuclear freeze movement thereafter.

Reference Zaroulis, Nancy, and Gerald Sullivan, *Who Spoke Up? American Protest against the War in Vietnam 1963–1975* (1984).

Woolley, Mary Emma (1863–1947)

Mary Woolley served as president of Mount Holyoke College for 36 years, leaving an indelible mark on the first woman's college in the United States. Woolley, born in South Norwalk, Connecticut, graduated from Wheaton Seminary in 1882 and remained there another four years as a teacher. After a brief trip to Europe, and with the encouragement of her father, Woolley applied to and was accepted at Brown University. She became one of the first seven women to graduate from Brown, earning a B.A. in 1894 and an M.A. in 1895. From there, Woolley went on to Wellesley College to teach history. Within four years she had advanced from instructor to professor and department chairwoman. Her reputation within the academic community prompted an invitation to become president of Mount Holyoke College, a position that she held from 1901 to 1936. During her tenure as

Women Strike for Peace members protest the war in Vietnam and Laos, 1970.

president, the student body doubled, the curriculum became both more flexible and more rigorous, housecleaning chores for students were abandoned, and the college's physical plant underwent a substantial building program. Woolley was also responsible for shifting the religious focus of the college from the local Congregational church to the nondenominational college chapel. Woolley often used chapel services to speak to her students, urging them make the most of their educational opportunity and to find that one thing in their lives that would make the world a richer place. She demanded of her students that they learn to think, and she inspired them to public service. Woolley believed wholeheartedly in women's rights. She supported the women's suffrage movement and, later, the Equal Rights Amendment. She also believed that women could be most effective in the cause of peace. She was a member of the APS and served as its vice-president from 1907 to 1913. She was also a member of the League of Nations Association and the Institute for Pacific Relations. She was the only woman to serve as a U.S. delegate to the Geneva Disarmament Conference in 1932. Both as a college president and in the years following her retirement, Woolley continued to work for permanent world peace. During World War II she organized the Committee on the Participation of Women in Post-War Policy.

When Woolley resigned from Mount Holyoke in 1936, a controversy over her successor engulfed the campus. The trustees wanted to appoint a man to replace her. Woolley and many members of the faculty and alumnae believed that the tradition of women presidents should be maintained. The trustees won out, and Woolley left Mount Holyoke never to return to the campus again. She died in West Port, New York, on 5 September 1947.

References Garraty, John A. and Edward T. James, eds., *Dictionary of American Biography*, supp. 4 (1974); James, Edward T., et al., eds., *Notable American Women, 1607–1950: A Biographical Dictionary* (1971).

Mary Emma Woolley was president of Mount Holyoke College for 36 years.

Workshop for Non-Violence

Founded in 1965, the Workshop for Non-Violence was an outgrowth of the War Resisters League (WRL) and the Committee for Non-Violent Action (CNVA). It focused on the tactics and strategies of nonviolent, direct-action protests. The organization's publication, *WIN*, had a wide readership among antiwar activists and was, consequently, an influential forum for antiwar activities.

Reference Zaroulis, Nancy, and Gerald Sullivan, *Who Spoke Up? American Protest against the War in Vietnam 1963–1975* (1984).

World Citizen, Inc. (WC)

The purpose of World Citizen, Inc.(WC), is to develop a global perspective in school and community youth groups. WC was founded in 1983 in Minneapolis, Minnesota, by teachers, parents, and business leaders from the Twin Cities area. Through the formation of WC clubs for children from ages five to 13, WC has developed a program whereby children can learn to deal with local, national, and international problems by using a global perspective to understand the concerns of others.

The organization assists any group desiring to start a WC club by sending out advisors and educational materials developed by WC, which include a short film written by and featuring singer John Denver, entitled *Alpha or Omega*. Another film, *Spaceship Earth*, features schoolchildren from Minneapolis. Educational materials are also provided through WC from Global Education, the Minneapolis-based publishing group that specializes in peace-oriented issues, and through WC's newsletter, *World Citizen News*, which is written by student reporters from various WC clubs.

Reference Meyer, Robert S., *Peace Organizations Past and Present* (1988).

World Citizens Assembly (WCA)

To commemorate the thirtieth anniversary of the founding of the United Nations (U.N.), and to emphasize that the goal of securing world peace had not yet been achieved, the World Citizens Assembly (WCA) was founded in San Francisco in 1975. A gathering of 500 people from 22 countries around the world met to work out a mutual set of goals and strategies. As the organization's name implies, the founders planned to create a world assembly of elected delegates whose purpose would be to seek permanent peace through a global political system.

After the initial meeting, regional assemblies were held in Europe, Central America, and Asia, while subsequent World Citizen assemblies were held in 1977, 1980, and 1984. In 1975 the WCA submitted an Ongoing Global Ceasefire statement, intended to declare a truce on all wars, to the U.N. General Assembly for consideration. On its tenth anniversary, the WCA returned to San Francisco, holding its largest public gathering at Golden Gate Park. Assistant secretary general of the U.N., Robert Muller, delivered the keynote address. Television and Hollywood actor Ed Asner also spoke, and a children's choir sang what by then had become the anthem of world citizenship, "We Are the World." The WCA launched a new campaign to create a People's House in the U.N., a body analagous to the U.S. House of Representatives. In addition, the WCA inaugurated a Let's Abolish War Campaign, geared to promote greater acceptance of law and order as an alternative to war for resolving world conflicts. The Peace and Environment Campaign, initiated in 1985, attempted to move away from the arms race, with its emphasis on destruction, and toward an environmental race, with an emphasis on restoring ecological balance.

Reference Meyer, Robert S., *Peace Organizations Past and Present* (1988).

World Conference on Religion and Peace

The third World Conference on Religion and Peace was held in Princeton, New Jersey, in 1979. Three hundred and fifty-eight delegates representing religions from Buddhism to Zoroastrianism, from 47 countries around the world, met to discuss the conference theme, Religion in the Struggle for World Community. The conference mobilization for peace was organized around four goals: (1) a just international economic order; (2) nuclear and conventional disarmament; (3) human rights; and (4) environment and energy crises, and education for peace. The Princeton Declaration issued by the conference stated, in part: "We believe that as religious people, we have a special responsibility for building a peaceful world community, and a special contribution to make. . . . We believe that peace is not only possible, but it is the way of life for human beings on earth." Members of the conference have joined with scientists, physicians, educators, and students to take an active role in opposing the arms race. Seeking the elimination of both nuclear and conventional arms, the conference's commitment to peace is grounded in the belief that there is a relationship between disarmament and development and that development can not take place until people are free from fear, insecurity, hunger, poverty, and oppression.

Reference Meyer, Robert S., *Peace Organizations Past and Present* (1988).

World Federalist Association (WFA)

In 1947 members of five organizations met in Asheville, North Carolina, for the purpose of merging into a single organization. The five groups—Americans United for World Government, Massachusetts Committee for World Federation, World Citizens of Georgia, Americans United for World Government, and World Federalists USA—became the United World Federalists. The United World Federalists functioned primarily as a lobbying group, and when that organization changed its name to World Federalists, USA it retained its lobbying function. In 1975 the World Federalist Association (WFA) became a tax-deductible organization, carrying out the political agenda of its parent organization, the World Federalists, USA. At the same time, the Campaign for UN Reform was founded to take over political and electioneering programs within the World Federalists, USA. The WFA has long advocated substituting world law for world war as a means of resolving international conflicts.

Noted peace advocate Norman Cousins served the WFA as its president for many years, as did executive director Walter Hoffman. Under their tutelage, the WFA experienced marked growth, including 90 local chapters nationwide and several networking groups.

In addition to initiating and securing sponsors for congressional resolutions promoting a fully disarmed world, the WFA was instrumental in the creation of a National Peace Academy, which ultimately led to funding for a United States Institute of Peace. In 1986, a publication entitled *Creative Solutions to Meet Six Current Crises* was issued by the WFA. The six crises to which the title referred included terrorism, South Africa, the arms race, Central America, pollution, and U.N. funding. All six crises illustrated the need for settling conflicts through strong international "law with justice." To illustrate its point, the WFA initiated a lawsuit in federal court on 23 September 1986. The lawsuit petitioned for enforcement of the judgement handed down by the World Court, which had held that the U.S. policy of supplying aid to the Nicaraguan contras was a violation of international law.

In 1987, the WFA was one of three initiating sponsors, along with the Common Heritage Institute of Villanova and the World Association of World Federalists, of a three-day International Bicentennial Symposium on Strengthening the United Nations. Cosponsors included major peace groups, such as Clergy and Laity Concerned (CALC), the Friends Peace Committee, and the Women's International League for Peace and Freedom (WILPF). Some 22 other groups also cosponsored the symposium, held at Independence Hall at the University of Pennsylvania. The symposium's aim was to focus scholarly and public attention on the premise that a stronger United Nations (U.N.), capable of maintaining peace and promoting human rights and economic and social justice, was a necessary prerequisite to establishing a truly permanent world peace. Although sponsors did not demand that participants agree with the premise, they were asked to consider its merits. The resulting exchange of ideas led to the *Declaration of Philadelphia*, which all participants were asked to sign. The declaration essentially outlined the reasons for strengthening and properly funding the U.N. in order to help promote a world of law and justice.

Reference Meyer, Robert S., *Peace Organizations Past and Present* (1988).

World Government of World Citizens (WGWC)

When Garry Davis, a World War II bomber pilot who flew missions over Germany, began to question the authority and wisdom of nations sending off their citizens to engage in wars against each other, the seed for the World Government of World Citizens (WGWC) was planted. Davis, driven to find rationalism in an irrational world, concluded that the arbitrary divison of the world into sovereign nations lay at the root of humankind's inability to maintain a lasting peace.

To protest the concept of nationalism, Davis renounced his U.S. citizenship in 1948 and declared himself a citizen of the world. The following year, Davis, along with fellow world government enthusiasts, established an International Registry of World Citizens in Paris, France. A World Service Authority, charged with administering the WGWC program, operates out of Washington, D.C. The abiding premise of WGWC is that there is only one "physical human family" and that arbitrarily instituted borders cannot separate the common interests held by all members of that human family. Therefore, sovereign nations and nationalisms only serve to create situations in which humans are manipulated for causes that are not in their own best interest. Since its founding nearly 50 years ago, the WGWC has attracted over 750,000 members who proclaim themselves to be citizens of the world.

Reference Meyer, Robert S., *Peace Organizations Past and Present* (1988).

World Peace Foundation

Founded by Boston publisher Edwin Ginn in 1910, the World Peace Foundation was created to educate the public through conferences on international issues affecting peace. The findings of the conferences were published and widely disseminated, thereby advancing the cause of peace. The early focus of the foundation was on the development of international law and on advocating support for the League of Nations. Later, the focus shifted to the United Nations (U.N.). Still operating as a privately funded organization, the foundation more recently has focused on regional issues. Recent studies have concerned United States–Canada relations, dissension in South Africa, and collective security in the Western Hemisphere. Current studies dealing with Latin America and Africa include analyses of U.S. policy in Africa in the 1990s and economic development in Latin America. The foundation sponsors monthly foreign policy luncheons and publishes a quarterly journal, *International Organization*. Foundation archives are located in the Swarthmore College Peace Collection.

Reference Meyer, Robert S., *Peace Organizations Past and Present* (1988).

World Peace through Law Center

Operating on the premise that world peace is not possible without first ensuring a system of enforceable world law, the World Peace through Law Center, founded in 1963, was the first worldwide organization that brought together lawyers, judges, and law students in order to establish a model system of world laws that would ultimately promote world peace.

World Peace has one world president and four regional presidents. Members of the organization can choose one of four areas in which to concentrate their efforts: human rights, intellectual property, legal education, and law and computer technology. Members are also invited to join one of four professional branches in the organization, including the World Association of Lawyers, the World Association of Judges, the World Associaton of Law

Professors, or the World Association of Law Students. The center holds world conferences to discuss a broad range of issues affecting international law, including terrorism, hijacking, refugees, human rights, the environment, drug regulation, urban development, and multinational business. It also stages mock trials in order to demonstrate how conflicts can be resolved short of war. In addition, a Treaty Acceptance Committee was established in each participating country to support ratification of multilateral treaties and conventions.

Reference Meyer, Robert S., *Peace Organizations Past and Present* (1988).

World Peacemakers

A religiously grounded organization started by several members of the Church of the Saviour in Washington, D.C., in 1978, World Peacemakers was a response to the arms race. The founders—Gordon Cosby, Richard Barnet, Bill Branner, and Bill Price—took seriously their church's admonition to live "in a manner which will end all war, personal and public." Alarmed at the crisis presented by an escalating arms buildup, the founders sought to engage Americans in a campaign to pray for world peace and to work within their church communities toward that end. World Peacemakers issued a series of publications that urged congregations to appeal to the government to negotiate a bilateral cessation of developing and deploying nuclear weapons. World Peacemakers adopted this ecumenical approach to world peace in the belief that true grass-roots support for an end to the arms buildup could produce results politically.

Reference Meyer, Robert S., *Peace Organizations Past and Present* (1988).

World Pen Pals (WPP)

The World Pen Pals (WPP) organization began in 1950 when a group of ninth-grade students in Minneapolis, Min-

nesota, wrote to then-President Harry S Truman, asking that Truman "keep talking until you find some way to agree" on a peaceful solution to the Cold War. The appeal from the students, who described themselves as "the generation of children who have never known peace" brought widespread positive response. The letter-writing organization, founded as a result of the Minneapolis students's action, has since become the largest in the United States. It matches worldwide pen pals between the ages of 12 and 20. Taken on as a project of the International Institute of Minnesota, WPP each year links more than 15,000 students from countries and territories around the world with students in the United States. Supporters of the project believe that the person-to-person friendships developed through letter writing help to promote peace and international understanding.

Reference Meyer, Robert S., *Peace Organizations Past and Present* (1988).

World Policy Institute (WPI)

Founded as the Institute for World Order in 1948, the World Policy Institute (WPI) advocates peaceful resolution of global conflict, a sound and equitable world economy, and the protection of human rights. The WPI publishes the *World Policy Journal*, a forum for the evaluation of U.S. and world economic and security policies. The journal is made available to members of Congress as well as to domestic and foreign governments, journalists, academics, and organization leaders. The WPI also sponsors a Security Project, initiated in 1983, which is charged with analyzing for consistency—and with integrating—U.S. economic, political, and military policies. The information is shared with presidential and congressional candidates and incumbents as well as with journalists, civic organizations, universities, and national organizations. The WPI, a nonprofit organization, also publishes and distributes books and curriculum guides and delivers speeches and briefings to public, congressional, and university audiences.

Reference Meyer, Robert S., *Peace Organizations Past and Present* (1988).

World War I, Anti-War Sentiment

Although World War I had been fought as the war to make the world safe for democracy and as the war to end all wars, the enthusiasm with which Americans had supported Wilsonian ideals and Allied goals began to turn to disillusionment on a grand scale shortly after the Treaty of Versailles. Disillusionment was fueled by a growing belief that Americans had been manipulated emotionally and had been lied to by those who sought war for their own selfish reasons.

A series of books that began to appear shortly after the war, and which continued to appear through the mid-1930s, helped to solidify the feeling of betrayal. First-hand accounts of what the war had really been like became available to the public, including *Under Fire* by Henri Barbusse, *Three Soldiers* by John Dos Passos, *A Farewell to Arms* by Ernest Hemingway, and Erich Maria Remarque's *All Quiet on the Western Front*. Realistic, sometimes graphic, descriptions of the horrors of war shocked readers, but they might have been accepted as necessary horrors if these accounts had not been accompanied by a series of nonfiction works that emphasized the deceptions and selfishness on the part of Allied leaders. This latter group of books included *Falsehood in Wartime* by Arthur Ponsonby, *Now It Can Be Told* by Sir Philip Gibbs, and *Propaganda Techniques in the World War* by Harold D. Lasswell. The combination of first-hand accounts and exposés convinced the public that idealistic young men had been led into a senseless and unnecessary slaughter on the battlefield through lies and deception. This belief grew stronger throughout the 1920s and culminated with the publication in 1934 of two books that fixed the blame on businessmen intent on profits from war, specifically mu-

nitions manufacturers and arms traffickers. *Iron, Blood, and Profits* by George Seldes and *Merchants of Death* by Helmuth Engelbrecht and Frank Hanighen promoted the thesis that it was the arms manufacturers who had maneuvered events for their own profit. *Merchants of Death*, in particular, gained widespread readership throughout the country and was selected as a Book-of-the-Month Club offering.

The charges sparked a congressional investigation and were addressed by officials at the highest level of government, giving credence to a pacifist ideal that had long been held by a small group throughout U.S. history but which now gained wider acceptance as people vowed "never again." A 1937 poll asked "if another war like the World War develops in Europe, should Americans take part again?" An unprecedented 95 percent of all respondents said "no."

Reference Wittner, Lawrence S., *Rebels against War: The American Peace Movement 1941–1960* (1969).

World Without War Council (WWWC)

This organization had two previous incarnations. Acts for Peace, founded in 1958, was a northern California organization that existed until 1961. It then changed its name to Turn toward Peace after the movement spread to Oregon and Washington as well as throughout California. In 1967 it became the World Without War Council (WWWC), with affiliations in Chicago, New York, and Washington, D.C. The goal of all three organizations was always the same: the development of an international legal and political institution capable of resolving conflicts. The means to achieve the goal have changed with each incarnation.

The WWWC is primarily a consulting and management organization rather than a membership organization. It brings to the table a variety of viewpoints within the peace movement in an effort to find ways in which the institutions it sees as necessary to ensuring peace will thrive when they come into being. In addition to providing excellent overview information, the WWWC also works directly with institutions and organizations, helping to initiate projects and structures that will help make the United States a leader in moving toward a world in which international conflict is solved peacefully.

Among the WWWC's more specific tasks are: improving relations among various agency heads in order to promote a common sense of purpose and direction for the country, developing sophisticated leadership in the philanthropic commu-

nity, recruiting and training leadership in a range of nongovernmental organizations, and developing a commitment to sound and creative local work. Robert Pickus, the president of WWWC, clarified his organization's approach to world peace in *Reflections on the Freeze and a Peace Worthy of the Name:* "An effective peace strategy would not focus on weapons alone. It would recognize the central problem: the absence of legal and political alternatives to weapons in the resolution of conflict."

Reference Meyer, Robert S., *Peace Organizations Past and Present* (1988).

Chronology

1828 The American Peace Society is founded in Boston, Massachusetts. Under the leadership of Benjamin Franklin Trueblood, general secretary from 1892 to 1915, the Society will grow to become the most influential peace organization in the United States in the years leading up to World War I.

1895 Albert Smiley organizes and hosts the first Lake Mohonk Peace Conference. The conference, which will be held annually for 22 years, provides a common meeting place for American peace activists.

1905 The Intercollegiate Socialist Society is formed. Its founders include such notables as Upton Sinclair, Clarence Darrow, John Reed, Jack London, Walter Lippman, and Edna St. Vincent Millay. It will languish during World War I, to be revitalized in 1921 as the League for Industrial Democracy. The League's student arm, the Student League for Industrial Democracy, will later change its name to Students for a Democratic Society.

1908 The American School Peace League, later called the American School Citizenship League, is founded by Fannie Fern Phillips Andrews. Its purpose is to promote peace by making principles of international justice and fraternity part of school curricula. Most active in its early years, the organization will remain viable until 1950.

1910 Boston publisher Edwin Ginn founds the World Peace Foundation.

1912 Elihu Root is awarded the Nobel Peace Prize.

1914 World War I begins in Europe.

The Fellowship of Reconciliation is founded in Great Britain. Meetings of the religious pacifist organization will begin in the United States during the following year.

1915 Reformer Jane Addams is elected first chairwoman of the newly formed Women's Peace Party, which works toward a peaceful solution to the war in Europe. She is also elected president of the International Congress of Women at The Hague, which seeks to persuade world statesmen to enlist neutral nations to mediate the conflict.

The American Union against Militarism (originally called the American League for the Limitation of Armaments) is organized to oppose Woodrow Wilson's military preparedness program. The group's Civil Liberties Bureau, reorganized as the American Civil Liberties Union, will survive the parent organization's dissolution in 1921.

1917 The United States enters World War I.

The American Friends Service Committee is formed to provide relief to victims of World War I and to provide alternative service for members of the Society of Friends (Quakers) and other conscientious objectors.

1918 Eugene V. Debs, the 1912 Socialist party candidate for the presidency, is arrested for making an antiwar speech in Canton, Ohio. Sentenced to prison, Debs will run a second presidential campaign from his jail cell in 1920.

World War I ends as the German army collapses.

1919 Jane Addams is elected president of the Women's International League for Peace and Freedom, a post she will hold until her death in 1935.

Led by Carrie Chapman Catt and others, the National American Woman Suffrage Association establishes the League of Women Voters, which will become active in such issues as U.S. membership in the League of Nations and the World Court, and support for the United Nations.

The Women's Peace Society is founded by Fanny Garrison Villard.

President Woodrow Wilson is awarded the Nobel Peace Prize for his efforts to negotiate a lasting peace in Europe in the aftermath of World War I. His Fourteen Points for peace form the basis for the Versailles Treaty.

1920 The Versailles Treaty, which establishes the conditions of the peace ending World War I, authorizes the creation of the League of Nations, a world peacekeeping body. Opposition to the League in the U.S. Senate prevents ratification of the treaty; consequently, the United States does not join. Ironically, the terms imposed on Germany by the victorious Allies under the Treaty of Versailles will be used as nationalist propaganda in the Nazi drive to power in Germany in the 1930s.

1921 Frederick Libby founds the National Council for the Prevention of War. He will serve as the organization's executive secretary until 1970.

The United States, Great Britain, Japan, France, and Italy sign the Five-Power Treaty, limiting naval tonnage and the fortification of island possessions in the Pacific.

The Four-Power Treaty, signed by the United States, Japan, Great Britain, and France, nullifies the Anglo-Japanese Alliance and provides that the signatories will mutually respect Pacific possessions.

The Wartime Prohibition Treaty outlaws the use of poison gas and prohibits the use of submarines to destroy international commerce during wartime.

1923 The War Resisters League is founded by Jessie Wallace Hughan.

1924 Charles Herbert Levermore wins the Edward Bok American Peace Award for his plan to prevent war between the United States and other nations.

1928 The Kellogg-Briand Treaty is signed by most of the major powers. In essence, the signatories renounce the use of violence to resolve international disputes.

1931 Jane Addams is awarded the Nobel Peace Prize, sharing the honor with Nicholas Murray Butler.

1933 The American League against War and Fascism, a coalition of liberal and leftist organizations opposed to the rise of Fascism in Europe, is organized. Despite internal conflicts among member groups, the League will remain active though the 1930s.

1934 The first nationwide peace strike occurs with simultaneous demonstrations on college campuses.

1938 Norman Mattoon Thomas founds the Keep America Out of War Committee.

The United Pacifists Committee is organized by Jessie Wallace Hughan to support conscientious objectors and to implement a peace education program.

1939 World War II begins with the invasion of Poland by Germany and the Soviet Union.

1940 The America First Committee is formed to counter the growing American intervention in the war in Europe. Participants include such prominent individuals as Robert E. Wood, Charles Lindbergh, and Gerald Nye. The committee, which supports isolationism and a strong defense, will be dissolved after the Japanese attack on Pearl Harbor.

France, Belgium, Denmark, Norway, and the Netherlands fall to invading German forces.

Americans for Democratic Action (originally called the Union for Democratic Action) is organized following the 1940 Socialist party convention, and ultimately supports U.S. participation in the war. Reorganized in 1947, the organization will become a forum for liberal views on the Vietnam War.

1941 Germany invades the Soviet Union.

The United States declares war on Japan and the European Axis powers in the aftermath of Japanese attacks on Pearl Harbor and other U.S. Pacific bases.

Isador Hoffman is cofounder of the Jewish Peace Fellowship, established to provide a place of support and counsel for Jewish conscientious objectors.

1943 The National Council of American-Soviet Friendship is founded to promote peace and cooperation between the United States and the Soviet Union.

1945 Germany and Japan surrender to Allied forces, bringing an end to World War II.

The United Nations is formally organized in San Francisco. The organization is dedicated to human rights, the peaceful resolution of international disputes, and the economic and social advancement of all peoples.

1946 John R. Mott is awarded the Nobel Peace Prize for his efforts in uniting "millions of young people in work for the Christian ideals of peace and tolerance among nations."

1948 The Central Committee for Conscientious Objectors is formed to oppose the Selective Service Act of 1948. The Committee provides counseling and legal assistance to conscientious objectors, as well as information to potential draftees.

The Women's International League for Peace and Freedom incorporates the Jane Addams Peace Association as the parent organization's educational arm.

The Institute for World Order, later renamed the World Policy Institute, is founded, advocating peaceful resolution of international conflict, the protection of human rights, and a sound and equitable world economy.

1950 Ralph J. Bunche receives the Nobel Peace Prize for his 1949 negotiation of the armistice ending Arab-Jewish hostilities in Palestine.

W. E. B. DuBois, one of the founders of the National Association for the Advancement of Colored People and a peace activist, is indicted on federal charges as an unregistered foreign agent. DuBois is acquitted.

The Korean War begins.

1954 Emily Greene Balch is awarded the Nobel Peace Prize for a lifetime of peace activism.

1955 The Russell-Einstein Manifesto criticizes the United States and the Soviet Union for the arms race.

1957 The Committee for Non-Violent Action is founded by members of the War Resisters League to protest the testing, building, and proliferation of nuclear weapons. It will later become involved in protests against the Vietnam War, and will merge with the War Resisters League in 1967.

The first of the Pugwash Conferences, meetings designed to rebuild the international scientific community that had been torn apart by the cold war, is held in Pugwash, Nova Scotia.

Linus Pauling, Homer Jack, and Norman Cousins found the Committee for a Sane Nuclear Policy, also known as SANE, which opposes the nuclear arms race and nuclear testing. It will merge with the Nuclear Weapons Freeze Campaign in 1987 to form SANE/FREEZE.

1958 President Eisenhower unilaterally suspends nuclear weapons testing. Atmospheric testing will be resumed in 1962.

1959 In the Omaha Action, protesters at the Mead ICBM base in Omaha, Nebraska, create publicity for the movement to ban nuclear weapons.

The campus-based Student Peace Union is formed, drawing its membership primarily from the Fellowship of Reconciliation, the American Friends Service Committee, and the Young People's Socialist Alliance. It will sponsor a series of peace demonstrations in the nation's capital.

1960 The Students for a Democratic Society is formed from the old Student League for Industrial Democracy. Al Haber and Tom Hayden are among its key organizers. By the late 1960s, a radical group within the SDS, calling itself the Weathermen and later the Weather Underground, will resort to terrorist tactics against government policy in Vietnam.

1961 President John F. Kennedy establishes the Peace Corps to further understanding between the United States and other nations.

Bella Abzug founds the Women's Strike for Peace; she will serve as the organization's national legislative director until 1970.

American negotiator John McCloy and Soviet diplomat Valerian Zorin sign the *Joint Statement of Agreed Principles for Disarmament Negotiations*. A significant step toward bilateral arms control, the initiative withers after the assassination of President Kennedy in 1963.

Physicians for Social Responsibility is formed in response to atmospheric nuclear weapons testing and the threat of nuclear war.

1962 The Port Huron Statement, authored by Tom Hayden, outlines the goals of the Students for a Democratic Society.

Linus Pauling wins the Nobel Peace Prize for his efforts toward nuclear disarmament.

1963 The first protest against American involvement in Vietnam is organized in New York City by Thomas Cornell, a member of the Catholic Worker movement.

Some 70,000 people march in the annual Easter Peace Walk in New York City, protesting the arms race.

The United States, the Soviet Union, and other nations sign the Limited Nuclear Test Ban Treaty, prohibiting nuclear weapons tests in the atmosphere, underwater, and in outer space. The Senate ratifies the treaty later that year. France and China refuse to sign.

1964 The Catholic Peace Fellowship is founded by a group of Catholic activists, including Daniel and Philip Berrigan, Martin Corbin, Thomas Cornell, and James Forest.

Peace activists, including such notables as Joan Baez, David Dellinger, and Daniel and Philip Berrigan, hold a rally in Washington, D.C., protesting the Vietnam War.

The Tonkin Gulf Resolution opens the way for massive U.S. intervention in Vietnam.

The May 2 Movement is founded among students at Yale University to protest American involvement in Vietnam.

The International Peace Research Association, a worldwide organization of peace researchers, is formed.

1965 Clergy and Laity Concerned is formed, joining activists from different faiths in opposition to the Vietnam War and the arms race.

Alice Herz, a Quaker and once a refugee from Nazi Germany, burns herself to death in protest against the arms race and U.S. actions in Vietnam. Over the next five years, several other peace protesters will turn to self-immolation in response to the Vietnam War.

The first antiwar "teach-in" is organized by faculty at the University of Michigan.

The Workshop for Non-Violence is formed. It will focus on nonviolent, direct-action protests. Its publication, *WIN*, will be an influential forum for opponents to U.S. intervention in Vietnam.

1966 The Center for War/Peace Studies is founded, guided by their motto, "Applied research toward a world of peace with justice."

1967 The first large mobilization of opponents of the Vietnam War takes place in New York City and San Francisco.

Philip Berrigan and three associates damage selective service records in Baltimore, Maryland, in protest against U.S. military involvement in Vietnam. The protesters become known as the "Baltimore Four."

The Common Heritage Institute, a think tank for the study of peace issues, is founded at Villanova University.

The Fund for Peace is established. In time the Fund will establish such influential projects as the Center for Defense Information, the Center for National Security Studies, the Alternative Defense Project, and the Institute for the Study of World Politics.

1968 Daniel and Philip Berrigan, with seven associates (they would collectively become known as the "Catonsville Nine"), burn records at the selective service office in Catonsville, Maryland. Convicted on charges of destroying government property, both of the Berrigan brothers spend time as fugitives before being taken into custody and sent to prison. Their action, however, precipitates a series of similar protests by Catholic antiwar activists.

Dr. Benjamin Spock, the Reverend William Sloane Coffin, and three others are indicted for conspiracy to violate the draft laws. Found guilty, their verdicts will be reversed on appeal.

The Reverend Dr. Martin Luther King, Jr., a champion of nonviolent resistance in the civil rights struggle and a critic of the Vietnam War, is assassinated in Memphis, Tennessee.

Robert Kennedy, running for the Democratic nomination for the presidency on a platform opposed to U.S. policy in Vietnam, is assassinated in California.

The Nuclear Nonproliferation Treaty is signed by representatives of 62 countries, including the Soviet Union and the United States, but excluding France and China. The

U.S. Senate will ratify the treaty the following year.

The Democratic National Convention in Chicago, Illinois, becomes the scene of a "police riot" against antiwar demonstrators. The following year, several of the most prominent protesters are tried on charges arising from the demonstrations; the "Chicago Seven" trial becomes a legal circus as the defendants spar with Judge Julius Hoffman.

1969   Nine Catholic activists (the "D.C. Nine") raid the Dow Chemical offices in Washington, D.C., in protest against Dow's production of napalm for use in the Vietnam conflict.

The International Association of Educators for World Peace is founded by Charles Mercieca of Alabama.

Some 500,000 antiwar protesters descend on Washington, D.C. to demonstrate against the Vietnam War.

The Union of Concerned Scientists is formed at the Massachusetts Institute of Technology. Its key concerns are an environmentally safe nuclear energy program and the prevention of nuclear war.

1970   The American Movement for World Government is formally organized. Its origins can be traced to the 1945 publication of Emery Reves's *The Anatomy of Peace*, which argues that technology has rendered the sovereign nation-state obsolete.

The deployment of American forces in Cambodia leads to widespread and sometimes violent antiwar demonstrations on college campuses across the country. At Kent State University in Kent, Ohio, four student protesters are killed in a confrontation with Ohio National Guard troops.

Norman Borlaug wins the Nobel Peace Prize for his work on agricultural productivity.

John Gardner founds Common Cause.

Kathy and Jim McGinnis found the Institute for Peace and Justice, a center for peace studies at Saint Louis University in Missouri.

The International Peace Academy, a leading institution in the study of international peacekeeping methods, is founded in New York City.

1972   The United States and the Soviet Union agree to limit the deployment of antiballistic missile systems and to freeze the deployment of ICBMs in the first Strategic Arms Limitation Talks agreement, also known as SALT I.

Artists for Survival is founded in Waltham, Massachusetts, in opposition to the nuclear arms race.

The Center for Defense Information, a project of the Fund for Peace, is founded.

1973   U.S. forces are pulled out of Vietnam. Two years later, the South Vietnamese army will collapse in the face of a North Vietnamese offensive, resulting in the reunification of the country under a Communist government and an end to the Vietnam War.

1978   The Center on Law and Pacifism is founded in Philadelphia, Pennsylvania, providing legal services to religious pacifists.

1979   President Jimmy Carter and Leonid Brezhnev sign the SALT II treaty in Vienna, limiting ICBMs, but Congress will not ratify the treaty in the aftermath of the Soviet invasion of Afghanistan.

1980   Dr. Bernard Lown of the United States and Dr. Yevgeny Chazov of the Soviet Union form International Physicians for the Prevention of Nuclear War. The organization will win the Nobel Peace Prize in 1985.

Randall Forsberg, the director of the Institute of Defence and

Disarmament studies, issues an appeal to the United States and the Soviet Union to halt all testing, production, and deployment of nuclear weapons. Within a year, the idea of a "nuclear freeze" will gather widespread support, and in 1982 nearly a million people will turn out at a nuclear freeze campaign rally in New York City.

1981   Former Iran hostage Moorhead Kennedy founds the Council for International Understanding.

Roger Molander organizes Ground Zero to enlist grassroots opposition to the arms race.

High Technology Professionals for Peace is founded.

The Lawyer's Alliance for Nuclear Arms Control is organized to educate legal professionals and the public regarding the dangers of nuclear war. The Alliance also sponsors conferences that bring together lawyers from the United States and the Soviet Union.

1982   The Children of the Peacemakers Foundation (originally called the Round Table Foundation) is founded in San Francisco, California.

Psychologists for Social Responsibility is formed to organize professional psychologists to promote peaceful solutions to world conflicts.

1983   Athletes United for Peace is founded to promote peace though sports contacts between the United States and the Soviet Union.

U.S. Catholic bishops issue a pastoral letter on nuclear weapons and war. The document, *The Challenge of Peace: God's Promise and Our Response*, breaks with a tradition of official church policy supporting the government in defense matters.

The Institute on Global Conflict and Cooperation is established by the University of California.

Bibliography

Abrams, Irwin. *The Nobel Peace Prize and the Laureates: An Illustrated Biographical History 1901–1987*. Boston: G. K. Hall, 1988.

Abzug, Bella. *Ms. Abzug Goes to Washington*. New York: Saturday Review Press, 1972.

Addams, Jane. *The Second Twenty Years at Hull-House*. New York: Macmillan, 1930.

———. *Twenty Years at Hull House*. New York: Macmillan, 1910.

Album of American History, 6 vols. New York: Charles Scribner's Sons, 1960–1985.

Altbach, Philip G. *Student Politics in America: A Historical Analysis*. New York: McGraw-Hill, 1974.

The American Annual: An Encyclopedia of the Events of 1968, 1969, 1970. New York: 1969, 1970, 1971.

Andrews, Fannie Fern Phillips. *Memory Pages of My Life*. Boston: Houghton-Mifflin, 1948.

Aptheker, Herbert. "W. E. B. Du Bois—A Man for Peace." *Political Affairs* 41 (August 1982): 31–35.

Bacon, Margaret. *Let This Life Speak: The Legacy of Henry Cadbury*. Philadelphia: University of Pennsylvania Press, 1987.

Baez, Joan. *And a Voice to Sing With* New York: Summit Books, 1987.

———. *Daybreak*. New York: Dial Press, 1968.

Balch, Emily Greene. *Beyond Nationalism*. New York: Twayne Publishers, 1972.

Bentley, Judith. *The Nuclear Freeze Movement*. New York: Franklin Watts, 1984.

Berrigan, Daniel. *The Trial of the Catonsville Nine*. Boston: Beacon Press, 1970.

Berrigan, Phillip. *Prison Journals of a Priest Revolutionary*. New York: Ballantine Books, 1970.

Brown, Ira V. *Lyman Abbott, Christian Evolutionist*. Cambridge, MA: Harvard University Press, 1953.

Chambers, Clark A. *Paul U. Kellogg and the Survey: Voices for Social Welfare and Social Justice*. Minneapolis: University of Minnesota Press, 1971.

Chatfield, Charles. *For Peace and Justice: Pacifism in America, 1914–1941*. Knoxville: University of Tennessee Press, 1971.

———, ed. *Peace Movements in America*. New York: Schocken Books, 1973.

Christian Science Monitor.

Coffin, William Sloane. *Once to Every Man*. New York: Atheneum, 1977.

Cole, Wayne S. *Roosevelt and the Isolationists, 1932–1945*. Lincoln: University of Nebraska Press, 1983.

Coletta, Paola. *William Jennings Bryan*. 3 vols. Lincoln: University of Nebraska Press, 1964–1969.

Cook, Blanche Weisen. *Crystal Eastman on Women and Revolution*. New York: Oxford University Press, 1978.

Cornell, Julien D. *Conscientious Objectors and the Law*. New York: J. Day Co., 1972.

Cousins, Norman. *Who Speaks for Man?* New York: Viking Press, 1945.

Cousins, Norman, and J. Garry Clifford, eds. *Memoirs of a Man*. New York : Norton Press, 1975.

Current Biography.

Day, Alan, ed. *Peace Movements of the World: An International Directory*. London: Longman House, 1986.

Day, Dorothy. *Loaves and Fishes*. New York: Harper & Row, 1963.

DeBenedetti, Charles, ed. *Peace Heroes in Twentieth Century America*. Bloomington: Indiana University Press, 1988.

Detzer, Dorothy. *Appointment on the Hill*. New York: Henry Holt and Company, 1948.

Dictionary of American Biography. 22 volumes. New York: Charles Scribner's Sons, 1928–1958.

Duffas, Robert L. *Lillian Wald: Neighbor and Crusader*. New York: Macmillan, 1938.

Eddy, Sherwood. *Eighty Adventurous Years: An Autobiography*. New York: Harper & Brothers, 1953.

Eiseman, Alberta. *Rebels and Reformers: Biographies of Four Jewish Americans*. Garden City, NY: Zenith Books, 1976.

Erb, B. Paul. *Orie O. Miller: The Story of a Man and an Era*. Scottdale, PA: 1969.

Flexner, Eleanor. *Century of Struggle: The Women's Rights Movement in the United States*. Cambridge: The Belknap Press of Harvard University, 1975.

Foner, Eric, and John Garraty, eds. *The Reader's Companion to American History*. Boston: Houghton Mifflin Co., 1991.

Franklin, John Hope, and August Meier, eds. *Black Leaders of the Twentieth Century*. Urbana: University of Illinois Press, 1982.

Fulbright, J. William. *The Arrogance of Power*. New York: Random House, 1966.

Garrow, David J. *Bearing the Cross: Martin Luther King, Jr. and the Southern Leadership Conference*. New York: Morrow, 1986.

Giles, K. S. *Flight of the Dove*. Beaverton, OR: Touchstone Press, 1980.

Gilpin, Robert. *American Scientists and Nuclear Weapons Policy*. Princeton, NJ: Princeton University Press, 1962.

Ginger, Ray. *The Bending Cross: A Biography of Eugene Victor Debs*. New Brunswick, NJ: Rutgers University Press, 1949.

Harmon, Nolan B., ed. *The Encyclopedia of World Methodism*. Nashville: United Methodist Publishing House, 1974.

Haskins, James. *Barbara Jordan*. New York, Dial Books, 1977.

Hayden, Tom. *Rebellion and Repression*. New York: Meridian Books, 1969.

Hayden, Thomas. *Trial*. New York: Holt, Rinehart, and Winston, 1970.

Hayden, Tom. *Tom Hayden: A Memoir*. New York: Random House, 1990.

Hennacy, Ammon. *Autobiography of a Catholic Anarchist*. New York: Catholic Worker Press, 1954.

Hentoff, Nat. *Peace Agitator: The Story of A. J. Muste*. New York: Macmillan, 1963.

Howlett, Charles F. *Troubled Philosopher: John Dewey and the Struggle for World Peace*. Port Washington, NY: Kennikak Press, 1977.

Humes, D. J. *Oswald Garrison Villard: Liberal of the 1920s*. Syracuse: Syracuse University Press, 1960.

Irwin, Inez Haynes. *Up Hill with Banners Flying*. Penobscot, ME: Traversity Press, 1964.

Isserman, Maurice. *If I Had a Hammer . . . The Death of the Old Left and the Birth of the New Left*. New York: Basic Books, 1987.

Jacob, Philip E. *The Origins of Civilian Public Service*. Washington, DC: National Service Board for Religious Objectors, 1946.

James, Edward T., et al., eds. *Notable American Women, 1607–1950: A Biographical Dictionary*. Cambridge, MA: The Belknap Press of Harvard University, 1971.

Jones, Mary Hoxie. *Swords into Ploughshares: An Account of the American Friends Service Committee 1917–1937*. New York: Macmillan, 1937.

Josephson, Hannah. *Jeannette Rankin, First Lady in Congress: A Biography*. Indianapolis, IN: Bobbs Merrill, 1974.

Josephson, Harold, ed. *Biographical Dictionary of Modern Peace Leaders*. Westport, CT: Greenwood Press, 1985.

Kahn, E. J., Jr. "A Soldier's Slant on Compulsory Military Training." *Saturday Evening Post* (19 May 1945).

Kaltefleiter, Werner, and Robert L. Pfaltzgraff, eds. *The Peace Movement in Europe and the United States*. New York: St. Martin's Press, 1985.

Kennedy, David M. *Birth Control in America: The Career of Margaret Sanger*. New Haven, CT: Yale University Press, 1970.

Kennedy, Moorhead. *The Ayatollah in the Cathedral: Reflections of a Hostage*. New York: Hill and Wang, 1983.

King, Martin Luther, Jr. *Why We Can't Wait*. New York: Harper & Row, 1963.

Klejment, Anne. "The Berrigans: Revolutionary Christian Nonviolence." In *Peace Heroes in Twentieth Century America*, edited by Charles DeBenedetti. Bloomington: Indiana University Press, 1988.

Knock, Thomas J. *To End All Wars: Woodrow Wilson and the Quest for World Order*. New York: Oxford University Press, 1992.

Lamparski, Richard. *Whatever Became of . . . ?* New York: Crown Publishers, 1967.

Lasch, Christopher. *The New Radicalism in America, 1889–1963: The Intellectual as a Social Type*. New York: Knopf, 1965.

Lash, Joseph. *Eleanor: The Years Alone*. New York: W. W. Norton, 1972.

———. *Eleanor and Franklin*. New York: W. W. Norton, 1971.

Lewis, David L. *King: A Critical Biography*. Urbana: University of Illinois Press, 1978.

Lieberman, Mark. *The Pacifists: Soldiers without Guns*. New York: Praeger Publishing, 1972.

Link, Arthur S., et al., eds. *The American People: A History*. Arlington Heights, IL: AHM Publishing, 1981.

Lunardini, Christine A. *From Equal Suffrage to Equal Rights: Alice Paul and the National Woman's Party 1910–1928*. New York: New York University Press, 1986.

Manahan, Nancy. "Future Old Maids and Pacifist Agitators: The Story of Tracy Mygatt and Frances Witherspoon." *Women's Studies Quarterly* 10 (Spring 1982).

Marchland, C. Roland. *The American Peace Movement and Social Reform, 1898–1918*. Princeton, NJ: Princeton University Press, 1972.

Meyer, Robert S. *Peace Organizations Past and Present*. Jefferson, NC: McFarland, 1988.

Miller, Sally M. *Victor Berger and the Promise of Constructive Socialism*. Westport, CT: Greenwood Press, 1973.

Miller, W. D. *Dorothy Day*. San Fransisco: Harper & Row, 1982.

Mills, C. Wright. "On the New Left." *Studies on the Left* II (1961).

Mills, C. Wright. *The Causes of World War III*. Westport, CT: Greenwood Press, 1976.

———. "Listen Yankee." *Harpers Magazine* (December 1960).

Morris, Richard B., ed. *Encyclopedia of American History*. Bicentennial Edition. New York: Harper & Row, 1976.

National Cyclopaedia of American Biography. Ann Arbor, MI: University Microfilms, 1967.

New York Times.

New York Times Biographical Service.

Newfield, Jack. *Robert Kennedy: A Memoir*. New York: Dutton Press, 1969.

Newsweek.

Patterson, David S. "An Interpretation of the American Peace Movement, 1898–1914." In *Peace Movements in America,* edited by Charles Chatfield. New York: Schocken Books, 1973.

———. *Toward a Warless World: The Travail of the American Peace Movement 1887–1914.* Bloomington: Indiana University Press, 1976.

Pauling, Linus. *No More War!* New York: Dodd, Mead & Co., 1958.

Pauling, Linus, et al., eds. *World Encyclopedia of Peace.* New York: Pergamon Press, 1986.

Peck, Mary Grey. *Carrie Chapman Catt.* New York: Octagon Books, 1975.

Perkins, Dexter. *Charles Evans Hughes and American Democratic Statesmanship.* Boston: Little Brown and Company, 1956.

Petersen, Patti McGill. "Student Organizations and the Antiwar Movement in America 1900–1960." In *Peace Movements in America,* edited by Charles Chatfield. New York: Schocken Books, 1973.

Pickett, Clarence Evan. *For More Than Bread.* Boston: Little Brown and Company, 1953.

Randall, M. M. *Improper Bostonian: Emily Greene Balch, Nobel Peace Laureate.* New York: Twayne Publishers, 1964.

Roosevelt, Eleanor. *The Autobiography of Eleanor Roosevelt.* New York: Harper & Row, 1958.

———. *This I Remember.* New York: Harper & Brothers, 1949.

———. *This Is My Story.* New York: Garden City Publishing, 1937.

Schell, Jonathan. *The Fate of the Earth.* New York: Knopf, 1982.

———. *The Time of Illusion.* New York: Knopf, 1976.

Schlesinger, Arthur, Jr. *The Crises of the Old Order.* Boston: Houghton Mifflin, 1988.

———. *Robert Kennedy and His Times.* Boston: Houghton Mifflin, 1978.

———. *A Thousand Days.* Boston: Houghton Mifflin, 1965.

Seeley, Robert. *The Handbook of Nonviolence.* Great Neck, NY: Lakeville Press, 1986.

Sicherman, Barbara, et al., eds. *Notable American Women, The Modern Period: A Biographical Dictionary.* Cambridge: The Belknap Press of Harvard University, 1980.

Sochen, June. *Movers and Shakers: American Women Thinkers and Activists, 1900–1970.* New York: Quadrangle Books, 1972.

———. *The New Woman: Feminism in Greenwich Village 1910–1920.* New York: Quadrangle Books, 1972.

Spock, Benjamin. *Decent and Indecent: Our Personal and Political Behavior.* New York: McCall Publishing, 1970.

Stanton, Elizabeth Cady, et al., eds. *History of Woman Suffrage.* 6 vols. New York: Foster and Wells, 1881–1922.

Stevens, Doris. *Jailed for Freedom.* New York: Boni and Livewright, 1920.

Stineman, Esther. *American Political Women: Contemporary and Historical Profiles.* Littleton, CO: Libraries Unlimited, 1980.

Szulc, Tad. *The Illusion of Peace.* New York: Viking Press, 1978.

Thomas, Evan W. *The Radical "No"— Correspondence and Writing of Evan Thomas on War.* Edited by Charles Chatfield. New York: Garland, 1974

Uglow, Jennifer S., ed. *The Continuum Dictionary of Women's Biography.* New York: Continuum, 1989.

U.S. Congress, House Committee on Un-American Activities. *Report on the Communist "Peace" Offensive: A Campaign to Disarm and Defeat the United States.* 82nd Cong., 1st Sess., 1951.

Van Doren, Charles, ed. *Webster's American Biographies.* Springfield, MA: G&C Merriam Co., 1974.

Vicker, George. *The Formation of the New Left: The Early Years.* Lexington, MA: Lexington Books, 1975.

Wall Street Journal.

Wank, Solomon, ed. *Doves and Diplomats: Foreign Offices and Peace Movements in Europe and America in the Twentieth Century.* Westport, CT: Greenwood Press, 1978.

Ware, Louise. *George Foster Peabody: Banker, Philanthropist, Publicist.* Athens: University of Georgia Press, 1951.

Washington Post.

White, Theodore. *The Making of the President 1968.* New York: Atheneum, 1969.

Whitman, Alden, ed. *American Reformers: An H. W. Wilson Biographical Dictionary.* New York: The H. W. Wilson Co., 1985.

Who Was Who in America. Chicago: Marquis.

Who's Who in America. Chicago: Marquis.

Whitney, Sharon, and Tom Raynor. *Women in Politics.* New York: Franklin Watts, 1986.

Wittner, Lawrence S. *Rebels against War: The American Peace Movement 1941–1960.* New York: Columbia University Press, 1969.

Wreszin, Michael. *Oswald Garrison Villard: Pacifist at War.* Bloomington: Indiana University Press, 1965.

Wynner, Edith, and Georgia Lloyd. *Searchlight on Peace Plans: Choose Your Road to World Government.* New York: E. P. Dutton and Co., 1944.

Zaroulis, Nancy, and Gerald Sullivan. *Who Spoke Up? American Protest against the War in Vietnam 1963–1975.* New York: Doubleday, 1984.

Index